The World of
Japanese Fiction

The World of Japanese Fiction

Edited, and with an Introduction
and Headnotes, by
YOSHINOBU HAKUTANI
and
ARTHUR O. LEWIS

 A Dutton Paperback

E. P. Dutton & Co., Inc., New York, 1973

This paperback edition of "THE WORLD OF JAPANESE FICTION"
First published in 1973 by E. P. Dutton & Co., Inc.

Copyright © 1973 by Yoshinobu Hakutani and Arthur O. Lewis
All rights reserved. Printed in the U.S.A.
FIRST EDITION

No part of this publication may be reproduced or transmitted in any form or by any means, electronic or mechanical, including photocopy, recording, or any information storage and retrieval system now known or to be invented, without permission in writing from the publisher, except by a reviewer who wishes to quote brief passages in connection with a review written for inclusion in a magazine, newspaper or broadcast.

Published simultaneously in Canada by
Clarke, Irwin & Company Limited, Toronto and Vancouver

SBN 0-525-47342-4

INDIVIDUAL COPYRIGHTS AND ACKNOWLEDGMENTS

Grateful acknowledgment is made to the following for permission to quote from copyright material:

Saikaku Ihara: "The Almanac-Maker's Tale." Reprinted from *The Life of an Amorous Woman and Other Writings* by Saikaku Ihara by permission of New Directions Publishing Corporation, New York, and Laurence Pollinger Limited, London. Copyright © 1963 by UNESCO.

Ogai Mori: *The Wild Geese*. Reprinted by permission of Charles E. Tuttle Publishing Co., Inc. Copyright © 1959 by Charles E. Tuttle Co., Inc.

Ryunosuke Akutagawa: "The Hell Screen." Reprinted from *Japanese Short Stories* by Ryunosuke Akutagawa by permission of Liveright Publishers, New York. Copyright © 1961 by Liveright Publishing Corporation.

Riichi Yokomitsu: "Machine." Reprinted from *Modern Japanese Stories*, edited by Ivan Morris, by permission of Charles E. Tuttle Publishing Co., Inc. Copyright © 1962 by Charles E. Tuttle Co., Inc.

Ango Sakaguchi: "The Idiot." Reprinted from *Modern Japanese Stories*, edited by Ivan Morris, by permission of Charles E. Tuttle Publishing Co., Inc. Copyright © 1962 by Charles E. Tuttle Co., Inc.

Copyrights and Acknowledgments v

Osamu Dazai: "The Courtesy Call." Reprinted from *Modern Japanese Stories,* edited by Ivan Morris, by permission of Charles E. Tuttle Publishing Co., Inc. Copyright © 1962 by Charles E. Tuttle Co., Inc.

Yasunari Kawabata: "The Moon on the Water." Reprinted from *Modern Japanese Stories,* edited by Ivan Morris, by permission of Charles E. Tuttle Publishing Co., Inc. Copyright © 1962 by Charles E. Tuttle Co., Inc.

Yukio Mishima: "The Priest of Shiga Temple and His Love." Reprinted from *Modern Japanese Stories,* edited by Ivan Morris, by permission of Charles E. Tuttle Publishing Co., Inc. Copyright © 1962 by Charles E. Tuttle Co., Inc.

Junichiro Tanizaki: "The Bridge of Dreams." Reprinted from *Seven Japanese Tales* by Junichiro Tanizaki, translated by Howard Hibbett, by permission of Alfred A. Knopf, Inc., New York, and Martin Secker & Warburg Limited, London. Copyright © 1963 by Alfred A. Knopf, Inc.

Acknowledgment

Many people helped us in preparing this book, but we want to thank particularly Professor David R. Ewbank of Kent State University and Mrs. Michiko Hakutani for reading the manuscript, suggesting corrections, and giving us valuable criticisms.

Contents

Introduction ix

SHIKIBU MURASAKI (978?–1016?)
The Tale of Genji (*Genji Monogatari*,
    Eleventh Century) 1
  "The Chamber of Kiri"
  "Evening Glory"
  "Exile at Akashi"

ANONYMOUS
Tales of the Heike (*Heike Monogatari*,
    Thirteen Century) 56
  "The Fight at Dan-no-ura"
  "The Drowning of the Emperor"
  "The Six Paths"

SAIKAKU IHARA (1642–93?)
Five Women Who Chose Love (*Koshoku Gonin Onna*,
    1686) 67
  "The Almanac-Maker's Tale"

OGAI MORI (1862–1922)
The Wild Geese (*Gan*, 1911) 89

RYUNOSUKE AKUTAGAWA (1892–1947)
"The Hell Screen" ("Jigokuhen," 1918) 180

RIICHI YOKOMITSU (1898–1947)
"Machine" ("Kikai," 1930) 211

ANGO SAKAGUCHI (1906–55)
"The Idiot" ("Hakuchi," 1946) 232

OSAMU DAZAI (1909–48)
"The Courtesy Call" ("Shinyu Kokan," 1946)   265

YASUNARI KAWABATA (1899–1972)
"The Moon on the Water" ("Suigetsu," 1953)   280

YUKIO MISHIMA (1925–70)
"The Priest of Shiga Temple and His Love"
   ("Shigadera Shonin no Koi," 1954)   291

JUNICHIRO TANIZAKI (1886–1965)
"The Bridge of Dreams" ("Yume no Ukihashi," 1959)   308

Introduction

Few readers disagree that fiction is perhaps the most widely read literary form in the world today. It would, therefore, be no surprise to anyone that *shosetsu*—which means both the novel and the short story—has also enjoyed great popularity in modern Japan. Each year scores of novels and short stories are published and attract serious attention from the reading public. Many are quickly translated into the major languages of the world. At the same time, an equally large number of well-known books of fiction written elsewhere are translated into Japanese. This rapid exchange of ideas and literature is not motivated by a superficial fascination with the exotic, but by a growing desire to share insights into the common problems of twentieth-century life.

The interest in Japanese fiction both in Japan and in the West has often given rise to the notion that its form and technique are solely a result of Western influences. Some of the great works of fiction by Japanese writers certainly bear the mark of such influences, and it is quite true that a great majority of the novels have been written since Japan opened its door to the world a little over a century ago. But it would be an oversimplification for anyone to interpret modern Japanese writings merely in terms of Western literature. In fact, the Japanese novel dates back to the medieval Heian period (794–1185). *The Tale of Genji (Genji Monogatari)*, the superb literary achievement of that period, has exerted a steady and profound influence upon all subsequent Japanese literature. *Tales of the Heike (Heike Monogatari)*, a thirteenth-century historical novel, has been the source of numerous Noh and Kabuki plays. The best-seller popularity accorded to a modern version of the legend entitled *The New*

Tales of the Heike (*Shin Heike Monogatari*) by Eiji Yoshikawa speaks eloquently of the contemporary significance of this myth. Also in the long tradition of Japanese fiction the importance of the realistic work of the seventeenth-century writer Saikaku Ihara cannot be disregarded. The medium of expression employed by modern Japanese novelists is not, of course, the older form of the language cultivated by the men of letters in the seventeenth, eighteenth, and early nineteenth centuries, but it is still a pure native tongue. Thus, in Japan as in Western nations important literary studies today cannot be carried out without conceiving of literature as a part of the culture of a nation. Critics tend to concern themselves with formal doctrines, with questions of borrowed style and technique, but it is often more essential and rewarding for general readers to discover the wellspring of modern fiction in its nation's literary background.

A literary historian can hardly imagine the creation of so superb a novel as *The Tale of Genji* without considering what preceded it. Whether or not its predecessors had any impact on it is a difficult question to answer, but the fact remains that at least two works of fiction existed before Murasaki wrote her novel. The anonymous *Bamboo-Cutter's Tale* (*Taketori Monogatari*), written sometime in the late ninth century, is fanciful folklore. While at work a childless man discovers a diminutive maiden in a bamboo. He takes her home and names her Kaguya Hime (Shining Princess). She quickly grows up to womanhood and is wooed by many men including the Emperor, but all in vain. She is finally taken back in a chariot to the moon, from which she has apparently strayed. The manner of the narrative is highly primitive and the story lacks the psychological depth of later works of the Heian period. But the charming naïveté and simplicity of the tale are so compelling that every schoolchild in Japan remembers this fairy tale. The other writing, *The Tale of Ise* (*Ise Monogatari*), was composed by a poet named Ariwara-no-Narihira (825–880) about the same time as *Bamboo-Cutter's Tale*. Narihira's story, apparently based largely on his own experiences as a nobleman, is concerned with a series of love affairs. Its uniqueness lies in its inclusion of various poems, some of them quoted from *Manyoshu* (an eighth-century collection of over four thousand poems), which are dispersed throughout the narrative as a structural device.

Although many minor tales of the Heian period are characterized by their extravagant fantasies, *The Tale of Genji* (written by Shikibu Murasaki in the early eleventh century) is a meticulously realistic depiction of Court life. Murasaki gives her views on the art of the novel in a passage spoken by her hero Genji. He argues that the novel is neither a fantastic tale like the *Bamboo-Cutter's Tale* nor a historical record like *Kojiki*, the oldest known compilation of Japanese myths, historical legends, and genealogies, which was completed in 712. For Murasaki, the novel must concern itself with the feelings of a living person. Since a character is also a historical person, Murasaki admits that a novelist must present facts, but she insists that the facts must be carefully selected and arranged. Indeed, names, dates, places, and events in a novel may be fictitious, but this does not mean they are false. Fictionalization is also a necessary part of the process of re-creating reality. Furthermore, a novelist's expression of feeling stemming from facts should be more indirect than a poet's, for Murasaki realizes that a novelist is obligated to describe in detail the circumstances that prompted his feelings.

It is interesting to note here Murasaki's definition of the novel stated by Genji in one of his leisurely conversations with his adopted daughter:

> But I have a theory of my own about what this art of the novel is, and how it came into being. To begin with, it does not simply consist in the author's telling a story about the adventures of some other person. On the contrary, it happens because the storyteller's own experience of men and things, whether for good or ill—not only what he has passed through himself, but even events which he has only witnessed or been told of—has moved him to an emotion so passionate that he can no longer keep it shut up in his heart. Again and again something in his own life or in that around him will seem to the writer so important that he cannot bear to let it pass into oblivion. There must never come a time, he feels, when men do not know about it. That is my view of how this art arose.

Clearly then, it is no part of the storyteller's craft to describe only what is good or beautiful. Sometimes, of course, virtue will be his theme, and he may then make such play with it as he will. But he is just as likely to have been struck by numerous examples of vice and folly in the world around him, and about them he has exactly the same feelings as about the pre-eminently good deeds which he encounters: they are important and must all be garnered in. Thus anything whatsoever may become the subject of a novel, provided only that it happens in this mundane life and not in some fairyland beyond our human ken.[1]

The statement that a novelist must emotionally involve himself with his character's life suggests that *The Tale of Genji* is not necessarily a realistic account of the decadent, Heian Court society. Murasaki's picture of conditions is perhaps more accurately called an idealistic and highly romantic vision of the world that noblemen and courtiers of the day wished to attain but never did. The time of the events that occur to a character is, therefore, indefinite, as the author declares at the beginning of her tale: "He lived it matters not when." After describing the bizarre experience that Genji has had with Yugao, the author confesses that although the hero has recently gone through his acts of indiscretion, she must still present him in a favorable light by deleting some of them. Genji, the author says, "was supposed to be an Emperor's son"; she is well aware of the probability that some readers will accuse her of whitewashing her protagonist in order to improve his future reputation. She says, however, "If I am accused of too much loquacity, I cannot help it."

As the excerpts in this collection demonstrate, the predominant theme of *The Tale of Genji* is love. There are no pivotal actions to speak of; the story develops as its main character moves from one experience to another. The movement is not, however, linear in the manner of a well-made Western novel, but cyclical. Genji is never allowed to grow old but participates in an insatiable quest for love. Yet he never becomes a rebellious and rugged Don Juan; he is never an egotist; and despite his ill-fated amorous adventures, he is adored by all men and women of his society. As many critics have pointed

[1] *The Tale of Genji*, trans. Arthur Waley (Boston: Houghton Mifflin Company, 1935), pp. 501–502.

out, Murasaki has endowed her hero with her own feminine sensibility. His actions and sentiments are always portrayed with great subtlety and refinement. In every one of his love affairs, Murasaki remarkably penetrates and tellingly describes his motives. And these motives are never sordid or inhuman; his thoughtfulness and constant courtesy are far too deeply engrained. Even though his amour may turn out to be whimsical or lighthearted, we are not left without a sense of enlightenment. The author is totally committed to a sense of beauty in presenting the portrait of a prince against a colorful, rich culture.

From the end of the twelfth to the early part of the fourteenth century, Imperial authority was handed over to military men. During their protracted struggle for power, the country experienced long turmoil and hardship. Under these conditions, the literary productions were minimum; the refinement and reflectiveness of the previous period were completely forgotten. Although many intellectual activities were replaced by the propagation of practical knowledge and military glory, the Buddhist monks still maintained their refined traditions. Thus, in medieval Japan, Buddhism, rather than the Heian aristocracy, played a more important role for the development of culture. The ecclesiastics in the Kamakura period (1185-1333) taught men to resign themselves to fate, to minimize the values of heroism and valor, and to anticipate a spiritual happiness possible only in the next world.

This religious outlook is prominent in much of the literature produced during the period. Although *Tales of the Heike* (three excerpts are included in this collection) is a celebrated war novel in which we read descriptions of many of the fiercest battles in Japanese history, it is also a human story. The mother who grieves for her dying son; the nurse who is determined to drown the child Emperor rather than endanger his life at the hands of the enemy; the warrior who resolves to defect only because his son has been captured—all these characters show the human side of the battle. While the Heike clan disintegrates when confronted by the stronger forces of the Genji, we are shown that the warrior Shigeyoshi, the nurse Nii, and the former Empress are, nevertheless, able to achieve their salvation.[2] Ironically, as related in another of the tales, the winner of the battle, Yoshitsune, falls into disfavor with his half-brother Yoritomo and eventually dies an ignominious death. Since the novel concentrates on the tragedy of the Heike rather than on the glory of the Genji, it can be interpreted as an antiwar document. As the former Empress tells us, old parents were left behind by their young ones, husbands separated from their wives, and children severed from their mothers. Everyone involved with war went day and night without proper food or shelter and stood daily on the verge of total annihilation; to them, hope for the future salvation became the only reality.

The authorship of *Tales of the Heike* is not known. It is based on an earlier version of the battle, *The Rise and Fall of the Genji and the Heike* (*Genpei Seisuiki*), a more historically accurate work completed some time in the early part of the Kamakura period. Traditionally, the well-known stories from *Tales of the Heike* were recited to the accompaniment of a lute called "biwa," so that the tone of the dialogues provided the listener with deep sorrow and remorse. The phrasing of sentences is extremely smooth and cadenced, and the episodes are usually brief and stark, a stylistic reminder of the short, fleeting life of mortal man.

After the Kamakura period, there was still another long stretch of the Middle Ages in Japanese history. The Muromachi period (1333–1600), during which the internal military struggles of the preceding era continued, was hardly conducive to the production of the novel. The emperors and shoguns (military dictators) were frequently at odds over control of the central government until the Tokugawa regime came into power, establishing its capital in Tokyo in 1600. During this period some poetry was written at the courts of the Emperor and the shogun, but the greatest contribution to literature was the Noh plays, religious works that conveyed a sense of melancholy and resignation. It was also in

[2] Genji in *Tales of the Heike* is the name of a clan in medieval Japanese history and should not be confused with the name of a fictional character in *The Tale of Genji*.

this period that a recluse named Kenko Yoshida (1283–1350) wrote *The Grass of Leisure* (*Tsurezure-Gusa*), a famous collection of essays describing the public as well as private life of a medieval monk.

For the next two hundred fifty years, a succession of Tokugawa shoguns provided Japan with an unprecedented peace and security, even to the extent of sealing off the country from a surge of European influences. In the meantime, a great wave of learning was stimulated by the importation of various kinds of knowledge from China. This period saw the rise of business activity among the people and consequently a material progress never before experienced. In the field of fiction, the subdued tales of medieval warfare or the refined romances of the Heian aristocracy no longer suited the mood of the new era. The novel had to deal not only with noblemen or warriors but with common people—merchants, storekeepers, workers, artisans, entertainers, maids, and even prostitutes. The greatest novelist of the age was Saikaku Ihara (1642–1693?), who began as a haiku poet but turned to fiction. His first success came with *A Man Who Devoted His Entire Life to Lovemaking* (*Koshoku Ichidai Otoko*, 1682). The book consists of fifty-four chapters, an indication that Saikaku [3] wanted to emulate the greatest romance of love, *The Tale of Genji*, which has the same number of chapters. Although the historical and stylistic differences between the two are unmistakable, both works deal with love: Saikaku details the amorous pursuits of a self-made man in the new age just as his predecessor had dealt with princely love in an aristocratic society.

Saikaku's prose reflects the free spirit of the age; it is realistic and even, according to some critics, pornographic. He strongly emphasizes sexual love. Unlike any other prose writers before him, Saikaku also treats homo- and bisexuality. No matter what subjects he is concerned with, he does not share the medieval author's interest in moralizing; rather, he carefully detaches himself from the scenes he describes. In his episodes we rarely see an emotional involvement of the author with his characters neither do we notice an idealization of

[3] A Japanese writer is often called by his first name.

them. Saikaku is curious rather than affectionate toward them; his comments are filled with humor and often with irony.

"The Almanac-Maker's Tale," an episode (selected for this collection) from *Five Women Who Chose Love* (*Koshoku Gonin Onna*, 1686), relates a tragedy deriving from an act of love. Though he implies at the end of the story that there is no mercy for an illicit love, he cites a passage from *The Tale of Genji:* "That which in this world lies quite past our control is the way of love." Saikaku is more concerned with a mundane truth than with the expression of moral and religious precepts. In this tale he quite deliberately describes the circumstances under which man can be easily tempted to the way of love. Man is placed in this ephemeral world, a weak moral agent pitted against the overwhelming forces of love and sex. The heroine Osan, in fact, has had no intention of having an affair with Moemon; she has acted only to save her maid from an embarrassment. As if it were a punishment for her act, Osan's intrigue turns into a natural license for the adultery. Significantly, the story is pervaded with a sense of evanescence in the life of man: seasons revolve to show the passage of time, people enjoy viewing flowers that last only a few days, and the boat in which the lovers ride floats in the bay but must return to the shore at dusk. Only a cold winter keeps the lovers in exile, and another spring will bring a chestnut vendor back to the almanac-maker. Though from time to time the author hints at another world awaiting all men, his mind is always on the present, however brief and imperfect it may be.

One might expect that in Japan, as in England, this promising new kind of novel would grow and flourish in the eighteenth and nineteenth centuries. Instead, fiction sank to its lowest ebb. The reason for this is obvious. Instead of encouraging the trend of freedom and democracy, which existed in the seventeenth century, the Tokugawa government became more authoritative and censorious of the activities of literary men. The only works esteemed then were those written under the influence of Chinese models. Akinari Ueda (1734–1809) and Bakin Takizawa (1767–1848), both indebted to Chinese novels, were famous in their day but are now almost completely forgotten. In direct contrast to his predecessor Saikaku, Bakin constantly built his stories on a simplistic moral code, rewarding good and punishing vice. His plots are full of supernatural and unimaginable incidents; his writing is completely devoid of wit and humor. Ikku Jippensha (1766–1831), who was less valued than Bakin in his lifetime, has a more lasting appeal for today's audience. His *Hizakurige* (1802–22), reminiscent of a Western picaresque novel, relates the humorous adventures of two hobos on the road from Tokyo to Kyoto. Their names, Yaji and Kita, are as well remembered by Japanese as are Huck and Jim by Americans.

Japan entered the modern era when Commodore Perry opened the door to Japan, and trade with Europe and the United States began. In 1868, six centuries of military rule came to an end and the country was reunited under Emperor Meiji. With this historical event came a sudden upsurge of Western influences in all fields. Men of letters were eager to read whatever books were available to them. Their complete isolation from, and ignorance of, the great works of European literature is evidenced by the fact that their first reading list consisted of such books as Samuel Smiles's *Self-Help* (1871) and Edward Bulwer-Lytton's *Ernest Maltravers* (1878).[4] But later they progressed from Sir Walter Scott's *The Bride of Lammermoor* (1880) to Sir Thomas More's *Utopia* (1882), the first half of Friedrich Schiller's *Wilhelm Tell* (1882), Giovanni Boccaccio's *Decameron* (1882), Alexander Pushkin's *The Captain's Daughter* (1883), and eventually Shakespeare's plays (1883–86).

In 1885, a young graduate of Tokyo University, Shoyo Tsubouchi (1859–1935), published a book entitled *The Essence of the Novel (Shosetsu Shinzui)*. Shoyo not only had read the works of Alexander Dumas *père*, Walter Scott, Victor Hugo, and Edgar Allan Poe, but was well versed in Chaucer, Spenser, Shakespeare, and Milton. His knowledge of literary criticism was unsurpassed in his day; later he translated Shakespeare's complete works. Although *The Essence of the Novel* may not be as original as Henry James's "The

---

[4] Dates are those of translation into Japanese.

Art of Fiction" (1884) or Émile Zola's *Le Roman expérimental* (1880), Shoyo's theories were instrumental in shaping the modern Japanese novel. He argued that the traditional prejudice against fiction as an inferior art, which was fostered by Confucianism and even admitted by such a popular novelist as Robun Kanagaki (1829–1894), must be completely eliminated. For Shoyo, the novel was as noble an art as painting, music, and poetry. He warned against using the novel for narrow political or utilitarian ends. In attacking Bakin's writing he advocated that the first element of the novel is "human feeling," manners and customs in society being only secondary. A novelist must penetrate into the heart of man and describe his feeling with minuteness and fidelity: "The novel is an art; in order to be an art, it must be realistic."

The first to respond to Shoyo's manifesto was Shimei Futabatei (1864–1909). Futabatei's first masterpiece—and the first modern Japanese novel—*Floating Cloud* (*Ukigumo*, 1886–89), describes a pure but timid young man's feelings and reaction to the changes brought by the Meiji Restoration. As a student of Russian in college, Futabatei had earlier read critical works by Vissarion Belinski and Alexander Herzen, tales by Nicolai Gogol, and translated parts of Ivan Turgenev's *A Sportsman's Sketches.* As demonstrated in his own novels, *Floating Cloud* and *An Adopted Husband* (*Sono Omokage,* 1906), he succeeds in the minute psychological delineation of character. His greatest contribution to Japanese fiction, however, is not in technique or subject matter, but in language. He insisted that the language of the novel must be identical with that which is spoken, and his realistic dialogue became influential in the works of later novelists.

At the turn of the century naturalism was in the air. Originating in France, this new literary *Zeitgeist* spread all over the world, though its impact upon Japan was less marked than it was on Europe or America. The importance of tradition for Japanese novelists might account for the fact that literary naturalism failed to engage major novelists in Japan. In France, for instance, the great works of Balzac and Zola could not have been written without the tradition of Blaise Pascal, who developed the field of mathematics, and of Louis Pasteur, who experimented in bacteriology. The Japanese tradition in question lacked not only a Pascal and a Pasteur but also philosophers like Auguste Comte and Hippolyte Taine who interpreted the works of scientists for literary men. But when modern Japanese novelists became interested in Western fiction, they usually, and rightly, absorbed only those elements that were close to their traditions. The earliest reaction to French naturalism came from two major novelists, Soseki Natsume (1867–1916) and Ogai Mori (1862–1922). Soseki had no objection to the naturalist writers' detailed and objective treatment of material, but he was not at all convinced of the effect of the overpowering forces of heredity and environment on characters. He could not believe, at the dawn of enlightenment in Japan, that a good novel was to be made of the misery and littleness of man; what could enrich the spirit of the new era, he thought, was the discovery of aesthetic and humanistic values in tradition. Thus, he was more interested in the perfection of style and the architectonic structure of a well-made novel.

Ogai Mori, the other influential novelist of the times, was the first Japanese writer to spend his life in the West. Ogai went to Germany in 1884 to study medicine and remained a surgeon after his return. But while in Germany he became interested in its romantic literature and, on the basis of Karl Robert Eduard von Hartmann's aesthetic theory, developed an idealistic theory of fiction. In a direct attack against Shoyo's contention that a literary critic must judge objectively like a botanist or a biologist, Ogai asserted: "Making a judgment, which is the essence of criticism, must be preceded by the existence of idealism and of standard." Although romantic in his attitude toward fictional material, he insisted that a novel be closely based on personal experience. This type of novel, known as *shi-shosetsu* (*Ich roman*, or "I novel"), was to become a major genre in modern Japanese literature. Ogai's best-known novel, *The Wild Geese* (*Gan*, 1911), included in this book in its entirety, is based on his own experience in 1880, when he was a young university student in Tokyo. The heroine Otama, despite her poor, unhappy background, is presented as a morally strong and genuinely beautiful woman whose goodness prevents her from attaining the freedom she longs for. Because she is humble and innocent, she fails to communicate with her knight Okada at a crucial point in her liberation. Because of her sincere love for her father, she agrees to become the mistress of a wealthy moneylender. Even at her last chance for meeting Okada, she dares not disturb him and his friends, who are trying to hide a stolen goose from the eyes of a nearby policeman. Time runs out and cruel fate destroys her. If Stephen Crane, dealing with a similar predicament in his *Maggie: A Girl of the Streets* (1893), focuses his attention on the environment of his heroine, Ogai in this novel dramatizes the ideal qualities of his heroine with proper detachment and nuance.

The tradition started by Soseki and Ogai as a reaction to naturalism was carried on by a group of novelists who called themselves *tanbiha* (indulgent aesthetes). The most distinguished of them was Junichiro Tanizaki (1886–1965), who enjoyed one of the longest careers as a novelist. His preoccupation with sensual beauty as seen in his earlier works has often led critics to call his writing "fetishistic" or "masochistic." His most ambitious work is *The Makioka Sisters* (*Sasame Yuki*, 1943–48), completed after World War II. The novel tells of the lives that four sisters spent in the late thirties before the war. This long novel, lacking in an overall plot, is an introspective account of a past world Tanizaki knew best. It has a romantic vision that can only be created by an old man but is portrayed with the painstaking detail of a young realist. Tanizaki had earlier translated into modern Japanese the entire twenty-five hundred pages of *The Tale of Genji*, with which *The Makioka Sisters* is frequently compared.

Tanizaki's style and theme can easily be recognized in "The Bridge of Dreams" ("Yume no Ukihashi," 1959), another masterpiece from his later work. This story, included in the present collection, exhibits a keen psychological penetration into the personality of an extremely sensitive youth. The theme is his sexual awareness of his mother, which is now transferred to his stepmother. Tanizaki's success is not simply in illustrating a convincing Freudian view of a son's love for his mother; it is rather in providing the story with a symbolic fusion of maternal, paternal, and brotherly love into the memory of his now-deceased mother. Otokuni's remembrances of the past are elaborated with beautiful images: the sound of waterfalls, the movement of fish, the setting of Heron's Nest, the color of landscapes. The hero's utterance of the old word *"nenunawa,"* for instance, marks a passage of time, and his occasional references to old Japanese poems remind him of change in the world and in himself. But what remains is his unfading dream of his mother. This short story is, indeed, a work of art by a master and makes a unique contribution to the development of modern Japanese fiction.

As the country approached the twenties another literary movement arose, this time against the romanticists and aesthetes who had dominated the early decades of the twentieth century in Japan. The new movement was supported by a group of young fledgling writers who contributed their works to a literary magazine called *New Current of Thought* (*Shin Shicho*). By the time this magazine reached its third and fourth series, notable works by such writers as Ryunosuke Akutagawa (1892–1927), Kan Kikuchi (1888–1948), and Yuzo Yamamoto (1887–) had been published in it. For example, Akutagawa's weird story "The Nose" ("Hana," 1916), praised by Soseki Natsume, set a significant pattern for his later writing. Their common maxim was the use of reason instead of emotion: a novelist must neither be obsessed with beauty nor influenced by idealism. They were mostly intellectuals who were determined to perfect style and technique without reference to theme. Their leader was Akutagawa, whose achievement as short-story writer deserves an eminent place in Japanese, if not in world, literature. Outside of Japan, he is best known as the author of the stories on which the film *Rashomon* (1951) is based. In these stories, Akutagawa experiments with point of view. Remaining coldly detached himself, he tells his stories through the perspectives of his characters; for him, there are as many "true" accounts of any event as there are observers.

Akutagawa traveled in China and read the works of Anatole France, Charles Baudelaire, August Strindberg, and Edgar Allan Poe, but his sole purpose in living was to re-create in the form of short, intensified fiction the traditional legends and stories of the past. His ideal was to create art for art's sake, and his writing often turned to the bizarre and the grotesque. The power of his genius for presenting scenes of horror and human tragedy with detachment and restraint is amply demonstrated by "The Hell Screen" ("Jigokuhen," 1918). Akutagawa's story, selected for this collection, is based on the famous legend of a painter from the Heian period who could sacrifice anything but his love for his only daughter. Faithful to his own conviction in creating authentic art, Yoshihide is commissioned by his lord to paint a burning chariot with a real woman in it, who is later revealed to be none other than his own daughter. The hero's single-mindedness is characteristic of the extreme argument of an artist's position. For Yoshihide, this painting has become the end of the road and there is no escape for him but to hang himself. The insoluble conflict of art and life that Akutagawa himself saw in his own day was soon to produce a story of a gruesome society nourished only by intellectualism. His *Kappa* (1927; the name of imaginary animals in Japanese folklore that live in rivers and lakes) is an anti-utopian novel narrated by a patient of a lunatic asylum who once lived among the Kappa. Akutagawa's later years were characterized by a sense of conflict and futility, and he could not justify his own existence. Finally, in 1927, he poisoned himself and died at the age of thirty-five.

The twenties in Japan saw the appearance of proletarian literature, a movement that continued well into the early thirties. Reflecting the sentiments of an early labor movement and later developing into a close cooperation with anarchists and bolsheviks, many young writers found a worthy cause to which they could devote their literary talents. Despite some ideological conflicts within their organization, they published literary magazines under such titles as *Literary Front* (*Bungei Sensen*) and *War Flag* (*Senki*). Yoshiki Hayama (1894–1945) wrote his long novel, *Men Who Live at Sea* (*Umi ni Ikuru Hitobito*, 1926), while in a prison; in it he describes the appalling working conditions of seamen. Unlike many of the novels of this school, it is not merely a social protest, but also an excellent novel. Unfortunately, however, proletarian writing failed to attract the attention and concern of major novelists in Japan. Those in the movement, furthermore, neglected to perfect style and technique and were often solely concerned with sentimentalizing the poor and the oppressed. As World War II approached, the government began to restrict their activities. The authorities suppressed their writings, and even persecuted such influential leaders as Takiji Kobayashi (1903–1933), the author of *Cannery Boat* (*Kani Kosen*, 1929), who was murdered at the hands of police in 1933. Because of such persecution, the movement gradually disappeared.

But, as if it were a replacement for the proletarian writers, another school of writers calling themselves "neo-perceptionists" came into their maturity in the thirties. They were directly opposed to using the novel as a forum for social protest and at the same time dissatisfied with the form of the *shishosetsu* often used in Japanese fiction. For them, the novel could thrive on startling images and direct sense impressions rather than on the expression of ideologies or personal reflections. Although this movement was short-lived, it produced two of the major writers represented in the present volume. Riichi Yokomitsu (1898–1947) was eager to absorb whatever was new in the works of André Gide, Marcel Proust, Paul Valéry, and James Joyce, but he was always interested in developing his own technique in dealing with the psychology of modern man. His "Machine" ("Kikai," 1930), included in the present collection, is an experiment in which he attempted to reduce human relationships to a petty brawl at a workshop. No matter how intelligently one tries to understand his own behavior and his relationship with others, the result is predetermined by the machine. In this constrained scheme of things, man looks absurd trying to exert his will. In his struggle to outwit the machine, man can only twist himself, becoming even more grotesque than he is. Modern man's egotism shows itself in his greed for money, fame, or love. Curiously enough, the one who has the least ego in the story is Yashiki, an innocent mechanic who meets a tragic end. In the final scene the narrator thus confesses: "I no longer understand myself. I only feel the sharp menace of an approaching machine, aimed at me. Someone must judge me. How can I know what I have done?"

The other major novelist of the school is Yasunari Kawabata

(1899–1972), the first Japanese writer to receive the Nobel Prize. Like Yokomitsu, he is terse and direct in his description of sense impressions, but his writing shows more restraint and is more delicate than Yokomitsu's. It is often compared with haiku poetry for its abrupt but evocative imagery. His early success came with the short story "A Dancer of Izu" ("Izu no Odoriko," 1926). The story describes a young dancer whom the author as a young student meets on a trip down the Izu Peninsula. Kawabata's best-known novel, *Snow Country* (*Yukiguni*, 1934–47), started in 1934 and completed after the war, also deals with the love that develops between a man and woman on a tour, this time between a middle-aged ballet expert and a young geisha, in the northern region. Even though the protagonists of both novels are women, both works contain autobiographical elements. In both stories, the hero is merely an observer, and this makes the stories quite different from the "I novel" discussed earlier. The author succeeds in introducing, not himself, but another person as the central character who is impressionistically portrayed. Thus, the hero becomes only a perceiving center who observes the story unfold. In "The Moon on the Water" ("Suigetsu," 1953), and included herein, the author uses a mirror to convey an intense impression of the love between a woman and her dead husband:

> Kyoko thought of, indeed longed for, the image of herself working in the garden, seen through the mirror in her husband's hand, and for the white of the lilies, the crowd of village children playing in the field, and the morning sun rising above the far-off snowy mountains—for that separate world she had shared with him. For the sake of her present husband, Kyoko suppressed this feeling, which seemed about to become an almost physical yearning, and tried to take it for something like a distant view of the celestial world.

The story centers on a woman's discovery of herself, and of the beauty of her past world contrasted with the ugliness of mundane life. Just as the moon's reflection on the water with its clear outline and color is as genuinely beautiful, the now-vanished world reflected on Kyoko's mirror with its memories and background acquires a spirit of its own.

Writers like Kawabata outlived the war, which had a devastating effect on literary activities in Japan. Those novelists, however, who were not drafted during the war kept on writing despite governmental surveillance and censorship. Thus, such older novelists as Toson Shimazaki (1872–9143), Naoya Shiga (1883–1971), and Tanizaki managed to publish some of their works in the early forties. Once the war was over, many of the established writers revived their activities in earnest, and with them a number of new important novelists appeared on the scene. Most fundamental to men of letters at that time was the long-denied freedom of speech and thought. Japanese literature since the Meiji Restoration had been constrained in one way or another: in the field of politics, commentary on the royal family had been severely restricted; and since the thirties, mention of the word "communism" had been prohibited. Works that described sexual relations, or even kissing, were usually banned, and adultery was taboo. Writers in their new-found freedom rejoiced like hungry men admitted to a feast. Despite a shortage of paper, literary magazines, some of which were discontinued under the censorship during the war, began to appear in numbers. The earliest issues included works by established novelists like Kafu Nagai (1879–1959), Hakucho Masamune (1879–1962), and Naoya Shiga, who, refusing to cooperate with the war efforts, had privately continued their writing.

Important work was, however, accomplished by younger writers, who can be divided into two main groups: those who had done some writing before but were interrupted during the war, and those who were mostly in their twenties during the war. To the first group belong Ango Sakaguchi (1906–1955) and Osamu Dazai (1909–1948), two novelists who were most successful in describing the chaotic human conditions prevailing during and after the war. Reflecting a breakdown of the traditional values, their philosophy was existentialism. These writers were not interested in social mores of the day; neither were they concerned with the future. They professed to live only for the present moment, and dared perish with it; one ended his life in great poverty and the other by suicide. Sakaguchi thus insisted that there should never be on the part of a novelist any consciously applied effort to create beauty; beauty comes, not from intention, but from what he cannot help but write by necessity. He wrote about himself in a unique style that disregarded all the existing standards of prose writing. In contrast to the modern tradition of Akutagawa or Kawabata, Sakaguchi argued that there should never be a distance between a novelist and his material; he believed that a novel is produced only by involving the self with the material.

"The Idiot" ("Hakuchi," 1946), a selection in this volume, is about Sakaguchi's war experience and reflects his own view of writing. The story is perhaps one of the most accurate pictures of the closing days of the war in Japan. War is hideous and cruel but man must preserve his life. As we see in the story, soldiers, politicians, city officials, and shopkeepers all hide their true selves to make their lives endurable. Only during the air raid do they reveal their true selves. The story is focused on the artist Izawa, who sees nothing but emptiness in these conditions. Later, however, his compassion, and unpretentious feeling of love, for an idiot woman who happens to run into his house during an air raid, awakens him and gives his existence meaning. The idiot not only provides the story with a symbol of escape from a writer's painful solitude as he wanders in the wasteland, but presents a realistic picture of his own experience.

Dazai, like Sakaguchi, was born of a wealthy country squire in northern Japan but spent a bohemian life in the city during his formative years. Dazai's novels reflect the problems and anguish of youth in the postwar era. In his writing, as well as in his suicide, he resembles Akutagawa. But his writing is more personal and lacks Akutagawa's objective detachment. Dazai's best works are generally considered to be *The Setting Sun* (*Shayo*, 1947) and *No Longer Human* (*Ningen Shikkaku*, 1948). *No Longer Human* is, perhaps, his most powerful expression of the nihilistic mood that prevailed among many of the writers of the younger generation after the war. The fall of the hero Yozo is precipitated by his tragic impulse for vile and inhuman acts, but his life is presented with an intense human sorrow and suffering that appeals to a fellow human being.

There is also another side to Dazai's pessimism. For Dazai

lying and laughing were useful means through which men could alleviate the burden of their lives and forget the emptiness of existence. Japanese farmers, who do not regard lying as a vice, are in marked contrast to warriors, who considered it the greatest offense a samurai could commit. This traditional difference between the two classes of men in Japan is in the background of "The Courtesy Call" ("Shinyu Kokan," 1946). This story, included herein, humorously satirizes the conceit of a modern intellectual, the host of the visitor in the story. Hirata, however arrogant he may be toward city intellectuals, comes to the realization that he is only a farmer, not a sharp marksman who can shoot down dozens of ducks before breakfast. The intellectual, on the other hand, always turning into cynicism and despair, can only end in self-annihilation. Although the event in the story is treated with levity, its implications are grave. Ironically, Hirata visits the writer to make plans for a class reunion. But the distance between the classmates is immense; one can hardly bridge the gulf with a token gesture of friendship or material support. The desert of debris, which litters even the countryside, suggests a sense of alienation. The distance between men, Dazai thinks, can be narrowed only by a certain code of behavior nurtured by tradition. Thus we are told that the visitor voted for the host's brother out of friendship as an old classmate. Although the visitor acts as if to take a revenge on the host, the visitor nevertheless talks to his wife with civility and even with a sense of humor.

The works of Sartre and Camus were translated shortly after the war, and the strong influence of these French writers on novelists like Sakaguchi and Dazai was undeniable. French existentialism, though often oversimplified and misinterpreted, suited the sense of futility and absurdity they felt about life. This view is held even today by many young writers, notably Kenzaburo Oe (1935–), whose *A Personal Matter* (*Kojintekina Taiken*, 1964) has attracted critics' attention. However, the year 1948, when Dazai committed suicide, marks the end of that postwar era of chaos and confusion. The gloom that hovered over Japan after the war gradually dissipated as its economic, social, and political conditions steadily improved. Since then, works of major and some minor foreign novelists (like Anaïs Nin) have been translated into Japanese or reissued. Another remarkable phenomenon was the new work produced by many of the older novelists. Tanizaki, for example, had written, besides *The Makioka Sisters*, two more major works—*The Key* (*Kagi*, 1956) and *Diary of a Mad Old Man* (*Futen Rojin Nikki*, 1961–62)—before his death in 1965 after a long and distinguished career.

Finally, Yukio Mishima (1925–1970), though unique in his style and philosophy, belongs to the younger generation of writers. If Dazai was the idol of youth shortly after the war, Mishima has become their champion since the fifties. His dramatic *seppuku* at the headquarters of the Japanese Self-Defense Forces in protest against the nation's apathy about military glory shocked the entire nation and puzzled his audience abroad. In 1970, after an extraordinarily prolific career as novelist, playwright, essayist, and even film director and actor, Mishima felt he was no longer young. He confessed to his friends and in his letters that, having expended all his energy for his last work, a tetralogy entitled *The Sea of Fertility* (*Hojo no Umi*, 1967–71), he had nothing more to say and nothing else to do but kill himself. In an article published in September, 1970, he further glorified the forthcoming action, quoting the sixteenth-century Chinese philosopher Wang Yang-ming and the Japanese scholar Heihachiro Oshio who pierced his throat and burned himself to death after the failure of a poor men's revolt in 1837. Whatever glory Mishima might have found in his final act in relation to his art will be discussed in years to come. But, to be sure, he was an idealist who sought beauty in death. At the same time, he was a man of action who, doggedly pursuing beauty and truth in the traditional values, was balked by ever increasing materialism —the spurious dream of contemporary Japanese.

From the beginning, Mishima was repulsed by the humanistic and liberal ideas common to all the writers of the younger generation. Instead, he was greatly attracted to the romantic tradition of Ogai and Tanizaki. Immediately after the war his talent was discovered by his mentor Kawabata, and by the end of the forties with the publication of *Confessions of a Mask* (*Kamen no Kokuhaku,* 1949) he had established his reputation as the most gifted novelist to appear in the postwar era. This novel is a frank confession of a young boy who gradually becomes aware of his homosexuality. His next major novel is *Forbidden Colors* (*Kinjiki,* 1952), published in two volumes. Like his previous novel it deals with the problems of homosexuality, this time studied against the background of a decadent underground life in Tokyo. Undoubtedly autobiographical, both novels avoid morbid sensationalism. His greatest achievement, however, is *The Temple of the Golden Pavilion* (*Kinkakuji,* 1956), which is the least autobiographical of his writings. Based on a real incident, the novel penetrates into the dark, complex psychology of a deranged young monk who, obsessed with the beauty of the temple— a national treasure—finally sets fire to it.

Mishima's style is characterized by his elaborate phrases and artificial images, some of which can be found in "The Priest of Shiga Temple and His Love" ("Shigadera Shonin no Koi," 1954), a short story included in the present volume. His ornate but flowing prose may owe to his earlier reading in the work of the eighteenth-century dramatist Chikamatsu. It is of some interest to note here that Mishima also wrote modern versions of Noh plays. Although he is said to have been influenced by French writers like Guy de Maupassant, Raymond Radiguet, and François Mauriac, and much taken with Oscar Wilde and W. B. Yeats, the fact remains that he had a lifelong fascination with older Japanese literature. "The Priest of Shiga Temple and His Love" is based on an episode contained in the medieval chronicle *The Record of Great Peace* (*Taiheiki*). The language of this chronicle, like that of *Tales of the Heike,* included in this book, is highly poetic and owes nothing to Chinese models or ideas. In this myth, Mishima is concerned with the motivation of two characters regarded as occupying the opposite ends of society: a priest and a "prostitute." At the beginning of the story neither the priest nor the concubine is aware of the conflict between sexual love and religious faith. Thus the priest has long determined to achieve the Pure Land by abandoning the thoughts of the Floating World. Similarly, the concubine has given up her attempt to attain the Pure Land by resigning herself to being the mistress of the Emperor. But when they meet, each succeeds in attaining what has been forbidden to him. The story can be taken as a farcical, if not witty, allegory concerning the road to human happiness, which the author thinks could be built at the crossroad of heaven and earth.

It was almost a century ago that the work of modern Japanese fiction was started by young men of the Meiji Restoration who made contact with Western culture for the first time. Since then Japanese novelists have carried out numerous experiments as is shown by all kinds of "isms," arguments, and counterarguments. At no crucial points, however, in the course of the development of their fiction were they oblivious of their native traditions. Major novelists like Ogai, Akutagawa, Tanizaki, Kawabata, Mishima, not to mention the much earlier Murasaki and Saikaku, all looked back to, and attempted to assimilate, classical Japanese literature. Interestingly enough, the last work Tanizaki produced before he died at the age of seventy-nine was his third complete translation of *The Tale of Genji* into modern Japanese.

Critics have often observed that although the content of modern Japanese fiction arises from the native material, its forms are basically Western. This point of view may be analogous to the assertion that machines produced in Japan today are essentially Western models, but that their manufacturers are Japanese. These critics might wish that fiction written in Japan were purely Japanese both in form and in content. But the age in which we live, be it in the East or in the West, is not conducive to such a mode of writing. Rather, the novels and short stories as they are written in Japan today are the products of the twentieth century as well as of the native tradition.

SHIKIBU MURASAKI
The Tale of Genji
(Genji Monogatari, Eleventh century)

Translated by Suematsu Kenchio

Little is known about the life of Shikibu Murasaki (978?–1016?), though she was already famous in Japan toward the end of the twelfth century as the author of *The Tale of Genji*. Daughter of the classical Chinese scholar Tametoki Fujiwara, she entered the service of Empress Akiko after the death of her husband. According to her *Diary*, Murasaki was able to read chronicles faster than her elder brother, who was educated as a Chinese scholar; her father used to sigh and say to her, "If only you were a boy." Her talent in classical Chinese is further shown by another entry in the diary, in which she quotes Emperor Ichijo (reigned 986–1011), who read *The Tale of Genji*, as saying, "The author must be a person devoted to fine scholarship; she could probably read the annals of Japan with great ease." Thereafter, at Court, she was nicknamed "Dame of Japanese Annals." In the early eleventh century in Japan, novels were supposed to be ignored by men, read only by women and children. The fact that the Emperor read her novel and even mentioned it in public must have given Murasaki a great honor. Before the eleventh century in Japan, literary works had always been transcribed in Chinese ideographs. A work of art in Japanese letters, therefore, would not have won a male audience. *The Tale of Genji* was the first writing done substantially in Japanese letters, called "hiragana," and, more importantly, the first major work read by men.

Not much is known of the actual writing of the novel. Certainly by 1008, at least the first chapters had been completed, for it was in that year that the Emperor made his statement about the author. Some critics regard the later sections of the work as evidence of greater maturity on the part of the author, thus presenting the possibility that it was not finished until just before her death; but the proof is inconclusive. Chronologically, *The Tale of Genji* is often divided into three parts: the first, thirty-three chapters from "Kiritsubo" through "Fuji no Uraba"; the second, eight chapters from "Wakana Part One" through "Maboroshi"; and the third, thirteen chapters from "Niou" through "Yume no Ukihashi." The first part deals with the life of the hero Genji from his birth to his fortieth year, during which he falls into disfavor at Court after his father's retirement from the throne but later regains power and enjoys the prime of his life with his second wife Murasaki. In the meantime, Genji is secretly in love with his step-mother Fujitsubo, who gives birth to the Crown Prince. In this period of his life, Genji is characterized as a scrupulous politician as well as a passionate lover. The second part of the tale is concerned with his later years ending in the life of a hermit at the age of fifty-two. In contrast to his earlier flourishing career, this part of his life is filled with gloom and sadness. His wife Murasaki, grieved by his acceptance of Nyosan as his legitimate wife, falls ill and finally dies. Genji's reputation is further marred by the illegitimate child of Nyosan, Kaoru, who is supposed by the world to be his son. The last part of the story, beginning with the death of Genji, relates the life of Kaoru, a well-cultivated man, who, unlike Genji, experiences a sense of conflict between religious faith and human love.

The three chapters selected here, from the first part of the tale, present Genji as an immature youth, then as an irresponsible lover, and finally as a cautious politician. The hero's emotional entanglements with women result in misery and unhappiness: Yugao dies bewitched; Akashi is vexed by an inferiority complex due to her rank; and Murasaki endures deep loneliness during her husband's banishment. In each case, the woman feels helpless and, having become involved with Genji, has no further control over her life. Genji is described as a born lover, but at the same time as a political figure entirely governed by his society. Thus, Yugao would not have died a mysterious death if Genji had not been an important public figure; Akashi would not have been left with a child if Genji had not been the guardian of the government;

Murasaki would not have been replaced by Nyosan if her mother's rank had been higher. Genji, the shining one, is thus both his own person and a man of his time, and it is this interplay of private and public character that gives the novel much of its appeal.

THE CHAMBER OF KIRI [1]

In the reign of a certain Emperor, whose name is unknown to us, there was, among the Niogo [2] and Koyi [2] of the Imperial Court, one who, though she was not of high birth, enjoyed the full tide of Royal favor. Hence her superiors, each one of whom had always been thinking—"I shall be the *one*," gazed upon her disdainfully with malignant eyes, and her equals and inferiors were more indignant still.

Such being the state of affairs, the anxiety which she had to endure was great and constant, and this was probably the reason that her health was at last so much affected, that she was often compelled to absent herself from Court, and to retire to the residence of her mother.

Her father, who was a Dainagon,[3] was dead; but her mother, being a woman of good sense, gave her every possible guidance in the due performance of Court ceremony, so that in this respect she seemed but little different from those whose fathers and mothers were still alive to bring them before public notice, yet, nevertheless, her friendliness made her oftentimes feel very diffident from the want of any patron of influence.

These circumstances, however, only tended to make the favor shown to her by the Emperor wax warmer and warmer, and it was even shown to such an extent as to become a warning to after-generations. There had been instances in China in which favoritism such as this had caused national disturbance and disaster; and thus the matter became a subject of public animadversion, and it seemed not improbable

[1] The beautiful tree, called Kiri, has been named *Paulownia imperialis*, by botanists.
[2] Official titles held by Court ladies.
[3] The name of a Court office.

that people would begin to allude even to the example of Yo-ki-hi.[4]

In due course, and in consequence, we may suppose, of the Divine blessing on the sincerity of their affection, a jewel of a little prince was born to her. The first prince who had been born to the Emperor was the child of Koki-den-Niogo,[5] the daughter of the Udaijin (a great officer of State). Not only was he first in point of age, but his influence on his mother's side was so great that public opinion had almost unanimously fixed upon him as Heir-apparent. Of this the Emperor was fully conscious, and he only regarded the newborn child with that affection which one lavishes on a domestic favorite. Nevertheless, the mother of the first prince had, not unnaturally, a foreboding that unless matters were managed adroitly her child might be superseded by the younger one. She, we may observe, had been established at Court before any other lady, and had more children than one. The Emperor, therefore, was obliged to treat her with due respect, and reproaches from her always affected him more keenly than those of any others.

To return to her rival. Her constitution was extremely delicate, as we have seen already, and she was surrounded by those who would fain lay bare, so to say, her hidden scars. Her apartments in the palace were Kiri-Tsubo (the chamber of Kiri); so called from the trees that were planted around. In visiting her there the Emperor had to pass before several other chambers, whose occupants universally chafed when they saw it. And again, when it was her turn to attend upon the Emperor, it often happened that they played off mischievous pranks upon her at different points in the corridor which leads to the Imperial quarters. Sometimes they would soil the skirts of her attendants, sometimes they would shut against her the door of the covered portico, where no other passage existed; and thus, in every possible way, they one and all combined to annoy her.

[4] A celebrated and beautiful favorite of an Emperor of the Thang dynasty in China, whose administration was disturbed by a rebellion, said to have been caused by the neglect of his duties for her sake.

[5] A Niogo who resided in a part of the Imperial palace called "Koki-den."

The Emperor at length became aware of this, and gave her, for her special chamber, another apartment, which was in the Koro-Den, and which was quite close to those in which he himself resided. It had been originally occupied by another lady who was now removed, and thus fresh resentment was aroused.

When the young prince was three years old the Hakamagi [6] took place. It was celebrated with a pomp scarcely inferior to that which adorned the investiture of the first prince. In fact, all available treasures were exhausted on the occasion. And again the public manifested its disapprobation. In the summer of the same year the Kiri-Tsubo-Koyi became ill, and wished to retire from the palace. The Emperor, however, who was accustomed to see her indisposed, strove to induce her to remain. But her illness increased day by day; and she had drooped and pined away until she was now but a shadow of her former self. She made scarcely any response to the affectionate words and expressions of tenderness which her Royal lover caressingly bestowed upon her. Her eyes were half-closed: she lay like a fading flower in the last stage of exhaustion, and she became so much enfeebled that her mother appeared before the Emperor and entreated with tears that she might be allowed to leave. Distracted by his vain endeavors to devise means to aid her, the Emperor at length ordered a Te-gruma [7] to be in readiness to convey her to her own home, but even then he went to her apartment and cried despairingly: "Did not we vow that we would neither of us be either before or after the other even in traveling the last long journey of life? And can you find it in your heart to leave me now?" Sadly and tenderly looking up, she thus replied, with almost failing breath:—

> Since my departure for this dark journey,
> Makes you so sad and lonely,
> Fain would I stay though weak and weary,
> And live for your sake only!

[6] The Hakamagi is the investiture of boys with trousers, when they pass from childhood to boyhood. In ordinary cases, this is done when about five years old, but in the Royal Family, it usually takes place earlier.

[7] A carriage drawn by hands. Its use in the Courtyard of the palace was only allowed to persons of distinction.

"Had I but known this before——"

She appeared to have much more to say, but was too weak to continue. Overpowered with grief, the Emperor at one moment would fain accompany her himself, and at another moment would have her remain to the end where she then was.

At the last, her departure was hurried, because the exorcism for the sick had been appointed to take place on that evening at her home, and she went. The child prince, however, had been left in the palace, as his mother wished, even at that time, to make her withdrawal as privately as possible, so as to avoid any invidious observations on the part of her rivals. To the Emperor the night now became black with gloom. He sent messenger after messenger to make inquiries, and could not await their return with patience. Midnight came, and with it the sound of lamentation. The messenger, who could do nothing else, hurried back with the sad tidings of the truth. From that moment the mind of the Emperor was darkened, and he confined himself to his private apartments.

He would still have kept with himself the young prince now motherless, but there was no precedent for this, and it was arranged that he should be sent to his grandmother for the mourning. The child, who understood nothing, looked with amazement at the sad countenances of the Emperor, and of those around him. All separations have their sting, but sharp indeed was the sting in a case like this.

Now the funeral took place. The weeping and wailing mother, who might have longed to mingle in the same flames,[8] entered a carriage, accompanied by female mourners. The procession arrived at the cemetery of Otagi, and the solemn rites commenced. What were then the thoughts of the desolate mother? The image of her dead daughter was still vividly present to her—still seemed animated with life. She must see her remains become ashes to convince herself that she was really dead. During the ceremony, an Imperial messenger came from the palace, and invested the dead with the title of Sammi. The letters patent were read, and listened to in solemn silence. The Emperor conferred this title now in regret that during her lifetime he had not even promoted her posi-

[8] Cremation was very common in these days.

tion from a Koyi to a Niogo, and wishing at this last moment to raise her title at least one step higher. Once more several tokens of disapprobation were manifested against the proceeding. But, in other respects, the beauty of the departed, and her gracious bearing, which had ever commanded admiration, made people begin to think of her with sympathy. It was the excess of the Emperor's favor which had created so many detractors during her lifetime; but now even rivals felt pity for her; and if any did not, it was in the Koki-den. "When one is no more, the memory becomes so dear," may be an illustration of a case such as this.

Some days passed, and due requiem services were carefully performed. The Emperor was still plunged in thought, and no society had attractions for him. His constant consolation was to send messengers to the grandmother of the child, and to make inquiries after them. It was now autumn, and the evening winds blew chill and cold. The Emperor—who, when he saw the first prince, could not refrain from thinking of the younger one—became more thoughtful than ever; and, on this evening, he sent Yugei-no-Miobu [9] to repeat his inquiries. She went as the new moon just rose, and the Emperor stood and contemplated from his veranda the prospect spread before him. At such moments he had usually been surrounded by a few chosen friends, one of whom was almost invariably his lost love. Now she was no more. The thrilling notes of her music, the touching strains of her melodies, stole over him in his dark and dreary reverie.

The Miobu arrived at her destination; and, as she drove in, a sense of sadness seized upon her.

The owner of the house had long been a widow; but the residence, in former times, had been made beautiful for the pleasure of her only daughter. Now, bereaved of this daughter, she dwelt alone; and the grounds were overgrown with weeds, which here and there lay prostrated by the violence of the winds; while over them, fair as elsewhere, gleamed the mild luster of the impartial moon. The Miobu entered, and was led into a front room in the southern part of the building. At first the hostess and the messenger were equally

[9] A Court lady, whose name was Yugei, holding an office called "Miobu."

at a loss for words. At length the silence was broken by the hostess, who said:—

"Already have I felt that I have lived too long, but doubly do I feel it now that I am visited by such a messenger as you." Here she paused, and seemed unable to contend with her emotion.

"When Naishi-no-Ske returned from you," said the Miobu, "she reported to the Emperor that when she saw you, face to face, her sympathy for you was irresistible. I, too, see now how true it is!" A moment's hesitation, and she proceeded to deliver the Imperial message:—

"The Emperor commanded me to say that for some time he had wandered in his fancy, and imagined he was but in a dream; and that, though he was now more tranquil, he could not find that it was only a dream. Again, that there is no one who can really sympathize with him; and he hopes that you will come to the palace, and talk with him. His Majesty said also that the absence of the prince made him anxious, and that he is desirous that you should speedily make up your mind. In giving me this message, he did not speak with readiness. He seemed to fear to be considered unmanly, and strove to exercise reserve. I could not help experiencing sympathy with him, and hurried away here, almost fearing that, perhaps, I had not quite caught his full meaning."

So saying, she presented to her a letter from the Emperor. The lady's sight was dim and indistinct. Taking it, therefore, to the lamp, she said, "Perhaps the light will help me to decipher," and then read as follows, much in unison with the oral message: "I thought that time only would assuage my grief; but time only brings before me more vividly my recollection of the lost one. Yet, it is inevitable. How is my boy? Of him, too, I am always thinking. Time once was when we both hoped to bring him up together. May he still be to you a memento of his mother!"

Such was the brief outline of the letter, and it contained the following:—

    The sound of the wind is dull and drear
    Across Miyagi's [10] dewy lea,

[10] Miyagi is the name of a field which is famous for the Hagi or Lespedeza, a small and pretty shrub, which blooms in the autumn.

And makes me mourn for the motherless deer
That sleeps beneath the Hagi tree.

She put gently the letter aside, and said, "Life and the world are irksome to me; and you can see, then, how reluctantly I should present myself at the palace. I cannot go myself, though it is painful to me to seem to neglect the honored command. As for the little prince, I know not why he thought of it, but he seems quite willing to go. This is very natural. Please inform his Majesty that this is our position. Very possibly, when one remembers the birth of the young prince, it would not be well for him to spend too much of his time as he does now."

Then she wrote quickly a short answer, and handed it to the Miobu. At this time her grandson was sleeping soundly.

"I should like to see the boy awake, and to tell the Emperor all about him, but he will already be impatiently awaiting my return," said the messenger. And she prepared to depart.

"It would be a relief to me to tell you how a mother laments over her departed child. Visit me, then, sometimes, if you can, as a friend, when you are not engaged or pressed for time. Formerly, when you came here, your visit was ever glad and welcome; now I see in you the messenger of woe. More and more my life seems aimless to me. From the time of my child's birth, her father always looked forward to her being presented at Court, and when dying he repeatedly enjoined me to carry out that wish. You know that my daughter had no patron to watch over her, and I well knew how difficult would be her position among her fellow maidens. Yet, I did not disobey her father's request, and she went to Court. There the Emperor showed her a kindness beyond our hopes. For the sake of that kindness she uncomplainingly endured all the cruel taunts of envious companions. But their envy ever deepening, and her troubles ever increasing, at last she passed away, worn out, as it were, with care. When I think of the matter in that light, the kindest favors seem to me fraught with misfortune. Ah! that the blind affection of a mother should make me talk in this way!"

In poetry it is associated with deer, and a male and female deer are often compared to a lover and his love, and their young to their children.

"The thoughts of his Majesty may be even as your own," said the Miobu. "Often when he alluded to his overpowering affection for her, he said that perhaps all this might have been because their love was destined not to last long. And that though he ever strove not to injure any subject, yet for Kiri-Tsubo, and for her alone, he had sometimes caused the ill-will of others; that when all this has been done, she was no more! All this he told me in deep gloom, and added that it made him ponder on their previous existence."

The night was now far advanced, and again the Miobu rose to take leave. The moon was sailing down westward and the cool breeze was waving the herbage to and fro, in which numerous *mushi* were plaintively singing.[11] The messenger, being still somehow unready to start, hummed:

> Fain would one weep the whole night long,
> As weeps the Sudu-Mushi's song,
> Who chants her melancholy lay,
> Till night and darkness pass away.

As she still lingered, the lady took up the refrain—

> To the heath where the Suzu-Mushi sings,
>   From beyond the clouds [12] one comes from on high
> And more dews on the grass around she flings,
>   And adds her own, to the night wind's sigh.

A Court dress and a set of beautiful ornamental hairpins, which had belonged to Kiri-Tsubo, were presented to the Miobu by her hostess, who thought that these things, which her daughter had left to be available on such occasions, would be a more suitable gift, under present circumstances, than any other.

On the return of the Miobu she found that the Emperor had not yet retired to rest. He was really awaiting her return, but was apparently engaged in admiring the Tsubo-Senzai— or stands of flowers—which were placed in front of the palaces, and in which the flowers were in full bloom. With him were

---

[11] In Japan there are a great number of "*mushi*" or insects, which sing in herbage grass, especially in the evenings of autumn. They are constantly alluded to in poetry.

[12] In Japanese poetry, persons connected with the Court, are spoken of as "the people above the clouds."

four or five ladies, his intimate friends, with whom he was conversing. In these days his favorite topic of conversation was the "Long Regret."[13] Nothing pleased him more than to gaze upon the picture of that poem, which had been painted by Prince Teishi-In, or to talk about the native poems on the same subject, which had been composed, at the Royal command, by Ise, the poetess, and by Tsurayuki, the poet. And it was in this way that he was engaged on this particular evening.

To him the Miobu now went immediately, and she faithfully reported to him all that she had seen, and she gave to him also the answer to his letter. That letter stated that the mother of Kiri-Tsubo felt honored by his gracious inquiries, and that she was so truly grateful that she scarcely knew how to express herself. She proceeded to say that his condescension made her feel at liberty to offer to him the following:

> Since now no fostering love is found,
> And the Hagi tree is dead and sere,
> The motherless deer lies on the ground,
> Helpless and weak, no shelter near.

The Emperor strove in vain to repress his own emotion; and old memories, dating from the time when he first saw his favorite, rose up before him fast and thick. "How precious has been each moment to me, but yet what a long time has elapsed since then," thought he, and he said to the Miobu, "How often have I, too, desired to see the daughter of the Dainagon in such a position as her father would have desired to see her. 'Tis in vain to speak of that now!"

A pause, and he continued, "The child, however, may survive, and fortune may have some boon in store for him; and his grandmother's prayer should rather be for long life."

The presents were then shown to him. "Ah," thought he, "could they be the souvenirs sent by the once lost love," as he murmured:

[13] A famous Chinese poem, by Hak-rak-ten. The heroine of the poem was Yo-ki-hi, to whom we have made reference before. The story is, that after death she became a fairy, and the Emperor sent a magician to find her. The works of the poet Peh-lo-tien, as it is pronounced by modern Chinese, were the only poems in vogue at that time. Hence, perhaps, the reason for its being frequently quoted.

> Oh, could I find some wizard spirit,
>   To bear my words to her I love,
> Beyond the shades of envious night,
>   To where she dwells in realms above!

Now the picture of beautiful Yo-ki-hi, however skillful the painter may have been, is after all only a picture. It lacks life and animation. Her features may have been worthily compared to the lotus and to the willow of the Imperial gardens, but the style after all was Chinese, and to the Emperor his lost love was all in all, nor, in his eyes, was any other object comparable to her. Who doubts that they, too, had vowed to unite wings, and intertwine branches! But to what end? The murmur of winds, the music of insects, now only served to cause him melancholy.

In the meantime, in the Koki-den was heard the sound of music. She who dwelt there, and who had not now for a long time been with the Emperor, was heedlessly protracting her strains until this late hour of the evening.

How painfully must these have sounded to the Emperor!

> Moonlight is gone, and darkness reigns
>   E'en in the realms 'above the clouds,'
> Ah! how can light, or tranquil peace,
>   Shine o'er that lone and lowly home!

Thus thought the Emperor, and he did not retire until "the lamps were trimmed to the end!" The sound of the night watch of the right guard [14] was now heard. It was five o'clock in the morning. So, to avoid notice, he withdrew to his bedroom, but calm slumber hardly visited his eyes. This now became a common occurrence.

When he rose in the morning he would reflect on the time gone by when "they knew not even that the casement was bright." But now, too, he would neglect "Morning Court." His appetite failed him. The delicacies of the so-called great table had no temptation for him. Men pitied him much. "There must have been some divine mystery that predetermined the course of their love," said they, "for in matters in which she is concerned he is powerless to reason, and wisdom deserts him. The welfare of the State ceases to interest him."

---

[14] There were two divisions of the Imperial guard, right and left.

And now people actually began to quote instances that had occurred in a foreign court.

Weeks and months had elapsed, and the son of Kiri-Tsubo was again at the palace. In the spring of the following year the first prince was proclaimed Heir-apparent to the throne. Had the Emperor consulted his private feelings, he would have substituted the younger prince for the elder one. But this was not possible, and, especially for this reason:—There was no influential party to support him, and, moreover, public opinion would also have been strongly opposed to such a measure, which, if effected by arbitrary power, would have become a source of danger. The Emperor, therefore, betrayed no such desire, and repressed all outward appearance of it. And now the public expressed its satisfaction at the self-restraint of the Emperor, and the mother of the first prince felt at ease.

In this year, the mother of Kiri-Tsubo departed this life. She may not improbably have longed to follow her daughter at an earlier period; and the only regret to which she gave utterance, was that she was forced to leave her grandson, whom she had so tenderly loved.

From this time the young prince took up his residence in the Imperial palace; and next year, at the age of seven, he began to learn to read and write under the personal superintendence of the Emperor. He now began to take him into the private apartments, among others, of the Koki-den, saying, "The mother is gone! now at least, let the child be received with better feeling." And if even stonyhearted warriors, or bitter enemies, if any such there were, smiled when they saw the boy, the mother of the Heir-apparent, too, could not entirely exclude him from her sympathies. This lady had two daughters, and they found in their half-brother a pleasant playmate. Every one was pleased to greet him, and there was already a winning coquetry in his manners, which amused people, and made them like to play with him. We need not allude to his studies in detail, but on musical instruments, such as the flute and the koto,[15] he also showed great proficiency.

About this time there arrived an embassy from Korea, and

[15] The general name for a species of musical instrument resembling the zither, but longer.

among them was an excellent physiognomist. When the Emperor heard of this, he wished to have the prince examined by him. It was, however, contrary to the warnings of the Emperor Wuda, to call in foreigners to the palace. The prince was, therefore, disguised as the son of one Udaiben, his instructor, with whom he was sent to the Koro-Kwan, where foreign embassies are entertained.

When the physiognomist saw him, he was amazed, and, turning his own head from side to side, seemed at first to be unable to comprehend the lines of his features, and then said, "His physiognomy argues that he might ascend to the highest position in the State, but, in that case, his reign will be disturbed, and many misfortunes will ensue. If, however, his position should only be that of a great personage in the country, his fortune may be different."

This Udaiben was a clever scholar. He had with the Korean pleasant conversations, and they also interchanged with one another some Chinese poems, in one of which the Korean said what great pleasure it had given him to have seen before his departure, which was now imminent, a youth of such remarkable promise. The Koreans made some valuable presents to the prince, who had also composed a few lines, and to them, too, many costly gifts were offered from the Imperial treasures.

In spite of all the precautions which were taken to keep all this rigidly secret, it did, somehow or other, become known to others, and among those to the Udaijin, who, not unnaturally, viewed it with suspicion, and began to entertain doubts of the Emperor's intentions. The latter, however, acted with great prudence. It must be remembered that, as yet, he had not even created the boy a Royal prince. He now sent for a native physiognomist, who approved of his delay in doing so, and whose observations to this effect, the Emperor did not receive unfavorably. He wisely thought to be a Royal prince, without having any influential support on the mother's side, would be of no real advantage to his son. Moreover, his own tenure of power seemed precarious, and he, therefore, thought it better for his own dynasty, as well as for the prince, to keep him in a private station, and to constitute him an outside supporter of the Royal cause.

And now he took more and more pains with his education in different branches of learning; and the more the boy studied the more talent did he evince—talent almost too great for one destined to remain in a private station. Nevertheless, as we have said, suspicions would have been aroused had Royal rank been conferred upon him, and the astrologists, whom also the Emperor consulted, having expressed their disapproval of such a measure, the Emperor finally made up his mind to create a new family. To this family he assigned the name of Gen, and he made the young prince the founder of it.[16]

Some time had now elapsed since the death of the Emperor's favorite, but he was still often haunted by her image. Ladies were introduced into his presence, in order, if possible, to divert his attention, but without success.

There was, however, living at this time a young princess, the fourth child of a late Emperor. She had great promise of beauty, and was guarded with jealous care by her mother, the Empress-Dowager. The Naishi-no-Ske, who had been at the Court from the time of the said Emperor, was intimately acquainted with the Empress and familiar with the princess, her daughter, from her very childhood. This person now recommended the Emperor to see the princess, because her features closely resembled those of Kiri-Tsubo.

"I have now fulfilled," she said, "the duties of my office under three reigns, and, as yet, I have seen but one person who resembles the departed. The daughter of the Empress-Dowager does resemble her, and she is singularly beautiful."

"There may be some truth in this," thought the Emperor, and he began to regard her with awakening interest.

This was related to the Empress-Dowager. She, however, gave no encouragement whatever to the idea. "How terrible!" she said. "Do we not remember the cruel harshness of the mother of the Heir-apparent, which hastened the fate of Kiri-Tsubo!"

While thus discountenancing any intimacy between her

[16] In these days Imperial princes were often created founders of new families, and with some given names, the Gen being one most frequently used. These princes had no longer a claim to the throne.

daughter and the Emperor, she too died, and the princess was left parentless. The Emperor acted with great kindness, and intimated his wish to regard her as his own daughter. In consequence of this her guardian, and her brother, Prince Hiob-Kio, considering that life at Court would be better for her and more attractive for her than the quiet of her own home, obtained for her an introduction there.

She was styled the Princess Fuji-Tsubo (of the Chamber of Wisteria), from the name of the chamber which was assigned to her.

There was, indeed, both in features and manners a strange resemblance between her and Kiri-Tsubo. The rivals of the latter constantly caused pain both to herself and to the Emperor; but the illustrious birth of the princess prevented any one from ever daring to humiliate her, and she uniformly maintained the dignity of her position. And to her alas! the Emperor's thoughts were now gradually drawn, though he could not yet be said to have forgotten Kiri-Tsubo.

The young prince, whom we now style Genji (the Gen), was still with the Emperor, and passed his time pleasantly enough in visiting the various apartments where the inmates of the palace resided. He found the companionship of all of them sufficiently agreeable; but beside the many who were now of maturer years, there was one who was still in the bloom of her youthful beauty, and who more particularly caught his fancy, the Princess Wisteria. He had no recollection of his mother, but he had been told by Naishi-no-Ske that this lady was exceedingly like her; and for this reason he often yearned to see her and to be with her.

The Emperor showed equal affection to both of them, and he sometimes told her that he hoped she would not treat the boy with coldness or think him forward. He said that his affection for the one made him feel the same for the other too, and that the mutual resemblance of her own and of his mother's face easily accounted for Genji's partiality to her. And thus as a result of this generous feeling on the part of the Emperor, a warmer tinge was gradually imparted both to the boyish humor and to the awakening sentiment of the young prince.

The mother of the Heir-apparent was not unnaturally

averse to the princess, and this revived her old antipathy to Genji also. The beauty of her son, the Heir-apparent, though remarkable, could not be compared to his, and so bright and radiant was his face that Genji was called by the public Hikal-Genji-no-Kimi (the shining Prince Gen).

When he attained the age of twelve the ceremony of Gembuk [17] (or crowning) took place. This was also performed with all possible magnificence. Various fetes, which were to take place in public, were arranged by special order by responsible officers of the Household. The Royal chair was placed in the eastern wing of the Seirio-Den, where the Emperor dwells, and in front of it were the seats of the hero of the ceremony and of the Sadaijin, who was to crown him and to regulate the ceremonial.

At three o'clock in the afternoon Genji appeared on the scene. The boyish style of his hair and dress excellently became his features; and it almost seemed a matter for regret that it should be altered. The Okura-Kio-Kurahito, whose office it was to rearrange the hair of Genji, faltered as he did so. As to the Emperor, a sudden thought stole into his mind. "Ah! could his mother but have lived to have seen him now!" This thought, however, he at once suppressed. After he had been crowned the prince withdrew to a dressing room, where he attired himself in the full robes of manhood. Then descending to the Court-yard he performed a measured dance in grateful acknowledgment. This he did with so much grace and skill that all present were filled with admiration; and his beauty, which some feared might be lessened, seemed only more remarkable from the change. And the Emperor, who had before tried to resist them, now found old memories irresistible.

Sadaijin had by his wife, who was a Royal princess, an only daughter. The Heir-apparent had taken some notice of her, but her father did not encourage him. He had, on the other hand, some idea of Genji, and had sounded the Emperor on the subject. He regarded the idea with favor, and especially

[17] The ceremony of placing a crown or coronet upon the head of a boy. This was an ancient custom observed by the upper and middle classes in both Japan and China, to mark the transition from boyhood to youth.

on the ground that such a union would be of advantage to Genji, who had not yet any influential supporters.

Now all the Court and the distinguished visitors were assembled in the palace, where a great festival was held; Genji occupied a seat next to that of the Royal princess. During the entertainment Sadaijin whispered something several times into his ear, but he was too young and diffident to make any answer.

Sadaijin was now summoned before the dais of the Emperor, and, according to custom, an Imperial gift, a white O-Uchiki (grand robe), and a suit of silk vestments were presented to him by a lady. Then proffering his own saké cup, the Emperor addressed him thus:

> In the first hair-knot [18] of youth,
> Let love that lasts for age be bound!

This evidently implied an idea of matrimony. Sadaijin feigned surprise and responded:

> Aye! if the purple [19] of the cord,
> I bound so anxiously, endure!

He then descended into the Court-yard, and gave expression to his thanks in the same manner in which Genji had previously done. A horse from the Imperial stables and a falcon from the Kurand-Dokoro [20] were on view in the yard, and were now presented to him. The princes and nobles were all gathered together in front of the grand staircase, and appropriate gifts were also presented to each one of them. Among the crowd baskets and trays of fruits and delicacies were distributed by the Emperor's order, under the direction of Udaiben; and more rice cakes and other things were given away now than at the Gembuk of the Heir-apparent.

In the evening the young prince went to the mansion of the Sadaijin, where the espousal with the young daughter of the

---

[18] Before the crown was placed upon the head at the Gembuk, the hair was gathered up in a conical form from all sides of the head, and then fastened securely in that form with a knot of silken cords of which the color was always purple.

[19] The color of purple typifies, and is emblematical of, love.

[20] A body of men who resembled "Gentlemen-at-arms," and a part of whose duty it was to attend to the falcons.

latter was celebrated with much splendor. The youthfulness of the beautiful boy was well pleasing to Sadaijin; but the bride, who was some years older than he was, and who considered the disparity in their age to be unsuitable, blushed when she thought of it.

Not only was this Sadaijin himself a distinguished personage in the State, but his wife was also the sister of the Emperor by the same mother, the late Empress; and her rank therefore was unequivocal. When to this we add the union of their daughter with Genji, it was easy to understand that the influence of Udaijin, the grandfather of the Heir-apparent, and who therefore seemed likely to attain great power, was not after all of very much moment.

Sadaijin had several children. One of them, who was the issue of his Royal wife, was the Kurand Shioshio.

Udaijin was not, for political reasons, on good terms with his family; but nevertheless he did not wish to estrange the youthful Kurand. On the contrary, he endeavored to establish friendly relations with him, as was indeed desirable, and he went so far as to introduce him to his fourth daughter, the younger sister of the Koki-den.

Genji still resided in the palace, where his society was a source of much pleasure to the Emperor, and he did not take up his abode in a private house. Indeed, his bride, Lady Aoi (Lady Hollyhock), though her position insured her every attention from others, had few charms for him, and the Princess Wisteria much more frequently occupied his thoughts. "How pleasant her society, and how few like her!" he was always thinking; and a hidden bitterness blended with his constant reveries.

The years rolled on, and Genji being now older was no longer allowed to continue his visits to the private rooms of the princess as before. But the pleasure of overhearing her sweet voice, as its strains flowed occasionally through the curtained casement, and blended with the music of the flute and koto, made him still glad to reside in the palace. Under these circumstances he seldom visited the home of his bride, sometimes only for a day or two after an absence of five or six at Court.

His father-in-law, however, did not attach much importance

to this, on account of his youth; and whenever they did receive a visit from him, pleasant companions were invited to meet him, and various games likely to suit his taste were provided for his entertainment.

In the palace, Shigeisa, his late mother's quarters, was allotted to him, and those who had waited on her waited on him. The private house, where his grandmother had resided, was beautifully repaired for him by the Shuri Takmi—the Imperial Repairing Committee—in obedience to the wishes of the Emperor. In addition to the original loveliness of the landscape and the noble forest ranges, the basin of the lake was now enlarged, and similar improvements were effected throughout with the greatest pains. "Oh, how delightful would it not be to be in a place like that which such a one as one might choose!" thought Genji within himself.

We may here also note that the name Hikal Genji is said to have been originated by the Korean who examined his physiognomy.

EVENING GLORY

It happened that when Genji was driving about in the Rokjio quarter, he was informed that his old nurse, Daini, was ill, and had become a nun. Her residence was in Gojio. He wished to visit her, and drove to the house. The main gate was closed, so that his carriage could not drive up; therefore, he sent in a servant to call out Koremitz, a son of the nurse.

Meantime, while awaiting him, he looked round on the deserted terrace. He noticed close by a small and rather dilapidated dwelling, with a wooden fence round a newly made enclosure. The upper part, for eight or ten yards in length, was surrounded by a trelliswork, over which some white reed blinds—rude, but new—were thrown. Through these blinds the indistinct outline of some fair heads were faintly delineated, and the owners were evidently peeping down the roadway from their retreat. "Ah," thought Genji, "they can never be so tall as to look over the blind. They must be standing on something within. But whose residence is it? What sort of people are they?" His equipage was strictly private and unostentatious. There were, of course, no outriders; hence he had no fear of being recognized by them. And so he still watched the house. The gate was also constructed of something like trelliswork, and stood half open, revealing the loneliness of the interior. The line "Where do we seek our home?" came first into his mind, and he then thought that "even this must be as comfortable as golden palaces to its inmates."

A long wooden rail, covered with luxuriant creepers, which, fresh and green, climbed over it in full vigor, arrested his eye; their white blossoms, one after another disclosing their smiling lips in unconscious beauty. Genji began humming to himself: "Ah! stranger crossing there." When his attendant informed him that these lovely white flowers were called "Yugao" (evening-glory), adding, and at the same time pointing to the flowers, "See the flowers *only*, flourishing in that glorious state."

"What beautiful flowers they are," exclaimed Genji. "Go and beg a bunch."

The attendant thereupon entered the half-opened gate and asked for some of them, on which a young girl, dressed in a long tunic, came out, taking an old fan in her hand, and saying, "Let us put them on this, those with strong stems," plucked off a few stalks and laid them on the fan.

These were given to the attendant, who walked slowly back. Just as he came near to Genji, the gate of Koremitz's courtyard opened and Koremitz himself appeared, who took the flowers from him and handed them to Genji, at the same moment saying, "I am very sorry I could not find the gate key, and that I made you wait so long in the public road, though there is no one hereabouts to stare at, or recognize you, I sincerely beg your pardon."

The carriage was now driven in, and Genji alighted. The Ajari,[1] elder brother of Koremitz; Mikawa-no-Kami, his brother-in-law; and the daughter of Daini, all assembled and greeted him. The nun also rose from her couch to welcome him.

"How pleased I am to see you," she said, "but you see I have quite altered, I have become a nun. I have given up the world. I had no reluctance in doing this. If I had any un-

[1] Name of an ecclesiastical office.

easiness, it was on your account alone. My health, however, is beginning to improve; evidently the divine blessing is on this sacrifice."

"I was so sorry," replied Genji, "to hear you were ill, and now still more so to find you have given up the world. I hope that you may live to witness my success and prosperity. It grieves me to think you were compelled to make such a change; yet, I believe, this will secure your enjoyment of happiness hereafter. It is said that when one leaves this world without a single regret, one passes straight to Paradise." As he said these words his eyes became moistened.

Now, it is common for nurses to regard their foster children with blind affection, whatever may be their faults, thinking, so to speak, that what is crooked is straight. So in Genji's case, who, in Daini's eyes, was next door to perfection, this blindness was still more strongly apparent, and she always regarded her office as his nurse, as an honor, and while Genji was discoursing in the above manner, a tear began to trickle from her eyes.

"You know," he continued, "at what an early age I was deprived of my dearest ties; there were, indeed, several who looked after me, but you were the one to whom I was most attached. In due course, after I grew up, I ceased to see you regularly. I could not visit you as often as I thought of you, yet, when I did not see you for a long time, I often felt very lonely. Ah! if there were no such things as partings in the world!"

He then enjoined them earnestly to persevere in prayer for their mother's health, and said, "Good-bye."

At the moment of quitting the house he remembered that something was written on the fan that held the flowers. It was already twilight, and he asked Koremitz to bring a taper, that he might see to read it. It seemed to him as if the fragrance of some fair hand that had used it still remained, and on it was written the following couplets:

> The crystal dew at Evening's hour
> Sleeps on the Yugao's beauteous flower,
> Will this please him, whose glances bright,
> Gave to the flowers a dearer light?

With apparent carelessness, without any indication to show who the writer was, it bore, however, the marks of a certain excellence. Genji thought, "this is singular, coming from whence it does," and turning to Koremitz, he asked, "Who lives in this house to your right?" "Ah," exclaimed Koremitz mentally, "as usual, I see," but replied with indifference, "Truly I have been here some days, but I have been so busy in attending my mother that I neither know nor have asked about the neighbors." "You may probably be surprised at my inquisitiveness," said Genji, "but I have reasons for asking this on account of this fan. I request you to call on them, and make inquiries what sort of people they are."

Koremitz thereupon proceeded to the house, and, calling out a servant, sought from him the information he wanted, when he was told that, "This is the house of Mr. Yomei-no-Ske. He is at present in the country; his lady is still young; her brothers are in the Court service, and often come here to see her. The whole history of the family I am not acquainted with." With this answer Koremitz returned, and repeated it to Genji, who thought, "Ah! the sending of this verse may be a trick of these conceited Court fellows!" but he could not entirely free his mind from the idea of its having been sent especially to himself. This was consistent with the characteristic vanity of his disposition. He, therefore, took out a paper, and disguising his handwriting (lest it should be identified), indited the following:

> Were I the flower to see more near,
> Which once at dusky eve I saw,
> It might have charms for me more dear,
> And look more beauteous than before.

And this he sent to the house by his servant, and set off on his way. He saw a faint light through the chinks of the blinds of the house, like the glimmer of the firefly. It gave him, as he passed, a silent sort of longing. The mansion in Rokjio, to which he was proceeding this evening, was a handsome building, standing amidst fine woods of rare growth and beauty, and all was of comfortable appearance. Its mistress was altogether in good circumstances, and here Genji spent the hours in full ease and comfort.

On his way home next morning he again passed the front of the house, where grew the Yugao flowers, and the recollection of flowers which he had received the previous evening, made him anxious to ascertain who the people were who lived there.

After the lapse of some time Koremitz came to pay him a visit, excusing himself for not having come before, on account of his mother's health being more unsatisfactory. He said, "In obedience to your commands to make further inquiries, I called on some people who know about my neighbors, but could not get much information. I was told, however, that there is a lady who has been living there since last May, but who she is even the people in the house do not know. Sometimes I looked over the hedges between our gardens, and saw the youthful figure of a lady, and a maiden attending her, in a style of dress which betrayed a good origin. Yesterday evening, after sunset, I saw the lady writing a letter, her face was very calm in expression, but full of thought, and her attendant was often sobbing secretly, as she waited on her. These things I saw distinctly."

Genji smiled. He seemed more anxious than before to know something about them, and Koremitz continued: "Hoping to get some fuller information, I took an opportunity which presented itself of sending a communication to the house. To this a speedy answer was returned, written by a skillful hand. I concluded from this and other circumstances that there was something worth seeing and knowing enclosed within those walls." Genji immediately exclaimed, "Do! do! try again; not to be able to find out is too provoking," and he thought to himself, "If in lowly life, which is often left unnoticed, we find something attractive and fair, as Uma-no-Kami said, how delightful it will be, and I think, perhaps, this may be such a one."

In the meantime his thoughts were occasionally reverting to Cicada.[2] His nature was not, perhaps, so perverted as to think about persons of such condition and position in life as

[2] Cicada: "the lady of the scarf," stepmother of one of Genji's gentlemen-in-waiting. Much younger than her husband, Iyo-no-Kami, she has been unsuccessfully courted by Genji; her younger brother, Kokimi, has become Genji's servant.

Cicada; but since he had heard the discussion about women, and their several classifications, he had somehow became speculative in his sentiments, and ambitious of testing all those different varieties by his own experience. While matters were in this state Iyo-no-Kami returned to the capital, and came in haste to pay his respects to Genji. He was a swarthy, repulsive looking man, bearing the traces of a long journey in his appearance, and of advanced age. Still there was nothing unpleasant in his natural character and manners. Genji was about to converse with him freely, but somehow or another an awkward feeling arose in his mind, and threw a restraint upon his cordiality. "Iyo is such an honest old man," he reflected, "it is too bad to take advantage of him. What Umano-Kami said is true, 'that to strive to carry out wrong desires is man's evil failing!' Her hardheartedness to me is unpleasant, but from the other side this deserves praise!"

It was announced after this that Iyo-no-Kami would return to his province, and take his wife with him, and that his daughter would be left behind to be soon married.

This intelligence was far from pleasing to Genji, and he longed once more, only once more to behold the lady of the scarf, and he concerted with Kokimi how to arrange a plan for obtaining an interview. The lady, however, was quite deaf to such proposals, and the only concession she vouchsafed was that she occasionally received a letter, and sometimes answered it.

Autumn had now come; Genji was still thoughtful. Lady Aoi saw him but seldom, and was constantly disquieted by his protracted absence from her. There was, as we have before hinted, at Rokjio, another person whom he had won with great difficulty, and it would have been a little inconsistent if he became too easily tired of her. He indeed had not become cool toward her, but the violence of his passion had somewhat abated. The cause of this seems to have been that this lady was rather too zealous, or, we may say, jealous; besides, her age exceeded that of Genji by some years. The following incident will illustrate the state of matters between them:—

One morning early Genji was about to take his departure, with sleepy eyes, listless and weary, from her mansion at Rokjio. A slight mist spread over the scene. A maiden attendant of the mistress opened the door for his departure, and led him forth. The shrubbery of flowering trees struck refreshingly on the sight, with interlacing branches in rich confusion, among which was some Asagao [3] in full blossom. Genji was tempted to dally, and looked contemplatively over them. The maiden still accompanied him. She wore a thin silk tunic of light green colors, showing off her graceful waist and figure, which it covered. Her appearance was attractive. Genji looked at her tenderly, and led her to a seat in the garden, and sat down by her side. Her countenance was modest and quiet; her wavy hair was neatly and prettily arranged. Genji began humming in a low tone:

> The heart that roams from flower to flower,
>   Would fain its wanderings not betray,
> Yet 'Asagao,' in morning's hour,
>   Impels my tender wish to stray.

So saying, he gently took her hand; she, however, without appearing to understand his real meaning, answered thus:

> You stay not till the mist be o'er,
>   But hurry to depart,
> Say can the flower you leave, no more
>   Detain your changeful heart?

At this juncture a young attendant in sasinuki [4] entered the garden, brushing away the dewy mist from the flowers, and began to gather some bunches of Asagao. The scene was one which we might desire to paint, so full of quiet beauty, and Genji rose from his seat, and slowly passed homeward. In those days Genji was becoming more and more an object of popular admiration in society, and we might even attribute the eccentricity of some of his adventures to the favor he enjoyed, combined with his great personal attractions. Where beautiful flowers expand their blossoms even the rugged mountaineer loves to rest under their shade, so wherever Genji showed himself people sought his notice.

[3] Asagao: morning glory.
[4] Sasinuki is a sort of loose trousers, and properly worn by men only, hence some commentators conclude, the attendant here mentioned to mean a boy, others contend, this garment was worn by females also when they rode.

Now with regard to the fair one about whom Koremitz was making inquiries. After some still further investigations, he came to Genji and told him that "there is someone who often visits there. Who he was I could not at first find out, for he comes with the utmost privacy. I made up my mind to discover him; so one evening I concealed myself outside the house, and waited. Presently the sound of an approaching carriage was heard, and the inmates of the house began to peep out. The lady I mentioned before was also to be seen; I could not see her very plainly, but I can tell you so much: she looked charming. The carriage itself was now seen approaching, and it apparently belonged to someone of rank. A little girl who was peeping out exclaimed, 'Ukon, look here, quick, Chiujio is coming.' Then one older came forward rubbing her hands and saying to the child, 'Don't be so foolish, don't be excited.' How could they tell, I wondered, that the carriage was a Chiujio's. I stole forth cautiously and reconnoitered. Near the house there is a small stream, over which a plank had been thrown by way of a bridge. The visitor was rapidly approaching this bridge when an amusing incident occurred: The elder girl came out in haste to meet him, and was passing the bridge, when the skirt of her dress caught in something, and she well-nigh fell into the water. 'Confound that bridge, what a bad Katzragi,'[5] she cried, and suddenly turned pale. How amusing it was, you may imagine. The visitor was dressed in plain style, he was followed by his page, whom I recognized as belonging to To-no-Chiujio."[6]

"I should like to see that same carriage," interrupted Genji eagerly, as he thought to himself, "that house may be the home of the very girl whom he (To-no-Chiujio) spoke about, perhaps he has discovered her hiding place."

"I have also made an acquaintance," Koremitz continued, "with a certain person in this house, and it was through these means that I made closer observations. The girl who nearly fell over the bridge is, no doubt, the lady's attendant, but

[5] A mythological repulsive deity who took part in the building of a bridge at the command of a powerful magician.

[6] To-no-Chiujio: Genji's brother-in-law and best friend. In an earlier episode To-no-Chiujio had described a mysterious and unhappy love affair, ended by misunderstandings and by threats made by unknown persons.

they pretend to be all on an equality. Even when the little child said anything to betray them by its remarks, they immediately turned it off." Koremitz laughed as he told this, adding, "this was an amusing trick indeed."

"Oh," exclaimed Genji, "I must have a look at them when I go to visit your mother; you must manage this," and with the words the picture of the "Evening-Glory" rose pleasantly before his eyes.

Now Koremitz not only was always prompt in attending to the wishes of Prince Genji, but also was by his own temperament fond of carrying on such intrigues. He tried every means to favor his designs, and to ingratiate himself with the lady, and at last succeeded in bringing her and Genji together. The details of the plans by which all this was brought about are too long to be given here. Genji visited her often, but it was with the greatest caution and privacy; he never asked her when they met any particulars about her past life, nor did he reveal his own to her. He would not drive to her in his own carriage, and Koremitz often lent him his own horse to ride. He took no attendant with him except the one who had asked for the "Evening-Glory." He would not even call on the nurse, lest it might lead to discoveries. The lady was puzzled at his reticence. She would sometimes send her servant to ascertain, if possible, what road he took, and where he went. But somehow, by chance or design, he always became lost to her watchful eye. His dress, also, was of the most ordinary description, and his visits were always paid late in the evening. To her all this seemed like the mysteries of old legends. True, she conjectured from his demeanor and ways that he was a person of rank, but she never ascertained exactly who he was. She sometimes reproached Koremitz for bringing her into such strange circumstances. But he cunningly kept himself aloof from such taunts.

Be this as it may, Genji still frequently visited her, though at the same time he was not unmindful that this kind of adventure was scarcely consistent with his position. The girl was simple and modest in nature, not certainly maneuvering, neither was she stately or dignified in mien, but everything about her had a peculiar charm and interest, impossible to describe, and in the full charm of youth not altogether void of experience.

"But by what charm in her," thought Genji, "am I so strongly affected; no matter, I am so," and thus his passion continued.

Her residence was only temporary, and this Genji soon became aware of. "If she leaves this place," thought he, "and I lose sight of her—for when this may happen is uncertain—what shall I do?" He at last decided to carry her off secretly to his own mansion in Nijio. True, if this became known it would be an awkward business; but such are love affairs; always some dangers to be risked! He therefore fondly entreated her to accompany him to some place where they could be freer.

Her answer, however, was "That such a proposal on his part only alarmed her." Genji was amused at her girlish mode of expression, and earnestly said, "Which of us is a fox?[7] I don't know, but anyhow be persuaded by me." And after repeated conversations of the same nature, she at last half-consented. He had much doubt of the propriety of inducing her to take this step, nevertheless her final compliance flattered his vanity. He recollected very well the Tokonatz (Pinks)[8] which To-no-Chiujio spoke of, but never betrayed that he had any knowledge of that circumstance.

It was on the evening of the fifteenth of August when they were together. The moonlight streamed through the crevices of the broken wall. To Genji such a scene was novel and peculiar. The dawn at length began to break, and from the surrounding houses the voices of the farmers might be heard talking.

One remarked, "How cool it is." Another, "There is not much hope for our crops this year." "My carrying business I do not expect to answer," responded the first speaker. "But are our neighbors listening!" Conversing in this way they proceeded to their work.

Had the lady been one to whom surrounding appearances were important, she might have felt disturbed, but she was far from being so, and seemed as if no outward circumstances

---

[7] A popular superstition in China and Japan believes foxes to have mysterious powers over men.
[8] Pinks: Because these flowers had been associated with her, To-no-Chiujio had called his mysterious lady, Tokonatz, just as Genji had called her Yugao.

could trouble her equanimity, which appeared to him an admirable trait. The noise of the threshing of the corn came indistinctly to their ears like distant thunder. The beating of the bleacher's hammer was also heard faintly from afar off.

They were in the front of the house. They opened the window and looked out on the dawn. In the small garden before their eyes was a pretty bamboo grove; its leaves, wet with dew, shone brilliantly, even as bright as in the gardens of the palace. The cricket sang cheerfully in the old walls as if it was at their very ears, and the flight of wild geese in the air rustled overhead. Everything spoke of rural scenes and business, different from what Genji was in the habit of seeing and hearing round him.

To him all these sights and sounds, from their novelty and variety, combined with the affection he had for the girl beside him, had a delightful charm. She wore a light dress of clear purple, not very costly; her figure was slight and delicate; the tones of her voice soft and insinuating. "If she were only a little more cultivated," thought he, but, in any case, he was determined to carry her off.

"Now is the time," said he, "let us go together, the place is not very far off."

"Why so soon?" she replied, gently. As her implied consent to his proposal was thus given without much thought, he, on his part, became bolder. He summoned her maid, Ukon, and ordered the carriage to be got ready. Dawn now fairly broke; the cocks had ceased to crow, and the voice of an aged man was heard repeating his orisons, probably during his fast. "His days will not be many," thought Genji, "what is he praying for?" And while so thinking, the aged mortal muttered, "Nam Torai no Doshi" (Oh! the Divine guide of the future). "Do listen to that prayer," said Genji, turning to the girl, "it shows our life is not limited to this world," and he hummed:

> Let us together, bind our soul
>   With vows that Woobasok [9] has given,
> That when this world from sight shall roll
>   Unparted we shall wake in heaven.

[9] Upasaka, a sect of the followers of Buddhism who are laymen though they observe the rules of clerical life.

And added, "By Mirok,[10] let us bind ourselves in love forever."

The girl, doubtful of the future, thus replied in a melancholy tone:

> When in my present lonely lot,
> I feel my past has not been free
> From sins which I remember not,
> I dread more, what to come, may be.

In the meantime a passing cloud had suddenly covered the sky, and made its face quite gray. Availing himself of this obscurity, Genji hurried her away and led her to the carriage, where Ukon also accompanied her.

They drove to an isolated mansion on the Rokjio embankment, which was at no great distance, and called out the steward who looked after it. The grounds were in great solitude, and over them lay a thick mist. The curtains of the carriage were not drawn close, so that the sleeves of their dresses were almost moistened. "I have never experienced this sort of trouble before," said Genji; "how painful are the sufferings of love.

> Oh! were the ancients, tell me pray,
> Thus led away, by love's keen smart,
> I ne'er such morning's misty ray
> Have felt before with beating heart.

Have you ever?"

The lady shyly averted her face and answered:

> I, like the wandering moon, may roam,
> Who knows not if her mountain love
> Be true or false, without a home,
> The mist below, the clouds above.

The steward presently came out and the carriage was driven inside the gates, and was brought close to the entrance, while the rooms were hurriedly prepared for their reception. They alighted just as the mist was clearing away.

This steward was in the habit of going to the mansion of Sadaijin, and was well acquainted with Genji.

"Oh!" he exclaimed, as they entered. "Without proper at-

---

[10] Meitreya, a Buddhisatva destined to reappear as a Buddha after the lapse of an incalculable series of years.

tendants!" And approaching near to Genji said, "Shall I call in some more servants?"

Genji replied at once and impressively, "I purposely chose a place where many people should not intrude. Don't trouble yourself, and be discreet."

Rice broth was served up for their breakfast, but no regular meal had been prepared.

The sun was now high in the heavens. Genji got up and opened the window. The gardens had been uncared for, and had run wild. The forest surrounding the mansion was dense and old, and the shrubberies were ravaged and torn by the autumn gales, and the bosom of the lake was hidden by rank weeds. The main part of the house had been for a long time uninhabited, except the servants' quarter, where there were only a few people living.

"How fearful the place looks; but let no demon molest us," thought Genji, and endeavored to direct the girl's attention by fond and caressing conversation. And now he began, little by little, to throw off the mask, and told her who he was, and then began humming:

> The flower that bloomed in evening's dew,
> Was the bright guide that led to you.

She looked at him askance, replying:

> The dew that on the Yugao lay,
> Was a false guide and led astray.

Thus a faint allusion was made to the circumstances which were the cause of their acquaintance, and it became known that the verse and the fan had been sent by her attendant mistaking Genji for her mistress' former lover.

In the course of a few hours the girl became more at her ease, and later on in the afternoon Koremitz came and presented some fruits. The latter, however, stayed with them only a short time.

The mansion gradually became very quiet, and the evening rapidly approached. The inner room was somewhat dark and gloomy. Yugao was nervous; she was too nervous to remain there alone, and Genji therefore drew back the curtains to let the twilight in, staying there with her. Here the lovers remained, enjoying each other's sight and company, yet the more the evening advanced, the more timid and restless she became, so he quickly closed the casement, and she drew by degrees closer and closer to his side. At these moments he also became distracted and thoughtful. How the Emperor would be asking after him, and know not where he might be! What would the lady, the jealous lady, in the neighboring mansion think or say if she discovered their secret? How painful it would be if her jealous rage should flash forth on him! Such were the reflections which made him melancholy; and as his eyes fell upon the girl affectionately sitting beside him, ignorant of all these matters, he could not but feel a kind of pity for her.

Night was now advancing, and they unconsciously dropped off to sleep, when suddenly over the pillow of Genji hovered the figure of a lady of threatening aspect. It said fiercely, "You faithless one, wandering astray with such a strange girl."

And then the apparition tried to pull away the sleeping girl near him. Genji awoke much agitated. The lamp had burned itself out. He drew his sword, and placed it beside him, and called aloud for Ukon, and she came to him also quite alarmed.

"Do call up the servants and procure a light," said Genji.

"How can I go, 'tis too dark," she replied, shaking with fear.

"How childish!" he exclaimed, with a false laugh, and clapped his hands to call a servant. The sound echoed drearily through the empty rooms, but no servant came. At this moment he found the girl beside him was also strangely affected. Her brow was covered with great drops of cold perspiration, and she appeared rapidly sinking into a state of unconsciousness.

"Ah! she is often troubled with the nightmare," said Ukon, "and perhaps this disturbs her now; but let us try and rouse her."

"Yes, very likely," said Genji; "she was very much fatigued, and since noon her eyes have often been riveted upward, like one suffering from some inward malady. I will go myself and call the servants"—he continued, "clapping one's hands is useless, besides it echoes fearfully. Do come here, Ukon, for a little while, and look after your mistress." So pulling Ukon near Yugao, he advanced to the entrance of the saloon. He saw all was dark in the adjoining chambers. The wind was high, and blew gustily round the mansion. The few servants, consisting of a son of the steward, footman, and page, were all buried in profound slumber. Genji called to them loudly, and they awoke with a start. "Come," said he, "bring a light. Valet, twang your bowstring, and drive away the fiend. How can you sleep so soundly in such a place? But has Koremitz come?"

"Sir, he came in the evening, but you had given no command, and so he went away, saying he would return in the morning," answered one.

The one who gave this reply was an old knight, and he twanged his bowstrings vigorously, "Hiyojin! hiyojin!" (Be careful of the fire! be careful of the fire!) as he walked round the rooms.

The mind of Genji instinctively reverted at this moment to the comfort of the palace. "At this hour of midnight," he thought, "the careful knights are patrolling round its walls. How different it is here!"

He returned to the room he had left; it was still dark. He found Yugao lying half dead and unconscious as before, and Ukon rendered helpless by fright.

"What is the matter? What does it mean? What foolish fear is this?" exclaimed Genji, greatly alarmed. "Perhaps in lonely places like this the fox, for instance, might try to exercise his sorcery to alarm us, but I am here, there is no cause for fear," and he pulled Ukon's sleeve as he spoke, to arouse her.

"I was so alarmed," she replied; "but my lady must be more so; pray attend to her."

"Well," said Genji, and bending over his beloved, shook her gently, but she neither spoke nor moved. She had apparently fainted, and he became seriously alarmed.

At this juncture the lights were brought. Genji threw a mantle over his mistress, and then called to the man to bring the light to him. The servant remained standing at a distance (according to etiquette), and would not approach.

"Come near," exclaimed Genji, testily. "Do act according

to circumstances," and taking the lamp from him threw its light full on the face of the lady, and gazed upon it anxiously, when at this very monent he beheld the apparition of the same woman he had seen before in his terrible dream, float before his eyes and vanish. "Ah!" he cried, "this is like the phantoms in old tales. What is the matter with the girl?" His own fears were all forgotten in his anxiety on her account. He leaned over and called upon her, but in vain. She answered not, and her glance was fixed. What was to be done? There was no one whom he could consult. The exorcisms of a priest, he thought, might do some good, but there was no priest. He tried to compose himself with all the resolution he could summon, but his anguish was too strong for his nerves. He threw himself beside her, and embracing her passionately, cried, "Come back! come back to me, my darling! Do not let us suffer such dreadful events." But she was gone; her soul had passed gently away.

The story of the mysterious power of the demon, who had threatened a certain courtier possessed of considerable strength of mind, suddenly occurred to Genji, who thought self-possession was the only remedy in present circumstances, and recovering his composure a little, said to Ukon, "She cannot be dead! She shall not die yet!" He then called the servant, and told him. "Here is one who has been strangely frightened by a vision. Go to Koremitz and tell him to come at once; and if his brother, the priest, is there, ask him to come also. Tell them cautiously; don't alarm their mother."

The midnight passed, and the wind blew louder, rushing amongst the branches of the old pines, and making them moan more and more sadly. The cries of strange weird birds were heard, probably the shrieks of the ill-omened screech owl, and the place seemed more and more remote from all human sympathy. Genji could only helplessly repeat, "How could I have chosen such a retreat." While Ukon, quite dismayed, cried pitifully at his side. To him it seemed even that this girl might become ill, might die! The light of the lamp flickered and burned dim. Each side of the walls seemed to his alarmed sight to present numberless openings one after another (where the demon might rush in), and the sound of mysterious footsteps seemed to approach along the deserted passages behind them. "Ah! were Koremitz but here," was the only thought of Genji; but it would seem that Koremitz was away from home, and the time Genji had to wait for him seemed an age. At last the crowing cocks announced the coming day, and gave him new courage.

He said to himself, "I must now admit this to be a punishment for all my inconsiderateness. However secretly we strive to conceal our faults, eventually they are discovered. First of all, what might not my father think! and then the general public? And what a subject for scandal the story of my escapades will become."

Koremitz now arrived, and all at once the courage with which Genji had fought against calamity gave way, and he burst into tears, and then slowly spoke. "Here a sad and singular event has happened; I cannot explain to you why. For such sudden afflictions prayers, I believe, are the only resource. For this reason I wish your brother to accompany you here."

"He returned to his monastery only yesterday," replied Koremitz. "But tell me what has happened; any unusual event to the girl?"

"She is dead," returned Genji in a broken voice; "dead without any apparent cause."

Koremitz, like the prince, was but young. If he had had greater experience he would have been more serviceable to Genji; indeed, they both were equally perplexed to decide what were the best steps to be taken under the trying circumstances of the case.

At last Koremitz said, "If the steward should learn this strange misfortune it might be awkward; as to the man himself he might be relied on, but his family, who probably would not be so discreet, might hear of the matter. It would, therefore, be better to quit this place at once."

"But where can we find a spot where there are fewer observers than here?" replied Genji.

"That is true. Suppose the old lodgings of the deceased. No, there are too many people there. I think a mountain convent would be better, because there they are accustomed to receive the dead within their walls, so that matters can be more easily concealed."

And after a little reflection, he continued, "There is a nun whom I know living in a mountain convent in Higashi-Yama. Let us take the corpse there. She was my father's nurse; she is living there in strict seclusion. That is the best plan I can think of."

This proposal was decided on, and the carriage was summoned.

Presuming that Genji would not like to carry the dead body in his arms, Koremitz covered it with a mantle, and lifted it into the carriage. Over the features of the dead maiden a charming calmness was still spread, unlike what usually happens, there being nothing repulsive. Her wavy hair fell outside the mantle, and her small mouth, still parted, wore a faint smile. The sight distressed both the eyes and heart of Genji. He fain would have followed the body; but this Koremitz would not permit.

"Do take my horse and ride back to Nijio at once," he said, and ordered the horse for him. Then taking Ukon away in the same carriage with the dead, he, girding up his dress, followed it on foot. It was by no means a pleasant task for Koremitiz, but he put up with it cheerfully.

Genji, sunk in apathy, now rode back to Nijio; he was greatly fatigued, and looked pale. The people of the mansion noticed his sad and haggard appearance.

Genji said nothing, but hurried straightaway to his own private apartment.

"Why did I not go with her?" he still vainly exclaimed. "What would she think of me were she to return to life?" And these thoughts affected him so deeply that he became ill, his head ached, his pulse beat high, and his body burned with fever. The sun rose high, but he did not leave his couch. His domestics were all perplexed. Rice gruel was served up to him, but he would not touch it. The news of his indisposition soon found its way out of the mansion, and in no time a messenger arrived from the Imperial palace to make inquiries. His brother-in-law also came, but Genji only allowed To-no-Chiujio to enter his room, saying to him, "My aged nurse has been ill since last May, and has been tonsured, and received consecration; it was, perhaps, from this sacrifice that at one time she became better, but lately she has had a relapse, and is again very bad. I was advised to visit her, moreover, she was always most kind to me, and if she had died without seeing me it would have pained her, so I went to see her. At this time a servant of her house, who had been ill, died suddenly. Being rendered 'unclean' by this event, I am passing the time privately. Besides, since the morning, I have become ill, evidently the effects of cold. By the bye, you must excuse me receiving you in this way."

"Well, sir," replied To-no-Chiujio, "I will represent these circumstances to his Majesty. Your absence last night has given much inquietude to the Emperor. He caused inquiries to be made for you everywhere, and his humor was not very good." And thereupon To-no-Chiujio took his leave, thinking as he went, "What sort of 'uncleanness' can this really be. I cannot put perfect faith in what he tells me."

Little did To-no-Chiujio imagine that the dead one was no other than his own long-lost Tokonatz (Pinks).

In the evening came Koremitz from the mountain, and was secretly introduced, though all general visitors were kept excluded on the pretext of the "uncleanness."

"What has become of her?" cried Genji, passionately, when he saw him. "Is she really gone?"

"Her end has come," replied Koremitz, in a tone of sadness; "and we must not keep the dead too long. Tomorrow we will place her in the grave: tomorrow 'is a good day.' I know a faithful old priest. I have consulted with him how to arrange all."

"And what has become of Ukon?" asked Genji. "How does she bear it?"

"That is, indeed, a question. She was really deeply affected, and she foolishly said, 'I will die with my mistress.' She was actually going to throw herself headlong from the cliff; but I warned, I advised, I consoled her, and she became more pacified."

"The state of her feelings may be easily conceived. I am myself not less deeply wounded than she. I do not even know what might become of myself."

"Why do you grieve so uselessly? Every uncertainty is the result of a certainty. There is nothing in this world really to be lamented. If you do not wish the public to know anything of this matter, I, Koremitz, will manage it."

"I, also, am aware that everything is fated. Still, I am deeply sorry to have brought this misfortune on this poor girl by my own inconsiderate rashness. The only thing I have now to ask you, is to keep these events in the dark. Do not mention them to anyone—nay, not even to your mother."

"Even from the priests to whom it must necessarily be known, I will conceal the reality," replied Koremitz.

"Do manage all this most skillfully!"

"Why, of course I shall manage it as secretly as possible," cried Koremitz; and he was about to take his departure, but Genji stopped him.

"I must see her once more," said Genji, sorrowfully. "I will go with you to behold her, before she is lost to my sight forever." And he insisted on accompanying him.

Koremitz, however, did not at all approve of this project; but his resistance gave way to the earnest desire of Genji, and he said, "If you think so much about it, I cannot help it."

"Let us hasten, then, and return before the night be far advanced."

"You shall have my horse to ride."

Genji rose, and dressed himself in the ordinary plain style he usually adopted for his private expeditions, and started away with one confidential servant, besides Koremitz.

They crossed the river Kamo, the torches carried before them burning dimly. They passed the gloomy cemetery of Toribeno, and at last reached the convent.

It was a rude wooden building, and adjoining was a small Buddha Hall, through whose walls votive tapers mysteriously twinkled. Within, nothing but the faint sound of a female's voice repeating prayers was to be heard. Outside, and around, the evening services in the surrounding temples were all finished, and all Nature was in silent repose. In the direction of Kiyomidz alone some scattered lights studding the dark scene betrayed human habitations.

They entered. Genji's heart was beating fast with emotion. He saw Ukon reclining beside a screen, with her back to the lamp. He did not speak to her, but proceeded straight to the body, and gently drew aside the mantle which covered its face. It still wore a look of tranquil calmness; no change had yet attacked the features. He took the cold hand in his own, crying out as he did so:

"Do let me hear thy voice once more! Why have you left me thus bereaved?" But the silence of death was unbroken!

He then, half sobbing, began to talk with Ukon, and invited her to come to his mansion, and help to console him. But Koremitz now admonished him to consider that time was passing quickly.

At this Genji threw a long sad farewell glance at the face of the dead, and rose to depart. He was so feeble and powerless that he could not mount his horse without the help of Koremitz. The countenance of the dead girl floated ever before his sight, with the look she wore when living, and it seemed as if he were being led on by some mysterious influence.

The banks of the river Kamo were reached, when Genji found himself too weak to support himself on horseback, and so dismounted.

"I am afraid," he exclaimed, "I shall not be able to reach home."

Koremitz was a little alarmed. "If I had only been firm," he thought, "and had prevented this journey, I should not have exposed him to such a trial." He descended to the river, and bathing his hands,[11] offered up a prayer to Kwannon of Kiyomidz, and again assisted Genji to mount, who struggled to recover his energy, and managed somehow to return to Nijio, praying in silence as he rode along.

The people of the mansion entertained grave apprehensions about him; and not unnaturally, seeing he had been unusually restless for some days, and had become suddenly ill since the day before, and they could never understand what urgency had called him out on that evening.

Genji now lay down on his couch, fatigued and exhausted, and continued in the same state for some days, when he became quite weak.

The Emperor was greatly concerned, as was also Sadaijin. Numerous prayers were offered, and exorcisms performed everywhere in his behalf, all with the most careful zeal. The public was afraid he was too beautiful to live long.

The only solace he had at this time was Ukon; he had sent for her, and made her stay in his mansion.

---

[11] It is the Oriental custom that when one offers up a prayer, he first washes his hands, to free them from all impurity.

And whenever he felt better he had her near him, and conversed with her about her dead mistress.

In the meantime, it might have been the result of his own energetic efforts to realize the ardent hopes of the Emperor and his father-in-law, that his condition became better, after a heavy trial of some three weeks; and toward the end of September he became convalescent. He now felt as though he had been restored to the world to which he had formerly belonged. He was, however, still thin and weak, and, for consolation, still resorted to talk with Ukon.

"How strange," he said to her, as they were conversing together one fine autumn evening. "Why did she not reveal to me all her past life? If she had but known how deeply I loved her, she might have been a little more frank with me."

"Ah! no," replied Ukon; "she would not intentionally have concealed anything from you; but it was, I imagine, more because she had no choice. You at first conducted yourself in such a mysterious manner; and she, on her part, regarded her acquaintance with you as something like a dream. That was the cause of her reticence."

"What a useless reticence it was," exclaimed Genji. "I was not so frank as, perhaps, I ought to have been; but you may be sure that made no difference in my affection toward her. Only, you must remember, there is my father, the Emperor, besides many others, whose vigilant admonitions I am bound to respect. That was the reason that I had to be careful. Nevertheless, my love to your mistress was singularly deep; too deep, perhaps, to last long. Do tell me now all you know about her; I do not see any reason that you should conceal it. I have carefully ordered the weekly requiem for the dead; but tell me in whose behalf it is, and what was her origin?"

"I have no intention of concealing anything from you. Why should I? I only thought it would be blamable if one should reveal after death what another had thought best to reserve," replied Ukon. "Her parents died when she was a mere girl. Her father was called Sammi-Chiujio, and loved her very dearly. He was always aspiring to better his position, and wore out his life in the struggle. After his death, she was left helpless and poor. She was however, by chance, introduced to To-no-Chiujio, when he was still Shioshio, and not Chiujio.

During three years they kept on very good terms, and he was very kind to her. But some wind or other attacks every fair flower; and, in the autumn of last year, she received a fearful menace from the house of Udaijin, to whose daughter, as you know, To-no-Chiujio is married. Poor girl, she was terrified at this. She knew not what to do, and hid herself, with her nurse, in an obscure part of the capital. It was not a very agreeable place, and she was about removing to a certain mountain hamlet, but, as its 'celestial direction' was closed this year, she was still hesitating, and while matters were in this state, you appeared on the scene. To do her justice, she had no thought of wandering from one to another; but circumstances often make things appear as if we did so. She was, by nature, extremely reserved, so that she did not like to speak out her feelings to others, but rather suffered in silence by herself. This, perhaps, you also have noticed."

"Then it was so, after all. She was the Tokonatz of To-no-Chiujio," thought Genji; and now it also transpired that all that Koremitz had stated about To-no-Chiujio's visiting her at the Yugao house was a pure invention, suggested by a slight acquaintance with the girl's previous history.

"The Chiujio told me once," said Genji, "that she had a little one. Was there any such?"

"Yes, she had one in the spring of the year before last—a girl, a nice child," replied Ukon.

"Where is she now?" asked Genji, "perhaps you will bring her to me some day. I should like to have her with me as a memento of her mother. I should not mind mentioning it to her father, but if I did so, I must reveal the whole sad story of her mother's fate, and this would not be advisable at present; however, I do not see any harm if I were to bring her up as my daughter. You might manage it somehow without my name being mentioned to anyone concerned."

"That would be a great happiness for the child," exclaimed Ukon, delighted, "I do not much appreciate her being brought up where she is."

"Well, I will do so, only let us wait for some better chance. For the present be discreet."

"Yes, of course. I cannot yet take any steps toward that object; we must not unfurl our sails before the storm is completely over."

The foliage of the ground, touched with autumnal tints, was beginning to fade, and the sounds of insects (*mushi*) were growing faint, and both Genji and Ukon were absorbed by the sad charm of the scene. As they meditated, they heard doves cooing among the bamboo woods.

To Genji it brought back the cries of that strange bird, which cry he had heard on that fearful night in Rokjio, and the subject recurred to his mind once more, and he said to Ukon, "How old was she?"

"Nineteen."

"And how came you to know her?"

"I was the daughter of her first nurse, and a great favorite of her father's, who brought me up with her, and from that time I never left her. When I come to think of those days I wonder how I can exist without her. The poet says truly, 'The deeper the love, the more bitter the parting.' Ah! how gentle and retiring she was. How much I loved her!"

"That retiring and gentle temperament," said Genji, "gives far greater beauty to women than all beside, for to have no natural pliability makes women utterly worthless."

The sky by this time became covered, and the wind blew chilly. Genji gazed intently on it and hummed:

> When we regard the clouds above,
>   Our souls are filled with fond desire,
> To me the smoke of my dead love,
>   Seems rising from the funeral pyre.

The distant sound of the bleacher's hammer reached their ears, and reminded him of the sound he had heard in the Yugao's house. He bade "Good night" to Ukon, and retired to rest, humming as he went:

> In the long nights of August and September.

On the forty-ninth day (after the death of the Yugao) he went to the Hokke Hall in the Hiye Mountain, and there had a service for the dead performed, with full ceremony and rich offerings. The monk-brother of Koremitz took every pains in its performance.

The composition of requiem prayers was made by Genji himself, and revised by a professor of literature, one of his intimate friends. He expressed in it the melancholy sentiment about the death of one whom he had dearly loved, and whom he had yielded to Buddha. But who she was was not stated. Among the offerings there was a dress. He took it up in his hands and sorrowfully murmured,

> With tears to-day, the dress she wore
> I fold together, when shall I
> Bright Elysium's far-off shore
> This robe of hers again untie?

And the thought that the soul of the deceased might be still wandering and unsettled to that very day, but that now the time had come when her final destiny would be decided,[12] made him pray for her more fervently.

So closed the sad event of Yugao.

Now Genji was always thinking that he should wish to see his beloved in a dream.

The evening after his visit to the Hokke Hall, he beheld her in his slumbers, as he wished, but at the same moment the terrible face of the woman that he had seen on that fearful evening in Rokjio again appeared before him; hence he concluded that the same mysterious being who tenanted that dreary mansion had taken advantage of his fears and had destroyed his beloved Yugao.

A few words more about the house in which she had lived. After her flight no communication had been sent to them even by Ukon, and they had no idea of where she had gone to. The mistress of the house was a daughter Yugao's nurse, who had three children of her own. Ukon was a stranger to them, and they imagined that her being so was the reason for her sending no intelligence to them. True they had entertained some suspicions about the gay prince, and pressed Koremitz to confide the truth to them, but the latter, as he had done before, kept himself skillfully aloof.

They then thought she might have been seduced and carried off by some gallant son of a local governor, who feared his intrigue might be discovered by To-no-Chiujio.

---

[12] According to the Buddhist's doctrine of the Hosso sect, all the souls of the dead pass, during seven weeks after death, into an intermediate state, and then their fate is decided. According to the Tendai sect, the best and the worst go immediately where they deserve, but those of a medium nature go through this process.

During these days Kokimi, of Ki-no-Kami's house, still used to come occasionally to Genji. But for some time past the latter had not sent any letter to Cicada. When she heard of his illness she not unnaturally felt for him, and also she had experienced a sort of disappointment in not seeing his writing for some time, especially as the time of her departure for the country was approaching. She therefore sent him a letter of inquiry with the following:

> If long time passes slow away,
>   Without a word from absent friend,
> Our fears no longer brook delay,
>   But must some kindly greeting send.

To this letter Genji returned a kind answer and also the following:

> This world to me did once appear
>   Like Cicada's shell, when cast away,
> Till words addressed by one so dear,
>   Have taught my hopes a brighter day.

This was written with a trembling hand, but still bearing nice traits, and when it reached Cicada, and she saw that he had not yet forgotten past events, and the scarf he had carried away, she was partly amused and partly pleased.

It was about this time that the daughter of Iyo-no-Kami was engaged to a certain Kurand Shioshio, and he was her frequent visitor. Genji heard of this, and without any intention of rivalry, sent her the following by Kokimi:

> Like the green reed that grows on high
>   By river's brink, our love has been,
> And still my wandering thoughts will fly
>   Back to that quickly passing scene.

She was a little flattered by it, and gave Kokimi a reply, as follows:

> The slender reed that feels the wind
>   That faintly stirs its humble leaf,
> Feels that too late it breathes its mind,
>   And only wakes, a useless grief.

Now the departure of Iyo-no-Kami was fixed for the beginning of October.

Genji sent several parting presents to his wife, and in addition to these some others, consisting of beautiful combs, fans, *nusa*,[13] and the scarf he had carried away, along with the following, privately through Kokimi:—

> I kept this pretty souvenir
> In hopes of meeting you again,
> I send it back with many a tear,
> Since now, alas! such hope is vain.

There were many other minute details, which I shall pass over as uninteresting to the reader.

Genji's official messenger returned, but her reply about the scarf was sent through Kokimi:

> When I behold the summer wings
> Cicada-like, I cast aside;
> Back to my heart fond memory springs,
> And on my eyes, a rising tide.

The day of the departure happened to be the commencement of the winter season. An October shower fell lightly, and the sky looked gloomy.

Genji stood gazing upon it and hummed:

> Sad and weary Autumn hours,
> Summer joys now passed away,
> Both departing, dark the hours,
> Whither speeding, who can say?

All these intrigues were safely kept in strict privacy, and to have boldly written all particulars concerning them is to me a matter of pain. So at first I intended to omit them, but had I done so my history would have become like a fiction, and the censure I should expect would be that I had done so intentionally, because my hero was the son of an Emperor; but, on the other hand, if I am accused of too much loquacity, I cannot help it.

---

[13] An offering made of paper, to the God of Roads, which travelers were accustomed to make before setting out on a journey.

The Tale of Genji   47

EXILE AT AKASHI [1]

The storm and thunder still continued for some days, and the same strange dream visited Genji over and over again.[2]

This made him miserable. To return to the capital was not yet to be thought of, as to do so before the Imperial permission was given, would only be to increase his disgrace. On the other hand, to render himself obscure by seeking further retreat was also not to be thought of, as it might cause another rumor that he had been driven away by mere fear of the disturbed state of the ocean.

In the meantime, a messenger arrived from the capital with a letter from Violet.[3] It was a letter of inquiry about himself. It was written in most affectionate terms, and stated that the weather there was extremely disagreeable, as rain was pouring down continuously, and that this made her especially gloomy in thinking of him. This letter gave Genji great pleasure.

The messenger was of the lowest class. At other times Genji would never have permitted such sort of people to approach him, but under the present circumstances of his life he was only too glad to put up with it. He summoned the man to his presence, and made him talk of all the latest news in the capital.

The messenger told him, in awkward terms, that in the capital these storms were considered to be a kind of heavenly warning, that a Nin-wo-ye [4] was going to be held; and that

[1] Having fallen from favor because of the enmity of Koki-den, mother of his half-brother, the new emperor, Genji has voluntarily gone into exile to avoid further injury to his friends and dependents. (This chapter has been considerably abbreviated in translation.)

[2] In a dream Genji was invited by the god of the ocean to return to the palace; his immediate joyful belief that the dream was a sign he should return to the Court has been replaced by the realization that the dream is a sign that he should remain by the sea.

[3] Violet: Murasaki, Genji's second wife, has remained at home.

[4] A religious feast in the Imperial palace, in which Nin-wo-kio, one of the Buddhist Bibles, was read, an event that rarely took place. Its object was to tranquillize the country.

many nobles who had to go to Court were prevented from doing so by the storms, adding that he never remembered such violent storms before.

From the dawn of the next day the winds blew louder, the tide flowed higher, and the sound of the waves resounded with a deafening noise. The thunder rolled and the lightning flashed, while everyone was trembling in alarm, and were all, including Genji, offering up prayers and vows to the God Sumiyoshi,[5] whose temple was at no great distance, and also to other gods. Meanwhile a thunderbolt struck the corridor of Genji's residence and set fire to it. The prince and his friends retired to a small house behind, which served as a kitchen. The sky was as if blackened with ink, and in that state of darkness the day ended. In the evening the wind gradually abated, the rain diminished to a thin shower, and even the stars began to blink out of the heavens.

This temporary retreat was now irksome, and they thought of returning to their dwelling quarters, but they saw nothing but ruins and confusion from the storm, so they remained where they were. Genji was occupied in prayer. The moon began to smile from above, the flow of the tide could be seen, and the rippling of the waves heard. He opened the rude wooden door, and contemplated the scene before him. He seemed to be alone in the world, having no one to participate in his feelings. He heard several fishermen talking in their peculiar dialect. Feeling much wearied by the events of the day, he soon retired, and resigned himself to slumber, reclining near one side of the room, in which there were none of the comforts of an ordinary bedchamber.

All at once his late father appeared before his eyes in the exact image of life, and said to him, "Why are you in so strange a place?" and taking his hand, continued, "Embark at once in a boat, as the God Sumiyoshi guides you, and leave this coast."

Genji was delighted at this, and replied, "Since I parted from you I have undergone many misfortunes, and I thought that I might be buried on this coast."

"It must not be thus," the phantom replied; "your being here is only a punishment for a trifling sin which you have committed. For my own part, when I was on the throne, I

[5] The God of the Sea.

did no wrong, but I have somehow been involved in some trifling sin, and before I expiated it I left the world. Hurt, however, at beholding you oppressed with such hardships I came up here, plunging into the waves, and rising on the shore. I am much fatigued; but I have something I wish to tell the Emperor, so I must haste away," and he left Genji, who felt very much affected, and cried out, "Let me accompany you!" With this exclamation he awoke, and looked up, when he saw nothing but the moon's face shining through the windows, with the clouds reposing in the sky.

The image of his father still vividly remained before his eyes, and he could not realize that it was only a dream. He became suddenly sad, and was filled with regret that he did not talk a little more, even though it was only in a dream. He could not sleep any more this night, and dawn broke, when a small boat was seen approaching the coast, with a few persons in it.

A man from the boat came up to the residence of Genji. When he was asked who he was, he replied that the priest of Akashi (the former governor) had come from Akashi in his boat, and that he wished to see Yoshikiyo,[6] and to tell him the reason of his coming. Yoshikiyo was surprised, and said, "I have known him for years, but there was a slight reason why we were not the best of friends, and some time has now passed without correspondence. What makes him come?"

As to Genji, however, the arrival of the boat made him think of its coincidence with the subject of his dream, so he hurried Yoshikiyo to go and see the newcomers. Thereupon the latter went to the boat, thinking as he went, "How could he come to this place amidst the storms which have been raging?"

The priest now told Yoshikiyo that in a dream which he had on the first day of the month, a strange being told him a strange thing, and, said he, "I thought it too credulous to believe in a dream, but the object appeared again, and told me that on the thirteenth of this month he will give me a supernatural sign, directing me also to prepare a boat, and as soon as the storm ceased, to sail out to this coast. Therefore, to test its truth I launched a boat, but strange to say, on this day the extraordinarily violent weather of rain, wind, and

[6] Yoshikiyo: a retainer who accompanied Genji into exile.

thunder occurred. I then thought that in China there had been several instances of people benefiting the country by believing in dreams, so though this may not exactly be the case with mine, yet I thought it my duty, at all events, to inform you of the fact. With these thoughts I started in the boat, when a slight miraculous breeze, as it were, blew, and drove me to this coast. I can have no doubt that this was divine direction. Perhaps there might have been some inspiration in this place, too; and I wish to trouble you to transmit this to the prince."

Yoshikiyo then returned and faithfully told Genji all about his conversation with the priest. When Genji came to reflect, he thought that so many dreams having visited him must have some significance. It might only increase his disgrace if he were to despise such divine warnings merely from worldly considerations, and from fear of consequences. It would be better to resign himself to one more advanced in age, and more experienced than himself. An ancient sage says, that "resigning oneself makes one happier"; besides, his father had also enjoined him in the dream to leave the coast of Suma, and there remained no further doubt for taking this step. He, therefore, gave this answer to the priest: "Coming into an unknown locality, plunged in solitude, receiving scarcely any visits from friends in the capital, the only thing I have to regard as friends of old times are the sun and the moon that pass over the boundless heavens. Under these circumstances, I shall be only too delighted to visit your part of the coast, and to find there such a suitable retreat."

This answer gave the priest great joy, and he pressed Genji to set out at once and come to him. The prince did so with his usual four or five confidential attendants. The same wind which had miraculously blown the vessel of the priest to Suma now changed, and carried them with equal favor and speed back to Akashi. On their landing they entered a carriage waiting for them, and went to the mansion of the priest.

The scenery around the coast was no less novel than that of Suma, the only difference being that there were more people there. The building was grand, and there was also a grand Buddha Hall adjoining for the service of the priest. The plantations of trees, the shrubberies, the rockwork, and the mimic lakes in the garden were so beautifully arranged as to exceed the power of an artist to depict, while the style of the dwelling was so tasteful that it was in no way inferior to any in the capital.

The wife and the daughter of the priest were not residing here, but were at another mansion on the hillside, where they had removed from fear of the recent high tides.

Genji now took up his quarters with the priest in this seaside mansion. The first thing he did when he felt a little settled was to write to the capital, and tell his friends of his change of residence. The priest was about sixty years old, and was very sincere in his religious service. The only subject of anxiety which he felt was, as we have already mentioned, the welfare of his daughter. When Genji became thoroughly settled he often joined the priest, and spent hours in conversing with him. The latter, from his age and experience, was full of information and anecdotes, many of which were quite new to Genji, but the narration of them seemed always to turn upon his daughter.

April had now come. The trees began to be clothed with a thick shade of leaves, which had a peculiar novelty of appearance, differing from that of the flowers of spring, or the bright dyes of autumn. The Kuina (a particular bird of summer) commenced their fluttering. The furniture and dresses were changed for those more suitable to the time of year. The comfort of the house was most agreeable. It was on one of these evenings that the surface of the broad ocean spread before the eye was unshadowed by the clouds, and the Isle of Awaji floated like foam on its face, just as it appeared to do at Suma. Genji took out his favorite kin,[7] on which he had not practiced for some time, and was playing an air called "Korio," when the priest joined him, having left for awhile his devotions, and said that his music recalled to his mind the old days and the capital which he had quitted so long. He sent for a biwa (mandolin) and a *soh-koto*[8] from the hillside mansion, and, after the fashion of a blind singer of ballads to the biwa, played two or three airs.

He then handed the *soh-koto* to Genji, who also played a

[7] Kin: a Chinese koto with seven strings.

[8] The "biwa," more than any other instrument, is played by blind performers, who accompany it with ballads. The *soh-koto*, with thirteen strings, is smaller than a modern koto.

few tunes, saying, as he did so, in a casual manner, "This sounds best when played upon by some fair hand." The priest smiled, and rejoined: "What better hand than yours need we wish to hear playing; for my part, my poor skill has been transmitted to me, through three generations, from the Royal hand of the Emperor Yenghi, though I now belong to the past; but, occasionally, when my loneliness oppresses me, I indulge in my old amusement, and there is one who, listening to my strains, has learnt to imitate them so well that they resemble those of the Emperor Yenghi himself. I shall be very happy, if you desire, to find an opportunity for you to hear them."

Genji at once laid aside the instrument, saying: "Ah, how bold! I did not know I was among proficients," and continued, "From olden time the *soh-koto* was peculiarly adopted by female musicians. The fifth daughter of the Emperor Saga, from whom she had received the secret, was a celebrated performer, but no one of equal skill succeeded her. Of course there are several players, but these merely strike or strum on the instrument; but in this retreat there is a skillful hand. How delightful it will be."

"If you desire to hear, there is no difficulty. I will introduce her to you. She also plays the biwa very well. The biwa has been considered from olden time very difficult to master, and I am proud of her doing so."

In this manner the priest led the conversation to his own daughter, while fruit and saké were brought in for refreshment. He then went on talking of his life since he first came to the coast of Akashi, and of his devotion to religion, for the sake of future happiness, and also out of solicitude for his daughter. He continued: "Although I feel rather awkward in saying it, I am almost inclined to think your coming to this remote vicinity has something providential in it, as an answer, as it were, to our earnest prayers, and it may give you some consolation and pleasure. The reason that I think so is this—it is nearly eighteen years since we began to pray for the blessing of the God Sumiyoshi on our daughter, and we have sent her twice a year, in spring and autumn, to his temple. At the 'six-time' service,[9] also, the prayers for my own repose on

[9] The services performed by rigid priests were six times daily—

the lotus flower,[10] are only secondary to those which I put up for the happiness of my daughter. My father, as you may know, held a good office in the capital, but I am now a plain countryman, and if I leave matters in their present state, the status of my family will soon become lower and lower. Fortunately this girl was promising from her childhood, and my desire was to present her to some distinguished personage in the capital, not without disappointment to many suitors, and I have often told her that if my desire is not fulfilled she had better throw herself into the sea."

Such was the tedious discourse which the priest held on the subject of his family affairs; yet it is not surprising that it awakened an interest in the susceptible mind of Genji for the fair maiden thus described as so promising. The priest at last, in spite of the shyness and reserve of the daughter, and the unwillingness of the mother, conducted Genji to the hillside mansion, and introduced him to the maiden. In the course of time they gradually became more than mere acquaintances to each other. For some time Genji often found himself at the hillside mansion, and her society appeared to afford him greater pleasure than anything else, but this did not quite meet with the approval of his conscience, and the girl in the mansion at Nijio returned to his thoughts. If this flirtation of his should become known to her, he thought, it perhaps would be very annoying to her. True, she was not much given to be jealous, but he well remembered the occasional complaints she had now and then made to him while in the capital. These feelings induced him to write more frequently and more minutely to her, and he soon began to frequent the hillside mansion less often. His leisure hours were spent in sketching, as he used to do in Suma, and writing short poetic effusions explanatory of the scenery. This was also going on in the mansion at Nijio, where Violet passed the long hours away in painting different pictures, and also in writing, in the form of a diary, what she saw and did. What will be the issue of all these things?

---

namely, at early morn, midday, sunset, early evening, midnight, and after midnight.

[10] The Buddhist idea that when we get into Paradise we take our seat upon the lotus flower.

Now, since the spring of the year there had been several heavenly warnings in the capital, and things in general were somewhat unsettled. On the evening of the thirteenth of March, when the rain and wind had raged, the late Emperor appeared in a dream to his son the Emperor, in front of the palace, looking reproachfully upon him. The Emperor showed every token of submission and respect when the dead Emperor told him of many things, all of which concerned Genji's interests. The Emperor became alarmed, and when he awoke he told his mother all about his dream. She, however, told him that on such occasions, when the storm rages, and the sky is obscured by the disturbance of the elements, all things, especially on which our thoughts have been long occupied, appear to us in a dream in a disturbed sleep; and she continued, "I further counsel you not to be too hastily alarmed by such trifles." From this time he began to suffer from sore eyes, which may have resulted from the angry glances of his father's spirit. About the same time the father of the Empress-mother died. His death was by no means premature; but yet, when such events take place repeatedly, it causes the mind to imagine there is something more than natural going on, and this made the Empress-mother feel a little indisposed.

The Emperor then constantly told her that if Genji were left in his present condition it might induce evil, and, therefore, it would be better to recall him, and restore his titles and honors to him. She obstinately opposed these ideas, saying, "If a person who proved to be guilty, and has retired from the capital, were to be recalled before the expiration of at least three years, it would naturally show the weakness of authority."

She gained her point, and thus the days were spent and the year changed.

The Emperor still continually suffered from indisposition, and the unsettled state of things remained the same as before. A prince had been born to him, who was now about two years old, and he began to think of abdicating the throne in favor of the Heir-apparent, the child of the Princess Wisteria. When he looked around to see who would best minister public affairs, he came to think that the disgrace of Genji was a matter not to be allowed to continue, and at last, contrary to the advice of his mother, he issued a public permission for Genji's return to the capital, which was repeated at the end of July. Genji therefore prepared to come back. Before, however, he started, a month passed away, which time was mostly spent in the society of the lady of the hillside mansion. The expected journey of Genji was now auspicious, even to him, and ought also to have been so to the family of the priest, but parting has always something painful in its nature. This was more so because the girl had by this time the witness of their love in her bosom, but he told her that he would send for her when his position was assured in the capital.

Toward the middle of August everything was in readiness, and Genji started on his journey homeward. He went to Naniwa, where he had the ceremony of Horai performed. To the temple of Sumiyoshi he sent a messenger to say that the haste of his journey prevented him coming at this time, but that he would fulfill his vows as soon as circumstances would permit. From Naniwa he proceeded to the capital, and returned once more, after an absence of nearly three years, to his mansion at Nijio. The joy and excitement of the inmates of the mansion were unbounded, and the development of Violet charmed his eyes. His delight was great and the pleasure of his mind was of the most agreeable nature; still, from time to time, in the midst of this very pleasure, the recollection of the maiden whom he had left at Akashi occurred to his thoughts. But this kind of perturbation was only the result of what had arisen from the very nature of Genji's character.

Before the lapse of many days all his titles and honors were restored to him, and he was soon created an extra Vice-Dainagon.

All those who had lost dignities or office on account of Genji's complications were also restored to them. It seemed to these like a sudden and unexpected return of spring to the leafless tree.

In the course of a few days Genji was invited by the Emperor to come and see him. The latter had scarcely recovered from his indisposition, and was still looking weak and thin. When Genji appeared before him, he manifested great pleasure, and they conversed together in a friendly way till the evening.

ANONYMOUS
Tales of the Heike
(*Heike Monogatari,* Thirteenth century)

Translated by A. W. Sadler

Several historical works dealing with the twelfth-century civil wars survive from the Kamakura period (1185–1333). Of these the greatest literary achievement is *Tales of the Heike,* a historical novel that emphasizes the pathos and the tragedy in the fall of the Heike clan. By the middle of the twelfth century, a military clan called the Heike (the House of Taira) rose under the leadership of Kiyomori and overpowered the Fujiwara family, which ruled the Heian Court, as well as their rival the Genji (the House of Minamoto). The Heike's failure to evolve a new system of government led to a military struggle for power between the two clans in the last quarter of the century. *Tales of the Heike* recounts a series of wars between 1180 and 1185 in which the Heike was finally crushed.

Tales of the Heike is a collection of various episodes dealing with the war as is shown by the present selections. Who composed and assembled these tales, probably completed by the middle of the thirteenth century, is unknown. The text of the work exists in numerous copies none of which is complete in itself. "The Fight at Dan-no-ura" describes one of the fiercest battles fought between the two forces. The Heike had earlier been chased out of the capital by their eastern enemy the Genji, led by the hero Yoshitsune, and in this episode have retreated to the Inland Sea along the shores of Shikoku and Kyushu, two southwest islands. Although the Heike were successful in defending their fortress at certain positions, they suffered major losses at Ichi-no-Tani and other places, and were finally driven to the sea. "The Drowning of the Emperor" is a well-known episode that occurred in the midst of this losing battle at sea. "The Six Paths" is a story of the former Empress, mother of the late child Emperor, who lived in the capital as a recluse after the war. Relating a brief history of the defeat of the Heike and the agonizing path she had taken, she was nevertheless assured by her visitor that she achieved her own salvation.

The language of *Tales of the Heike* is more poetic than that of *The Tale of Genji,* since some of the passages were obviously intended for recitation with a musical instrument. Such lines are thus composed of an alternation of five and seven syllables, the traditional Japanese meter. This style is reflected in Noh plays like *Atsumori* by the celebrated fifteenth-century playwright Zeami Motokiyo, which is based on *Tales of the Heike.*

THE FIGHT AT DAN-NO-URA

Now the two hosts of the Genji and Heike faced each other scarcely thirty cho [1] distant on the water; and as the tide was running strongly through Moji, Akama, and Dan-no-ura, the Heike ships were carried down by the current against their will, while the Genji were naturally able to advance on them with the tide. Kajiwara with his sons and retainers to the number of fourteen or fifteen, stuck close to the shore, and catching on with rakes to some ships of the Heike that went astray, they boarded them and sprang from one ship to the other, cutting their men down both at bow and stern and doing great deeds. And their merit that day has been specially recorded.

Thus both armies joined battle all along the line, and the roar of their war cries was such as to be heard even to the highest heavens of Brahma, and to cause the deity deep under the earth to start in amazement. Then Tomomori, coming forth on to the deckhouse of his ship, shouted to his men in a mighty voice: "Even in India and China and also in our own country, with the most renowned leader and the bravest warriors an army cannot prevail if fate be against it. Yet must our honor be dear to us, and we must show a bold front to these Eastern soldiers. Let us then pay no heed to our lives, but think of nothing but fighting as bravely as we may." Hida-no-Saburo Saemon Kagetsune again repeated this proclamation to the samurai. "Ho! these Eastern fellows may

[1] A cho is approximately one hundred meters.

have a great name for their horsemanship," shouted Aku-shichibyoye Kagekiyo, "but they know nothing about sea fights, and they will be like fish up a tree, so that we will pick them up one by one and pitch them into the sea!" "And let their Commander Kuro Yoshitsune be the special object of your attack," added Etchu-no-Jirohyoye Moritsugu, "he is a little fellow with a fair complexion and his front teeth stick out a bit, so you will know him by that. He often changes his clothes and armor, so take care he doesn't escape you!" "Who cares for that wretched little fellow?" replied Aku-shichi, "Cheer up, my brave comrades; we'll soon pick him up under our arms and fling him into the sea!"

After Shin-Chunagon Tomomori had thus addressed his men he took a small boat and rowed across to the ship of Munemori. "Our own men look well enough," said he, "only Awa-no-Mimbu Shigeyoshi seems doubtful in his allegiance. I pray you let me take off his head." "But he has served us well so far," replied Munemori, "so how can we do this only on suspicion? Anyhow, let him be summoned."

So Shigeyoshi came into the presence of Munemori. He was attired in a hitatare [2] of yellowish red color with a little black in it, and armor laced with light-red leather. "How now, Shigeyoshi? Do you intend treachery?" said Munemori, "for your conduct today has a suspicious look. Do you tell your men of Shikoku to bear themselves well in the fight, and don't play the dastard." "Why should I play the dastard?" said Shigeyoshi as he retired. Meanwhile Tomomori had been standing by with his hand gripping his sword hilt hard enough to break it, casting meaning looks at Munemori to intimate his wish to cut Shigeyoshi down, but as the latter gave no sign he could do nothing.

So the Heike divided their thousand vessels into three fleets. In the van rowed Yamaga-no-Hyotoji Hideto with five hundred ships, and after him came the Matsuura with three hundred more; last of all came the Heike nobles with two hundred. Now Yamaga-no-Hyotoji who led the van was the strongest archer in all Kyushu, and he chose five hundred men who drew the bow better than most, though not equal to himself, and placed them in the bows of his ships, shoulder

[2] Hitatare: a ceremonial robe worn by both warriors and commoners in ancient Japan.

to shoulder, so that they let fly a volley of five hundred arrows at once.

The fleet of the Genji was the more numerous with its three thousand ships, but as their men shot from various places here and there, their force did not show to advantage. Yoshitsune himself, who was fighting in the forefront of the battle, was greatly embarrassed by the arrows of the foe that fell like rain on his shield and armor. So, elated by their victory in the first attack, the Heike pressed onward, and the roar of their shouting mingled with the booming of their war drums that continuously sounded the onset.

Now on the side of the Genji, Wada-no-Kotaro Yoshimori did not go on shipboard, but mounted his horse and sat himself firmly in the saddle with his feet deep in the stirrups, riding into the midst of the Heike host and letting fly his arrows right and left. A famous archer he had always been, and no enemy within the space of three cho escaped his arrows, but one shaft he shot an extraordinary distance on which was a request to return it to the marksman. When it was withdrawn by order of Tomomori it was seen to be feathered with white wing feathers of the crane mixed with black ones of the wild goose, a plain bamboo shaft thirteen handbreadths and three fingers long, inscribed at the space of a handbreadth from the lashing on the butt with the name Wada-no-Kotaro Yoshimori painted in lacquer.

Among the Heike too there were some fine archers, but none who could do a feat like this. After a while however, Nii-no-Kishiro Chikakiyo of Iyo stepped forward and shot it back again. It flew to a distance of more than three cho and struck deep into the left arm of Miura-no-Ishi Sakon-no-Taro, who was standing about a *tan*[3] behind Wada. "Ha-ha!" laughed Miura's men as they came crowding round, "Wada-no-Kotaro boasts no one can equal him at shooting, and now he has been put to shame openly." Then Yoshimori, angered at this, sprang into a small boat and pressed on into the midst of the foe, drawing his bow lustily so that very many of his adversaries were killed and wounded.

After this both sides set their faces against each other and fought grimly without a thought for their lives, neither giving way an inch. But as the Heike had on their side an Emperor

[3] A *tan* is equivalent to about ten meters.

endowed with the Ten Virtues and the Three Sacred Treasures of the Realm, things went hard with the Genji and their hearts were beginning to fail them, when suddenly something that they at first took for a white cloud, but which soon appeared to be a white banner floating in the breeze, came drifting over the two fleets from the upper air and finally settled on the stern of one of the Genji ships, hanging on by the rope.

THE DROWNING OF THE EMPEROR

When he saw this, Yoshitsune, regarding it as a sign from Hachiman Dai-bosatsu, removed his helmet, and after washing his hands, did obeisance; his men all following his example. Moreover a shoal of some thousands of dolphins also made its appearance from the offing and made straight for the ships of the Heike. Then Munemori called the diviner Ko-hakase Harunobu and said: "There are always many dolphins about here, but I have never seen so many as these before; what may it portend?" "If they turn back," replied Harunobu, "the Genji will be destroyed; but if they go on then our own side will be in danger." No sooner had he finished speaking than the dolphins dived under the Heike ships and passed on.

Then, as things had come to this pass, Awa-no-Mimbu Shigeyoshi, who for three years had been a loyal supporter of the Heike, now that his son Dennai Saemon Noriyoshi had been captured, made up his mind that all was lost, and suddenly forsook his allegiance and deserted to the enemy. Great was the regret of Tomomori that he had not cut off the head of "that villain Shigeyoshi," but now it was unavailing.

Now the strategy of the Heike had been to put the stoutest warriors on board the ordinary fighting ships and the inferior soldiers on the big ships of Chinese build, so that the Genji should be induced to attack the big ships, thinking that the commanders were on board them, when they would be able to surround and destroy them. But when Shigeyoshi went over and joined the Genji he revealed this plan to them, with the result that they immediately left the big ships alone and concentrated their attacks on the smaller ones on which were the Heike champions.

Later on the men of Shikoku and Kyushu all left the Heike in a body and went over to the Genji. Those who had so far been their faithful retainers now turned their bows against their lords and drew the sword against their own masters. On one shore the heavy seas beat on the cliff so as to forbid any landing, while on the other stood the serried ranks of the enemy waiting with leveled arrows to receive them. And so on this day the struggle for supremacy between the houses of Gen and Hei was at last decided.

Meanwhile the Genji warriors sprang from one Heike vessel to the other, shooting and cutting down the sailors and helmsmen, so that they flung themselves in panic to the bottom of the ships unable to navigate them any longer. Then Shin-Chunagon Tomomori rowed in a small boat to the Imperial vessel and cried out: "You see what affairs have come to! Clean up the ship, and throw everything unsightly into the sea!" And he ran about the ship from bow to stern, sweeping and cleaning and gathering up the dust with his own hands. "But how goes the battle, Chunagon Dono?" asked the Court ladies. "Oh, you'll soon see some rare gallants from the East," he replied, bursting into loud laughter. "What? Is this a time for joking?" they answered, and they lifted up their voices and wept aloud.

Then the Nii Dono, who had already resolved what she would do, donning a double outer dress of dark-gray mourning color, and tucking up the long skirts of her glossy silk hakama,[4] put the Sacred Jewel under her arm, and the Sacred Sword in her girdle, and taking the Emperor in her arms, spoke thus: "Though I am but a woman I will not fall into the hands of the foe, but will accompany our Sovereign Lord. Let those of you who will, follow me." And she glided softly to the gunwale of the vessel.

The Emperor was eight years old that year, but looked much older than his age, and his appearance was so lovely that he shed as it were a brilliant radiance about him, and his long black hair hung loose far down his back. With a look of surprise and anxiety on his face he inquired of the Nii Dono: "Where is it that you are going to take me?"

Turning to her youthful Sovereign with tears streaming down her cheeks, she answered: "Perchance our Lord does

[4] Hakama: a formal attire worn mostly by men.

not know that, though through the merit of the Ten Virtues practiced in former lives you have been reborn to the Imperial throne in this world, yet by the power of some evil karma destiny now claims you. So now turn to the east and bid farewell to the deity of the Great Shrine of Ise, and then to the west and say the Nembutsu that Amida Buddha and the Holy Ones may come to welcome you to the Pure Western Land. This land is called small as a grain of millet, but yet is it now but a vale of misery. There is a Pure Land of happiness beneath the waves, another capital where no sorrow is. Thither it is that I am taking our Lord."

And thus comforting him, she bound his long hair up in his dove-colored robe, and blinded with tears the child-Sovereign put his beautiful little hands together and turned first to the east to say farewell to the deity of Ise and to Sho-Hachimangu, and then to the west and repeated the Nembutsu, after which the Nii Dono, holding him tightly in her arms and saying consolingly: "In the depths of the ocean we have a capital" sank with him at last beneath the waves.

Ah, the pity of it! That the gust of the spring wind of Impermanence should so suddenly sweep away his flower form. That the cruel billows should thus engulf his Jewel Person. Since his palace was called the Palace of Longevity, he should have passed a long life therein. Its gate was called the Gate of Eternal Youth, the barrier that old age should not pass; and yet, ere he had reached the age of ten years, he had become like the refuse that sinks to the bottom of the sea.

How vain it was to proclaim him as one who sat on the throne as a reward of the Ten Virtues! It was like the dragon that rides on the clouds descending to become a fish at the bottom of the ocean. He who abode in a palace fair as the terraced pavilions of the highest heaven of Brahma, or the paradise where S'akya Muni dwells, among his ministers and nobles of the Nine Families who did him humble obeisance, thus came to a miserable end beneath the ocean waves.

THE SIX PATHS [5]

"Since you have renounced the world," said Awa-no-Naiji, "what does it matter about your appearance? I pray you

[5] Hell, Pretas, Beasts, Asuras, Men, and Heaven.

come and greet his Majesty, for he will soon return." So the former Empress repressed her emotion and entered her cell. "Before my window in prayer I await the coming of Amida," she said, "and at my lowly door I look for the Savior of mankind; but your Majesty's gracious visit I did not expect."

The Ho-o, looking upon her, thus replied: "Even those who live for eighty thousand kalpas in the highest heaven of the World of Formlessness must surely die, and the denizens of the Six Celestial Worlds of Desire cannot escape the Five Changes. The wondrous bliss of the city of delight of the heavens of Indra, and the passionless serenity of the high pavilions of the mid-Dyana world of the heavens of Brahma, even these, like the rewards of dreamland or the pleasures of a vision, eternally change and dissolve, turning and revolving like the wheels of a chariot. And since the Celestial Beings are subject to the Five Changes, how shall men escape? But I hope that you still hear tidings from your old acquaintances, for you must think much of old times."

"There are none from whom I hear anything now," replied the Empress, "except from the wives of Nobutaka and of Takafusa, who continually send me help; but in former days I never even dreamed of being assisted by people such as they." And as she spoke her tears flowed, and her lady companions also hid their faces in their sleeves.

After a while she controlled her emotion and continued: "Though I need not say that being reduced to such a condition has been a great grief to me, yet I feel gladness on account of my enlightenment in the next world. By the help of S'akya Muni, reverently relying on the Great Vow of Amida, I may escape the troubles of the Five Hindrances and the Three Obediences, and in this latter age purify the Six Senses, so that, fixing my hopes on the highest heaven, and fervently praying for the enlightenment of our whole family, I may await the coming of the Saving Host.

"But the thing that I can never forget is the image of the late Emperor, and even though I try to bear his loss with patience, I cannot, for truly there is nothing that wrings the heart like parental affection. And so I pass both day and night in ceaseless prayer for his enlightenment, and this will be my guide also in the True Way." "Verily this our Empire is but a petty country," answered the Ho-o, "but since by observance of the Ten Virtues he became its Emperor, everything must be in accordance with his will. And though all who are born in an age when the Law of Buddha has been widely spread, if they have the desire to practice the Law, without doubt will be hereafter reborn in bliss, yet when I regard your present condition, though it is in accordance with the vanity of human affairs, I cannot but be overcome with grief." And as he spoke his Majesty burst into tears.

"Born the daughter of the Taira Chancellor," continued the former Empress, "and having become the mother of the Emperor, the whole Empire lay in the hollow of my hand. Clad in my varied robes of state, from the New Year Festival to the Year End Ceremonies I was surrounded by the great ministers and courtiers in brilliant throng, even as above the clouds the Six Heavens of Desire and the Four Dhyana Heavens are encircled by eight myriads of lesser heavens.

"Dwelling in the Seiryoden and the Shishinden behind the Jewel Curtain, I gladdened my eyes in spring with the blossoms of the Imperial Cherry Tree. In the hot months of summer I refreshed myself with crystal streams, and in the autumn I viewed the moon in the midst of my ladies. In the cold nights of winter soft bed quilts were heaped up to warm me, and I thought that I had only to wish for the draught of immortality, and the magic potion of eternal life and youth brought from Horai the Elysian isle, for it to be immediately forthcoming. So full was my life of joy and happiness, both by day and by night, that perchance even in heaven nothing could surpass it.

"Then in the autumn of Ju-ei when Yoshinaka came up to attack us, after setting fire to their ancient homes, our family fled from the capital where they had lived so long, looking sadly back at the Imperial palace. Going down to the shore of Suma and Akashi, of which I before knew only the name, we set sail on the boundless ocean, and so from island to island and from shore to shore, our sleeves wet with the salt spray by day, and the cry of the seabirds mingling with our sobs by night, we rowed about seeking some favorable refuge, but never forgetting our ancient home. Left thus with none to help us, the anguish of the Five Changes of our dissolution came upon us. We speak of the 'Pain of the Grief of Parting' and the 'Pain of the Regret of Meeting,' and both of these in one I have known to the full. For when we came to Dazaifu in the island of Kyushu, thinking that there we might find safety for a while, Koreyoshi drove us out again, so that we could find no rest for our foot throughout all the length and breadth of the land.

"And so the next autumn arrived, and we who had always been wont to view the moon from the sacred enclosure of the Ninefold Palace, now spent our nights watching it on the eightfold sea road. And in the tenth month, seeing that the Genji had driven us from the capital, and we had been expelled from Kyushu by Koreyoshi, so that we were like a fish in a net having no place whither to escape, the Chujo Kiyotsune, hating to live any longer, threw himself into the sea in despair. And this was but the beginning of our afflictions. Tossing on the waves by day, and spending our sleepless nights in the ships, we had no tribute of rice with which to prepare the Imperial food, and sometimes, when we wished to prepare it, we had no water with which to do so. Afloat on the vast ocean we could not drink its salt water, and thus we underwent all the suffering of the Preta world. Then, after we had won two fights at Muroyama and Mizushima, the spirits of our family were revived, and building a fortress at Ichi-no-tani in the province of Settsu, all the courtiers and nobles doffed their Court robes and clad themselves in armor for the fight, and the din of battle was incessant both by day and night, even like unto the battle of the Asuras with Indra and his Devas.

"Then in our flight after the defeat at Ichi-no-tani, parents were left behind by their children and wives separated from their husbands, and if we saw a fishing boat in the offing we trembled lest it should be a ship of the enemy, while a flock of white herons in the pine trees threw us into panic lest it should be the white flag of the Genji. And at last, when in the fight at Moji, Akama, and Dan-no-ura she saw that our doom was sealed, the Nii-no-Ama weeping exclaimed: 'Now it seems our last hour has come, and in this fight there is little hope of any of the men surviving. Even if any of our distant relations are left alive they will scarcely be able to perform the services for our departed spirits, but from of old time it has been the custom to spare the women, so you must live to pray for the spirit of the Emperor, and I beg you also to say a prayer for my future salvation.'

"And as in a dream we listened to her words, of a sudden a great wind blew, and the drifting mist came down upon us, so that the hearts of the warriors were confounded, and in the face of heaven they could do nothing. Then the Nii-no-Ama took the Emperor into her arms and went to the gunwale of the vessel, and holding him tightly in her arms, leaped with him into the sea. My eyes darkened and my heart stood still, and it is a thing I can never forget or bear to think of. And at that moment from all those who still lived there went up so great and terrible a cry, that the shrieks of all the damned burning amid the hottest hell of Avichi could not exceed it.

"And so, after being roughly dragged out of the sea by the soldiers, as I was being sent back again to the capital, I came to the shore of Akashi in the province of Harima. And as I chanced to fall asleep there for a space, I saw in a dream as it were our former palace, but of greater and more surpassing beauty, and there sat our late Emperor with the courtiers and nobles of our house ranged about him in all their ceremonial grace and dignity; such a sight as I had not seen since we left our ancient capital. And when I asked where this place might be, the Nii-no-Ama answered and said: 'This is called Ryugu, the Palace of the Dragon King of the sea.'

"'Ah, how blessed!' I replied, 'and is it then a land where is no more sorrow?' 'In the Ryu-chiku Kyo you may read,' she said, 'and never neglect to pray fervently for our future happiness.' And as she said this I awoke, and since that time I have done nothing but read the sutras and say the prayers for their future bliss. And all this, I think, is nothing else but the Six Paths." "In China," said the Ho-o, "Hiuen Tsiang saw the Six Paths before he received enlightenment, and in this country Nichizo Shonin, by the power of Zo-o Gongen, is said to have seen them. That you have been permitted to have gazed on them with mortal eyes is a blessing indeed."

SAIKAKU IHARA
Five Women Who Chose Love
(Koshoku Gonin Onna, 1686)
Translated by Ivan Morris

Saikaku Ihara (1642–1693?) was born in the city of Osaka, the country's commercial center in his day as well as today. Very little is known about his life, except that his wife and one of their children died early in his career. As shown in his writings, Saikaku traveled widely and was well acquainted with people and places. His early popularity came from the people who were enormously impressed by his ability to turn out a great number of poems at a great speed. He is said to have composed, at one time, more than two thousand haiku poems in a day-and-night performance. Basho Matsuo, his contemporary and perhaps the most famous haiku poet, naturally despised his commonplace and often vulgar poems. Saikaku also tried his hand at drama, the genre in which Monzaemon Chikamatsu, another of his contemporaries, became famous, but his greatest contribution to Japanese literature was in realistic fiction that reflected the manners and sentiments of common people of his day. His later works show an increasing sense of gloom, and in his last poem he expressed his regret at having lived too long; he had seen too much of *ukiyo*—the floating world—about which he wrote so well.

Chronologically, Saikaku's works may be roughly classified into three periods: *koshokubon* (books of sexual love) in the early and middle 1680s; miscellany in the late 1680s; and *choninmono* (things for townsmen) in the late 1680s and early 1690s. To the first group belong *A Man Who Devoted His Entire Life to Lovemaking (Koshoku Ichidai Otoko,* 1682, *The Great Mirror of Beauties (Shoen Okagami,* 1684), *The Tale of Wankyu's Life (Wankyu Isse no Monogatari,* 1685), *Five Women Who Chose Love,* and *A Woman Who Devoted Her Entire Life to Lovemaking (Koshoku*

Ichidai Onna, 1686). The writings of the second period describe local legends and anecdotes in such works as *Saikaku's Tales from Various Provinces* (*Saikaku Shokoku Banashi*, 1685) and *Pocket Inkstone* (*Futokoro Suzuri*, 1687). To this period belongs *The Great Mirror of Manly Love* (*Nanshoku Okagami*, 1687), which deals with homosexuality practiced among samurai and Kabuki actors. During this period Saikaku was also concerned with the morale of the warrior class; *Tales of the Warrior's Responsibilities* (*Bukegiri Monogatari*, 1688), for example, describes the traditional code of loyalty, honor, and revenge but the author often satirizes it as anachronistic. Finally, the third period of his prose fiction includes *The Eternal Treasury of Japan* (*Nippon Eitaigura*, 1688) and *Reckoning in This World* (*Seken Munazanyo*, 1692). In both works the author—like Defoe, with whom he is often compared—is primarily concerned with the love of money with which his townsmen seemed to be preoccupied in the new age.

"The Almanac-Maker's Tale," included here, is the third of the five independent stories making up *Five Women Who Chose Love*. All the heroines, like Osan in "The Almanac-Maker's Tale," are passionate individuals and, except one, meet a tragic end. Saikaku is interested here in the discrepancy existing between human love and the prevailing moral code.

Saikaku's language has its own style: the sentences are usually long but composed of short and often abbreviated phrases. It combines the colloquialism of his times with conventional allusions and expressions. His prose is perhaps more difficult for contemporary Japanese than is Defoe's for contemporary English readers.

THE ALMANAC-MAKER'S TALE IN THE MIDDLE PART [1]

1. THE INSPECTION OF BEAUTIES

Thus is it written in the almanac for the second year of Tenna: "The first day of the First Moon: New Year's Writing, an aus-

[1] The translation of this tale originally had many scholarly footnotes that have been omitted from this edition.

picious day for all things. The second day: men first lie with women."

As to this latter practice, it has from the age of the Gods been taught by the wagtail; since those ancient times dalliance between men and women has never ceased.

Now there lived in Kyoto a woman known as the Beautiful Wife of the Almanac-Maker. Her fame had spread far and wide, and by her beauty she had stirred up a mountain of love in the capital. Her eyebrows, delicately shaped like a new moon, rivaled in loveliness the crescent float displayed through the streets at the time of the Gion Festival; her figure was fresh like the early cherry blossoms at the Kiyomizu Temple when gradually they begin to unfold; and the beauty of her lips appeared no less than that of the maples in Takao at the height of their crimson glory. She dwelt in Muromachi-dori and in her attire she displayed the latest tastes. She was indeed the very acme of fashion; nor was there any woman to equal her in the entire capital.

It was full spring, the season that gladdens the hearts of men, and the wisteria blossoms in the Eastern Hills by Yasui were at their loveliest. Billowing out like clouds of purple, they robbed even the pine trees of their color. As dusk fell, the crowds began to return to the city from their flower viewing, and as the fair women flocked down the slopes of the Eastern Hills, they made them into veritable hills of beauty.

There was in Kyoto at that time a band of young pleasure-seekers, famous under the name of the Four Heavenly Kings, who stood out from the common ruck of men by the handsomeness of their features. Relying on their fathers' generosity, these men gave themselves over to enjoyment, and from one New Year's Day to the next New Year's Eve they did not let a single day pass without engaging in some amorous delight.

On the preceding night they had visited the gay quarters of Shimabara and indulged themselves until dawn with the courtesans Morokoshi, Hanasaki, Kaoru, and Takahashi; today they had repaired to Shijogawara, there to practice another form of love with men like Takenaka Kichisaburo, Karamatsu Kasen, Fujita Kichisaburo, and Mitsuse Sakon. Now, having engrossed themselves both in the love of men and in the love of women, without regard for day or night, they had exhausted the full range of their diversions; and in the evening, after the theatre had finished, they repaired to the teahouse called Matsuya and sat down side by side.

"Outside the company of courtesans," one of them remarked, "it is rare indeed to see so many pretty women as one can today. I wonder whether we may find one now who really dazzles us with her beauty."

And so, choosing a discerning actor in their group as judge, they prepared for their evening inspection of the beauties who were now returning from the Eastern Hills. Here was a new diversion for the Heavenly Kings!

To their dismay, most of the ladies were riding in closed palanquins and remained therefore invisible. Presently, however, a group of women came by on foot, all passably attractive, though none strikingly so.

"At all events," said one of the young men, "let us record only those who are truly beautiful."

Then, calling for inkstone and paper, they embarked on a catalogue of the passing beauties.

First came a woman of some thirty-three years. Slender was the nape of her neck, and there was ardor in her eyes. The line of the hair on her brow was of a natural beauty, and though her nose stood rather high, this was not sufficient to mar her other charms. This lady's undergarment was of white satin, above which she wore a kimono of pale blue and, over this, one of reddish yellow, all these being lined with the same fine silk. On her left sleeve, painted in classical style, was a likeness of the bonze Yoshida, above the words, "To sit alone in the lamplight with a book spread out before you . . ." Clearly this was a woman of ingenious fancies. Her sash was of woven velvet with a checkered pattern, and gracefully draped over her kimono was a cloak of the fashion favored by Court ladies. Her feet, encased in a pair of light-mauve socks and shod with sandals of three-colored braids, glided noiselessly over the street. Struck by her natural elegance, they could not help exclaiming, "Lucky devil—that husband of hers!" But at that very moment the lady opened her mouth to speak to an attendant, and they became aware of a missing lower tooth. And at that their ardor instantly cooled.

Following close behind her, came a maiden of not more

than about fourteen, accompanied on one side by a woman who may have been her mother and on the other by a black-gowned nun. In close attendance were a number of serving women and lackeys. For a girl to be thus carefully escorted, thought the young men, she must be still unmarried; but then it struck them that her teeth were blackened and her eyebrows shaved. Her face was round and well favored; her eyes shone with intelligence; her ears elegantly framed the pretty head. The men also observed her slender fingers, smooth-skinned and white. Her style of dress was of the most matchless elegance. Underneath she wore a yellow garment lined with the same rich silk, above this a purple robe of fully dappled design, and over it all a kimono of gray satin sewn onto which was the design of many sparrows. Her sash, of single thickness, was dyed with multicolored stripes. She walked along with splendid bearing, her dress slightly opened at the top. The cords fastened to her well-lined lacquered sedge hat were plaited with twists of paper. A beauty indeed—or so they thought at first sight; but a second look revealed an inch-long blemish upon her face. This could be no ordinary birthmark, thought the young blades. "How she must detest that nurse of hers!" said one of them, and they all laughed as she passed them by.

Then came a girl of some twenty years, wearing a striped garment of handwoven cotton. So threadbare was it that when the wind blew it back, one could see that even the lining was covered with patches and her shame was exposed to all. Her sash appeared to have been made from leftover pieces of a coat and was pitifully thin. On her feet she wore purple leather-soled socks, evidently the only type at her disposal, and an unmatched pair of Nara sandals. An old cloth kerchief covered her head. The hair escaping underneath had clearly seen no comb for many a long day, and its dishevelment was hardly relieved by an artless effort to tie it into a knot. With utter lack of coquetry she walked along, quite self-contained, it seemed, and caring nothing for what people thought. Now when they turned their eyes on her, they saw that her features lacked none of the requisites of beauty, and the young men were all enchanted to find a girl so uniquely endowed with natural charms.

"Were she but attired in proper clothes," said one of them, "she would surely capture some man's heart. But there's no help for poverty!"

They were all touched by the poor girl, and after she had gone her way, they had someone follow her in secret to make inquiries. Thus they learned that she lived at the end of the Seiganji-dori, where she worked at chopping tobacco leaves. The young bucks felt heavyhearted at this report. Here indeed was food for smoke!

Next to catch their eye was a woman of about twenty-seven, decked in the greatest elegance. Her triple-layered garments were of rich black silk; their hems were trimmed with crimson. The outer kimono was adorned with an informal crest in gold. All this was secured with a wide Yorishima sash, woven of Nishijin brocade in Chinese style and knotted in front. Her hair, adorned with a pair of combs, was tied with a wide paper cord in a Shimada coiffure, so shaped that it fell down in the back; round it was draped a kerchief decorated with a delicately dyed pattern; and over this a Kichiya-style sedge hat, enlivened with four-colored braid, rested on her head—but lightly, so as not to conceal the fair looks of which she was so obviously proud. Seeing her move toward them with soft-footed gait, her hips voluptuously swaying, the young men exclaimed, "Here, here, here she is—the woman we've been waiting for! Peace, so that we may observe her closely!"

They waited for her to approach, then perceived that the three maids who accompanied her each held a child in her arms. Small children they were, to boot, probably born within the space of three short years. The young blades were amused.

"Mama, Mama!" cried the children from behind, but the lady walked on, feigning not to hear them.

"Though they be her children," remarked one of the men, "she assuredly finds their presence now most vexing. The flower of a woman's beauty ill survives her motherhood!"

At these words they all laughed boisterously, hearing which the lady would fain have been quit of this fleeting world.

Next, attended in lordly manner by lackeys carrying a palanquin, came a girl barely thirteen years of age. Her long hair was combed out in back, turned slightly up at the ends and secured with a scarlet band. Her forelock stood out and was parted like a young boy's, the coiffure being tied with a paper cord of gold and decorated with a half-inch comb of immaculate beauty—all of which displayed such perfect grace that it would be idle to catalogue her charms one by one. Her under-kimono was of white satin relieved with a black-and-white design; the outer garment was a silken veil of Chinese lace, elegantly contrived so that beneath it one could perceive the iridescent satin of the middle kimono, on which had been sewn a peacock pattern. All this was fastened with an unpadded sash of many colors. Her bare feet were encased in a pair of sandals with paper braids and one of her attendants carried her stylish sedge hat. In her hands she held high a rich spray of trailing wisteria and her expression seemed to say that this was "for those who had not seen the blossoms."

Of all the lovely women they had singled out, she was the very nonpareil. When the young men fondly inquired of one of her attendants what the lady's name might be, he replied over his shoulder, "She is the daughter of our master in Muromachi. And she is called the Present-Day Komachi."

They knew that evening that hers was the beauteous "color of the flowers." Only later were they to understand that hers too was a singular wantonness of spirit.

2. THE PILLOW DREAM THAT WAS THRUST UPON A LADY

Jolly though a bachelor's house may be, when evenings come, a home without a wife can be a dismal place indeed. A certain almanac-maker in these parts had for the past many years lived in unmarried state. This man aspired after a wife of such excellent beauty that even in the capital with all its colorful women his ideal was hard to realize. Yet so forlorn he was that he recommended himself "like a floating weed" to the good offices of his acquaintances; and thus it was that he was led to gaze fondly on the Present-Day Komachi, she who on that springtime day had carried in her hand the spray of wisteria and whose "fragile loveliness" had shone so brightly during the inspection at the Shijogawara Barrier.

Most odd it was to see how this inveterate bachelor now let nothing stand in the way of speeding his betrothal. At the time there was a woman, known for the fluency of her tongue as the Glib Arranger, who dwelt above Karasumaru off Shimo-tachiuri Street, and who practiced the trade of go-between. The almanac-maker called on her, earnestly requesting that she arrange the match, and forthwith he sent the two-handled keg of saké so that the betrothal might be sealed. His suit having been favorably answered and an auspicious day picked out, Osan—for such was this young beauty's name—was welcomed to his house as wife.

For three full years they lived together in connubial bliss. He was so steeped in the beauty of his spouse that he never cast his eyes afield, caring neither for the flower-fragrant evenings, nor for the early moonlit dawns. Osan, for her part, day and night faithfully carried out her wifely duties: for which end she took especial pains to exercise economy in the preparation of her husband's attire, herself assiduously plaiting strands of red ochre thread by hand and supervising her maids in the task of weaving the pongee silk; in the kitchen, too, she was frugal in her use of fuel, and made all entries in her housewife's cashbook with the utmost care: here indeed was a wife that any townsman would covet for himself.

By and by the household came to flourish and the master's joy knew no bounds. It happened then that he was obliged to journey to the Eastern provinces on business. It grieved him sorely to leave the capital, but there was no help for it. Harsh indeed are the calls of a man's livelihood!

Having at length resolved on his departure, he had his traveling clothes made ready. Before leaving, he visited Muromachi and called on his wife's father to inform him of the circumstances. This gentleman was much concerned at how his daughter would manage all the duties that her husband's absence would entail—concern, indeed, that any parent would be bound to feel.

"If we could but find some clever fellow," he said, "who could take charge of things while you are gone—someone who might look after the shop and help Osan with the household bookkeeping." Then he bethought himself of Moemon, a clerk who had served him well for many years, and, summoning this man, he dispatched him to his son-in-law's house.

Now this Moemon was of that honest breed of men of whom it is said that their head is the seat of God—though, be it added, in the styling of the hair upon his head he took not the slightest interest, leaving such fripperies to others; he let it grow at will, thus giving his brow a narrow look. The sleeves of his kimono measured barely more than seven inches at the wrist; he took scant care of the appearance of his sword; and so far as the lighter diversions were concerned, not once since the Ceremony of Boyhood had he donned a sedge hat. Instead, he lived all day only for making money, and at night he placed an abacus under his pillow, so that in his dreams he might conceive some profitable scheme.

It was now the autumn season, when storms blow harshly at night, and Moemon bethought himself with concern of the coming winter months. Resolving for the sake of his health to undergo cauterization, and hearing that the parlormaid Rin was adept at laying on the moxa, he requested her help. Several twists of the herb were then prepared and a striped cotton quilt spread over Rin's mirror stand, against which Moemon might lean. The first few applications of the burning herb were almost more than he could bear, and those about him—the nurse, the housemaid, and even the scullery maid Take—pressed the afflicted regions to alleviate the pain; at the same time, they could not forbear laughing as they saw the patient twist his face in agony.

After the treatment had continued for some time, the moxa was smoking violently and Moemon could hardly wait for the final application of salt. It was then that a pellet of the burning herb by ill luck slipped down his spine, puckering up the skin over which it passed. The pain was of no short duration, but out of regard for the girl who had treated him, Moemon merely closed his eyes and clenched his teeth. For all the patient's fortitude, Rin was moved with pity for his suffering as she crushed out the embers on his body. It was from having thus touched his skin that she suddenly conceived an infatuation for Moemon. At first she kept her longing for him secret, but it did not take long for her feelings to become known and to reach the ears of her mistress, Osan. Yet even then she could not quench her fondness.

It was a source of special grief to the poor maid that, being of the meanest education and unversed in putting words to paper, she was unable to express her love in writing. She looked with envy at the manservant Kyushichi, who could at least contrive to scribble down his thoughts with clumsy strokes. Secretly she besought his help; whereat he conceived the desire—a most odious one for Rin—to taste her charms himself before she could bestow them on Moemon.

Vainly the days flowed by, and soon it was the beginning of the Tenth Moon—that season of winter rains and deception. One day, after Osan had finished writing a letter to her husband in Edo, she said, "Now let us compose a love letter for Rin." Quickly her brush ran along the paper; then folding the note into a wish-knot, she simply wrote on the outside, "To Mister Moemon—from myself," and handed it to the girl. The latter received it with joy, and was eagerly awaiting a favorable moment for its delivery when from within the shop came the cry, "Some fire to light my tobacco!" Using this as a pretext and taking advantage of the fact that no one else was in the kitchen, she went into the shop and personally handed the note to Moemon. He, for his part, had not the remotest idea that the writing was in fact Osan's. Having read the message, he could only think that this Rin was truly a girl of some charm. He therefore penned a suitable reply and had it delivered to the girl. Rin, hard put to read Moemon's words herself, sought out an occasion when her mistress was in good humor to show the missive to her.

"That you should have cast your tender thoughts on me," it read, "was unexpected news indeed. I too am still in my youthful years and matters such as these are far from odious. Yet when our attachment deepens, it may forsooth bear fruit and we shall be faced with all the trouble of calling on a midwife. For all that, if you will take upon yourself the expenses of the clothing, the baths, and all the rest, I shall accede to your desires despite my doubts."

"Well, really!" exclaimed Osan, after reading these blunt words. "What a hateful man he is! Does he fancy that there is a dearth of males in the world? Rin is no such ill-favored girl and I'll warrant she could find herself a man as good as this Moemon any day."

So saying, she resolved that in letter after letter she would sue the young man for pity and, having finally won him over, serve him a fine trick. With this design, she now used every means to snare his heart by tender missives; to such effect, indeed, that before long Moemon's feelings were aroused, and regretting his earlier asperity, he dispatched this earnest note: "The fourteenth night of the Fifth Moon is fixed for the Vigil. Let us use that night as the occasion for our tryst."

Seeing this, Osan and her maid held their sides with laughter. "Rather than enjoy a night of love," said she, "that evening he'll become good sport for all of us!"

On the appointed night, then, Osan changed places with Rin, and, disguising herself in an unlined cotton dress, lay down in the bed where the girl was wont to sleep. Here she waited until close to dawn, when she could not help falling into a pleasant doze. Meanwhile the various maids had been standing ready here and there with cudgels, staves, and candlesticks, waiting to rush out in a body at the agreed word of command from their mistress; but, being weary from the excitement of the previous evening, they too were soon emitting drowsy snores.

It was after the seven bells had sounded that Moemon made his way stealthily through the darkness, undoing his loincloth as he went. Reaching Rin's chamber, he stripped himself naked and slipped in between the bedclothes, his heart pounding with excitement. In his eagerness for enjoyment, he dispensed with all verbal preliminaries and soon he had acquitted himself to his manly credit.

As Moemon replaced the covers and left the room on tiptoe, he was aware of the elegant scent that lingered on the lady's clothing.

"Odd indeed," he pondered to himself, "and brazen the ways of this floating world! I should scarcely have thought that this Rin would already have known a man's love. Yet someone has surely been here ahead of me and done the deed!" And, apprehensive of discovery, he resolved to return to the charge no more.

Later when Osan awoke of her own accord, she found to her surprise that the pillow was out of place and in disorder, while her sash too was undone and not at hand. Then she saw paper handkerchiefs scattered about the bed and was overcome with shame at the knowledge that Moemon had taken his pleasure with her while she slept.

"What has been done," she reflected, "cannot possibly remain secret, and now that it has come to such a pass, I can but continue on this course and throw away my life. For the remainder of my days, this amour of mine will be the gossip of the world, until at last I tread the paths of Hades in company with Moemon."

She disclosed this firm intention to the young man, who realized now the unforeseen mistake that he had made that night. Dismissing, then, "the horse he once had rid" for her whom he now "so dearly craved," he took to visiting Osan each night, and cared naught for the censure of reproving tongues.

Thus having both wandered astray in their own fashion, Osan and Moemon gave themselves over to the consequences of their error, and soon they were braving a most perilous toss of the coin between life and death.

3. THE LAKE THAT TOOK PEOPLE IN

"That which in this world lies quite past our control is the way of love"—so it is recorded in *The Tale of Genji*.

At this time there was being performed at the Ishiyama Temple the Ceremony of Exhibiting the Holy Image, and people were thronging to see it, having quite put out of their minds the cherries that blossomed in the Eastern Hills. Yet, as one observed them, having crossed the Osaka Barrier, with its "people leaving the capital and others returning," it appeared that not one of all these women in their fashionable attire was bent on visiting that temple to seek her salvation in the world to come; instead, each had on her face a self-admiring look produced by the elegance of her own apparel. Gazing into their hearts, even the Goddess Kannon could hardly have forborne from laughter.

It was at this season that Osan herself visited the temple, with Moemon in attendance. Seeing the flowers in bloom, they likened them to their own lives; for who could tell when they too would fall? Little knowing whether this might not be the last time that they would set their eyes on these fair bays and hills, they hired a dragnet fishing boat in Seta, so that this day might remain as a happy memory in their minds. As they rowed off, they saw the Long Bridge of Seta and wished that it might bode them well. And yet they knew that this joy of theirs was bound to be short-lived. Floating past Mount Toko, they made the rippling waves serve as the pillow of their couch, and soon the disorder of Osan's hair bespoke the nature of their pleasure. Later, as they drifted by Kagami Mountain, their pensive expression must have been mirrored on its slopes and caused it to be overcast with tears. Nearing Cape Wani, they bethought themselves that to escape their fate would be as hard as to be delivered from a crocodile's mouth, and when they heard someone hailing a boat from Katada, their spirits froze at the idea that these might be pursuers who had come after them from Kyoto. Now Mount Nagara came into view, calling to the lovers' minds the brevity of their own lives; and gazing into the distance at the Fuji of the Capital, which, if one were to compare it to that other Fuji, must be "piled up twenty-fold," time after time they wet their sleeves with tears, thinking that "if there be snow," it presently must melt. Seeing the town of Shiga, they recalled that people spoke of how it had flourished in ancient times as a capital; just so were they fated to be spoken of after they were dead and gone. At this thought they fell into still deeper gloom.

When evening came and the lanterns of the Dragon God were lit, they betook themselves to the Shirahige Shrine; yet as the lovers offered up their prayers, the evanescence of their lives became ever clearer in their minds.

"Come what may," said Osan, "the longer we linger in this world, the more bitter will be our hardships. Should we not throw ourselves into this lake and in the Land of Buddha plight our lasting troth?"

"I don't cling to this life of mine," replied Moemon. "Yet, being ignorant of what may come hereafter, I have bethought myself of a plan. Let us both leave messages of farewell for those in the capital, and have it reported that we are drowned. Meanwhile we can quit this spot, betake ourselves to some place in the country—it matters not where—and spend our years together."

Hearing these words, Osan rejoiced and said, "Even such was my intention from the time I left my home—and for this purpose I brought along in this box five hundred gold *koban*."

"That will indeed provide us with our livelihood," said Moemon. "So let us now escape and go into hiding."

They each then set to preparing notes. "Having succumbed," they wrote, "to evil inclinations and indulged in adulterous pleasure, we cannot escape the doom of Heaven, nor is there any place for us in this world. On this day of the present month we take our leave of the floating world."

In addition they each arranged to leave behind various tokens that people would clearly recognize as having belonged to them. Osan added a few strands of her black hair to the two-inch image of the Buddha that she was wont to wear next to her skin as an amulet, while Moemon left the twenty-inch sword that he carried by his side, with its iron guard of coiled-dragon design wrought by the swordsmith Seki-no-Izumi-no-Kami. They even carried their precautions to the point of placing their coats, Osan's straw slippers and Moemon's leather-soled sandals under a willow tree by the water's edge. Next they secretly engaged two fishermen from those shores, who, being skillful divers, were in the habit of displaying Rock Leaps. Handing them money, they explained their circumstances to the men, and the latter gladly undertook the task. Then the two lovers waited for the onset of darkness.

The time having come and all their preparations being made, Osan and Moemon left open the bamboo gate of their lodging, then went to shake the attendants out of their sleep.

"For reasons of our own we are resolved to die forthwith!" So saying, they rushed out of doors.

A moment later from the height of the craggy cliffs the sound could be faintly heard of voices invoking the Sacred Name of Buddha. Then two bodies hurtled down through space, ending in a splash of water; whereat the people in the house put up a great wailing. Meanwhile Moemon, carrying Osan on his shoulders, was making his way through the undergrowth at the foot of the mountains, where he took refuge in a dense grove of pine trees. The fishermen, for their part, had dived under the waves, to reappear at some other point along the beach.

Osan's companions clapped their hands in lamentation. With the help of the villagers, they searched high and low, but to no avail. When dawn broke, however, they discovered the keepsakes; these they collected, weeping bitterly the while, and returned with them to Kyoto. When they related what had befallen, the people of the household, fearful of the family's reputation, directed them to keep these matters secret. But in our world of prying eyes precautions of this kind are bootless, and soon the gossip spread far and wide, being a fine topic for springtime tattle. Such was the outcome of this wanton couple's deed; and none could deflect them from their folly.

4. THE TEAHOUSE WHICH KNEW NOT OF GOLD PIECES

Now these two lovers had entered the ranks of those who fly across the hills to Tamba. Moemon held Osan's hand as they made their own path across the trackless heath. Finally they dragged themselves to the top of a steep hill. From here the way ahead looked even more foreboding and, thinking of their plight, it seemed as though, while still alive, they had already joined the dead. All this, to be sure, proceeded from their own free choice, yet that did not make it one jot less grievous.

Pursuing their course, they came to a place so desolate that not even the mark of woodcutters' footsteps could be seen. Now they truly knew to their cost the sorrows of losing one's way. Osan with her woman's frailty could no longer continue the journey. Seeing the girl in this suffering state, her breath now coming but weakly, and all color gone from her face, Moemon was sorely moved. He gathered on a leaf the drops of water that had trickled on a rock and poured them in her mouth. In various other ways he sought to nurse her, but for all his cares she gradually lost strength and the beating of her pulse grew faint. It seemed as if the end was not far off, and, having nothing at hand to use as medicine, they could but wait for the final breath. It was then that Moemon approached his mistress and murmured dolefully in her ear, "If you could but have gone a little farther! In a village that lies ahead I have acquaintances. There we could forget these present hardships, rest to our hearts' content and, lying side by side, engage in the most intimate converse."

"What happy words!" Osan replied. "You are indeed a man for whom one would gladly pay one's life." And forthwith her spirits revived.

Seeing this girl, so prepossessed with lust that all else had been cast out in its favor, Moemon could not forbear from being moved. He lifted her again upon his shoulders, and they had not gone far before they reached the fences of a little village.

Through this village ran the highway to the capital and along the mountain edge a road wide enough for two horses to pass each other. Here they came upon a straw-thatched hut, from whose eaves hung a sheaf of cedar leaves and on a sign the inscription, "First-Grade Saké." Entering this place, they saw a tray of rice cakes adorned with the dust of many days and quite lacking in their pristine whiteness. In the corner of the shop, however, were displayed for sale tea whisks, clay dolls, bean drums, and other such objects, which, being quite familiar to the young couple and savoring of the capital, served to heighten their spirits. They stayed there and rested for a while, after which, being in a contented frame of mind, they handed the old shopkeeper a gold *koban*. But this was to show an umbrella to a cat, and the man, seeing it, made a wry face and said, "Please pay me for the tea you drank."

Thoroughly amused by the thought that a place like this, not even forty miles from the capital, should be unfamiliar with gold coins, they set forth for the village of Kayabara. Here Moemon visited the house of his mother's sister. It was many years since they had last had tidings of each other, and neither knew how the other had fared. Moemon spoke to her of the past, and she, mindful of their connection, gave him no cold welcome, but regaled him with talk of his father, Mosuke. Thus, with tears in their eyes, Moemon and his aunt spent the night in fond recollections of their family.

When dawn broke, however, his aunt, growing suspicious of the fair young lady who had journeyed in his company, inquired, "And who may she be?"

Not having prepared himself for such a question, Moemon was taken off his guard. "She is a younger sister of mine," he replied, "who for many years held service in the household of a Court official. But growing indisposed and wearying of the formality of life in the capital, she thought that if she could find a suitable match in some peaceful mountain village such as this, she would gladly lower her status and in some rustic field pursue the humble work of country folk. For this reason I have brought her here with me. She brings a dowry of some two hundred gold *koban*."

Thus he blurted out his makeshift story. But this is a world where avarice holds sway in every corner, and his aunt promptly marked the mention of a dowry.

"A happy circumstance indeed!" said she. "My only son is yet unbetrothed and as you are my very flesh and blood, let us make this girl his wife."

Hearing her plead in this manner, the young couple was more troubled than ever, and Osan secretly shed bitter tears.

"How will this end?" she was lamenting to herself, when the son himself returned home, the night being now well advanced. And what a fearful sight he was! Towering above the common run of men, he stood there, his hair ruffled like a lion's mane, his beard like a shaggy bear's, his eyes bloodshot and strangely gleaming, his limbs knotted with sinews like a very pine tree. The fellow's clothes were sewn together from old rags and his sash was made of a twisted rope of wisteria vines. A bunch of matchlocks hung from his rifle and in his straw bag were thrust the bodies of rabbits and badgers, all of which proclaimed that he made his living as a hunter. His name was Zetaro the Rock Leaper, and he was known in the whole village as a notorious ruffian.

Hearing his mother say that he was to be married to a city girl, the young stalwart was much elated. "Strike while the iron's hot!" said he. "Let's have the ceremony this very evening." Bringing out his pocket mirror, he set to examining his face—pretty doings for such a churl!

His mother meantime produced a salted fish stew and a saké bottle with a broken spout—all in readiness, as she said, for the coming nuptials. To serve as bridal chamber, she enclosed a small corner of the room, using straw matting for a screen. Here she placed two wooden pillows, two thin mats and striped bedding. Then she burned some kindling in the brazier. That night she was indeed in the very height of spirits.

Not so Osan and Moemon, the one of whom was sunk in sorrow, the other in perplexity.

"This is what comes of my heedless words," said Moemon. "And how vexing it is to know that all this is the inescapable consequence of my own folly! So once again we have come to grief. After all, the Gods will not forgive us for living on, when we should have died beneath the waters of that lake in Oini."

He lay hold of his sword and stood up. But Osan restrained him, saying, "So hasty-spirited, Moemon! But stop, for I have many thoughts. Tomorrow at daybreak we must quit this place. Leave all to me." Thus did she calm his spirits.

That evening, after she and her intended spouse had cheerfully exchanged their nuptial cups, Osan announced, "I was born under that sign that men most abhor—the Fiery Horse."

"It wouldn't worry me in the least," answered Zetaro, "if you were born in the year of the Fiery Cat or the Fiery Wolf! I'm a fellow who even eats blue lizards—likes them, for that matter—and I've managed to survive. In fact, in all my twenty-seven years I've never once had as much as the slightest bellyache. You should try and take after me, Moemon my lad! Now, when it comes to wiving, I can tell you I wouldn't myself have chosen any soft, city-bred wench for my mate. But since we're related, I'll just have to put up with you!"

With these words he lay his head on Osan's lap and lolled there comfortably. Even in the midst of their distress, Osan and Moemon could not but be amused at his uncouth demeanor.

They waited impatiently for Zetaro to fall asleep, then stole out of the house and once more hid themselves in the depths of Tamba. Slowly the days passed and they reached the Tango Way. One evening they kept vigil in the Monju Temple at Kiredo. It appeared to be the middle of the night when Osan, having dozed off, was confronted with a miraculous vision of the guardian God, who addressed them in these words: "Ye have displayed an unexampled wantonness, and fly where'er ye will, ye shall ne'er escape the adversity that followeth on such deeds. Nor can ye in any way contrive to redeem the past. Yet if thou, Osan, shouldst hereafter abandon the ways of the floating world, cut off those black tresses that thou dost value so, join the Holy Priesthood, live forever apart from this man that thou lovest, cleanse thy heart of all evil designs and enter the Way of Salvation, then it may be that men will spare thy life."

Hearing these gracious words as in a trance, Osan replied,

"Do not concern yourself, I pray you, for what may befall me in the future. I like what I am doing and should gladly give my life for the illicit love that I now enjoy. You may indeed, Lord Monju, understand love between men, but so far as womanly passion is concerned, you cannot have the slightest knowledge."

No sooner had she spoken than she awoke from her unpleasant dream. The wind was soughing in the pines at Hashidate. Hearing it, Osan bethought herself of "this fragile world of dust which the very wind can blow away"; and still more she gave herself over to her aberrant passion.

5. THE EAVESDROPPER WHO HEARD ABOUT HIMSELF

Men know only too well the bad things that befall them and seek to hide these from their neighbors. Thus it is that the gambler is silent about his losses, that the man who has been cozened by a trollop assumes a knowing look as if nothing untoward has happened, that the brawler who has been worsted in a fight keeps it a secret and that the merchant who has suffered loss in some speculation conceals the knowledge from the world. All these are cases of "a dog's dung in the darkness." But among the several misfortunes that can befall a man, none is so cruel as to have a wanton wife.

"Osan is dead and nothing can be done to change the past." Thus accepting the report of her drowning, the almanac-maker put up a good front to the world. As his thoughts went back to the happy years that they had spent together, he could not but feel bitter at the outcome. Yet, summoning a priest, he would direct that masses be read for the repose of his dead wife's soul. Most pitiably, Osan's colorful silk garments were offered to the family temple, where, having been made into banners and baldachins, they fluttered in the uncertain wind of death, thus to become a further source of grief.

Now in this wide world there is nothing so intrepid as man. Moemon, who had at first exercised such prudence that he durst not issue abroad even under the cover of darkness, had now in the course of time quite lost himself in the desire to see the capital again. One day, then, he dressed himself in humble attire, and, pulling his sedge hat down to hide his face, set forth on a "useless journey to the capital," commending Osan to the care of the people in the village.

Walking along the road, more fearful even than one who dreads the onslaught of his enemy, Moemon presently approached the Hirosawa Pond as dusk was gathering. He gazed at the double image of the moon that shimmered on the waters, and, bethinking himself of Osan, wet his sleeves with doleful tears—tears that fell onto the stone and broke like pearls; like scattered pearls, too, glittered the drops of water on the rocks of Mount Narutaki, which Moemon now left behind him as he hastened through the familiar quarters of Omuro and Kitano. Entering the city itself, he was overcome with a vague sense of apprehension, and every now and then was chilled with terror at the sight of his own shadow reflected in the light of the seventeen-day-old moon. At length, then, he came near to the house of Osan's father, the place where he himself had dwelt so long. Approaching the shop, he crouched down out of sight and eavesdropped, so that he might learn the recent state of things. One group of men was talking of the delay in the arrival of silver payment from the branch shop at Edo. Some of the clerks had gathered to discuss the various ways of styling hair and were exchanging critical remarks about the workmanship of each other's cotton clothes and other matters of manly fashion; all this proceeded from the wish to appear pleasing to women and thus to satisfy their own lust. Having listened to them discuss these various topics, Moemon heard their conversation turn, much as expected, to himself.

"Well indeed," said one of the clerks, "that fellow Moemon made off with a beauty whose equal one could hardly find in this wide world. Worth paying for with one's life, in troth! I'll warrant he counted himself a lucky man even though he had to die for it."

"Aye, to be sure," said another, "to have had a girl like that would be the memory of a lifetime for any man!"

Then up spake one of the other clerks with a knowing look: "That Moemon was a scurvy rogue and fouled the very air we breathed! What wretch in this world would have tricked both master and husband as he has done?"

Overhearing the censure of this man, for whom chill reason

was unrelieved with any human warmth, Moemon muttered to himself, "Assuredly that was the voice of Kisuke from the Daimonji Shop. Unfeeling wretch that he is with all his hateful talk! To think that he borrowed eighty *momme* of silver from me and that I even have his bond of loan! I'd like to wring his neck to pay him for those callous words of his."

Grinding his teeth with anger, Moemon rose to his feet. But those who are hiding from the world must bear such hurts in silence, and Moemon restrained himself despite his rage. Just then his blood froze as one of the men said, "Moemon is no more dead than me or you! They say he's hiding somewhere in the region of Ise with Mistress Osan—and having a fine time with her, I'll be bound!"

Overhearing these words, Moemon started to tremble. He left the place with rapid steps and made his way to the Hatago Inn by the Third Avenue, where he rented a room, and, without so much as taking a bath, lay down to rest.

It being the seventeenth night of the month, the Begging Proxies were abroad, and, calling one of them, Moemon wrapped up twelve coppers and gave them to him, commending to the Gods his earnest prayer that he might for many years make good his hiding. Yet how could even the God of Atago Shrine redeem him from his errant ways when he continued to enjoy the fruits thereof?

On the following day, thinking to have a final look at the capital, Moemon stole down the Eastern Hills and visited the Shijogawara district. Here he was met by a crier who announced, "See the actor Fujita appear in a modern drama. The three-part programme will presently begin!"

Moemon did not know what this drama might be, but he resolved to visit the theatre, considering that Osan might on his return enjoy a description of the play. Accordingly he rented a round cushion and took his place with the other spectators, peering about nervously the while, for fear that someone there might recognize him. Looking at the stage, he was seized with a vague apprehension as he saw that the play dealt with the story of a man whose daughter was abducted. This, however, was as nothing to his horror when he noticed that at the end of his very row sat none other than Osan's husband. He felt as though one foot were dangling over the chasm of Hell; his blood ran cold and beads of sweat broke out over his body. Rushing for the entrance, he left the theatre, and hardly slowed his pace until he had reached his village in Tango. From that day forth Kyoto to him spelled naught but fear.

The Chrysanthemum Festival was now at hand, and, as was his yearly wont, a chestnut vendor from Tamba called at the almanac-maker's house. After he had rambled over sundry topics, he asked, "By the bye, how fares the mistress of this house?" A strained air fell over the company and no one answered him, until the almanac-maker with a bitter look said, "She is dead."

Hearing this, the chestnut vendor continued, "Strange indeed how people can resemble each other in this world! Not far from Kiredo in Tango I came across a lady who does not differ from your wife in the smallest particle, and a young fellow who was the living image of the clerk who worked here." So saying, he took his leave.

Now the husband, who had listened attentively to his words, sent a man to observe the couple. Having ascertained that they were indeed Osan and Moemon, he assembled a large company of his retainers and arrested the fugitives.

There was no escaping the consequences of their offense, and, after the inquest had been concluded, the two lovers, together with the girl who had acted as their confidante, were led together through the street and at the Execution Grounds of Awataguchi their lives vanished as the morning dew on the grass. Thus on the twenty-second day of the Ninth Moon their end came smoothly like an evanescent dream at dawn; nor was there aught ignoble in the way of their departing. The tale of how these two finished their lives was handed down to posterity; and Osan bequeathed her name of love to the world, so that even now men seem to see the image of the pale-blue silk she wore that morning.

OGAI MORI
The Wild Geese
(Gan, 1911)

Translated by Kingo Ochiai and Sanford Goldstein

Ogai Mori (1862–1922), coming from a southwestern province, was graduated from the Tokyo University Medical School in 1881, and became an army surgeon. He studied hygiene in Germany from 1884 to 1888. Upon his return, while remaining an army doctor, Ogai worked on translations of German poems as well as on his own stories. His first piece of fiction, "The Dancing Damsel" ("Mai Hime"), was published in 1890 in a literary magazine called *Friends of the Nationals (Kokumin no Tomo)*. This story deals with the conflict between a young Japanese student's love for a beautiful German dancer and his duties in Japan, to which he must return without her.

Ogai also published his autobiographical *Vita Sexualis (Ita Sekusuarisu,* 1909), in which he attacked the naturalists' contention that man has no control over his sexual instinct. His most productive period, however, was in the 1910s, when he published modern-life novels like *The Wild Geese,* the historical novels *The Abe Clan (Abe Ichizoku,* 1913), *Heihachiro Oshio* (1914), *Sanshodayu* (1915), and *The Boat on the Takase (Takase Bune,* 1916), and biographies like *Katei Hojo* (1918). He was influential in bringing Western literature to Japan through his translations from German and the Scandinavian languages. He is credited not only for stimulating a romantic tradition in modern Japanese fiction but also with developing an elegant but lucid prose style.

Ogai's later years are characterized by his concern over the character and morale of the contemporary Japanese. Unlike Soseki, he did not merely describe contemporary personages but discussed the spirit of Confucian scholars in the Tokugawa period. When these efforts were not well received even by his close friends, his reply was: "I do not care to discuss whether or not my writing of these biographies has a utilitarian end. I write them only because I want to." On another occasion he argued that there is no difference between writing a biography of a hero like Bismarck and that of a "crippled Confucianist like Ranken." In 1916 he retired from the army after ten years as Surgeon-General to become director of the Imperial Museum; his death came six years later, when he was still at work on another historical writing, *A Study on Reign Names (Gengo Ko)*.

CHAPTER ONE

This story happened long ago, but by chance I remember that it occurred in 1880, the thirteenth year of Emperor Meiji's reign. That date comes back to me so precisely because at the time I lodged in the Kamijo, a boardinghouse which was just opposite the Iron Gate of Tokyo University, and because my room was right next to that of the hero of the story. When a fire broke out inside the house in the fourteenth year of Meiji, I was one of those who lost all of their possessions when the Kamijo burned to the ground. What I'm going to put down, I remember, took place just one year before that disaster.

Almost all the boarders in the Kamijo were medical students, except for the few patients who went to the hospital attached to the university. It's been my observation that a residence of this kind is controlled by one of its members, a lodger who rises to a position of authority because of his money and shrewdness. When he passes through the corridor before the landlady's room, he always makes it a point to speak to her as she sits by the square charcoal brazier. Sometimes he'll squat opposite her and exchange a few words of gossip. Sometimes he seems to think only of himself when he throws saké parties in his room and puts the landlady out by making her prepare special dishes, yet the truth is that he takes care to see that she gets something extra for her troubles. Usually this type of man wins respect and takes advantage of it by having his own way in the house.

The man in the room next to mine was also powerful in the Kamijo, but he was of a different breed.

This man, a student called Okada, was a year behind me, so he wasn't too far from graduating. In order to explain Okada's character, I must speak first of his striking appearance. What I really mean is that he was handsome. But not handsome in the sense of being pale and delicately thin and tall. He had a healthy color and a strong build. I have hardly ever come across a man with such a face. If you force me to make a comparison, he somewhat resembled the young Bizan Kawakami, whom I got to know later than the time of this story, and who became destitute and died in misery. Okada, a champion rower in those days, far surpassed the writer Bizan in physique.

A good-looking face may influence others, but it alone does not carry weight in a boardinghouse. Personal behavior must also be considered, and I doubt if many students lived as well-balanced a life as Okada did. He wasn't a bookworm who worked greedily for examination marks each term and who wanted to win a scholarship. Okada did the required amount of work and was never lower than the middle of his class. And in his free time he always relaxed. After supper he would take a walk and would return without fail before ten. On Sundays he rowed or set off on a long hike. Except for periods of living with his crew before a match or of returning to his home in the country for summer vacations, the time never varied when he was in or out of his room. Often a boarder who had forgotten to set his watch by the signal gun at noon went to Okada's room to find out the time. And occasionally even the office clock in the Kamijo was put right by Okada. The more we observed him, the stronger became our impression that he was reliable. Even though Okada didn't flatter the landlady or spend much money above his room and board, she began to praise him. Needless to say, the fact that he paid his rent regularly was one of the reasons for her attitude.

She often said: "Look at Mr. Okada!"

But, anticipating her words, some of the students would say: "Well, we can't all be like him."

Before anyone realized it, Okada had become a model tenant.

Okada had regular routes for his daily walks. He would go down the lonely slope called Muenzaka and travel north along Shinobazu Pond. Then he would stroll up the hill in Ueno

Park. Next he went down to Hirokoji and, turning into Naka-cho—narrow, crowded, full of activity—he would go through the compound of Yushima Shrine and set out for the Kamijo after passing the gloomy Karatachi Temple. Sometimes he made a slight variation in a particular route, such as a right turn at the end of Naka-cho, so that he would come back to his room along the silence and loneliness of Muenzaka.

There was another route. He occasionally entered the university campus by the exit used by the patients of the hospital attached to the medical school because the Iron Gate was closed early. Going through the Red Gate, he would proceed along Hongo-dori until he came to a shop where people were standing and watching the antics of some men pounding millet. Then he would continue his walk by turning into the compound of Kanda Shrine. After crossing the Megane-bashi, which was still a novelty in those days, he would wander for a short while through a street with houses on only one side along the river. And on his way back he went into one of the narrow side streets on the western side of Onarimichi and then came up to the front of the Karatachi Temple. This was an alternate route. Okada seldom took any other.

On these trips Okada did little more than browse now and then in the secondhand bookstores. Today only two or three out of many still remain. On Onarimichi, the same shops, little changed from what they formerly were, continue to run their businesses. Yet almost all the stores on Hongo-dori have changed their locations and their proprietors. On these walks Okada hardly ever turned right after leaving the Red Gate because most of the streets narrowed so much that it was annoying. Besides, only one secondhand bookshop could then be found along that way.

Okada stopped in such shops because, to use a term now in vogue, he had literary tastes. In those days the novels and plays of the new school had not yet been published; as for the lyric, neither the haiku of Shiki nor the waka of Tekkan had been created. So everyone read such magazines as the *Kagetsu Shinshi,* which printed the first translation of a Western novel. In his student days Okada read with interest the happenings of the new era written in the style of classical Chinese literature. This was the extent of his literary tastes.

Since I've never been very affable, I didn't even speak to

those students I met quite often on the campus except when I had a reason. As for the students in the boardinghouse, I seldom tipped my cap in greeting. But I became somewhat friendly with Okada because of the bookshops. On my walks I wasn't as rigid in my direction as Okada was, but since I had strong legs, I let them direct me through Hongo to Shitaya and Kanda, and I paused in every secondhand bookstore. On such occasions I often met Okada inside.

I don't remember who spoke first, but I do recall the first words between us: "How often we meet among old books!"

This was the start of our friendship.

In those days at the corner down the slope in front of Kanda Shrine, we came across a shop which sold books on its stalls. Once I discovered the *Kimpeibai,* and I asked the storekeeper how much it was.

"Seven yen."

"I'll give you five," I said.

"A while back Okada offered six."

Since I had enough money with me, I gave the dealer what he asked.

But when I met Okada a few days later, he said: "You acted quite selfishly—you know I found the *Kimpeibai* first."

"The man at the shop said you bargained, but that you couldn't agree. If you must have it, buy it from me."

"Why should I? We're neighbors, so I can borrow it when you're through."

I agreed.

In this way, Okada and I, who had not until now been acquainted even though we lived at such close quarters, often began to call on each other.

CHAPTER TWO

Even in the days I am writing about, the Iwasaki mansion was located, as it is today, on the southern side of Muenzaka, though it had not yet been fenced in with its present high wall of soil. At that time dirty stone walls had been put up, and ferns and horsetails grew among the moss-covered stones. Even now I don't know whether the land above the fence is flat or hilly, for I've never been inside the mansion. At any rate, in those days the copse grew thick and wild, and from the street we could see the roots of the trees, while the grass around them was seldom cut.

On the north side of the slope, small houses were constructed in clusters, and the best-looking among them had a clapboard fence. As for shops, there were only a kitchenware dealer's and a tobacconist's. Among the dwellings, the most attractive to the people who passed belonged to a sewing teacher, and during the day young women could be seen through the window going about their work. If the day was pleasant and the windows were open when we students passed, the girls, always talking, raised their faces and looked out into the street. And then once more they would continue their laughing and chattering.

Next to this house was a residence whose door was always wiped clean and whose granite walk I often saw sprinkled with water in the evening. During the cold weather the sliding doors were shut, but even during the hot weather the bamboo shutters were lowered. This house always seemed conspicuously quiet, the more so because of the noise in the neighboring one.

About September of the year of this story, Okada, soon after his return from his home in the country, went out after supper for his usual stroll, and as he walked down Muenzaka, he met by accident a woman on her way home from the public bath and saw her enter the lonely place next to the sewing teacher's. It was almost autumn, so people had less occasion to seek relief from the heat by sitting outside their houses, and the slope was now empty. The woman, who had just come to the entrance of that quiet house, was trying to open the door, but hearing the sound of Okada's clogs, stopped what she was doing and turned her face. The two stared at each other.

Okada was not very much attracted by the woman in kimono with her right hand on the door and her left hand holding her bamboo basket of toilet articles. But he did notice her hair freshly dressed in the ginkgo-leaf style with her sidelocks as thin as the wings of a cicada. He saw that her face was oval and somewhat lonely, her nose sharp, her forehead to her cheeks conveying an impression of flatness, though it was difficult to say exactly what made him think so. Since these were no more than momentary impressions, he had completely forgotten about her when he came to the bottom of the slope.

But about two days later he again took the same direction, and when he came near the house with the lattice door, he glanced at it, suddenly remembering the stranger from the public bath. He looked at the bow window with its vertically nailed bamboo canes and two thin, horizontal pieces of wood wound with vines. The window screen had been left open about a foot and revealed a potted plant. As he gave some attention to these details, he slowed down somewhat, and it took a few moments before he reached the front of the house.

Suddenly above the plant a white face appeared in the background where nothing but gray darkness had been. Furthermore, the face smiled at him.

From that time on, whenever Okada went out walking and passed this house, he seldom missed seeing the woman's face. Sometimes she broke into his imagination, and there she gradually started to take liberties. He began to wonder if she was waiting for him to pass or was simply looking outside with indifference and accidentally noticed him. He thought about the days before he had first come upon her, trying to recall if she had ever glanced out of the house or not, but all he could remember was that the house next to the noisy sewing teacher's was always swept clean and looked lonely. He told himself that he must have wondered about the kind of person who lived there, but he could not even be certain of that. It seemed to him that the screens were always shut or the bamboo blinds were drawn to reinforce the quiet behind them. He finally concluded that perhaps the woman had recently come to look outside and had opened the window to wait for his passing.

Each time he came by, they looked at each other, and all the while thinking about these events, Okada gradually felt he was on friendly terms with "the woman of the window." One evening, two weeks later, he unconsciously took off his cap and bowed when he passed her house. Her faintly white face turned red, and her lonely smile changed into a beaming one.

From that moment on, Okada always bowed to the woman of the window when he went by.

CHAPTER THREE

Okada's admiration of old Chinese romantic tales had caused him to take an interest in military sports, but since he had no opportunities for practicing them, this desire had never been satisfied. This might, however, explain his interest in rowing, which he had taken to a few years before. He had been so enthusiastic and had made so much progress that he became a champion rower. Obviously, this activity was a manifestation of his desire to practice martial arts.

A type of woman in these romantic tales also appealed to Okada. She is the woman who makes beauty her sole aim in life so that, with perfect ease, she goes through an elaborate toilet even while the angel of death waits outside her door. Okada felt that a woman should be only a beautiful object, something lovable, a being who keeps her beauty and loveliness no matter what situation she is in. Okada probably picked up this sentiment unconsciously, partly under the influence of his habitual reading of old Chinese romantic love poetry and the sentimental and fatalistic prose works of the so-called wits of the Ming and Ch'ing dynasties.

Even though a long interval had passed since Okada started bowing to the woman of the window, he would not investigate her personal history. From the appearance of the house and the way she dressed, he guessed that she might be someone's mistress. But this did not disturb him. He did not even know her name, and he made no effort to learn it. All he had to do was look at the nameplate, but he couldn't bring himself to do this in her presence. At other times, when she wasn't there, he hesitated because of the neighbors and the passersby. As a result, he never looked at the characters written on the small wooden sign shadowed by the eaves.

CHAPTER FOUR

Although the events of this story that have Okada for their hero took place before I learned the earlier history of the woman of the window, it will be convenient to give an outline of that history here.

The narrative goes back to the days when the medical school of the university was located at Shitaya and the old guardhouse of Lord Todo's estate was turned into a student dormitory. Its windows, of vertical wooden bars as thick as a man's arms, were set at wide intervals in a wall of gray tiles plastered in checkerboard fashion. If I may phrase it this way, the students lived there like so many beasts, though I'm sorry to make such a comparison. Of course you can't see windows like those now except in the castle turrets of the Emperor's palace, and even the bars of the lion and tiger cages in the Ueno Zoo are more slenderly made than those were.

The dormitory had servants whom the students could use for errands. They usually sent out to buy something cheap to eat, like baked beans or roasted sweet potatoes. For each trip the servant received two sen. One of these workers was called Suezo. The other men had loud mouths buried in burlike beards, but this man kept his mouth shut and always shaved. The others wore dirty clothes of rough cotton; Suezo's were always neat, and sometimes he came to work wearing silk.

I don't know who told me or when, but I heard that Suezo lent money to needy students. Of course it only amounted to fifty sen or one yen at a time. But when the debt gradually grew to five or ten yen, Suezo would make the borrower draw up a note, and if it wasn't yet paid at the end of the term, a new one was written. Suezo became what can really be called a professional moneylender. I haven't any idea how he obtained such capital. Certainly not from picking up two sen for each student errand. But perhaps nothing is impossible if a man concentrates all of his energies on what he wants.

At any rate, when the medical school moved from Shitaya to Hongo, Suezo no longer remained a servant, but his house, newly located on Ike-no-hata, was continually visited by a great number of indiscreet students. When he began working for the university, he was already over thirty, was poor, and had a wife and child to support. But since he had made quite a fortune through moneylending and had moved to his new house, he began to feel dissatisfied with his wife, who was ugly and quarrelsome.

At that time he remembered a certain woman he had seen every so often while he was still going to the university through a narrow alley from his house at the back of Neribeicho. There was a dark house whose ditchboards in that alley were always partly broken and half of whose sliding shutters were closed all year round. At night, when anyone passed, he had to go sideways because of a wheeled stall drawn up under the eaves.

What first attracted Suezo's attention to this house was the music of the samisen inside. And then he learned that the person playing the instrument was a lovely girl about sixteen or seventeen years old. The neat kimono she wore was quite different from the shabby appearance of her house.

If the girl happened to be in the doorway, as soon as she saw a man approaching she went back into the dark interior. Suezo, with his characteristic alertness, though without particularly investigating the matter, found out that the girl's name was Otama, that her mother was dead, and that she lived alone with her father, who sold sugary, sticky candies molded into figures in his stall.

But eventually a change took place in this back-street house. The wheeled stall vanished from its set place under the eaves. And the house and its surroundings, which were always modest, seemed suddenly attacked by what was then fashionably called "civilization," for new boards over the ditch replaced the broken and warped ones, and a new lattice door had been installed at the entrance.

Once Suezo noticed a pair of Western shoes in the doorway. Soon after, a new nameplate bearing a policeman's title was put up. Suezo also made certain, while shopping on the neighboring streets and yet without seeming to pry, that the old candy dealer had acquired a son-in-law.

To the old man, who loved his daughter more than sight itself, the loss of Otama to a policeman with terrifying looks was like having her carried off by a monster with a long nose and a red face. Otama's father had feared the discomfort he would incur by the intrusion of such a formidable son-in-law, and after meeting the suitor, had consulted with several confidants, but none of them had told him to reject the offer.

Someone said: "You see, I told you so, didn't I? When I took the trouble to arrange a good match, you were too particular, saying you couldn't part with your only child, so that finally a son-in-law you couldn't say no to is going to move in on you!"

And another said threateningly: "If you can't stand the man, the only other solution is to move far away, but since he's a policeman, he'll be able to catch up with you and make his offer again. There's no escaping him."

A wife who had a reputation for using her head was believed to have told the old man: "Didn't I advise you to sell her off to a geisha house since her looks were good and her samisen master praised her skill? A policeman without a wife can go from door to door, and when he finds a pretty face, he takes her off whether you like it or not. You can't do anything but make the best of the bad luck that such a man took a fancy to your daughter."

No more than three months after Suezo had heard these rumors, he discovered one morning that the doors of the old candy dealer's house were locked and that an attached piece of paper gave notice that the house was for rent. Then, on inquiring further into the neighbors' talk while shopping, Suezo heard that the policeman had in his own native place a wife and children who had turned up on a surprise visit, whereupon a fight followed, and Otama ran from the house. A neighbor who overheard the quarrel stopped the girl from doing something rash. Not one of the old man's friends had enough knowledge about legal matters, so the old man had been quite indifferent about seeing if the marriage had been legally registered, and when the son-in-law told him he would completely handle the legal end of the marriage, the old man had had no suspicions or fears.

A girl at Kitazumi's grocery said to Suezo: "I really feel sorry for Taa-chan—she's honest and she had no doubt about the policeman, but he said he was only looking for a place to live."

And with his hand circling his cropped head of hair, the storekeeper interrupted her: "It's a pity about the old man too. He moved away because he couldn't stand meeting his neighbors and he couldn't stay here as before. But he still sells candy where he used to, saying he can't do business in places where there are no little customers. A while back he sold his stall, but now he has it again from the secondhand dealer, after telling him the situation. I think he's got financial troubles because of the moving and such. It's as though the old man lived for only a short time in a world of dreams, freeing himself into easy retirement and keeping company with the policeman, who drank saké, acting like a god, while, in fact, he starved his wife and children in the country."

After that, the candy dealer's daughter slipped from Suezo's mind, but when he became financially well off and could do more of what he wanted, he happened to remember the girl.

Suezo, now with a wide circle of acquaintances to do his bidding, had them look for the old candy dealer and finally located his mean quarters next to a ricksha garage behind a theatre. He learned also that the daughter wasn't married. So Suezo sent a woman to make overtures with an offer from a wealthy merchant disposed to have the girl for his mistress. In spite of Otama's objections at first, the old woman kept reminding the meek and reluctant girl of the advantages her father would get from the arrangement, and the negotiations reached the point where the parties agreed to meet at the Matsugen restaurant.

CHAPTER FIVE

Before this new interest in Suezo's life, his only thoughts had centered on the students, their loans, and his returns, but he had no sooner located Otama and her father than he began to search his neighborhood for a house to establish his mistress in. He did not know whether or not he would succeed with his plan, but he was so eager to advance the scheme that he began to put it into operation. Two of the many houses he investigated pleased him. One of them was on his own street, halfway between his house, which was right next to the famous writer Fukuchi's, and the Rengyokuan, which sold the best bowl of noodles in the area. A short distance from the Shinobazu Pond was the house that had first appealed to him, for it stood somewhat back from the road, was fenced about with bamboo canes, and had a thick-needled parasol pine and a few cypresses.

The other house, in the middle of Muenzaka, was smaller. He did not find any notice on the door when he arrived, but he had heard that the house was for sale. Almost immediately upon entering, he discovered the noise from the neighboring house and the group of young ladies at work. "I don't like that," he said to himself, but on inspecting the interior with more care, he could not help appreciating the high quality of the timber. He knew that the former occupant, a wealthy merchant who had just died, had built the house with care in order to spend his retirement there. The place, with its front garden and granite doorway, was comfortable, neat, and superior in taste.

One night, as Suezo lay in bed, he thought about the two houses. His wife, who had tried to put her child to sleep, had herself dozed off while the infant suckled at her breast. Suezo turned away from her, her mouth open, snoring, the child pulling at the exposed breast.

Usually Suezo would lie awake in bed while devising new schemes for increasing the interest on his loans. His wife never complained about this habit, and she was usually asleep long before her husband.

Once more he glanced at her, thinking to himself: "Is that a woman's face? I doubt it. Take Otama's face. That's a woman's face, but I haven't seen her for a long time. You couldn't even call her a woman then. I wouldn't think she was more than a child. Yet even then—what a face! Gentle—yes. But with something smart in it too. It couldn't be worse now—better, I should think. How I'd love to see her now instead of that thing!"

Once more he looked down at the snoring woman. "Poor devil!" he thought. "Sleeping there and not knowing a thing. She believes I'm adding up sums, but how wrong! How stupid and wrong! If you only knew—"

He suddenly slapped at his leg. "What! Mosquitoes out already! That's what's wrong with this section. Too many pests. We'll have to put up the net soon. Let the old she-devil get eaten alive, but I've got to think about the children."

His mind returned again to the question of the houses, and only after one o'clock in the morning had he made a decision. He had reasoned that he would prefer the Ike-no-hata place for its view, but what was the need of that when all he had to do was look out the window in the house he was now living in? One point in its favor was the cheap rent. That was true, but he remembered that a rented house has too many other expenses. Besides, it was not hidden enough. It would attract attention. What if one day he happened to leave the window open by mistake? He could just see the old devil on her way to market with the boy and girl. He could see them looking in and finding him there with Otama. There'd be more than that devil to pay!

When he thought about the Muenzaka house, he felt that it was somewhat gloomy, but the key point in its favor was its out-of-the-way location on a slope that only students seemed to stroll along at odd hours. But he didn't like the idea of putting up so much money for it. Still, with its timber. . . . And when he had it insured, he could at least get back what he paid at the beginning. "All right, then. That's it!" he told himself. "I'll take it. Take it and her."

Now he was especially pleased with it all. The future suddenly seemed real, and he saw himself on his evening of triumph. He had bathed carefully, had dressed smartly, had concocted an excuse to dodge his wife for the night. He saw himself rushing out of the house. He was free. He was almost to Muenzaka. He saw the light and wondered what it would be like when he went up the walk and opened the door. How radiantly beautiful her face would be! Poor Otama! There she was waiting for him, a kitten or some pet on her lap—ready to welcome him, of course—her face made up, of course. He would dress her in a gorgeous kimono, would give her whatever she had demanded for the occasion. But he checked himself a moment. He wouldn't play the fool. He wouldn't spend his money unwisely. He had his connections at the pawn shops. How stupid to squander money like some men, like Fukuchi for example. Suezo suddenly saw his famous neighbor Fukuchi strutting openly on the streets and followed by his expensive geishas. The students would see the writer and be envious, but Suezo knew that the dandy was actually ill-off. He was supposedly an intelligent man, a writer. But was he? If a clerk did the same kinds of nasty tricks with his pen as Fukuchi did, he would be discharged.

Suezo's thoughts returned to his Otama, and he suddenly remembered that she could play the samisen. Would she delight him with an intimate tune, plucking the strings with her fingers? No, it would be expecting too much of her, for she was young, inexperienced, only a policeman's temporary mistress. And he feared her shyness, feared she might say to him that evening: "I won't play. You'll only laugh at me." She might be shy in everything, in no matter what, and she might blush and fidget at the important moment.

Suezo's imagination shifted first one way and then another without restraint. The intensity increased until at last images shattered into fragments of flickering white skin and of whispered words tumbling into his ear.

With his wife still snoring beside him, he fell into a sweet sleep.

CHAPTER SIX

Suezo thought of the approaching meeting with his future mistress at the Matsugen as a celebration.

We often hear that misers will even skin flints, but men who make large fortunes by thrift are not uniform in their behavior. Perhaps, as a group, these men give attention to such trifles as cutting sheets of toilet paper in half or filling out postcards with characters you cannot decipher without the aid of a microscope. Some of the most covetous are thrifty in every aspect of living, yet a few give themselves a breath of fresh air by leaving a loophole in their tight moneybags. Up to the present time the misers we have read about in novels or have seen on the stage seem to belong to the absolute type. But those we meet in life are not like that. Some of the most frugal loosen their purse strings to the final notch for women, and others gorge themselves with sumptuous foods.

I have already referred to Suezo's passion for clothing. Even during his difficult days of university employment, he was often completely transformed on holidays, his weekday outfit of inferior cotton replaced by a handsome kimono. He seemed like a smart-looking, successful merchant instead of a dormitory servant. This was a pleasure to him, and occasionally he dressed himself up in costly taffeta clothes and startled students who happened to pass and recognize him.

Dress had been Suezo's only hobby. He had not associated with geishas or prostitutes, and a night of saké at one of the drinking houses had been an impossibility. Even a bowl of noodles at the Rengyokuan had been a luxury for himself alone, and only recently had he permitted his wife and children to share the treat. He had not taken his wife out because he had not let her dress in a kimono to match his own expensive one. When she wanted a costly item for herself, he denied it to her.

"Don't talk like that," he had argued. "You and I are quite different. I've got to dress this way because of the men I associate with."

When Suezo's loans had started to bring in large sums, he began eating out. Yet he always justified the expense by going to a restaurant with his friends and never alone. But now that he was about to see Otama at the Matsugen, he wanted to make it a special affair, something gay and impressive. He had chosen the restaurant for that reason.

When the day of days drew near, Suezo wondered how he would dress Otama for the occasion. He would have spent any sum on her for the purpose, but since he had to provide for her father as well, he hesitated. The old go-between was at her wit's end for a solution, yet they both agreed that they had to consider the old man because any possible oversight might end their chances of getting Otama as a mistress.

The old man had told the go-between about his only child: "No," he had said, "I have no other relatives. And I've had a lonely time of it without my wife. She was over thirty when our first child was born. Our first and last. I kept Otama alive after her mother died in childbirth by taking her to different women in the neighborhood. They gave her their milk. And I had other troubles. When Otama was four, she had the measles during the Edo epidemic. The doctor said she'd die, but I didn't believe him. I took care of her. I saved her life. I let my business go, everything, watching over her. What a year! All sorts of terrible things happened two years after Lord Ii was killed. In that year some Westerners were beheaded at Namamugi. I couldn't even keep up my shop. More than once I was going to kill myself and Otama too. But how could I harm Otama? You should have seen her then. She had the smallest hands. How they poked at my chest! And she smiled at me with the widest eyes! We barely managed to live from one day to the next. I don't think many others could have gone through what we did. I wasn't a young man then. I was forty-five when she was born and, what with the cares I had, must have looked older. Still, I could have started over. One of my friends kept repeating the old proverb: 'When a single man can't live, two can.' Then he said he knew a widow who was looking for a husband. And he'd recommend me. Oh, she had money too! But I would have had to give my child away to someone else. How could I? I refused the offer flat."

Suddenly the old man paused, but a moment later he continued: "You don't know how I want to curse! You can't know what it is to feel that you've been tricked! Being poor made me a dull old man! I was there when that policeman made a plaything out of Otama. Yet she's not a bad girl, and they still speak of her as a fine daughter. You know, I'd like to marry her to a good man in the right way. That's the truth. But who to? No one's willing to take me along with her. I often said to myself: 'Don't give her away as a mistress! Don't!' But you say your master's a good man, an honest man, one we can trust? And a gentleman too? You see, I have to remember that Otama will be twenty next year. She has to marry soon. They say that the young shoot must be eaten before it withers. I'm trying to understand your offer. You see, I'm going to give away one so dear to me. You see, she's my only child. She's all I care about. I've got to meet this gentleman myself!"

When the go-between repeated these words to Suezo, he was disappointed at the old man's insistence that he be present at the interview. Suezo had planned to dismiss the go-between as soon as she had brought Otama to the restaurant. He expected no one to interfere. But if the father came, what a formal scene it would be! True, Suezo's mind bordered on formality, but it extended only to himself, as though he deserved recognition and praise for bringing the meeting about and for taking the first step in satisfying his secret passion. For the event a tête-à-tête was essential. But the presence of a father would completely alter the tone of the holiday.

Previously the go-between had told him: "What a virtuous

pair they are! At first they said no. They wouldn't even listen to me. But I got the girl alone and talked about duty, duty to her father. 'Your hardworking father,' I said. 'Too old to keep earning his living.' And that made her listen. She agreed to it all right. She got her father to agree!"

When Suezo learned this, his spirits soared, for he admired the tenderness and obedience of the person he was to own. Yet finding that both were pillars of purity, he felt that this important meeting would be like that of a bridegroom in front of his father-in-law. And the thought that the celebration might shift in that direction made him feel as though someone were pouring a dipper of ice water on his overheated head.

But he knew he had to be consistent, that he had to show his wealth and generosity. At last he agreed to give both father and daughter the necessary clothing. When he had further time to reason out his actions, he comforted himself, saying: "Since I'll have to take care of the father eventually when I get the daughter, I'm only doing in advance what I'll have to do later."

In such situations the customary procedure was to send the other party a definite sum of money to cover expenses. But Suezo had his own methods. He knew what was appropriate for the occasion, so he confided all the details to his tailor and ordered him to make adequate kimonos for the father and daughter. At the same time the go-between rushed off to ask Otama their measurements.

After the crone had left, Otama said to her father: "At least the man is considerate."

"Not sending the money shows he respects us," said the old man.

These were their reactions to Suezo's shrewd, penny-pinching methods.

CHAPTER SEVEN

Since fires seldom break out in the vicinity of Ueno Square and since the Matsugen hasn't burned down as far as I can remember, I think you can still find the room where the two parties met.

"I want something small and quiet," Suezo had said when he made the reservations, and on the appointed day he was led from the south entrance through a straight corridor that turned left into a room with an area of six mats.

When he was alone, he sat down on the cushion with his back to the alcove, which was adorned with an ukiyoe on a small scroll and a vase with a single twig of jasmine in it. He looked about with his usual care, examining everything.

Outside he saw a wooden fence that shut off the view of the pond. Perhaps he should have taken an upstairs room. But in an upstairs room they might have been seen from the street. Some years later the area around the pond was ruined and made into a racetrack, and then again, by one of those unusual transformations of the world, into a bicycle track. A long thin strip of land lying between the room and the fence was too narrow for a garden. From where he sat he could see a few Paulownia trees, their trunks as smooth and glossy as if they had been polished with oiled rags. He also noticed a stone lantern and some small cypresses planted at intervals. In the busy street white clouds of dust rose, kicked up by the passersby, but here inside the enclosure the servants had sprinkled water over the moss to give the green an added freshness.

A maid came into the room carrying tea and an incense burner to drive away the mosquitoes. Placing the items before him, she asked: "And what dishes would you like served?"

"I'll tell you when my guests come," he said, dismissing her.

Once more alone, he took out his pipe. On entering, he had thought the room too warm, but after some time he put down the soiled fan the maid had given him, for occasional drafts of cool wind came through the corridors along with faint yet distinct odors from the kitchen and the toilets.

Leaning against the pillar of the alcove, Suezo watched the smoke drift. He thought of the earlier Otama, the pretty girl he had caught glimpses of as he passed her house. A pretty girl, yes, but really a child. What kind of woman had she changed into? What would she look like in her new kimono? A shame that the old man was coming with her! How long would he stay? Could he be sent home, removed somehow or other?

Suezo was startled out of his daydreaming by a samisen being tuned in the room above him.

Then he heard the footsteps of two or three persons along the corridor.

"Your guests," said the maid, thrusting her face into the room.

"Come now! Step in! Let's not have any distance between you! Our master's open-minded!" said the go-between in a voice as noisy as a cricket's.

Suezo got to his feet and hurried out to the corridor. He saw the stooped figure of the old man as he hesitated near the corner wall and, behind him, Otama. She stood calmly, not at all overwhelmed, her eyes taking in everything with curiosity. The vision of a chubby girl with a pretty face swept through Suezo's mind, but the woman who had appeared before him was totally different. Time had changed her. She was a thin, graceful beauty. She had arranged her hair in the style of a future bride and was without the customary makeup demanded on such occasions. Suezo had prepared himself for the pleasure, but he had not expected that the woman would be as she was. His eyes probed and registered. She was beyond anything he had imagined, and, for that, all the more beautiful.

Otama was also surprised. She had previously thought that she did not care what the merchant was like. She would sell herself to anyone, no matter what his personality. She would do anything for her father. But on seeing Suezo's dark features, his keen but engaging eyes, and his elegant yet restrained kimono, she felt momentarily relieved, like a person escaping from a hopeless situation.

"Please," said Suezo politely to the old man, "come in."

He spoke first to the old man and pointed to the interior of the room.

"Please," he repeated, turning to Otama.

After the father and daughter had entered the room, Suezo called the go-between to a sheltered part of the corridor, put some money wrapped in paper into her hand, and whispered into her ear. The woman smiled, her teeth stained with traces of black dye, and bowing her head several times in appreciation and laughing contemptuously, she hurried away along the corridor.

When Suezo returned, he found his guests huddled together at the entrance.

"Come now. Sit down. Please—on these cushions." This done, he called out: "And now for the dishes!"

Soon saké and some light refreshments were brought in. As Suezo filled the old man's cup and exchanged a few words with him, he could tell from his manner that he had seen better days and had not simply dressed up for his first visit to a fancy restaurant.

At the beginning, Suezo had thought of the old man as a nuisance and was annoyed at having him there, but when he began to talk confidentially, Suezo's attitude softened. He went out of his way to make himself pleasant to the old man and to show the good he had in him. Inwardly Suezo was glad that he had been offered an opportunity to win Otama's trust by treating her father in this way.

By the time the dishes had been carried into the room, it seemed as though all three of them had dropped in to dine after a family excursion. Suezo, who was usually a tyrant in his own home and who was alternately obeyed and resisted by his wife, felt a placid and delicate delight that he had never felt before when he saw Otama take up a saké bottle and fill his cup, her face blushing and revealing a modest smile. While Suezo knew intuitively and unconsciously a happiness whose shadow floated like a vision in Otama's presence, he lacked the fine reasoning that would have made him reflect why his home life was devoid of such happiness, nor could he calculate how much was required to maintain such an unusual feeling—in fact, whether or not the requirement might be satisfied by him and his wife.

"Please!" shouted a voice against the beating of a pair of wooden clappers just outside the fence. "Your favorite actors!"

Upstairs the music stopped, and a maid said something from the railing.

"Thank you," said the man outside. And he called out the names of two Kabuki players.

The actor-imitator began to perform at once.

"We're lucky," said the maid, entering the room with another container of saké. "A real mimic's come tonight!"

"What's that?" asked Suezo. "Are there false mimics along with the true ones?"

"Oh, yes. Lately, a university student's been going around."

"You mean he can actually play an instrument too?" asked Suezo.

"Of course, just like a professional. Even his costume's real. But we know him! We can tell who he is by his voice."

"Then there's only one deceiver," said Suezo.

"Yes, only one who dares!" said the maid, laughing.

"Do you know him personally?" Suezo asked.

"Why, yes! He often comes here to eat."

"He must have quite a skill then," said the old man. "And just think—he's only a student."

"But probably a bad one," said Suezo with an ironic smile as he thought of the students who came to his house. Some of them, he knew, disguised themselves as tradesmen and teased the prostitutes in the small houses. How they enjoyed using the jargon of these women! But it surprised him that a student did tour the neighborhood in earnest as a mimic.

"Who are your favorite actors, Otama-san?" Suezo said, turning to her suddenly.

"I don't have any favorites," she said. She had been quietly listening to the conversation.

"Oh!" interrupted her father, "she's never been inside a theatre!" And he added: "We live right next to one, and all the girls on our block go to see the plays. But not my Otama. Never. I hear the other girls rush out of their houses the minute they catch the first note!"

The old man, in spite of his intentions, was apt to revert to the praise of his daughter.

CHAPTER EIGHT

They reached an agreement. Otama would live in the house Suezo had bought on Muenzaka.

But the transfer, which Suezo had thought a simple matter, raised some difficulties.

"I want my father as close as possible," Otama had said. "I want to visit him often. I must look after him."

Her original intention had been to send her father, already over sixty, the greater part of her allowance and to provide him with a young maid who would make him comfortable. If her plan worked, he would no longer have to remain in their dismal home, its wall shared with that of a ricksha garage. "Why can't you put my father in a house near my own?" she had asked.

So it turned out that Suezo, who had thought that all he need do was to receive his mistress in the house he had purchased for her, now had, in addition, just as he had been forced to invite the father with the daughter at their first interview, to undertake the problem of the old man's living quarters.

She had told Suezo: "It's my own concern. I don't want to trouble you."

But since she had mentioned the problem, he could not avoid it. He wanted to show her how generous he was.

Finally Suezo had said: "Look. When you come to live at Muenzaka, I'll rent a house for your father at Ike-no-hata."

It had been forced on him. When Suezo saw how Otama would have to save and pinch on her allowance after she had said that she would manage the arrangement herself, he couldn't allow her to do so.

Thus Suezo had to pay more than he had calculated. But he paid without bitterness, much to the bewilderment of the old go-between.

By the middle of July, Otama and her father had settled in their new homes. Suezo was so bewitched by the modesty of the girl's manner and her maidenly way of speaking that he visited her almost every night. He had been capable of complete ruthlessness in his dealings, and still was, but now he tried every trick of tenderness to gain Otama's affection. This, I believe, is what historians have often called the touch of weakness in a man of iron will.

On these visits Suezo made it a point to appear almost every evening, though he never stayed the entire night. With the help of the go-between, Otama had hired a maid. Ume was only thirteen, and she did the kitchen work, which, Otama could not help feeling, was little more than having a child play a pleasant game. The result was that Otama did not have enough to do during the day and was left without anyone to talk to.

She would find herself wishing for her master to come earlier in the evening and would smile at the change taking place in herself. Before, the situation had been different. She had also been alone while her father was out selling his candies, but during his absence she had taken in piecework. She had not even had the friendship of the girls in the neighborhood, yet she had never regretted the loss, had never even been bored. She would think only of the sum she would receive upon completing the task. There would be her father's surprise, his smile of pleasure because of her diligence. Yes, she had worked hard in those days. But now it was different, and she was beginning to feel the pains of ennui.

Yet her weariness was not unbearable, relieved as it was by Suezo's evening calls. Her father's position in the new house was a more difficult one than her own. Overnight he had been given luxuries he had never had before. At odd times during the day he would say to himself: "Am I bewitched? Yes! Bewitched by a fox!"

But the change was not enough to satisfy him, and he began to miss those earlier days when he and Otama would spend their evenings together, the oil lamp lit, their small talk about the ways of the world begun, the silence without disturbance from others infiltrating their room.

"A pretty dream that was," said the old man to himself. "It'll never come back."

At other times he said to himself: "When will she come? I expect her. But when?"

A number of days had passed since their separation, and he had not received even a short visit from her.

For the first few days the old man was delighted with the house, the maid from the country, the conveniences. The girl cooked his meals and did the heavy task of carrying in the water from the well. He tried to keep busy too and helped the girl put the rooms in order. Sometimes he swept. Occasionally he sent her out to shop for him. And in the evening when he heard her working in the kitchen, he sprinkled the ground around the parasol pine. Later, his figure framed in the low window, his arms on the sill, a pipe in his mouth, he watched the movements of the noisy crows over Ueno Hill and looked at the shrine on the wooded island in the pond, the lotus flowers in the water blurred by degrees in the thickening haze of evening.

He said to himself that he was grateful for his good fortune, that he was satisfied with his circumstances, yet at the same time he could not help thinking: "I raised her without anyone's help. I kept her from the moment she was born. We didn't even need words. We could understand each other without talk. A daughter who was always kind, always waiting for me when I came home."

He would sit at the window for hours, his eyes on the pond or the people walking along the street.

At times he wanted to shout: "Otama! Look at that! Did you see that carp jump?"

When a stranger was passing, he wanted to call his daughter to the window, wanted to tell her: "A foreigner! What a hat she's got on! A whole bird on top of it!"

How he wished he could say that to Otama, to cry: "Did you ever see such a sight?"

And it pained him that he could not.

With each passing day he became increasingly irritable. He began to find fault with the maid when she brought him his meals. He had not had a servant for many years, and since he was a tenderhearted man, he refrained from scolding her. But he was uneasy in her presence, for no matter what she did, it went against him. To do justice to the girl—just up to Tokyo from the country—it was unfortunate for her to be compared with Otama, who bore herself so well and did everything gently and quietly.

Finally, on the fourth day after moving to his new house, he was shocked to find that the maid had her thumb in his soup as she brought it to him at breakfast.

"No more serving me! Go away!" He found the courage to say that much.

After the meal he took his usual position at the window. He didn't think it would rain, and with the weather so cool, he thought he would go out for a walk. As he went around the pond he kept speculating: "She may come while I'm out."

And he turned several times to look at his house.

Eventually he came to a small bridge leading toward Muenzaka. Should he go to his daughter's house? But he couldn't bring himself to take that direction. It seemed as though he felt hindered by a barrier suddenly rising between him and his daughter, an awareness of their altered positions, something. A mother might never have such a feeling toward an only child. Wondering why a father should, he continued around the pond instead of crossing the bridge. Suddenly he discovered he was standing in front of Suezo's place. The go-between had previously pointed to it from his own house. From close up, it seemed better looking, surrounded by its high mud wall with bamboo strips nailed diagonally at the top of the barrier. The neighboring house, which he had been told belonged to the scholar Fukuchi, had more extensive grounds, but the residence itself was old-fashioned and not as gaudy and pretentious as Suezo's.

For a while the old man stood in front of Suezo's house, his eyes on the service gate of white woodwork, yet his mind definite that he did not want to enter it.

The old man was not thinking of anything in particular, but for some time he seemed dazed, attacked by a rush of feeling, a kind of loneliness coming over him and mixed with the sudden awareness of life's brevity, its change. If you force me to define these emotions more specifically, they were those of a parent who has debased himself by selling his daughter as a mistress.

A week passed, and still Otama had not come. He was annoyed at himself for wanting to see her so badly, and he wondered: "Has she forgotten me? She's comfortable now. Why not?"

These suspicions were so faint that he alone could have brought them about and played with them in his own mind. Suspicions they were, and yet not such as to make him hate her. But superficially at least, with the irony that one often uses in conversation, he murmured: "I'd be happier if I could."

Then his reasoning took another direction: "I leave the house so that I don't have to think too much. Let her come when I'm not there! She'll be sorry she missed me. But what if she doesn't care if I'm out? Well, at least her visit was a waste of time. That should annoy her. It would serve her right too!" And on his walks he repeated these conclusions a number of times.

He would go to the park, rest on a bench in the shade, and then get up and walk again. If he happened to see a covered ricksha, he would say to himself: "Ah! she's visited me! Oh, she'll be upset all right not to find me in. That'll teach her!" And if, as he half wished, it did punish her, he knew that he was also putting himself to a test.

In the evening he began to go to the theatre to listen to the storyteller and the recitations of dramatic ballads. Inside, he imagined his daughter on one of her futile visits to his house, but the thought would suddenly occur to him that she was also in the hall, and he would look around at the young women with the same hair style as Otama's. Once he was certain he had seen her. The woman had entered during the intermission, her companion in *yukata* and with a panama hat, quite a new fashion in those days. The old man watched her take a seat in the gallery, put her hands on the railing, and look down into the pit below. But as he looked more closely, he said to himself: "No, her face is too round. Besides, she's smaller than Otama." In addition, her escort was accompanied not only by that woman but by others who sat behind him.

They were all geisha girls and apprentices.

And he heard a student near him whisper: "That's Fukuchi!"

As Otama's father left the hall after the performance, he saw the man followed by his troop of geishas and novices and led by a woman holding a long-handled lantern with the name of the theatre written in red characters.

He walked on in the same direction as this party, sometimes going ahead, sometimes falling behind.

At last he reached his own house and went in.

CHAPTER NINE

Otama, who had never been away from her father, was eager to know how he was. Yet, in spite of this desire, several days had passed without her being able to visit him. She was afraid that Suezo might come when she was out, and she feared that he would be annoyed if he did not find her. Usually he came at night and stayed until eleven, but he began to appear briefly at odd hours.

The first time he came during the day he said, sitting down opposite her in front of the charcoal brazier: "I've dropped in on my way to an appointment. I'll just smoke a cigarette and go."

As a matter of fact, Otama seldom knew when he would come, so she didn't have the courage to leave. She might have slipped out in the morning, but she considered Ume an unreliable child. Moreover, Otama didn't want to be seen then or in the afternoon, for she didn't like the thought of the neighbors staring at her. She was so shy that at first she went to the bathhouse below the slope only after she had sent Ume out to see that it was not crowded.

To make matters worse, on the third day after she had moved in, she had been frightened. She was already timid enough to give the situation more attention than it deserved. On first moving into Muenzaka, she had been called on by the vegetable dealer and the fishmonger. When she agreed to be their customer, they gave her an account book. On the day in question, when the fish had not been delivered, she sent Ume down the slope to get a few slices for lunch. Otama was not used to eating fish every day, having taken her meals without such delicacies. Nor had her father been particular about food as long as she had prepared it well and it was healthy for him. But once she had heard one of her neighbors at their old house saying that she and her father had bought no fish for several days. Remembering how embarrassed she had been then, Otama decided to send the girl for some. "If Ume thinks I'm trying to save money," she reasoned, "then I'm being unfair to Suezo. He's not like that."

But a short while later the maid returned crying.

"What is it? Tell me," Otama said a number of times before the girl would speak.

"I went into a fish market, but not the one we buy from. I looked around but couldn't see the dealer. And I thought: 'Why, he's probably calling on customers after buying fresh fish at the waterfront.' And then I saw some mackerel looking like they'd just been pulled out of the water. 'How much?' I ask the wife. 'I've never seen you around here,' she says to me, not even telling me how much. 'Whose house you from?' she asks. And when I told her, she began to make a face like she was angry. 'Why!' she says. 'Then I'm sorry for you. Go on back where you're from and tell your mistress we don't sell fish to the—whore of a usurer!' And then she turned her back on me, smoking her pipe, pretending I wasn't even there!"

Ume had been too shocked and hurt to go to another shop and had run all the way back. And the simple girl, all the while making sympathetic gestures, told her mistress the entire story line by line.

As Ume spoke, Otama's face turned pale, and for a while she could not answer. A mixture of feelings tumbled inside the inexperienced girl. It was impossible for her to disentangle her confused thoughts, but the total confusion put so heavy a strain upon the heart of a pure girl sold that all her blood seemed to be drawn into it, draining the color from her face and leaving her back chilled with cold perspiration.

On these occasions an insignificant thought seems to take hold of us. Would Ume continue to serve her after this disgrace?

As the girl watched Otama she could see that her words had upset her mistress. But she could not guess what had caused Otama such dismay. The girl had returned to the house in a fit, but now it seemed that the food for lunch was indispensable, and she still carried the coins in the folds of her sash.

"I never met such a nasty person!" Ume said, a look of compassion on her face. "Why! who'd shop at such a place? Not me. There's another shop up ahead of that one. Near a fox-shrine. That's where I'll go. And right away too." And she got up from the mats to run out.

Otama gave her an automatic smile and a nod, moved at finding a friend in Ume, who hurried out of the room.

Otama remained seated. As the strain became less intense, she began to cry quietly and reached into her kimono sleeve for a handkerchief. She heard a voice cry out: "It's not fair! How cruel!" It was her own confusion. By these words she did not mean that she hated the woman who refused to sell her the fish, nor did she feel sad or mortified in recognizing that her status had barred her from a simple fish market. She did not even feel resentment toward Suezo, who had purchased her and who had now turned out to be a usurer. It was humiliating to belong to such a man, but she did not even feel that. She had heard that usurers were disgusting persons, looked down on, feared, detested. But her father's only experience in that direction had been with pawnbrokers. And when their clerks had not been kind enough to give him the sum he needed, he had never complained in spite of the inconvenience. So, even though she had been told that such men existed, her fear was similar to that of a child toward an ogre or a policeman—not a particularly keen one. What then was this despair she suddenly felt?

In her feeling, the sense of injustice done by the world in general and men in particular was almost absent. If she had such a sense, it was that of the unfairness of her own destiny. She had done nothing wrong, yet she was to be persecuted by the world. This pained her. This was her despair. When she had learned that the policeman had deceived her and deserted her, she had used the same words for the first time in her life: "It's not fair! How cruel!" And she had used them again when she had been forced into becoming a mistress. And now that she realized she was not only a "whore" but one kept by a usurer whom the world detested, the feeling of humiliation that time and resignation had softened and toned down emerged once more with its sharp outline and strong colors. This was the substance of Otama's emotion, if you force me to describe it in any reasonable way.

Eventually she stood up, opened a closet, and from a bag of imitation leather took out a calico apron which she had made. Tying the apron around her waist, she entered the kitchen with a sigh. Her silk apron was more like a dress, and she never used it while working there. She was so fond of personal cleanliness that even when she wore an easy-to-wash summer kimono she would tie a towel around her hair in order to keep the neckband from getting soiled.

Gradually her thoughts settled. Resignation was the mental attitude she had most experienced. And in this direction her mind adjusted itself like a well-oiled machine.

CHAPTER TEN

One evening when Suezo came, he took his usual seat opposite Otama. From their first meeting in her new home she had put a cushion beside the charcoal brazier as soon as she knew he was there. He would go to it and sit down, and relaxing with his pipe, engage in small talk. From her own position on the mats she would answer him in monosyllables. She would say a few words, pass her hands along the frame of the brazier, toy with the charcoal tongs, do anything to keep herself busy. If she hadn't had a definite place before the brazier, she wouldn't have known what to do. It may be said that she was facing a formidable enemy with only the battlement of the brazier to protect her.

During their talks Suezo would get her to speak for a time, usually on trivial and sentimental matters about the years she had lived alone with her father. In spite of himself, Suezo would listen with a smile, not so much to what she was saying but rather to the pleasant melody of her voice. It was as though he were hearing the pure tones of a bell-insect. Then Otama would suddenly become self-conscious, blush at having run on about herself, and dash off the rest of her sentence before lapsing into her usual silence. With his penetration Suezo could see that her speech and behavior were so totally innocent that she seemed as transparent as fresh water in the bottom of a flat vase. His delight in their conversation was equal to his own joy in soaking his limbs in an agreeably warm bath after an exhausting day at work. The experience of this delight, quite a new one for him, had been giving him unconsciously a sort of "culture" since the start of his visits to her. After all, a primitive beast can be subdued by sensitive hands.

But a number of days after she had moved in, he became aware of her increasing restlessness. When he took his place before the brazier, she would get up, find some unnecessary task to do, occupy her hands. From the beginning of their relationship, she had avoided his glance and had hesitated in answering his questions. On this occasion her conduct was so strange that there had to be some explanation for it.

"Come now," he said, filling his pipe, "something's bothering you. What is it?"

"No," said Otama, her eyes widening, "there's nothing wrong."

She had pulled out one of the drawers from the frame of the brazier as if to arrange it, but she had already put it in order. She began to search for an item when obviously she had nothing to look for. Suezo could tell that her eyes could not keep very great secrets.

In spite of frowning unconsciously, he brightened instantly. "Come, Otama, you know you're worried. It's written all over your face. I can just make out the words. Let me see," he said, looking at her sharply. "Oh yes! 'I'm all confused. What'll I do? What'll I do?'"

Otama was embarrassed, and for a while she sat in silence as though she did not know how to begin. Suezo could clearly perceive the motion of this delicate instrument.

"I—well—it's my father. I've been thinking about visiting him—one of these days. . . . And it's been long since. . . ."

Though a man may see the particular movement of a highly intricate machine, he may not necessarily understand its total operation. An insect that must always ward off persecution from the bigger and stronger of the species is given the gift of mimicry. A woman tells lies.

"What!" said Suezo, smiling in spite of his scolding tone. "You haven't visited him yet? His house right at Ike-no-hata? In front of your nose? Why, just think of Iwasaki's estate on the other side. It's almost as if the two of you were living in the same house. If you wish, we'll go now, though tomorrow would be better."

"But—I've so many things to think of—to consider," she said, poking the ashes with the charcoal tongs and stealing a glance at him.

"Nonsense!" he interrupted. "Such a simple thing doesn't require a reason! What an infant you are!" he said, his voice nevertheless tender.

The matter ended there. Later, he even said with humorous gallantry: "If it's so much trouble, I'll come around in the morning and take you. After all, it *is* several hundred yards!"

Lately Otama had tried to think of him in several ways. When she saw him in front of her with his reliable and considerate manner, even tenderness, she wondered why he had chosen a base profession. And she said to herself: "I may change him, make him find something else to do." But she knew this was more than she could do. And yet she confessed to herself: "He's not detestable! Usurer or not, he's not detestable!"

As for Suezo, he had caught an image at the bottom of Otama's mind, had sounded her out regarding it, and had found it a childish trifle. But as he walked down Muenzaka after eleven that night, it seemed as though something were behind what he had already discovered. He was shrewd enough to locate part of the trouble. "Something," he conjectured, "someone's told her something. Something about me. And she's holding it against me."

But he did not know who had told what.

CHAPTER ELEVEN

When Otama reached her father's house the next morning, he had just finished breakfast. She had never spent a great deal of time getting ready to go out, and she hurried along thinking that perhaps she had come too early, but the old man, not a late sleeper, had already swept the entrance to his house and had sprinkled water over the grounds. And after washing his hands and feet, he was just taking his lonely meal on the new mats.

A few doors from her father's house, some places where geishas entertained had recently been constructed, and on certain evenings the neighborhood was noisy. But the houses to the right and left of the old man's, like his own, kept their doors closed and were quiet, especially in the morning.

As the old man looked out of his low window, he could see through the branches of the parasol pine in his front garden the stringlike willow trees faintly moving in the fresh breeze. Beyond them the lotus leaves covered the pond, their green color spotted here and there with light pink flowers blooming at that early hour. In the winter the old man's house would be cold since it faced north, but in the summer it was as good as anyone could wish to find.

Ever since Otama had been old enough to think for herself, she had hoped that if the opportunity arose she would do one thing or another for her father. And when she saw the house he was living in, she couldn't restrain her joy, couldn't help feeling her prayers realized. But even the happiness she felt had its bitter ingredient, an awareness of her altered position. "If I could see my father without that," she said to herself, "how happy I could be!"

She felt the frustration expressed in the proverb: "An unfulfilled wish is the world's way."

The old man had put down his chopsticks and was taking his tea when he heard a noise at the front door. Since it had never been opened by a visitor, he was surprised. And setting aside his teacup, he kept his eyes in that direction. He could not see anyone behind the folding screen of rush stalks, but when he heard his daughter call: "Otossan," he had a difficult time remaining seated instead of jumping up and rushing over to meet her. Yet he sat where he was, his mind busily trying to find the words to use and thinking he would begin with "It's a wonder you still remember your father!" But when he saw Otama hurry toward him, her face radiant as though experiencing a relief from pain after the interval of their separation, he couldn't have said those words. Yet he was dissatisfied with his weakness in not being able to say even that much, and he stared at her face in silence.

Yes, he thought, she was beautiful. Even when he had been poor, he had insisted that his only source of pride should always look her best, and he had even refused to let her do heavy tasks. But now that he was seeing her for the first time after an absence of ten days, she seemed reborn. Compared to the present Otama, who was consciously grooming and polishing herself, the daughter he remembered was a precious stone in the rough. A parent who sees his own daughter or an old man who sees a young girl cannot deny the beauty of a beautiful object. And such men cannot be exempt from feeling the power that beauty has in easing the heart.

The old man had consciously remained silent, had intended to make her see that he was sullen, but he couldn't help himself and softened against his will. Even Otama, who had never known a day of separation from her father before this new arrangement and who had not seen him for ten days, was speechless for a moment. She had much to tell him, but all she could do was look at his face with pleasure.

"Are you finished?" asked the maid, her tone quick and her voice rising as she appeared suddenly at the entrance to the kitchen.

Otama couldn't catch the girl's words. And when the maid, her hair rolled up around a comb so that it was out of proportion to her fat face, saw Otama, she stared at the visitor rudely.

"Take it away! And bring in fresh tea! Use the green on the shelf," the old man said, pushing the tray forward for her to take it into the kitchen.

"Oh, you don't have to trouble her to make special tea for me."

"What kind of nonsense is that! I've got some cake too." He went over to the closet and, taking out a tin of egg crackers, put some into a cake dish.

"There's a baker not too far from here who makes these. And guess what? You can buy Joen's cooked fish in soy sauce in an alley right next to it!"

"Ah, Joen! Do you remember, Otossan, when you took me to the music hall? And Joen was there? Talking about a feast he went to, saying the fish was as good as his own. And how we laughed! What a pleasingly plump man he was! Coming on stage and flinging up his kimono before sitting down. I could hardly keep myself from laughing out loud. I wish you'd get that fat!"

"What? Be as fat as him? Not me!" he said, putting the dish before her. Soon the maid brought the tea, and the father and daughter were talking as easily as if they had done the same thing yesterday and the day before.

"How are you getting along?" he asked suddenly, feeling the awkwardness of the question. "Does Suezo come dropping in every so often?"

"Yes—" she said, hesitating, not knowing what to reply. Suezo came not merely "often" but every night. If she had been Suezo's wife and someone had asked her how she was getting on with her husband, she would have said happily: "Wonderfully! Please don't worry about us." But since she was his mistress, her conscience prevented her from revealing Suezo's nightly appearance.

"We're managing," she said after a pause. "You shouldn't worry about me. Please don't."

"Everything's all right then—" His daughter's reply had not quite satisfied him, and the two of them unconsciously began speaking as though their mouths were full of paste. They had never kept anything from each other, but now they were speaking with formality, like unrelated persons having secrets to conceal from each other. When the policeman had duped them and they had felt embarrassed in the presence of their neighbors, they still had the greatest confidence in one another, convinced as they were that what had happened was not their fault. Yet this situation was different, for after the desperate decision that had put them in comfortable positions, they became painfully aware of a barrier thrown across their former intimacy.

A few moments of silence followed. The old man wanted a more definite answer and approached the question in a new way. "What sort of man is he?"

"Let me see," said Otama, inclining her head to the side almost as though she were speaking to herself. "I guess that after everything's said, he's not a bad man. He hasn't said anything cruel—though it's only been a few days."

The old man looked puzzled. "Hum—why should he be a *bad* man?"

She looked at her father, her heartbeat increasing. She realized that she now had her chance to tell him what she had learned, yet it pained her to bring him any new problems. She had put him at ease now. He was comfortable. And she suddenly decided: "I won't tell him!" She would keep the matter to herself, an unopened secret behind the one they shared of her serving as a mistress, even though in doing this she was aware that the gap between them was widening.

She diverged from the point, saying: "It's just that I heard he made his money in a clever way by doing various things. And that made me anxious about the kind of man he was.

Well, what should I say about him? Oh . . . he looks like a gentleman. I don't know whether he's really one or not. Still it seems to me that he tries to say and do things so that other people will think he is. And, Otossan, isn't it better to try to be that kind of man, even if it's only a matter of trying?"

After this speech she looked up at her father. However honest a woman may be, she feels less hesitation than a man in keeping back what is really on her mind at the moment and speaking about other things. And it may be said that those women who speak the most at such times are the more honest of their sex.

"Well, you may be right. But you talk as though you don't trust him."

"Ah, I'm getting smarter," she said with a smile, "bit by bit. From now on I'm not going to be made a fool of. Don't you think I'm a brave woman?"

These pointed remarks of opposition directed at him from the daughter he thought invariably meek surprised the old man, and he gazed at her with misgivings.

"Well, Otama," he said, "I've lived and been made a fool of all my life. But you know, you're better off being cheated than cheating. I don't care what situation a person's in, he has to pay back what he owes someone else. You've got to be faithful to your obligations."

"You never have to worry about that, Otossan. How often you used to say: 'Ta-bo's honest.' I know I am. But lately I've made up my mind, and I won't let myself be tricked again. I won't lie to anyone. I won't deceive anyone. But at the same time no one's going to deceive me either. I'll see to it that they don't."

"All of this, I suppose, means that you don't trust Suezo?"

"Just that. He treats me as though I were an infant. I'm not surprised that his type takes that approach with me. He thinks he can go through somebody's eye and nose without being seen. But I'm not as much of a child as that."

"You don't mean that he's lied to you?"

"Yes, he has. You remember, the go-between said he was a widower left with some children and that the woman he took under his care would be just like his wife though not in name. She said that it was only because of what the neighbors would say about our living in a poor district that he couldn't marry me. Well, he has a wife. He told me so himself. He didn't even hesitate. He didn't even feel ashamed. I was shocked."

The old man was shocked too. "Is it true? Then—then what she said was only a matchmaker's trick?"

"So I must be kept strictly secret from his wife. Since he's lying to her, how can I trust him completely?"

Otama seemed to have risen in the old man's estimation, and he looked at her so absentmindedly that he forgot to knock out the ashes in his pipe.

"I've got to go back now," Otama said, as though she had suddenly remembered something. "Since I've found my way here once, it'll be easy to come again. From now on I'll visit almost every day. The reason I haven't been here sooner was that I didn't think it right to come until Suezo made the suggestion. But last night I finally told him that I wanted to visit you and got his consent. And so here I am today! My maid's really a child. She can't even prepare lunch without my help."

"Well, if you got his permission, eat here."

"No, I don't feel safe about my house. I'll come again—very soon. Goodbye, Otossan."

When she stood up to leave, the maid rushed to the entrance to put her wooden clogs in the right direction. Even an ignorant woman has to make observations on any woman she comes across. A certain philosopher once said that one of that sex regards another she meets, if only on the street and for the first time, as a rival. And this country wench, who constantly put her thumb into a bowl of soup, seemed to have been eavesdropping on Otama, who was too beautiful to ignore.

"All right then," said Otama's father, remaining seated on his cushion. "Come soon. And give my regards to Suezo."

Otama took a small wallet from the layers of her black sash and gave the maid some money wrapped in paper, put on her low clogs, and left the house.

She had entered the gate with the intention of revealing her troubles to her father and gaining a partner in her misery, but she came out in high spirits that seemed strange even to herself. While she had talked to him, she was conscious of trying to appear strong and firm instead of adding any anxieties to the freedom he had found, and she sensed the release of some hidden quality in her. Previously she had depended on others, but now she knew the power of an unexpected self-reliance. And as she walked around the pond, she felt cheered.

Already high above Ueno Hill, the sun blazed with its heat and dyed the Benten Shrine on the pond's inner island a deeper red. In spite of the hot glare Otama walked on without opening the small parasol that she carried.

CHAPTER TWELVE

One night after his return from Muenzaka, Suezo found his wife, Otsune, sitting up alone after the children at her side had fallen asleep. Her usual practice was to doze off with them. On this occasion she knew her husband had come in under the mosquito net. She didn't turn her head toward him but kept it bent down.

His bed was laid out farther back near the wall and away from the other members of the family. A cushion, smoking set, and tea things had been arranged beside his pillow. He sat down, lit a cigarette over the charcoal fire in the smoking set, and said tenderly: "What's wrong? You're still awake?"

His wife said nothing.

Since she refused to accept this proposal of peace from him, he wouldn't make any further concessions. And deliberately ignoring her, he leaned back smoking.

"Where you been till now?" she asked, suddenly lifting her head and looking at him. Since they had hired a maid, her speech had gradually improved, but when alone with her husband, she lapsed into former vulgarities.

Suezo looked at her sharply, but remained silent. He realized that she had learned something, but since he couldn't measure its range, he could say nothing yet. He wasn't the kind of man who gives bait for the opposition's advantage.

"Now I know everything!" she cried, her voice shrill and trembling at the end of her words to the point of tears.

"You sound so mysterious. What do you know?" he said, like a man who is surprised by the unexpected but who still retains a gentle tone.

"You ask too much of a person! How can you pretend like that? Even without any shame!" Her husband's calm so excited her that her voice broke, and she was forced to wipe her eyes on the sleeve of her underwear.

"I still don't understand what you're talking about. Tell me what's on your mind. I can't even guess."

"Ah! Is that all you can say when I'm asking you where you been tonight? How could you do such a thing? Keeping a whore, telling me you got work to do!" Her red, flat-nosed face looked as if it had been boiled in tears, and a lock of hair was stuck to her cheek. Her wet, narrow eyes opened as wide as possible, and she looked directly into his face. Suddenly she crawled over and grabbed the hand holding his cigarette.

"Stop it!" he said, shaking her off. He put out the ashes that were scattered over the mats. But she grabbed his arm again and cried: "Is there another person like you in the whole world? You've made a lot of money, but is there anyone else who dresses up like a gentleman and leaves his wife with nothing? Without even a kimono? Letting her take care of the children! Yet—yet so conceited that he takes up with a whore!"

"Quit that crying! Do you hear?" Once more he brushed her hand away. "You'll wake the children. And your voice is carrying to the maid's room!" His wife could feel the force behind these whispered words.

Suddenly the younger child turned and spoke in his sleep, and Suezo's wife was forced to lower her voice. "After all," she said, pressing her face against her husband's chest and weeping silently, "what can I do?"

"You don't have to do a thing. Someone's got you all excited. Who told you I had a mistress or some secret woman or such nonsense?" As he spoke, he noticed her tangled hair against his body, and he speculated on a question one usually considers at a more leisurely moment: Why does an ugly woman insist on arranging her hair in a way that fits only a beautiful one? As the movement of her hair against him became less, he could at the same time feel the pressure from her heavy breasts, which had supplied ample nourishment for each of their children. "Who told you?" he asked again.

"Forget about that so long as it's true." The pressure of her breasts increased.

"But it's not true, so I do mind who's misinformed you. Tell me."

"All right. The wife of the fish dealer—Uwokin."

"What? What? I can't understand you chattering away like a monkey! Who's that? Who?"

Otsune pulled herself away from him and smiled in spite of herself.

"Uwokin's wife."

"That woman! Just as I thought." He took another cigarette and gazed tenderly at his wife's frantic face. "A newspaper is said to form the public's opinion against a particular person, but I've never seen it done. Maybe that gossip has done just that. She meddles with everything in the neighborhood. Who'd believe her words? Listen to me. I'll tell you the truth."

His wife felt as though she were stumbling in a fog, yet she wondered if she weren't being duped by his words, and she remained alert. Watching him closely, she tried to follow him carefully. But when her husband used the difficult words of a newspaper as he had done in speaking about public opinion, she was overwhelmed and submitted without comprehension.

He fixed his sympathetic face close to his wife's and, occasionally drawing on his cigarette, went on: "Well, do you remember that student Yoshida who used to visit us so often? Wears glasses with gold rims and silk clothes? He's working at Chiba now—in a hospital. But he still owes me more than he can pay in two or three years. He's become intimate with a woman he met while he was still a student at the dormitory. Up to a short while ago he kept her in a rented house in Nanamagari. Well, at the beginning he sent her a monthly allowance. But since the first of the year, she hasn't received even a note. So she came to me and asked me to get in touch with him for her. You might well wonder I know her! Yoshida told me to come over to Nanamagari to renew our agreement. He's afraid that if he comes here too often some of his friends will recognize him. And that's how she got to know me. I was embarrassed enough by what she asked me to do, but I took the trouble to look into this along with my own business. And it's still not settled. And the woman keeps begging me for things. Now I'm sorry to have gotten into this mess. It's getting to be more than I can handle. There was the question of money, and besides that, she asked me to find her a comfortable house—not too much rent—so I took the time to move her to a house that used to belong to the parents of a pawnbroker at Kiridoshi. What with this and that, I've stopped in at her new place several times for a smoke or two. And I guess that gave the neighbors something to talk about. A sewing teacher lives next door, and several young girls meet there. Naturally they like to gossip. Who'd be fool enough to hide a mistress in such a place?" He laughed contemptuously.

Suezo's wife had listened carefully, and a glow came into her small eyes. "Well," she said coquettishly, "maybe what you say's true, but you can't tell about visiting that kind of woman so often. I'm sure she'll give herself to any man for money."

"Don't talk as though you were stupid! Am I the kind of man who would make love to another woman when I have *you* for my wife? Can you point to a single time when I had anything to do with anyone else? We're too old to be jealous of each other. Isn't that so? Listen here! You'd better not go too far with this!"

Suezo sang a song of triumph in his heart, for his explanation had been more effective than he had hoped.

"But I can't help worrying. Women like your type."

"Nonsense! That's what people call adoring one's own idol."

"What?"

"I mean—you're the only one who likes me. Why! It's already past one. Come on, let's go to bed."

CHAPTER THIRTEEN

Suezo's explanation, a mixture of truth and fiction, reduced his wife's jealousy temporarily, but since its effect was naturally only palliative, the gossip and grumbling never stopped as long as the woman lived at Muenzaka. Even the maid told Suezo's wife about the scandal, saying among other things at different times: "Today, so-and-so saw our master go there." But Suezo was never at a loss for an excuse.

"Do you have to work at night?" his wife often asked him doubtfully.

"Who'd want to talk about loans in the early hours of the morning?" he retorted.

"But why," she continued, "didn't that kind of thing go on at night before this?"

"Because now my business is bigger."

Formerly Suezo had managed all the transactions by himself. Now, however, in addition to an office near his home, he had set up a kind of branch office at Ryusenji-machi in order to save the students time by letting them borrow money there instead of taking the long walk to his home. If a student wanted some money for a licensed prostitute at Nezu, he ran to Suezo's main office, but if he desired a Yoshiwara woman, he went to the branch office. And later on, by contacting this office, a student who wished to spend a night of rioting at the Nishinomiya, a restaurant in the Yoshiwara, could do so without paying if he had Suezo's permission. It was, so to speak, a commissariat organized at the frontier of debauchery.

About a month had passed without Suezo and his wife colliding into any battles. Until then his sophistry had been effective, but it was broken through from an unexpected quarter.

One cool morning when Suezo remained at home, Otsune and her maid went shopping. But as they were returning, the maid, who had been following her mistress, suddenly pulled at Otsune's sleeve.

"What are you up to?" Otsune demanded, her tone sharp and her eyes turning on the maid. But the servant stood silently and pointed to a young woman loitering in front of a shop on the left side of the street. Annoyed, Otsune looked in the direction indicated, but unconsciously she stopped short. At the same time the other woman turned around. She and Otsune stared at each other.

At first Otsune thought she was a geisha. "If she is," she said to herself as a first impression, "then no single geisha in Sukiya-machi can match her in beauty!" But a moment later

Otsune noticed that this woman lacked something that every geisha has—something that she was unable to define herself. If it could be described, I might explain it as exaggerated behavior. A geisha may dress herself in excellent taste, but it is more or less excessive. And this added quality deprives her of a certain degree of moderation, of gentility. Otsune felt that the other woman lacked this element of exaggerated behavior.

The woman in front of the shop, faintly conscious of some passerby stopping, had looked around. But not noticing anything special about the stranger, she had once more turned, and with her parasol propped between her knees, which were pulled inward, she looked for some small silver coins in the purse she had withdrawn from her sash.

The shop, on the southern side of Naka-cho, was called Tashigaraya, an unusual name that was parodied in an anonymous and satiric poem, for when it was read backwards it referred to an indecent act. Among the shop's goods was a kind of toothpowder packaged in a red paper bag with characters printed in gold. At that time toothpaste had not yet been imported, and this product was known for its smooth quality. After her early morning visit to her father, Otama had stopped to purchase some of it on the way home.

When Otsune had passed Otama by some several steps, her maid whispered: "Okusan! that's the woman of Muenzaka!" Otsune nodded silently, but the maid seemed disappointed, as though her words had no effect.

When Otsune had concluded that the woman was not a geisha, she had instinctively said: "Ah, the Muenzaka woman!" This intuition was aided by her recognition that the maid would not have tugged at her sleeve merely for the sake of calling her attention to a beautiful woman, but another unexpected item had influenced her: the parasol between Otama's knees.

A little more than a month ago, Otsune's husband had brought her a parasol as a gift on his return from Yokohama, one with a long handle out of proportion to the spread of the cloth. It would have been all right for a tall foreigner to toy with, but when the squat Otsune carried it, it resembled, to make an extreme comparison, a swaddling cloth attached to the top of a clothes rod. So Otsune had never used it. Its cloth was of white ground with a fine checkered pattern dyed in indigo. And Otsune had immediately recognized that the woman standing in front of the Tashigaraya owned the same kind of parasol.

Otsune and her maid turned toward the pond at the corner of a saké dealer's shop, and the maid said propitiatingly: "You see, Okusan, she's not a very pretty woman. Her face is flat and she's too tall!"

"You shouldn't speak ill of a person." This, said in a reprimanding tone, was the sole answer the maid got from her mistress, who walked on quickly. The maid followed with an injured expression on her face.

Otsune was inwardly raging. She was unable to think clearly. As she walked toward her house, she didn't know how to approach her husband or what to say to him, yet she felt compelled to attack him somehow, to speak, to say something. How delighted she had been when he had brought her that parasol, when he had actually given it to her! "I always had to ask for something from him," she thought. And when he had said: "For you. Take it," she couldn't help asking herself: "What's this for? Why's he turned kind so suddenly?" Now she knew that he had given it to her as an afterthought. That woman had asked him for one—she was certain of that now. And knowing nothing, she had thanked him, thanked him for a parasol she couldn't even use! "And not only that," she said to herself, "but he gave her that kimono and those ornaments in her hair. He gave them to her!"

Otsune glanced at her own sateen parasol. How different it was from that other one of foreign make! "Everything I'm wearing is different from hers!"

Nor did Otsune merely worry about herself. "A tight-sleeved kimono will do for the boy," Suezo had said. "As for the girl, don't waste money by dressing her up now. She's too young."

Were ever the wife and children of a man worth thousands and thousands of yen so poorly dressed as she and her children? And she thought that if Suezo had neglected them, that woman was to blame. Of course everything he had told her about Yoshida was a lie. And when Suezo had said: "She used to live at Nanamagari," he had been keeping her even then. Yes, that was the truth. He had made excuses for his own clothing and personal items, saying: "I have my position to think of," and Otsune thought how she might have said: "Yes, you have your woman to think of!"

He had taken that woman all over, but he had taken his own wife nowhere. "How unfair! And cruel!" she whispered.

Otsune was lost in these thoughts when she suddenly heard her maid cry out: "Why! where are you going, Okusan?"

Otsune stopped, startled. She had been walking with her head down and was about to pass her own house.

The maid laughed rudely.

CHAPTER FOURTEEN

Suezo had been at home reading his newspaper and smoking when Otsune went out shopping after clearing away the breakfast things, but when she returned, he was no longer there. This disappointed her, for on entering the house she had thought feverishly that if he were there, she would rush against him, and even though she couldn't speak to him, she would hold him somehow or other and strike with whatever words came into her mind.

But she had lunch to prepare and autumn kimonos to finish for the children. She mechanically went about these daily tasks, and eventually her wish to attack her husband subsided. How often she had challenged him violently! She was even prepared to crack her head against a stone wall if necessary, but when she attacked him, instead of the stone wall of resistance she expected, she found, to her surprise, a curtain that destroyed her energy. She would listen to her husband's sly reasoning stated with confidence, and then she would lose her resolution in spite of feeling that she hadn't been persuaded by him in the least. If she attacked him at such a time, she couldn't be certain that her first try would be successful.

She ate lunch with her children, settled a quarrel between them, sewed their clothes, prepared supper, gave them a bath, took one herself, and ate her dinner next to the burning mosquito smudge. After they had eaten, the children played themselves into tiredness outdoors. The maid finished her duties in the kitchen, laid out the beds, each in its appointed place, and hung the mosquito net. Otsune sent the children in to wash their hands and then to bed, spread a fly net over her husband's supper on his small table, and put a kettle on the fire in the charcoal brazier in the room next to the bedroom. This was the procedure she followed when Suezo did not return at night.

She had done all these tasks mechanically, and then taking a fan, got under the net and sat on her bed. Suddenly she imagined Suezo in the house of the woman. "I can't sit here," she said to herself. "But what can I do?"

Somehow at the center of her confusion she felt that she ought to walk to Muenzaka. Once when she had bought some bean cakes for the children, she had passed the house which Suezo had described as next to the sewing teacher's. She could identify it by its lattice door, the house that woman lived in. All she wanted was to see it. Would there be a light? Would she hear them whispering? If only she could know just that much! But no, she couldn't. In order to get out of her own house she would have to pass the maid's room along the corridor, and at this time of the year the paper sliding doors were removed. She was certain the maid was awake sewing.

"Where you going so late?" Matsu would ask her.

And what could she answer? She might say: "I'm just running out to buy something."

But Matsu would reply: "Certainly not! Let *me* go!"

No matter what Otsune wanted to do, she could not leave the house secretly. "Ah, what can I do?" she thought.

When she had returned home, she had wanted to go to her husband immediately, but what would she have said? She knew her own limitations, and her words would have been meaningless. And then her husband would have invented some tale to trick her and would have succeeded. "I'm not his match in a quarrel. He's too shrewd." She wondered if she weren't better off to keep quiet. But then what would the result have been? "He'd still have his Muenzaka whore, and he'd have no use for me!" What could she do? What?

Again and again her thoughts returned to the point from

which they had started. She felt muddled, and she was unable to separate one from the next. Yet somehow she realized that it would be useless to attack Suezo with violence, and she decided to give up that approach at least.

Suddenly her husband entered their room. Otsune intentionally picked up her round fan and, toying with its handle, remained silent.

"Oh?" said Suezo. "Strange looks again? What's wrong?" He was in such good humor that he wasn't in the least offended by his wife's failure to greet him as she usually did.

She still refused to speak. She had meant to avoid any sort of collision, yet upon seeing him she was so annoyed that it was almost impossible to keep herself from assailing him.

"Don't tell me you're worrying about nothing again? Forget it," he said, repeating the last words and putting his hand on his wife's shoulder. He shook her two or three times and then sat down on his bed.

"I'm thinking," she said, "about the future, about what to do with myself. I don't have a family to go back to, and I've got children too."

"What's that? Thinking about what to do with yourself? You don't have to do anything. The world's perfect as it is."

"Go on. You can speak in such a happy-go-lucky way because it's all the better for you if I become something else."

"You're really talking nonsense. That you should become something else? There's no need to change at all. Stay as you are!"

"Go ahead and mock me. You don't have to have anything more to do with me because you don't care if I'm here or not. No, that's wrong. I should have said that what you want is not having me around."

"You're all mixed up. Do you honestly mean that it'd be better for me if you weren't here? Just the opposite! I couldn't do without you. I need you for a number of things, not the least of which is to look after the children."

"Oh? A prettier mother will take my place and look after them. Though they'd be stepchildren."

"You're really confusing me. We're their parents. They can never be that."

"Are you sure? Do you really believe that? What an egotist

you are! Do you mean then to have everything just as it is?"

"Of course."

"Oh? Letting pretty and plain have the same parasols?"

"What did you say? Now what are you up to? Are you telling me the plot of a farce?"

"Yes. I'm not allowed to have a part in a serious play."

"Can't you talk about something more serious than a play? What do you mean by parasols?"

"You know what I mean."

"How can I? I haven't any idea about them."

"I'll tell you then. Do you remember when you bought me a parasol from Yokohama?"

"What about it?"

"You didn't buy it only for me."

"If I didn't, then who else did I buy it for?"

"No, that's not exactly what I mean, I suppose. You did buy it for me, isn't that right? Because the idea just occurred to you when you picked one out for the woman at Muenzaka."

Otsune had injected the subject of the parasols into their discussion, and now that the words had taken definite shape, she couldn't help remembering her earlier rage.

Suezo was startled by this direct hit from his wife, and he almost said aloud: "She's getting closer!" But he was able to look astonished and said: "Impossible! Do you mean, actually mean that—that the same parasol I bought for you is owned by Yoshida's woman?"

"Why not? Since you bought her the very same kind!" she said, her voice suddenly turning into a shriek.

"Is that the only thing you're getting excited about? What an idiot you are! Look. I'm warning you—don't carry your silliness too far. When I bought that parasol for you, they told me it had just come in as a sample. I'm certain of that. But the same kind must easily be available on the Ginza by now and in the neighborhood. I assure you that this case is the same as the play with the theme of the innocent man who was found guilty. Tell me, Otsune, have you met Yoshida's mistress? I don't see how you could have identified her.

"Nothing's easier than that. Everyone in the neighborhood knows her because she's such a *pearl!*"

Otsune's hatred was bound up in her words. Before this

she had let him take advantage of her with his lying, but now, as though she were vividly seeing the affair acted out in front of her eyes, nothing could make her feel that her husband's words were convincing enough.

All the while Suezo had been wondering how his wife had met his mistress and if they had spoken to each other, but he thought it would look bad for him at present if he asked Otsune any of the details.

"A *pearl* do you call her? Is that the kind of woman you call a pearl? I would think her face was too flat."

Otsune said nothing about this reply, but the fault Suezo had found with the fact of the hated woman appeased her somewhat.

During the night a conciliation again took place after the heated argument, but in Otsune's heart was the pain of a thorn not yet pulled out of flesh.

CHAPTER FIFTEEN

The atmosphere in Suezo's house was gradually becoming more and more gloomy. Otsune was often seen gazing absent-mindedly into space and neglecting her work. At such times she paid no attention to the children and scolded them if they bothered her. But then she suddenly realized what she had done and said to them: "I'm sorry. What was it you wanted?" And later she would cry alone.

When the maid said: "What shall I prepare today?" Otsune often failed to answer. Or she might say: "Oh? Anything, anything you wish."

Suezo's children were shunned by their classmates, who sometimes shouted at them: "Moneylenders! Moneylenders!" At Suezo's insistence Otsune had kept them unusually neat. But now they were seen playing in the streets with their hair full of dust and their clothing torn.

The maid went about grumbling at the carelessness of her mistress, and, like a horse that dawdles along the road with an unskilled rider on its back, also became negligent of her own duties so that the fish rotted in the cupboards and the vegetables dried up.

With his passion for order, Suezo found the slovenly state of his home painful. But he couldn't complain because he knew that the cause and the fault were his own. He had prided himself on his ability to correct others by alluding to their weaknesses in a lighthearted manner, but he found that his wife became even more violent when he tried to humor her.

He began to observe her secretly, and he was surprised to find that her strange behavior was more noticeable when he stayed at home, for when he was out of the house she seemed like a person who had awakened from a stupor, and she went about her household tasks. When he learned this fact after talking with the children and the maid, he was at first startled. With his shrewdness in logic he tried to account for her conduct. Her illness, he reasoned, grew worse in his presence because she was dissatisfied with his behavior. He had tried not to act like a coldhearted husband, and he had avoided any possibility of giving her the impression that there was any estrangement between them. But since he noticed that she was even more out of sorts when he purposely stayed at home, it seemed that his remedy only aggravated her illness. "I'll change my methods," he said to himself.

He began to leave earlier and return later than usual. But the results were worse. The first time he went away earlier, his wife merely looked up in surprise, but when he came back late, instead of giving him a moody glance, she marched upon him with "What you been doing out this long!" Her behavior suggested that she was no longer able to put up with the situation, that she had reached the limits of patience and suffering. And then she burst out crying.

From that time on, whenever he wanted to leave before the usual hour, she tried to stop him with force, saying: "Why so early?"

And when he began to explain, she said: "You're lying!"

But when he started outdoors in spite of her protests, she pleaded: "Wait! Don't go yet! There's something I must ask you!" She would keep him there by holding on to his clothes or by standing in front of the door and refusing to let him pass. She did this even in the presence of the maid.

Usually Suezo would pass over anything unpleasant by

joking about it in order not to make a great issue of a point, but sometimes the maid saw an ugly scene in which he shook off his clinging wife and she fell. But if Suezo said: "All right, I won't go. Tell me what you have to say," his wife would submit a series of difficult problems by no means solvable in a day.

"What," she would say, "do you want me to become?"

Sometimes she said: "The way things are, what will my future be?"

In short, Suezo's experiment of an early departure and a late return was totally ineffective in curing his wife of her illness.

He went about the problem in a different way. He realized that when he stayed at home his wife was worse. With this fact in mind he had attempted to be away, but then she had tried to force him to remain. This meant that she was deliberately making herself ill by deliberately keeping him at home. The situation reminded him of an experience he had had when the university medical school was still at Izumibashi.

A student, one Ikai, had borrowed money from him. The boy would pretend he was unconscious of his own appearance, wearing a pair of high clogs on his naked feet and striding with his left shoulder two or three inches higher than the other. Ikai had put off paying Suezo back, had even refused to rewrite his bond, and somehow had always evaded Suezo's pursuit.

One day at the corner of an alley Suezo had come upon him and asked: "Where are you running to?"

"Oh? Why—just over to the jujitsu master's across the way. I say—about that business of yours. You can expect me one of these days." And with that Ikai slipped away.

Suezo pretended to continue on ahead, but he secretly came back, stood at the corner, and spied on the boy. He saw him enter a high-class restaurant.

Suezo hurried through his business, and a short time later he dared to enter the restaurant, saying: "Where's that student Ikai?"

As you might have expected, Ikai was quite surprised to find Suezo there, but assuming his characteristic pose as a hero, called out: "Come into the room, Suezo! I've got a few geishas!" And then forcing the usurer to have some saké, he said: "Don't talk about business here. Just drink at my expense."

This had been Suezo's first experience with geishas, and he couldn't help thinking that one of them, Oshun by name, was quite a filly. She had been drinking too much and, sitting before Ikai, had begun to denounce him for some reason or other. Suezo hadn't forgotten her words: "Ikai-san, you want us to believe you're brave, the way you put on those grand airs of yours! But you're really nothing but a coward! Let me tell you something for your own benefit. A woman never loves a man who's not kind enough to hit her occasionally. Try to remember that!"

Suezo thought that this might be true not only of geishas but of women in general. Lately his own wife had tried to keep him near her with sulky looks and resistance. This meant that she wanted him to do something to her. "She wants me to hit her!" he said to himself. "Yes, that's it. To really strike her!"

He had forced her to work like an animal without giving her enough food, and, with her feminine qualities held back, she had been transformed into a kind of beast. But since she had moved into a new house and had acquired a servant to help her and to call her "Okusan," she had been raised to a human level and had actually become an ordinary woman. And now she wanted to be beaten like that geisha Oshun.

But what about him? He had pushed his own way through the world with a determination to make a fortune, and cared nothing about what others said of him. He had bowed before fledglings and called them master. It had been his principle that being kicked and trampled didn't matter as long as he made money. And for most of his life, no matter what place he was in or what person came to him, he had prostrated himself as flat as a spider. From what he had seen and learned of the men he had associated with, those who were very considerate of their superiors bullied the people below them and, when they were drunk, even struck their wives and children. But with him no one was higher or lower. He would have thrown himself at any man's feet if it had made him wealthier. Otherwise he had no use for such a person. He would have nothing to do with him, would ignore him. He wouldn't even take the trouble to lift his hand against him. He would rather think about his interest than waste his energies that way. He had treated his wife similarly.

Otsune wanted him to attack her. "Too bad for her, but she won't get that from me." If his debtors had been lemons, he would have squeezed them to the last drop of bitter juice, but he would fight no one.

These were Suezo's latest thoughts on the subject.

CHAPTER SIXTEEN

More and more people passed along Muenzaka. It was September, and the beginning of the term at the university saw the students returning from their homes to their lodgings.

The mornings were as cool as the nights, but the days were still hot. In Otama's house the bamboo blinds were still drawn, their unfaded green covering the window from top to bottom. Otama sat inside with nothing to do. She leaned against a post hung with fans and vacantly looked into the street. After three o'clock the students would pass in small groups. And she knew that whenever they came, the voices of the girls next door would rise like the sounds of so many young sparrows. And attracted by the noise, she would also glance out.

At that time most of the university students were of the type who were later to be called "henchmen." If there were a few gentlemen among them, they were about to graduate. Those who were fair and handsome were mostly unattractive to her, for they seemed shallow and conceited. And those who were not superficial and vain, even the bright students among them, were not preferable because from a woman's point of view they appeared too rough-mannered. Nevertheless, every afternoon Otama, without any particular interest, would look at the students walking past her window.

But one day she was startled by an awareness of something sprouting inside her. This embryo within her imagination had been conceived under the threshold of consciousness and, suddenly taking definite shape, had sprung out.

Her aim in life had been her father's happiness, so she had become a mistress, almost forcibly persuading the old man to accept. She knew she had degraded herself to the lowest limits, yet she had still sought a kind of spiritual comfort in the unselfishness of her choice. But when the person who supported her turned out to be a usurer, she did not know how to cope with this new source of misfortune. The thought tormented her, and she was unable to remove it. She had gone to her father to tell him about it and to ask him to share her pain. But when she had visited him and had seen him living comfortably for the first time, she didn't want to pour a drop of poison into the saké cup he held in his hand. Whatever pain the decision might cost her, she was determined to keep her sadness to herself. And when she had made this decision, the girl, who had always depended on others, had felt for the first time her own independence.

After that, she secretly began to watch what she said and did, and when Suezo came, she started to serve him self-consciously instead of accepting him frankly and sincerely as she had previously done. She would be with him in the room, but her real self was detached, watching the scene from the side. And there it would deride first Suezo and then the other Otama for being under his control. When she first became aware of this condition, she was shocked. But in time she accepted it, and she said to herself: "That's the way you should feel."

Her treatment of Suezo became more cordial but her heart more remote. She came to feel that he did not deserve her gratitude for the protection he gave her, nor could she feel obligated to him for what he did. She did not even feel sorry for him because of her indifference. Conversely, in spite of the fact that she had no accomplishment she could boast of, she couldn't help thinking: "Ah, to be only a usurer's possession all my life."

And watching the students in their walks along the street, she began to speculate: "Isn't there a hero out there? I'll be rescued!"

But when she suddenly found herself indulging in such fancies, she was startled.

It was at this point that Okada got to know her. She saw him as just another student who walked past her window, yet when she realized that even though he was eminently handsome, he didn't seem to be conceited, she suspected that there was something about him that made her feel tender toward him. She began to watch for him to pass in the street.

She didn't even know his name or address, but since they exchanged glances so often, she began to have a natural and familiar feeling toward the young man. Once, before she had realized what she was doing, she had even smiled at him, an act of the sort that eludes suppression at the moment when thought is relaxed and restraint paralyzed. She was not the kind of person who had any conscious intention of making him her lover.

When Okada took off his cap and greeted her for the first time, her heart seemed to lift, and she felt herself blushing. A woman has a keen intuition. And Otama clearly knew that Okada's action was done on impulse and not deliberately. She was pleased by this new phase of their friendship, which was casual and quiet and had the window as a sort of boundary. And she pictured to herself again and again the image of Okada at the moment he had bowed.

A mistress who resides in her keeper's home can have the usual protections, but one who lives by herself has troubles she alone knows about.

One day a man in a *happi* coat—a fellow about thirty years old—came to Otama's house and said: "I need some money. I've got to travel, but I can't walk with this wound on my foot."

Otama sent Ume out with a ten-sen piece wrapped in paper. The man opened the wrapper on the spot. "Ten sen? Is that all? It's a mistake!" And he tossed the coin back to her.

Ume was embarrassed, but picked it up and went back in, only to find the man rudely following her and taking a seat opposite Otama, who had been putting some charcoal into the fire. He talked incoherently at great length, bragging at first about having been in prison and then making sentimental complaints. Otama could smell saké on his breath.

She was afraid, yet she held back her tears. Under his eyes, she wrapped in a piece of paper two fifty-sen cardlike green notes current at that time and gave them to him. She found that he was more easily satisfied than she had hoped.

"They're halves, but two'll do. You're pretty clever. And you'll do all right in your life—you will." And with these words he swaggered out with faltering steps.

The incident made Otama feel helpless, and she learned to "buy" her neighbors. She would prepare a special dish and send it over to the sewing teacher, who lived alone.

Her name was Otei, and she was a matron over forty with a fair complexion. She still looked young, though it was difficult to say just why.

"Until I was thirty," she had told Otama, "I was a high-class servant at a marquis'. But I married and then lost my husband soon after." She spoke elegantly and boasted of her ability to write characters.

"Can you teach me how to write?" Otama had asked. So the woman lent her some copybooks.

One morning Otei came to the back door to thank Otama for what she had sent over the day before. In the course of their talk while Otei stood at the door, the woman said to Otama: "I believe you know Okada-san, isn't that so?"

Otama had never heard the name before, yet it flashed through her mind that the sewing teacher had referred to the student, that she had seen Okada greeting her, and that the situation compelled her to pretend she knew him. After a brief hesitation that was not perceptible to the other woman, Otama readily answered: "Yes, I do."

"He's handsome all right," said Otei, "and yet, I hear there's not a flaw in his conduct."

"You seem to know him well," said Otama boldly.

"Madame Kamijo tells me that none of the students at her lodging can match him." And with these words Otei returned to her house.

Otama felt as though she herself had been praised and repeated to herself: "Kamijo! Okada!"

CHAPTER SEVENTEEN

With the passing of time Suezo's visits to Otama grew even more frequent, for not only did he come without fail at night as he had previously done, but he began to visit at irregular periods during the day as well. These were moments of escape from his wife, who followed him about with the annoying demand: "You've got to do something for me!"

When he tried to persuade her that nothing had to be done and that it was all right to live as they had been living, she insisted: "I can't go on like this! I can't return to my parents' home! I can't give up my children! I'm getting old!" These were the objections she listed to any possible change in her life.

Suezo often repeated: "There's no need to make any change. We'll stay as we are."

And as they argued about these matters, Otsune would lose her temper and get so wrought up that Suezo would rush out of the house. He had always been able to reason logically and mathematically, so his wife's words were ridiculous and unintelligible to him. She seemed to him like a person struggling to find his way out of a room that has three walls and a door wide open behind him. All one could possibly say to such a creature was "Turn around!"

Her life was more comfortable than it had ever been, and she was neither oppressed nor restrained. True, the Muenzaka woman was a new factor for her, but Suezo had grown neither more cold nor more cruel because of the woman—examples to the contrary can certainly be found among other men—and he told himself: "I'm even kinder, more generous." Why, he wondered, didn't she see the door, still left wide open?

Of course there was a certain amount of selfishness in Suezo's thought, for even though Otsune was receiving more material comfort than she had in the past and her husband's words and attitude had not altered, it was unreasonable for him to expect his wife to think in the same way she had thought when Otama hadn't existed. Wasn't the woman a splinter in Otsune's eye? And didn't he have the slightest intention of pulling it out and giving his wife relief? Otsune was unable to think rationally and couldn't follow an argument; thus the door Suezo thought open was not so to her. In fact, a heavy shadow fell across the doorway where she had hoped to get a glimpse of ease for the present and hope for the future.

One morning after a quarrel Suezo rushed out of the house.

It was probably a few minutes past ten-thirty. He thought he would go directly to Muenzaka, but when he saw the maid and his children heading that way, he turned in another direction and hurried ahead aimlessly. Occasionally he muttered some foul words to himself.

As he reached Shohei-bashi, he saw a geisha coming from the opposite direction. He first imagined that she looked like Otama, but as he passed her he saw that her face was freckled. "My Otama's more beautiful," he thought. He was aware of an immediate sense of satisfaction, and stopping on the bridge, he watched the geisha's departure. Speculating that she was out shopping, he saw her disappear into an alley.

The Megane-bashi was a new bridge at that time, and Suezo walked along toward Yanagihara after crossing it. Suddenly he saw a man and a girl of twelve or thirteen at their customary places under a large parasol that had been planted in the soil by a willow tree near the river. The girl was doing a folk dance, and, as usual, a number of spectators were there. When Suezo stopped for a few minutes to watch, a man almost ran into him. Suezo's eyes detected the stranger quickly, and as Suezo turned back and met his gaze, the pickpocket hurried away. "What professional stupidity!" Suezo muttered to himself, at the same time feeling under his kimono to see if his wallet were still safe. The thief must have been an ignorant fellow, for when Suezo had had a quarrel with his wife, his nerves were so tense that he noticed things he wouldn't usually have seen. His natural sensitiveness was made the keener, so that a pickpocket could hardly conceive of robbing him before Suezo sensed his intention. But on such occasions his power of controlling himself—in which he took great pride —was lax to a slight degree, though so slight that ordinary people would not have noticed. A very sensitive observer might have discovered that Suezo was a little more talkative than usual and that there was something restless and unnatural about him as he spoke and behaved in an officiously kind manner.

Suezo thought he had been out for quite some time, but when he glanced at his watch as he continued along the edge of the river, it was eleven, only a half hour since his departure, perhaps less.

Though he didn't know where to go, he seemed, as he

passed along, like a person on an important business trip. A short distance before the turn at Imagawa Lane, he saw a house advertising "Rice-in-Tea." Inside, he could buy a tray of a few dishes with pickles and tea for only twenty sen. "I've a mind to go in," he thought, but since it was too early for lunch, he went on, turned right, and came into the broad street leading to Manaita-bashi.

Crossing, he noticed on the right side a shop dealing in various kinds of pet birds whose lively cries attracted the passersby. He stopped in front of the shop—you can still see it today—and looked up at the cages of parrots and parakeets hung high on the eaves, while on the floor he could see those of white doves and Korean pigeons. His glance moved to the cages of small songbirds piled up row after row at the back of the shop. These little birds sang the loudest and flew about in the liveliest fashion. Among them the greatest in number and the noisiest in their singing were the light-yellow imported canaries. And as his eye brushed past them, he was attracted to the linnets, which sat quietly in their vivid colors. It suddenly occurred to him to buy a pair for Otama. "She could feed them. How charming to see her with them!" he thought.

Suezo asked the price, and, although the old shopkeeper seemed indifferent to making a sale, bought a brace of linnets. After he had paid for them, the shopkeeper asked: "How will you carry them?"

"Don't they come with a cage?"

"Of course not."

Suezo almost had to beg the man to make another sale. The old man put his withered hand roughly into the cage and, catching two of the linnets, transferred them to an empty cage.

"Can you tell if they're male and female?" Suezo asked.

"I should think so," said the old man reluctantly.

As Suezo retraced his steps, he carried the cage with the two linnets. His pace was unhurried then, and every so often he would lift the cage and look inside. The mood in which he had fled his house seemed to have been wiped away, and the tender feeling usually hidden inside him came to the surface. Perhaps frightened by the swaying of the cage, the birds, sitting motionless with their wings folded, clung tightly to the perch.

Each time Suezo looked at them, he felt as though he wanted to hurry off to Muenzaka to hang the cage in Otama's window.

But coming along Imagawa Lane, he stopped at the house of "Rice-in-Tea" for lunch. He put the cage behind the tray the waitress brought him and looked at the pretty birds. And thinking all the while of Otama, he ate the rather inferior meal with gusto.

CHAPTER EIGHTEEN

Suezo's gift of the linnets to Otama provided the opportunity for Otama and Okada to speak to each other.

Their relationship reminds me of the weather of that autumn. At that time my father, who is now dead, had planted fall flowers in the garden behind his house, and one Sunday after returning from the Kamijo, I saw him tying stalks of flowers and agueweeds along with other types of plants to props of thin bamboo canes set in the ground, for a typhoon was expected September first, the so-called Two Hundred and Tenth Day. But the twenty-four hours passed calmly. Next we thought the Two Hundred and Twentieth Day would be the dreaded one, but it wasn't. For several days after that, restless and threatening clouds were seen. Sometimes it was so hot that people thought summer had come again. The southeast wind seemed to gather strength but died away. "Two Hundred and Tenth Day," said my father, "is being paid off in installments."

When I returned to the Kamijo from my home one Sunday evening, none of the students was in, and everything was quiet. I had gone to my room to relax, when I suddenly heard a match struck in the next room.

I wanted company, so I called out: "Is that you, Okada?"

I could hardly catch his reply. I had become friendly with him, and we had avoided all the polite formalities, but his answer struck me as odd.

I thought that he had been daydreaming. "Do you mind if I come in?" I asked, curious to see what was wrong.

"That's what I was hoping. I came back quite a while ago, and I've done nothing since. When I heard you, I was aroused and thought I'd light my lamp." This time he answered me in a clear voice.

I went into the corridor and opened the sliding doors to my friend's room. He was sitting with his elbows on his desk and was looking into the outside gloom through his open window, which directly faced the Iron Gate.

Okada turned to me, saying: "It's unusually sultry, isn't it? And with these two or three mosquitoes in my room. . . . Annoying pests!"

I went to the side of his desk and sat there informally, saying: "My father calls it paying for Two Hundred and Tenth in installments."

"What? Oh. That's an interesting way of putting it. Well, maybe he's right. The weather was so unsettled—first clouding and then clearing—that I couldn't decide whether to go out or stay in. So I spent all morning just lying here and reading the *Kimpeibai* you lent me. I got to the point where I couldn't think straight, so I went out for a walk after lunch. And something strange happened."

He said all this without looking at me. Instead he stared out the window.

"What was it?"

"I killed a snake," he said, turning toward me.

"And rescued a beauty, eh?"

"No, only a bird. But it had something to do with a beauty."

"Now this interests me! What's it about?"

CHAPTER NINETEEN

This is what Okada told me.

That afternoon the clouds moved quickly, and sporadic gusts of wind blew up the dust on the roads and then subsided. Okada's reading of his Chinese novel had given him a headache. He had gone out for some air and from habit had turned toward Muenzaka. He felt dizzy. In old Chinese novels, especially in the *Kimpeibai*, usually after every ten or twenty pages of innocent description, the author invariably throws in an indecent scene as if he were quite punctually fulfilling a promise.

"I must have looked awfully silly after reading that sort of book," said Okada.

When he came to the stone wall of Iwasaki's mansion on the right where the slope begins to descend, he saw a group of people on the left. They stood in front of the house he always looked at in passing. This was the only fact that Okada didn't tell me at that time. There were about ten women present, and more than half of them were young girls talking as noisily as a group of singing birds. Okada couldn't see anything, and without any particular curiosity he turned toward them and took two or three steps from the middle of the road.

The women were looking at a single point, and as he followed their glance, he discovered the cause of the confusion: a birdcage hung in the window of the house. No wonder the women were upset. When Okada saw the cage, he too was startled. A bird was rushing about inside, flapping its wings and shrieking. And looking more closely, Okada noticed a large snake with its head through the bars frightening the bird. The snake had wedged its way between two thin bamboo sticks without actually breaking the cage. But by forcing itself through, it had widened the gap between the bars as wide as its body.

Okada took a few steps forward to get a better view, and as a result he stood just behind the row of girls.

As if by common consent, the girls seemed relieved to have found a rescuer in him; they made room for him and pushed him forward, whereupon Okada discovered a new fact: the bird had not been alone.

The mate to the one fluttering about was trapped in the snake's mouth. And though only one of its wings was caught, it seemed to be dead, perhaps from fear, for its other wing drooped and its body looked like a piece of cotton.

At that moment a woman who was somewhat older than the rest and was apparently the mistress of the house said hurriedly to Okada, yet with modesty: "Can't you help? That awful snake!" And she added: "These girls from next door just came out, but it's beyond a woman's ability!"

"This lady here," one of the girls said, "heard the birds making noise, so she opened the sliding windows. We heard her scream when she saw the snake. So we dropped our work and ran over. But we can't do anything. And our teacher's stepped out for a moment. But even if she were here now, she couldn't help. She's too old." The sewing teacher took her holiday on every fifth day of the month instead of on Sunday. That was why the girls had come that day.

When Okada was telling me this, he said: "The woman was quite beautiful." But he didn't say that he had seen her before and that he had greeted her each time he passed her house.

Without answering, Okada stood under the cage and examined how the snake had got there. It had crawled up to the cage hanging in the window by approaching it from under the eaves between Otama's house and the house of the sewing teacher. Its body lay on a crossarm of the eave like a rope thrown over the support, and its tail was hidden around a post at the corner of the house. The snake was quite long. Probably, Okada thought, it had come from the thick growth of trees and grass on the estate across the street. And what with the strange weather, it had stayed out and come upon the birds.

Okada was temporarily confused by the situation. It was obvious that the women couldn't do anything.

"Do you have something sharp in the house?" he asked.

"Run in," said the mistress to a small girl, "and get a knife from the kitchen." Perhaps the girl was the maid, for even though she wore a summer kimono similar to the other girls', she had tucked up her sleeves with a purple sash.

The girl frowned as if to say: "I don't like the fish knife used for cutting snakes!"

"Don't worry," her mistress said, "I'll buy you a new one."

This satisfied the girl, and she ran in and quickly brought out the knife.

Okada took it from her impatiently, and letting his wooden clogs slip from his feet, he easily set one foot on the window sill; with gymnastic skill his left hand was already grasping the crossarm of the eave.

Okada knew that even though the knife was new it wasn't sharp, so he had no intention of cutting the snake in two at one blow. Pushing the snake's body against the beam with the knife, Okada moved the blade up and down a few times. He felt as though he were breaking glass as the scales of the body were pierced.

By this time the head of the bird had already been sucked into the snake's mouth, and when the snake felt itself being wounded, its body began writhing like the rise and fall of a wave. Yet it refused to disgorge its victim or to pull itself out of the cage.

After Okada had pushed and pulled the knife back and forth several times, the dull edge finally divided the snake in two like a chunk of meat on a chopping board. The lower part of its body, which had been in continual movement, first fell down with a thud on the beard grass just below the roof. But the other half, tumbling off the beam on which it had rested, dangled in the air, the head still stuck in the cage. The head had doubled in size because half the bird remained in the snake's mouth, and the bamboo bars, bent like bows, continued to hold it in place. The weight of the dead body inclined the cage about forty-five degrees. The surviving bird kept up its mad dance, its wings fluttering with an energy that was still wonderfully unexhausted.

Okada withdrew his hand from the supporting crossarm and jumped to the ground. At this point a few of the girls, who had watched breathlessly all the while, returned to the sewing teacher's house.

"We've got to take down the cage and pull out the snake's head," said Okada, looking at the mistress.

But neither she nor her maid had heart enough to go in to lower the linen string that kept the cage suspended, for the severed end of the dangling snake was bleeding on the windowsill.

Just then a madcap voice said: "Should I take it down?"

Everyone turned to the speaker, the errand boy of a saké dealer. He was the only one who had come along on this dreary Sunday afternoon while Okada was killing the snake. Holding a saké bottle bound with a rope in one hand and his account book in the other, the boy had stood there as an idle spectator. But when the lower portion of the snake landed on the grass, he had abandoned his bottle and book on the ground, and picking up a small stone, he had struck the raw flesh of the snake, every blow to the writhing body giving him much pleasure.

"I hate troubling you, but please do it for us," said the mistress politely. The maid took the boy inside, and soon he reappeared at the window, climbed on the board with the flowerpot on it, and stretching himself as far as he could, barely managed to reach the string with his outstretched arms.

"Do you want it?" he asked the maid, but when she shrank from the cage, he jumped off the windowsill and carried it through the house out to the entrance.

"I'm holding the cage, so you've got to wipe up the blood," the boy said. "It's on the mats too!" he proudly advised the girl, who followed him out.

"Oh, yes! Do that right away!" said her mistress, and the maid hurried back in.

Okada looked into the cage and saw the bird trembling on the perch. More than half of its mate's body was lost in the snake's mouth. Even as Okada had cut the snake apart, it had tried up to the last moment to swallow its victim.

"Do you want me to get the snake out?" the boy asked, turning to Okada.

"Think you can?" Okada said with a smile. "All right, but lift it to the middle of the bars first or else you'll break them."

The boy was successful, and pulling at the tail of the bird with his fingertips, he said: "Why! Even though it's dead, the devil won't let go!"

Thinking there was nothing further to see, the remaining pupils of the sewing teacher went inside.

"Well," said Okada, looking around, "I'd better go too."

Apparently lost in thought, the mistress suddenly turned to him on hearing his words. She tried to speak, but was forced to hesitate and turned her eyes away. At that moment she noticed a spot of blood on Okada's hand.

"Ah!" she cried. "You've stained your hand." And calling her girl, she had a wooden washbasin brought to the entrance.

When Okada told me the story, he did not give me a detailed account of the woman's attitude, but he said to me: "I don't know how she could have found a small stain of blood on my little finger."

While Okada was washing his hands, the errand boy, who had been attempting to pull the dead bird from the snake's throat, cried out: "Hey!"

The mistress of the house was standing beside Okada with a new towel folded in her hand, and hearing the boy's cry, she asked: "What's wrong?"

"The other bird nearly flew out the hole the snake made!" said the lad, putting his open hands on the cage.

"Keep your hand there," said Okada, wiping his fingers on the towel she had given him. Turning to her, he asked: "Do you have a piece of strong thread? We can tie up the damaged part of the cage and keep that other bird from flying out."

"Will a paper cord for tying hair do?" the mistress asked, after a moment's thought.

"All right," said Okada.

"Get it from the mirror stand," the woman said to her maid. When the girl came out, Okada took the cord from her and in a haphazard crisscross fashion tied up the opening left by the bent bars.

"Well," said Okada, going out the entrance, "I guess there's nothing more for me to do."

"I'm . . . then thank you," said the woman, unable to express herself as she followed him outside.

Turning to the boy, Okada said: "Since you've done so much already, how about throwing the snake away somewhere?"

"All right. I'll throw it in the deep part of the ditch at the bottom of the slope. Do you have a piece of rope?" he asked, looking around.

"I have some. Wait a minute please," said the mistress, whispering to her maid.

"Good-bye then," said Okada. And he went down the slope without turning his head.

Okada had gone this far, and facing me, he said: "You see, I exerted myself too much even for a beauty."

"I think you did," I said. But I added quite frankly: "Killing a snake for a beautiful woman is an interesting story. It's almost like a fairy tale. But it doesn't seem to me that your story's finished."

"What? Don't be foolish. If it weren't, do you think I'd have published it?"

I think he spoke without affectation, yet if it really ended there, I felt that he was sorry it did.

I had said that his story was similar to a fairy tale, but another idea occurred to me as I listened to him. But I didn't tell him this. It seemed to me that Okada, who had been reading the *Kimpeibai*, had met a woman like Kinren, the heroine of that novel.

All the students at the university, including those who never borrowed from Suezo, knew the usurer, the moneylender who had risen from the position of a school servant. But there were some who didn't know that the woman at Muenzaka was his mistress. Okada was among these. At that time I hadn't learned any of the details about her, yet I did know that the woman living next to the sewing teacher was Suezo's mistress.

In this instance I knew a little more than my friend.

CHAPTER TWENTY

On the day that Okada killed the snake, a sudden change took place in Otama after she had spoken to him, for up to that time they had only looked at one another.

A woman may have her heart set on a particular article, yet she may not go so far as to think of buying it. Each time she passes it, she may stop and look into the window where the article, say a ring or a watch, is on display. She doesn't go to that shop deliberately, but whenever she happens to be in the neighborhood on some business or other, she always makes it a point to examine it. Though she recognizes that she will never be able to buy the article, the renunciation and the desire to have it often give rise to a not too keen but rather faint and sweetly sad emotion. And she enjoys feeling it. On the other hand, a particular item she can afford and has determined to buy gives her acute pain. It troubles her so much that she gets restless. Even when she knows she can own it in a few days, she can hardly wait for the moment of possession. Occasionally she will even go out to get it on impulse—this in spite of heat or cold, darkness, rain, or snow. The woman who steals articles in a shop is not carved out of a different wood. But there is a distinction. A shoplifter blurs the line between the expensive items she yearns for and can't buy and articles she can buy if she has the money.

Otama's longing for Okada had been like that of a woman for an expensive article she admired from a distance, but he now turned into an article she wanted to buy.

His rescue of her bird had given her an opportunity for becoming better acquainted with him. Should she send Ume to him with some token of gratitude? And if so, what should it be? Perhaps some bean-jam buns from Fujimura's confectionery? But that would reveal a lack of wit: too commonplace, what anyone else would do. If she avoided the commonplace, say by making him an elbow-cushion sewed out of small pieces of colored cloth, he would smile at it as though it were a token of girlish love. She couldn't think of a good possibility. But supposing she had made a choice, would it be right for Ume to take it to him?

Only a few days ago at a shop on Naka-cho, she had had her name card printed, but only that attached to the gift would not be satisfactory. She wished to write a few lines, but how could she? She had only gone through elementary school, and since she had not had any time to improve her brushwork, she couldn't even write a note properly. The sewing teacher had told her she had worked at a lord's house, and if Otama had asked her to write, the sewing teacher would have done so at once. But Otama didn't want that. She had nothing to write that would have made her feel ashamed, yet she didn't want anyone else to know that she had written to Okada. Then what should she do?

In the same way that a route is followed back and forth along the same road, Otama thought this much through in straight order and then in reverse, abandoning the problem while she dressed and gave directions to Ume for the kitchen. But later she speculated about it once more.

And then Suezo arrived. While she poured him some saké, she began to think about the problem again.

"What's on your mind so much?" Suezo asked, reproaching her slightly.

"Why!" she said, smiling meaninglessly but with a hidden fluttering of her heart, "nothing at all."

Lately she had trained herself a great deal in not permitting her sharp-eyed lover to find out what she was concealing from him.

After Suezo had left, she dreamed that she had finally purchased a box of cakes and had rushed Ume out with it. But after the girl had gone, Otama discovered that she hadn't included a name card or a note. And she was startled into wakefulness.

Perhaps Okada had not taken a walk or she had missed him as he passed, for the day after the snake-killing, Otama didn't get a chance to look at the face she wanted so much to see. But the following day he was outside as usual. He glanced toward her window, yet it was so dark inside that he didn't recognize her. And the next day, at the time he usually came by, she took out a broom and swept the interior of the doorway. There was little dust to get rid of, and she occupied herself by placing first to the right and then to the left a pair of wooden clogs.

"Oh, dear!" said Ume, coming out of the kitchen. "Let me do that!"

"Don't trouble about it," said Otama. "You look after the cooking. I'm only doing this because I don't have anything else to do." And with these words the girl was driven back to the kitchen.

At that moment Okada came by with his usual greeting. Red to the ears, Otama stood bolt upright with the broom in her hand, but she let him walk on without saying a word.

She threw down her broom as though it were a pair of tongs that burned her hand, kicked off her sandals, and ran into the house.

Sitting before the charcoal brazier, she toyed with a pair of fire tongs over the kindled coals, thinking to herself: "I'm a fool! I thought that if I stared outside on such a cool day with the window open, it would look strange. So I purposely waited for him outside, pretending the place had to be swept. And yet—yet when he did come, I couldn't say a word! No matter how embarrassed I am in front of Suezo, I can say anything when I have a mind to. But why can't I speak to Okada-san? It's natural for me to thank him for his help. If I can't even give him my thanks, I'll never have the chance to talk to him. I'd be only too glad to send Ume with a gift, but since there's a problem in sending it to him and since I can't say anything to him, what else can I do? Why couldn't I speak just now? Well, yes, yes, I was about to. But I didn't know what to say! Calling his name would have been too familiar a way for me. It would be strange to say to a man who was looking at me: 'Why, good-day!' Now that I'm thinking about it, it's no wonder that I was so upset at the time. For even now when I've enough time to think, I don't have the right words. No, it's foolish to think in this way. I didn't have to say anything. All I had to do was run out to him at once. Then he certainly would have stopped. And once he had, I might have said: 'Please, I must thank you for your kindness of the other day.' That or some such thing."

Reasoning in this way and toying with the coals, she was surprised to find the lid of the iron kettle jumping up and down, and she slid it aside to let out the steam.

From that day on, she carried on a personal debate about the two alternatives, namely, to speak to Okada herself or to send Ume to him with a message. Meanwhile, with the days growing cooler in the evening, it would have looked strange to leave the window open. Usually the grounds were swept once in the morning, but after the broom incident Ume swept in the evening as well, leaving Otama no chance to do it herself.

Otama began to go to the public bath at a later hour in order to see Okada on the way, but the distance between her house and the bath at the foot of the slope was too short to give much of an opportunity for such a meeting. On the other hand, as the days advanced, it was becoming more awkward for her to send her maid to him.

She tried to resign herself temporarily by giving her thought a new direction: she hadn't yet thanked Okada. Since she hadn't returned the kindness which she was duty-bound to return, she was under an obligation to him. And it was obvious that he knew she was. It might be all the better for her to remain in that situation instead of trying to repay him in a clumsy way.

Still she wanted to get to know him better by using her obligation to him as a starting point for more contact. In fact, she was secretly giving the matter a great deal of thought in order to bring this about.

By nature Otama was a spirited woman, and in the few months since she had become Suezo's mistress, her painful experience of the outward contempt shown a mistress and the inward envy of the people around her enabled her to set the world at naught. Yet since she was basically a good woman and had not yet had too much experience in life, she felt it difficult to visit a university student at his lodging house.

There were some fine autumn days when she could keep her window open and exchange a salute with Okada, but their relationship remained unchanged since that memorable event, and no new state of intimacy developed from her having spoken to him once and having handed him a towel. And the situation was more than frustrating for her.

When Suezo came and talked with her over the charcoal brazier, she imagined what it would be like if Okada were there instead. At first, she felt she was being unfaithful, but she gradually came to feel no shame in speaking in tune with Suezo's words while thinking of Okada all the time. Moreover, when she submitted to Suezo, the image of Okada was behind her closed eyes. Sometimes they were together in her dreams. He was there without any troublesome arrangements to be made. But the moment she thought how happy she was, the man turned into Suezo instead of Okada. She would be startled and would awake, her nerves so strained that sometimes she cried out in a fret.

It was already November, and the days settled into Indian summer, so Otama had an excuse for keeping the window open to await Okada's daily walk. Previously a group of chilly and wet days had prevented her from seeing him for several days at a time, and she had become despondent. But she was of so mild a temperament that she didn't give her maid any trouble with unreasonable demands, nor did she give Suezo any sorry looks.

During these periods she would remain alone at the brazier with her elbows resting on its frame. She would sit silently and would seem so lost that one day Ume asked her: "Is anything wrong?"

But now that she could see Okada for many days in a row, she felt buoyant, and one morning she walked to her father's house with a light step.

She visited him without fail once a week, but she never stayed more than an hour. This was because her father refused to let her stay longer. When she called on him, he treated her always with the same kindness. And if he had any good things to serve, he brought them out and made tea for her. But, this finished, he said: "You'd better go now."

He said this not merely because of the impatience of an old man but also because he thought it selfish of him to detain his daughter for long when he had sent her out to do service. On her second or third visit she had informed him that she could stay longer because her master never came in the morning, but the old man wouldn't allow her to take her time.

"Well, it may be true," he had told her, "that as yet he hasn't come in the morning, but you can't be certain when he'll get there on some unexpected business. If you had asked him, and got his permission, it would be all right. But since you've only stopped here on your way from shopping, you shouldn't stay long. You wouldn't have any excuse if he thought you were idling away the time."

She knew her father would be offended if he learned about Suezo's profession, and she worried about this. When she visited him, she wanted to find out if he had discovered anything, but so far he was ignorant of the matter. It was natural that he remained so. Since moving here, he had started to rent books, and with his glasses on, he would sit all day and read. He borrowed histories with a romantic twist and biographies, both kinds of books exclusively printed in a particular script. If the keeper of the library showed him works of fiction and recommended them, the old man would say: "What? Those lies!"

At night, since he tired of reading, he would go to the variety hall where he would listen to the comic tales and hear the dramatic ballads being recited without questioning their truth or falsehood. But unless the teller was a particular favorite of his, he seldom went to the hall at Hirokoji, where the narratives were chiefly historical. These were his only hobbies, and since he never gossiped with outsiders, he didn't make any new friends. Therefore, he had little chance of hearing about Suezo's background.

Nevertheless, some of his neighbors wondered about the fair visitor to the old man's house, and at last they identified her as the usurer's mistress. If the neighbors on both sides of the old man's house had been chatterboxes, the unpleasant report might have somehow reached him in spite of the lack of communication between them. But fortunately they were not likely to disturb his peace of mind, for one of them was a minor clerk at a museum who spent all of his leisure hours collecting model copybooks of Chinese characters and learning how to use the brush, and the other man was an engraver who had remained at the old craft in spite of his fellow craftsmen's having abandoned the trade in order to make seals. Of the houses in the same row as the old man's, the trading places included only a noodle restaurant, a rice-cake shop, and a store dealing in combs.

Even before the old man heard his daughter's gentle greeting, he was conscious of her visit from the movement of the door and the light step of her clogs. He would put down the book he was reading and wait for her entrance into the room. If he could take off his glasses and look at his precious daughter, it was a festival day for him. Of course he could see better with his glasses on, but it seemed to him that they set up a barrier between him and Otama. Usually he had so much to tell her that after she had gone, he always remembered something or other left unsaid. But he never failed to say: "Give Suezo my greeting."

On that day when Otama had left her house in such a joyous mood, she also found her father in good humor, listened to him recite a Court tale, and ate a rice wafer of enormous size. "I bought it," he said, "at a branch shop that just opened at Hirokoji. It's from the famous bakery at O-senju."

He asked her many times during their talk: "Isn't it time to go?"

"Don't worry about it!" Otama said smiling. And she stayed there almost until noon.

She knew that if she had told her father that lately Suezo sometimes came at the most unexpected hours, the old man would have urged her more frequently to go back.

Otama had become more brazen and was not very anxious about Suezo's visits during her absence.

CHAPTER TWENTY-ONE

It was getting colder, and the boards outside the wooden drain from the sink were covered with a thick frost. Otama pitied Ume for having to draw water from the deep well with a long rope, and she bought the girl a pair of gloves. But Ume, who thought it too troublesome for her to put them on and take them off in doing kitchen work, guarded the gloves as a precious gift and still labored at the well with her bare hands. Otama would say: "Use hot water for washing clothes and for wiping the floors." But Ume's hands still got rough and chapped.

Otama said, sympathizing with her: "The worst thing's to keep your hands wet. Wipe them carefully and dry them each time you take them out of water."

She bought Ume a cake of soap for the purpose. But the girl's hands became rougher, and it pained Otama to see them in that condition. "Why do her hands get so red and cracked?" she wondered to herself. "I did as much work as she does now and mine weren't like that."

Otama had been in the habit of getting out of bed as soon as her eyes opened in the morning, but when Ume would say: "The sink's frozen. Stay where you are," her mistress remained under the covers.

As a safeguard against obscene thoughts, educators warn young people not to remain awake after going to bed and to get up as soon as they awaken, for in the vigors of youth, kept warm in bed, an image like the flower of a poisonous plant blooming in fire is apt to be engendered. At such times

Otama's imagination was unbridled. Her eyes would glow, and the flush would spread from her eyelids to her cheeks as though she had drunk too much saké.

One frosty morning after a starry night, Otama remained idly in bed for a long time—a habit she had acquired of late. Not until she saw the morning sun through the front window did she rise. And with only a narrow band around her kimono and a housecoat over it, she stood brushing her teeth in the open corridor outside her room. Suddenly the lattice door opened, and Ume's friendly voice greeted a visitor. Otama heard him enter the room.

"Hey there! You lazy riser!" said Suezo, sitting at the brazier.

"Oh! Excuse me," Otama said, hastily taking the toothbrush from her mouth. "You've come awfully early."

To Suezo's eyes, her smiling face, flushed somewhat as though the blood had rushed to her head, was lovelier than ever. Since coming to live at Muenzaka, she had become prettier by the day. At first Suezo admired the maiden-like naïveté of her manners. But lately they had changed, and he was even more enchanted. He saw this transformation as evidence of her understanding of love, and he was proud that she had learned what it was from him. In spite of his insight into reality, this was a ridiculous misunderstanding of his mistress' state of mind. At first she had served him faithfully, but as a result of her unhappiness and the reflectiveness caused by the sudden changes in her life, she had arrived at a self-consciousness which might almost be called impudent negligence. She had acquired that coolness of mind that most women in the world who do have it can reach only after experiences with many men. Suezo found it stimulating to be trifled with by her coolness. She had begun to neglect her duties with an increasing disregard for them, and she had become less tidy. But this untidiness fanned Suezo's passions to a higher intensity. He did not realize the basis for these alterations, so he was more charmed than before.

Squatting down and drawing a brass basin near her, Otama said: "Turn around, please."

"Why?" he asked, lighting a cigarette.

"Because I'm washing."

"Don't worry about me. Go ahead."

"But if you sit there staring at me, I can't."

"My, but you're proper. How's this? All right?" And with his back toward the corridor Suezo smoked his cigarette. "What an innocent thing she is," he thought.

Pushing back the top of her kimono and letting it slip off her shoulders, she washed herself quickly. She was not as careful as she usually was, but since she had no blemish to hide or smooth over by using makeup in secret, she had no reason to feel embarrassed at being observed.

Before long, Suezo turned around. While she was washing, she didn't notice that he had turned, but after finishing and drawing the mirror stand in front of her, she saw his face in it, the cigarette still in his mouth.

"Ah? So that's the kind of man you are!" she said, continuing to comb her hair.

A triangular patch of white skin revealing her neck and part of her back could be seen above the loosened kimono, and her soft arms, lifted high and exposed a few inches above the elbows, were sights Suezo never tired of.

"Don't rush," he said, fearing his silence would hurry her and making his tone deliberately easy. "I haven't come for anything in particular. When you asked me the other day when I'd be here, I told you this evening. But I've got to go to Chiba. If everything goes all right, I'll be able to come back tomorrow. If not, maybe the day after."

"Oh?" said Otama, wiping her comb and looking back at him. She made herself seem sad.

"Be a good child and wait for me," said Suezo humorously, putting his cigarette case in his kimono sleeve. Suddenly he got up and went out to the entrance.

Throwing her comb down, Otama said: "Oh, excuse me for not giving you even a cup of tea!" But when she stood up to see him off, he had already opened the door and was gone.

Ume brought Otama's breakfast in from the kitchen and, setting it down, bowed with her hands on the mats to apologize.

"What are you asking pardon for?" said Otama, sitting at

the brazier and knocking the ashes off the fire with a pair of charcoal tongs.

"For being late with the tea."

"Oh, is that all? Why, I was only being polite. Your master doesn't mind," she said, taking up her chopsticks.

Watching her eat, Ume thought Otama was unusually goodnatured, though for that matter her mistress was seldom in a bad temper. A trace of the smile with which Otama had said "What are you asking pardon for?" still remained on her faintly flushed cheeks. The maid wondered why Otama had smiled, but she was too simple to probe causes. And she felt infected by her mistress' happiness.

Looking at Ume's face and making herself even more cheerful, Otama said: "Ah, don't you want to go home?"

The maid's eyes rounded in wonder. As late as the second decade of the Meiji era, the customs of the tradesmen's houses in Edo were still kept up, although they were slowly dying out. As a result, even those servants whose families lived in the city were not easily allowed to go home except on Servants' Day.

"Well," Otama continued, "since your master's not expected this evening, you might as well go and spend the night with your family if you wish."

"Oh, do you mean it?" Ume did not doubt Otama's sincerity, but she felt that she was unworthy of the favor allowed her.

"Why should I lie? I'd never play tricks on you unfairly. Don't put away the breakfast things, but go on—now! Take all the time you want, and stay there for the night. But don't forget to come back early tomorrow morning."

"Oh, yes—I will!" Ume said, her face flushed with delight. She saw her father's house, his two or three rickshas in the entrance, her father resting on a cushion placed in a space scarcely wider than the cushion itself between a chest of drawers and the brazier. And, her father at work, Ume also pictured her mother there, her sidelocks hanging loosely over her cheeks, a thin sash holding up her sleeves and seldom taken off her shoulders. These images, like so many silhouettes, came alternately in rapid succession to Ume's mind.

When Otama had finished the meal, Ume took the tray

away. The girl felt she should wash the dishes even though she had been told to leave them, and when Otama came in with something folded in a piece of paper, Ume was rinsing the bowls and plates in a small wooden bucket filled with hot water.

"Oh, you're washing them even though I said not to? I'll do it for you. It's not much work for me to wash a few things. You did your hair last night, so it looks all right, don't you think? Hurry and dress. I've nothing to give you as a present for your parents, so take this."

Otama handed Ume the folded paper. Inside was a half-yen note, blue-colored and resembling a playing card.

Otama had hurried Ume off, and like a good maid with her sleeves tied up with a sash and her kimono ends tucked up under her obi, she went directly into the kitchen. She began the half-washed bowls and plates as though it were a pleasant pastime for her. She was used to such work and could do it far more quickly and thoroughly than Ume could, but now she went about it more slowly than a child playing with its toys. She cleaned one plate for five minutes. Her face was animated, rosy, her eyes distant.

Hopeful images entered her mind. Women pitiably waver in their decisions until they have made up their minds, yet once they have decided on their course of action, they rush forward like horses with blinders, looking neither to the right nor left. An obstacle which would frighten discreet men is nothing to determined women. They dare what men avoid, and sometimes they achieve an unusual success.

In Otama's desire to make overtures to Okada, she had delayed so long that a person observing her might have felt impatient because of her indecision. But now that Suezo had told her of his journey to Chiba, she made up her mind to dash toward the port like a ship under full sail in a favorable wind. Suezo, the obstacle in her way, was to remain overnight at Chiba, and the maid was to be at her parents'.

What a delight for Otama to find herself quite free of restraints until the following morning! Since everything had turned out so well for her, she thought that it could only be a good omen that she would attain her object. On that day of all days Okada would most certainly pass her house! Sometimes he came by twice, first in going and then in returning. And even if she missed him once, to do so twice was an impossibility. "I don't care what happens—I'll talk to him today! And once I speak, I'm sure he'll stop to talk," she told herself.

She was a degraded woman, true, a usurer's mistress. But she was even more beautiful than when she had been a virgin. In addition, misfortune had taught her what she wouldn't otherwise have known: somehow men were interested in her. And if this were the case, Okada could not look on her with absolute disfavor. No, that was out of the question. If he had disliked her, he would not have continued to bow to her whenever they saw each other. It was because of this same interest that he had killed the snake for her some time ago. She doubted that he would have offered his assistance if the event had happened at any other house. If it had not happened at her house, he wouldn't even have turned his eyes. Moreover, since she cared for him so much, at least some of her affection, if not all of it, must have been felt by him. "Why, even the birth of a child isn't as difficult as one thinks beforehand," she assured herself.

As she probed her thoughts, she was not aware that the water in the bucket had grown cold.

After she had put away the trays on the shelf, she sat down at her usual place before the charcoal brazier. She felt restless. She took up the pair of tongs and stirred the ashes that Ume had sifted smooth. Then she got up to change into her kimono.

"I'll go to the hairdresser's," she decided.

A good-natured woman who came to Otama to arrange her hair had recommended this shop for special occasions. But up to that time Otama had never gone there.

CHAPTER TWENTY-TWO

In a European book of children's stories, there is a tale about a peg. I can't remember it well, but it was about a farmer's son who got into a series of difficulties on his journey because the peg in his cartwheel kept coming out. In the story I'm telling now, a mackerel boiled in bean paste had the same effect as that peg.

I was barely able to keep from starving because of the meager dormitory and boardinghouse meals, yet there was one dish that made my flesh creep. No matter how much air there is in the room or how clean the serving tray is, the moment I see this food, I recall the indescribable odors of the dormitory dining room. When I am served boiled fish with cooked seaweed and wheat gluten cakes, I have that hallucination of smell. And if the boiled fish is mackerel made in bean paste, the sensation is at its peak.

This dish, much to my disgust, was once served for supper at the Kamijo. The maid had set my tray down, but seeing me hesitate in lifting up my chopsticks, which I usually didn't do, she said: "Don't you like mackerel?"

"Well, I don't dislike it. When it's broiled, I can eat it with pleasure. But not when it's boiled in bean paste."

"Oh, I'm sorry. The *okamisan* didn't know. Do you want some eggs instead?" she said, preparing to rise.

"Wait a while," I told her. "I'm not hungry yet, so I'll go out for a walk. Make it look all right to the landlady. Don't say I dislike it. I don't want to give her any trouble."

"But I feel so sorry—"

"Oh forget it."

Seeing me stand to put on my *hakama*, the maid took the tray out into the corridor.

"Are you in, Okada?" I said, calling out to my neighbor.

"Do you want anything?" he asked, his voice clear.

"Nothing in particular, but I'm off for a walk. And I'm going to get some sukiyaki at a restaurant on my way back. Come on along."

"All right. There's something I've been wanting to tell you anyway."

I took my cap off the hook and went out of the Kamijo with my friend. I guess it was after four. Neither of us had talked about the direction to take, but we turned right at the lodging house gate.

Just as we were about to go down Muenzaka, I nudged Okada, saying: "Look—there she is!"

"Who?" he asked, in spite of knowing whom I meant, for he turned to the left side to glance at the house with the lattice door.

Otama was standing in front of her house. She would have looked beautiful even if she had been ill. But a young, healthy beauty is made even more beautiful by using makeup, and she was just that. I couldn't tell why, but there was a difference from her usual appearance. I thought she was lovelier than ever. And the radiance of her face dazzled me.

I felt she was transformed as she fixed her eyes on Okada. When he took off his cap, I noticed how upset he was, and I saw him unconsciously quicken his step.

Having the liberty of a third party, I looked back several times and saw that she continued to watch Okada.

He went down the slope with his head bent and without relaxing his hurried gait. I followed him in silence. Opposing thoughts tumbled inside me. They arose from the desire to put myself in Okada's place. But the idea sickened me. Denying my wish, I thought to myself that I couldn't be that base—yet I was annoyed at not being able to repress it effectively.

The thought of putting myself in Okada's place was not that I wanted to surrender to the woman's temptations. I had simply felt that I would have been happy if, like Okada, I had been loved by such a beauty. But how would I have behaved then? I would have kept my freedom of choice, but I wouldn't have run as Okada had just done. I would have visited her, talked with her. I would have kept my virginity, but I would have gone so far as to stop at her house, have conversations with her, love her as one loves a sister. I would have helped her. I would have rescued her from the dirty mud. My imagination had gone that far!

We walked on without speaking until we came to the crossing at the bottom of the slope. After we had passed the police box, I was finally able to talk to Okada.

"Look here," I said, "the situation's getting dangerous."

"What? What's getting dangerous?"

"Don't pretend with me. Why, you must have been thinking about that woman ever since you saw her. I turned around a number of times, and she was always watching you. She's probably standing there right now and looking in this direction. It's just as it's described in the *Saden:* 'His eyes received her and saw her off.' Only in your case it's just the reverse."

"That's enough about her! Since you're the only person I confided in about how I got to know her, you shouldn't tease me."

We reached the edge of the pond and stopped for a moment.

"Should we go that way?" Okada asked, pointing to the northern end of the pond.

I agreed and turned to the left. About ten steps later, I looked at the two-storied houses on the side of the street and said as though talking to myself: "Those houses belong to Fukuchi and Suezo."

"They're a fine contrast. Though I hear the journalist hasn't much integrity either."

"He's a politician too, and a politician," I said without giving much thought to the question, "no matter how he may live, is not free from slander." Perhaps I wanted to make the distance between these two men as wide as possible.

As we talked on in this way and crossed a small bridge leading to the north end of the pond, we saw a young man in student uniform standing at the water's edge and watching something. At our approach he shouted: "Hello there."

It was Ishihara, a student who was interested in jujitsu and who read only those books related to his major subject. Neither Okada nor I knew him well, but we didn't dislike him.

"What are you looking at around here?" I asked.

Without answering he pointed across the water. We stared in that direction through the gray vagueness of the evening air. In those days, rushes grew all over the section of the pond from the Nezu Ditch to where we were now standing. The withered stalks became more and more sparse toward the center of the pond, where only dried-up lotus leaves like bunches of rags and seed sacs like sponges were seen here and there with stems broken at various heights into acute angles. They lent a picturesque desolation to the scene. Among these bitumen-colored stems and over the dark gray surface of the water reflecting faint lights, we saw a dozen wild geese slowly moving back and forth. Some rested motionless on the water.

"Can you throw that far with a stone?" Ishihara asked, turning to Okada.

"Of course, but I don't know if I can hit anything or not."

"Go ahead. Try."

Okada hesitated. "They're going to sleep, aren't they? It's cruel to throw at them."

Ishihara laughed. "Don't be sentimental! If you don't, then I will."

"Then I'll make them fly away," said Okada, reluctantly picking up a stone.

The small stone hissed faintly through the air. I watched where it landed, and I saw the neck of a goose drop down. At the same time a few flapped their wings and, uttering cries, dispersed and glided over the water. But they did not rise high into the air. The one that was hit remained where it was.

"Excellent shot!" Ishihara cried. He looked at the surface of the water for a short time and said: "I'll get it. But help me a little."

"How can you?" Okada asked. Like him, I was eager to hear the answer.

"Now's not a good time," said Ishihara. "In half an hour it'll be dark. And then I can easily get it. I won't need your help in actually going out there, but be here then and do what I tell you. And then I'll treat you to a feast!"

"It sounds all right," said Okada. "But what will you do until then?"

"I'll wander around here. You two go wherever you wish. If all three of us stay, it'll attract attention."

"Then let's go once around the pond," I suggested to Okada.

He agreed, and we started out.

CHAPTER TWENTY-THREE

Okada and I crossed the end of Hanazono-cho and went toward the stone steps leading to the Toshogu Shrine. For some time we walked in silence.

"Poor bird," said Okada, as if speaking to himself.

Without any logical connection the woman of Muenzaka came into my mind.

"You see," Okada said, this time to me, "I only meant to throw in their direction."

"I know," I said, still thinking of the woman.

After some time I added: "But it'll be interesting to see how Ishihara intends to get the bird."

"Yes," said Okada, walking on and thinking of something. Perhaps the wild goose occupied his thoughts.

As we turned south at the foot of the stone steps, we went on toward the Benten Shrine, but the death of the bird had depressed us and had broken our talk into fragments.

Passing before the entrance of the shrine, Okada suddenly said: "I almost forgot what I wanted to tell you." It seemed as though it were an effort for him to turn his thoughts in another direction.

His news startled me. He had planned to tell me in my room that night, but he had gone out at my invitation. And then it had occurred to him to reveal it at the restaurant, but since that now seemed unlikely, he had decided to explain it during our walk. It was this.

"I'm going abroad before graduation. I've already got my passport from the Foreign Ministry. And I've sent in the notice that I'm giving up graduating. You know the German professor who's been studying endemic diseases in the Orient. Well, he employed me under the arrangement that he would give me four thousand marks for the trip to Germany and back, along with two hundred marks each month. He was looking for a student who could read Chinese and also speak German. Professor Baelz had recommended me, so I went and took the examination. I had to translate several passages from classical Chinese medical books into German, but I passed. And I got the contract right then."

The Leipzig University professor would take Okada and help him pass his doctoral examinations. Okada had received permission to use as his graduation thesis the medical literature of the Orient to be translated by him for the doctor.

"I'm moving from the Kamijo tomorrow to the doctor's house at Tsukiji. I'll pack the books he's collected in China and Japan. Then I'll help him on a research project in Kyushu. And from there we take a Messageries Maritimes ship."

I paused often in our walk to say how surprised I was and to praise Okada's determination, but I was under the impression that we had gone very slowly as we spoke. Yet when he finished, I looked at my watch and found that only ten minutes had passed since we left Ishihara. And we had already walked two-thirds of the way around the pond and were coming to the end of Ike-no-hata Street.

"It's too soon to go on ahead," I said.

"Let's have a bowl of noodles," Okada suggested.

"All right," I said at once, and we retraced our steps to the restaurant.

While eating, Okada said: "It's too bad I have to give up graduation when I'm so near to it. But if I missed this chance, I'd never be able to go to Europe. I doubt if I could ever get abroad at government expense."

"Well, it's too good an opportunity to miss. Who cares about graduating? If you get a doctor's certificate in Europe, it's certainly no disadvantage. And even if you don't, it won't matter much."

"That's what I've been thinking. Going abroad will give me better qualifications—it's my one concession to the way of the world."

"Are you ready to go? I suppose you've been quite busy with preparations."

"No, I'm going in these clothes. The doctor told me that Western suits made by Japanese tailors won't do in Europe."

"I can imagine. I once remember reading that the editor of the *Kagetsu Shinshi* went aboard at Yokohama with no preparations at all."

"I read that article too. According to it, he didn't even let his family know he was leaving. But I wrote a long letter to my parents."

"How I envy you! You'll have the professor, and you'll never feel inconvenienced on your trip. I can't even imagine what it will be like."

"Neither can I. But yesterday I did visit Professor Shokei Shibata. He's taken an interest in me. And when I told him, he gave me a guidebook he had written."

"Oh? I didn't know he'd even written one."

"He wrote it all right, but it's not for sale. He told me he had it printed to give to country bumpkins!"

As we talked on in this way, I suddenly realized that we had only five minutes before our appointment. We hurried out of the restaurant and went to meet Ishihara, who was waiting for us. The pond was in darkness, and only the Benten Shrine's red color was visible in the gathering haze.

Ishihara, who had been looking for us, brought us to the edge of the water and said: "It's all right now. All the other geese have shifted their positions. I'll start now. You two stand here and give me directions. Look. About six yards from here you see a broken lotus stem falling to the right. Now in line with that is another stem lower than that one and falling to the left. I have to make my way along that line. Now, if you see me get off even a bit, shout out to me either 'right' or 'left' and put me straight."

"We understand," said Okada. "We've studied the principle of parallax! But isn't the water too deep for you?"

"Not enough to go over my head," Ishihara said, taking off his clothes.

When he stepped into the pond, the muddy water was just above his knees. Raising one leg at a time and planting each alternately, he plodded on like a heron. The water was deeper in certain areas than in others.

Soon Ishihara passed the two stems of lotus, and presently Okada directed him to the right, whereupon Ishihara went a little in that direction. "Left!" Okada shouted next, for Ishihara had gone too far over.

Suddenly Ishihara stopped short, stooped, and at once began to retrace his steps. And by the time he had passed the farther lotus stem, we could see the game hanging from his right hand.

He reached the edge of the water, the mud staining his legs only to the middle of his thighs. The prize was an uncommonly large bird. After Ishihara had washed carelessly, he dressed quickly. Few passersby ever came to this section of the pond, and no one had appeared during the time Ishihara was in the water and had come back.

"How should we carry it?" I asked.

Putting on his *hakama*, Ishihara said: "How about Okada's putting it under his cloak? It's bigger than ours. And I'll have the bird cooked at my lodging!"

He lived in a rented room of a private family. Apparently his landlady's only virtue was her wickedness, and we could stop her from telling what we had done by giving her a piece of the goose. The house was somewhere in the back part of a winding alley.

Ishihara briefly explained the course we would take. We could approach his house from two ways. One route lay south through Kiridoshi, the other north through Muenzaka. These two directions formed a circle around the Iwasaki mansion. There was little difference in the distance between them. But that wasn't the present question. It was the police box, and there was one each way.

We weighed the advantages and disadvantages, and we concluded that we had better not take the more frequented way through Kiridoshi but the less traveled one through Muenzaka. The best procedure was for Okada to carry the goose under his cloak and for the two of us to flank him and make him look less conspicuous.

Okada seemed resigned; he smiled and took the bird. But in whatever way he carried it, the tail feathers emerged a few inches from the edge of his cloak. In addition, the lower part of Okada's cloak was expanded in a curious way so that he looked like a circular cone.

It was up to Ishihara and me to make Okada appear as natural as possible.

CHAPTER TWENTY-FOUR

"All right," Ishihara said, "let's start." And we set out with Okada between us. From the first, our concern had been the police box at the crossing below Muenzaka. So Ishihara lectured us on our mental attitude in passing the box in question. It was, to sum up what I heard, that we should not waver in our equilibrium of mind; that if we wavered, there would be a gap; and that if there were a gap, it would give the antagonist the advantage.

"The tiger doesn't eat a drunken man," Ishihara said, quoting an old Chinese proverb.

It seemed to me that his speech was nothing more than what his jujitsu master had told him.

"Do you mean then," said Okada playfully, "that a policeman's a tiger and we are drunks?"

"*Silentium!*" exclaimed Ishihara.

We were approaching the corner to go to Muenzaka. As we turned up the slope, we saw a policeman standing at the crossing.

Ishihara, who was close to Okada's left side, said suddenly: "Do you know the formula for calculating the volume of a cone? What? You don't! It's simple. Since volume is one-third the area of the base times the height, if the base is a circle, you can get it by one-third of the radius squared times pi times the height. And if you remember that pi equals 3.1416, it's the simplest of problems. I know the value of pi up to the eighth decimal. 3.14159265! For all practical purposes, the figures after that are unnecessary."

During this speech we passed the crossing. The policeman was in front of his station on the left side of the narrow street we were coming along; stationed there, he was watching a ricksha running from Kaya-cho toward Nezu. He looked at us for only a moment.

"Why," I asked Ishihara, "did you start calculating the volume of a cone?"

But at the same time I recognized a woman in the middle of the slope looking toward us. My heart felt a strange shock. All the way from the northern end of the pond I had been thinking about her instead of the policeman at his box. I didn't know why, but I imagined she would be waiting for Okada. And I hadn't been wrong. She had come down the slope about two or three houses from her own.

I was careful not to attract Ishihara's attention, and I looked quickly at the woman and Okada, from one to the other. His delicate coloring was a shade deeper. He brushed the vizor of his cap, pretending to set it right. The woman's face seemed as hard as stone. But her eyes, opened beautifully wide, seemed to contain an infinite wistfulness of parting.

Ishihara's answer to my question was mere sound in my

ears. He had probably said that he thought of the formula because of the shape of Okada's cloak.

Ishihara had also noticed the woman, but his only comment was "There's a beauty!" And then he continued his speech, adding: "I taught you the secret of the mind's equilibrium. You've not had any training in it, and I was afraid you couldn't carry off our scheme at the critical moment. So I devised a plan to shift your attention. Anything might have done, but I thought of the cone as I just explained it. At any rate, my technique has met with success! Thanks to the formula of a cone, you were able to get beyond the policeman and maintain an *unbefangen* attitude!"

The three of us came to a portion of the road turning east along the Iwasaki mansion. In an alley that was not wide enough to accommodate two rickshas, we were in little danger of being seen. Ishihara left Okada's side and marched before us like a leader.

I looked back once more, but the woman was no longer in sight.

We stayed at Ishihara's until late that night. It might be said that we were forced to keep Ishihara company while he drank a great deal of saké and ate the flesh of the goose. And since Okada said nothing about his trip abroad, I had to hold back my desire to discuss it at length. Instead, I was forced to listen to their personal experiences in the regatta.

When we returned to the Kamijo, I went to bed at once. I was drunk and tired, so I couldn't talk to Okada. And when I came back from the university the next day, I found that he had already gone.

Just as great events happen because of a peg, a dish of boiled mackerel at a Kamijo supper prevented Otama and Okada from ever meeting each other. This is not all of that story. But the events beyond it are outside the present narrative.

Now that I have written this, I have counted on my fingers and discovered that thirty-five years have passed since then. I learned half the story during my close association with Okada. And I learned the other half from Otama, with whom I accidentally became acquainted after Okada had left the country.

In the same way that one receives an image through a stereoscope, the two pictures set together under the lens, I created this story by comparing and combining what I knew earlier and what I heard later.

Some of my readers may ask: "How did you get to know Otama? And when did you hear the story from her?"

But as I said before, the answers to those questions are beyond the scope of my story. It is unnecessary to say that I lack the requisites that would qualify me to be Otama's lover; still, let me warn my readers that it is best not to indulge in fruitless speculation.

RYUNOSUKE AKUTAGAWA
"The Hell Screen"
("Jigokuhen," 1918)

Translated by Takashi Kojima

Ryunosuke Akutagawa (1892–1927) was born in Tokyo and attended Tokyo University as a student of English literature. While in college, Akutagawa collaborated with his friends Masao Kume, Kan Kikuchi, Yuzo Yamamoto, and others in the publication of the literary magazine *New Current of Thought* (*Shin Shicho*). His early works appeared in this magazine as well as in others, and his mastery of fictional technique was immediately recognized. "Yam Porridge" ("Imogayu," 1916), "The Handkerchief" ("Hankechi," 1916), "Rashomon" (1917), "Tobacco and a Demon" ("Tabako to Akuma," 1917), "The Puppeteer" ("Kairaishi," 1919), and "The Revolving Lantern" ("Kagedoro", 1920), all belonging to his early period, are fresh, masterfully wrought short stories describing the ludicrousness of man unaware of his self-contradiction.

Akutagawa's belief that the sole purpose of living is to create art soon reduced his life to "hell." The insoluble conflict of life and art, already shown in "The Hell Screen," was the theme of such stories as "Genkaku's Mountain Retreat" ("Genkaku Sanbo," 1927) and *Kappa* (1927). His growing pessimism—the conviction that his own life was losing meaning—makes his later works gloomy. In his desperate struggle to find the meaning of life, Akutagawa produced semiconfessional works like "Cogwheels" ("Haguruma," 1927) and "The Life of a Certain Fool" ("Aru Aho no Issho," 1927), but all in vain, and he committed suicide in July, 1927.

In revolt against literary naturalism, Akutagawa was at times attracted to the works of Anatole France, Charles Baudelaire, August Strindberg, and Edgar Allan Poe. A large number of his stories, however, derive from old tales in Japanese, and sometimes Chinese, legends. In his short career as a short-story writer, Akutagawa produced well over a hundred stories and some essays. Most of his well-known stories have been translated into several Western languages.

Akutagawa's style of writing is characterized by a sense of precision in wording and construction, which may remind one of Poe. The Akutagawa Prize, established in his honor several years after his death, has attained in Japan much the same prestige as the Prix Goncourt in France.

I

The Grand Lord of Horikawa is the greatest lord that Japan ever had. Her later generations will never see such a great lord again. Rumor has it that before his birth, Daitoku-Myo-O [1] appeared to her ladyship, his mother, in a dream. From birth he was a most extraordinary man. Everything he did was beyond ordinary expectations. To mention just a few examples, the grandeur and bold design of his mansion at Horikawa are far beyond our mediocre conceptions. Some say that his character and conduct parallel those of the Emperor I [2] of China and the Emperor Yang.[3] But this comparison may well be likened to the blind man's description of the elephant. For it was far from his intention to enjoy a monopoly of all glory and luxury. He was a man of great stature who would rather share pleasures with all the people under his rule.

Only so great a ruler could have been able to pass unhurt through the gruesome scene of the veritable pandemonium enacted in front of the Imperial palace. Moreover, it was undoubtedly his authoritative command that exorcised the nightly hauntings of the spirit of the late Minister of the Left [4] to his mansion, the gardens of which were a famed

[1] Daitoku-Myo-O: A three-faced and six-armed god that guards the west, astride a large white bull, being one of the five great kings that appear in the Chanavyua sutra.

[2] The First Emperor of China established the great Chinese Empire in 221 B.C.

[3] The Chinese Emperor Yang established the Sui Dynasty in A.D. 604.

[4] The Minister of the Left was, next to the Premier, the highest Minister of State along with the Minister of the Right.

imitation of the picturesque scenery of Shiogama.[5] Horikawa had such great influence that all the people of Kyoto, young and old, respected him as highly as if he were a Buddha incarnate.

Once on his way home from a plum-blossom exhibit at the Imperial Court, one of the bulls pulling his cart broke away and injured an old man who happened to be passing by. It is rumored that even in such an accident the old man, clasping his hands together in reverence, expressed his gratitude for having been knocked over by the Grand Lord's bull.

Thus his life was full of memorable anecdotes which might well be handed down to posterity. At a certain Imperial banquet he made a gift of thirty white horses. Once when the construction work of the main bridge was snagged, he made a human pillar of his favorite boy attendant to propitiate the wrath of the god. Years ago he had a Chinese priest, who had introduced the medical art of a celebrated Chinese physician, lance a carbuncle on his hip. It is impossible to enumerate all such anecdotes. But of all these anecdotes, none inspires one with such overpowering horror as the history of the hell screen which is now among the Lord's family treasures. Even the Grand Lord, whose presence of mind had never been shaken, seemed to have been extraordinarily shocked. Furthermore, his attendants were all frightened out of their wits. Having served him for more than twenty years, I had never witnessed such a terrifying spectacle.

But before telling you the story, I have to tell you about Yoshihide who made a ghostly painting of Hell on the screen.

II

Now as for Yoshihide, some people still remember him. He was such a celebrated master of painting that no contemporary could equal him. When what I am going to relate happened, he must have been well past his fiftieth year. He was stunted in growth, and was a sinister-looking old man, all skin and bones. When he came to the Grand Lord's mansion,

[5] Shiogama is a picturesque fishing village in the northeast of Japan.

he would often wear a clove-dyed hunting suit and soft headgear. He was extremely mean in nature, and his noticeably red lips, unusually youthful for his age, reminded one of an uncanny animal-like mind. Some said, that he had got his red lips because of his habit of licking his paintbrush, although I doubt if this were true. Some slanderous people said that he was like a monkey in appearance and behavior, and nicknamed him "Saruhide" [6] (monkey hide).

This Saruhide had an only daughter, who was fifteen years old, and was serving as a lady's maid at the Grand Lord's mansion. Quite unlike her father, she was a charming girl and of extraordinary beauty. Having lost her mother in her very early years, she was precocious, and moreover, intelligent and observant beyond her age. Thus she won the good graces of her ladyship, and was a favorite with the attendants.

About that time, a tame monkey was presented to the Lord from the province of Tanba, west of Kyoto. The Lord's young son, who was at his most mischievous age, nicknamed the animal "Yoshihide."

This name so much the more added to the ridiculousness of the funny animal that everyone in the mansion laughed at him. If that had been all, all would have fared well with him. But as it was, whenever the monkey climbed up the pine tree in the garden or soiled the mat of the Little Lord's room, indeed, whatever he did, they shouted his name and teased him.

One day Yoshihide's daughter, Yuzuki, was passing along the long corridor, carrying in her hand a spray of pink winter plum blossoms, with a note attached to it, when she saw the monkey running toward her from beyond the sliding door. He seemed injured and had no desire to climb up the pillar with his usual agility. In all likelihood he had sprained one of his legs. Then whom should she see but the Little Lord running after him swinging a switch in his hand, shouting, "Stop tangerine thief! Stop! Stop!" At the sight of this, she hesitated a moment. Just then the monkey came running over, and giving a cry, clung to the bottom of her skirt. Suddenly, she could no longer find it in her heart to restrain

---

[6] "Hide" refers to Yoshihide's name and is *not* the same as the English word.

her pity. Holding the spray of plum blossom in one hand, she swung open the sleeve of her mauve-colored robe with the other, and gently took up the monkey.

"I beg your pardon, my lord," she said, in a sweet voice, making a respectful bow before the Little Lord. "He is only a beast, please pardon him, my lord."

"Why do you protect him?" Looking displeased, the Little Lord stamped his feet two or three times. "The monkey is a tangerine thief, I tell you."

"He is only a beast, my lord," she repeated.

Then with an innocent but sad smile, she made so bold as to say, "To hear the word Yoshihide called out, I am cut to the quick, as if my father were chastised." At this remark, naughty child that he was, he gave in.

"I see," the Little Lord said reluctantly. "Since you plead for your father's sake, I'll give him a special pardon."

Then throwing away his switch, he turned and went back toward the sliding door through which he had come.

III

From that time on the girl and the monkey became very good friends. She tied a beautiful crimson ribbon around the animal's neck, and also hung from it a little gold bell which the princess had given her. The animal on his part would on no account leave her presence. Once when the girl was laid up with a slight cold, the little monkey sat at her bedside, and, with apparent concern, he watched over her, gnawing on his nails.

After this time, strange as it might sound, no one would tease the little monkey as they used to. On the contrary, they all took to petting him. At last even the Little Lord himself came to toss him a persimmon or a chestnut. Once when he caught a knight in the very act of kicking the animal, he is said to have been extremely incensed. This news reaching his ears, the Lord is said to have given gracious orders that the girl should be brought before his presence with the little monkey in her arms. With reference to this incident, he must also have heard how it was that she had come to make a pet of the animal.

"You are a good and dutiful daughter. I am well pleased

with your conduct," the Lord said, and presented her with a scarlet robe as a reward. The monkey, mimicking her deferential obeisance in expressing her gratitude, raised the robe to his forehead, to the immense amusement and pleasure of the Lord. It should be recalled that the Lord took the girl into his good graces because he had been impressed with her filial piety which led her to make a pet of the monkey, and not because he was an admirer of the charms of the gentle sex, as rumor had it. There were some justifiable grounds for the rumor, but about these subjects I may have the opportunity of talking further later when I find more time. Now let me limit my description to saying that the Lord was not a personage to fall in love with such a lowly girl as a painter's daughter, no matter how charming she was.

Highly honored, the girl withdrew from the Lord's presence. Being a naturally wise and intelligent girl, she did nothing to incur the jealousy of her gossipy fellow maids. On the contrary, this honor won their favor and popularity for both herself and the monkey. She was, above all, received into such particular favor by the princess that she was hardly ever found away from the latter's presence and she never failed to share the latter's company in her excursion carriage.

Now setting aside the girl for the time being, let me tell you about her father, Yoshihide. Although the monkey, Yoshihide, came to be loved by everyone, the painter, Yoshihide, was as much hated by everyone as before, and continued to be called "Saruhide" behind his back.

The Abbot of Yokawa hated Yoshihide as if he were a devil. At the mere mention of his name, he would turn black with anger and abhorrence. Some say that this was because Yoshihide painted a caricature depicting the abbot's conduct. However, this was a mere rumor current among the common people and may have had no foundation in fact. Anyhow, he was unpopular with everybody who knew him. If there were any who did not speak ill of him, they were only two or three of his fellow painters or those who knew his paintings but knew nothing of his character.

Really he was not only mean to look at, but he had such shocking habits that they made him a repellent nuisance to all people. For this he had no one but himself to blame.

IV

Now let me mention his objectionable habits. He was stingy, harsh, shameless, lazy, and avaricious. And worst of all, he was so haughty and arrogant that "his being the greatest painter in the whole of Japan" was hanging from the tip of his nose. If his arrogance had been limited to painting, he would not have been so objectionable. Moreover, he was so conceited that he had a profound contempt for all customs and practices in life.

Here is an episode about him told by a man who had been under his apprenticeship for many years. One day a famous medium in the mansion of a certain lord fell into a trance under the curse of a spirit, and she delivered a horrible oracle. Turning a deaf ear to the oracle, he made a careful sketch of her ghastly face with a brush and ink which he found at hand. In his eyes, the curse by an evil spirit may have been nothing more than a jack-in-the-box for children.

This being his nature, he would in picturing a heavenly maiden, paint the face of a harlot, and in picturing the God of Fire, the figure of a villain. He committed many such sacrilegious acts. When he was brought to task, he declared with provoking indifference, "It's ridiculous for you to say that the gods and Buddhas I have painted should ever be able to punish their painter." This so amazed all his apprentices that many of them took leave of him immediately in fearful anticipation of terrible consequences. After all, he was arrogance incarnate who thought himself the greatest man under the sun.

Accordingly, one can understand how highly he esteemed himself as a painter. However, his brushwork and colorings were so completely different from those of other painters that many of his contemporaries who were on bad terms with him, would speak of him as a charlatan. They claimed that famous paintings by Kawanari, Kanaoka,[7] and other master artists of the past have graceful episodes attached to them. Rumor has it that you can almost smell the delicate fragrance of the plum blossoms on moonlight nights and almost

---

[7] Both Kawanari and Kanaoka are celebrated Japanese painters of the tenth century.

hear the courtier on the screen playing his flute. But all paintings by Yoshihide have the reputation of being unpleasant and uncanny. For example, take his painting representing the five phases of the transmigration of souls which he had painted on the gate of the Ryugai * Temple. If you pass under the gate late at night, you can almost hear the sighing and sobbing of the celestial maidens. Some say they even smelled the offensive odor of the rotting bodies. The Grand Lord's court ladies, whose likenesses Yoshihide painted at the Lord's command, all fell ill as if their souls had left them and died within three years. Those who disparage his paintings say that all this is because they are works of his black art.

Yet, as I told you, he was an extremely cross-grained crank, and was boastful of his very perversity. Once when the Grand Lord said to him, "You seem to have a strong partiality for the ugly," he replied, with a grin on his red lips, "Yes, my Lord, unaccomplished artists can't perceive beauty in the ugly." Admitting that he was the greatest painter in the whole country, how could he ever have been so presumptuous as to make such a haughty remark in the presence of the Grand Lord. His apprentices secretly nicknamed him "Chira-Eiju" to slander his arrogance. "Chira-Eiju" is, I presume you know, a vainglorious long-nosed goblin that flew over to Japan in olden times.

However, Yoshihide, who was a perverse scoundrel beyond description, had one tender side showing that he was not altogether lacking in human kindness.

v

He loved his only daughter, who was a lady-in-waiting, with a love bordering on madness. She was a girl of very sweet disposition, and devoted to her father. On the part of Yoshihide, incredible as it may sound, he doted on his daughter to the point of infatuation, and would lavish money upon her, kimonos, hairpins, and what not for her adornment, although he never contributed his tithes or mites to any Buddhist temple.

* The "u" is underscored in the original Japanese use of proper names, but has been omitted in this translation.

But all his love for his daughter was blind, and wild. He never gave a thought to finding her a good husband. On the contrary, if anyone had attempted to make any advances to her, he would have had no scruples in hiring street rascals to waylay him. Even when she was summoned to be a chambermaid at the gracious command of the Grand Lord, he was so displeased that he looked as sour as vinegar even when he was brought before the very presence of the Grand Lord. The rumor that the Grand Lord, enamored of the girl's beauty, summoned her to his service in the face of her father's strong disapproval, may probably have originated in the imagination of those who were acquainted with such circumstances.

Rumor aside, so much is certain that Yoshihide, out of his indulgent love for his daughter, had an irresistible desire that she should be released from her service. Once, when at the Grand Lord's command he painted a picture of a cherub, he accomplished a masterpiece by making a life sketch of the latter's favorite page.

Highly gratified, the Grand Lord said to the painter, "Yoshihide, I am pleased to grant any request of yours."

"If it pleases your Lordship," Yoshihide was audacious enough to say, "Allow me to request that my daughter be released from your service."

Apart from other households, whoever else under the sun could ever have made such a presumptuous request of the Grand Lord of Horikawa with regard to the favorite lady-in-waiting, no matter how dearly he may have loved her? With an air of some displeasure, the magnanimous Grand Lord remained silent for a while, staring Yoshihide hard in the face.

"No, I can't grant that," he spat out and left abruptly. There may have been some four or five such occasions. Now it seemed to me that each time his Lordship looked at Yoshihide with less favor and with growing coldness in his eyes. This must have caused his daughter to worry over her father. When she retired to her room, she was often found sobbing, biting the sleeve of her kimono. Thereafter rumor spread all the more that the Grand Lord was enamored of the girl. Some say that the whole history of the hell screen may be traced to her refusal to comply with the Grand Lord's wishes. However, I do not believe that this could have been true.

It seems in our eyes that his Lordship did not allow the girl to be dismissed from his service because he took pity on her family circumstances and had graciously considered to keep her in his mansion and let her live in ease and comfort rather than to send her back to her cross, obstinate father. Undoubtedly he had made a "favorite" of such a charming sweet-tempered girl. However, it is a farfetched distortion of the fact to attribute all this to the amorous motives of his Lordship. No, I dare say that it is an entirely unfounded lie.

Be that as it may, it was at the time when his Lordship came to look upon Yoshihide with considerable disfavor that he summoned him to his mansion and commanded him to paint on a screen a picture of Hell.

VI

The hell screen was a consummate work of art, presenting before our eyes the vivid and graphic portrayal of the terrible scenes of Hell.

First of all in its design, his painting of Hell was quite different from those of other artists. In a corner of the first leaf of the screen on a reduced scale were painted the ten Kings of Hell and their households while all the rest consisted of terrible flames of fire roaring and eddying around and around the Mountain of Swords and the Forest of Lances, which, too, seemed ready to blaze up and melt away into flames. Accordingly, except for the yellow and blue patches of the Chinese-designed costume of the infernal officials, wherever one might look, all was in blazing flames, black smoke swirling around and sparks shooting up like burning gold dust fanned in a holocaust of fire.

This brushwork alone was sufficient to startle the human eye. The criminals writhing in agony amidst the consuming Hell fire were not like those represented in ordinary pictures of Hell. For here in the portrayal of sinners was set forth a whole array of people in all walks of life from nobles and dignitaries to beggars and outcasts; courtiers in dignified Court dress, coquettish wives of knights in elaborate costumes, priests praying over the rosaries hanging from their necks, samurai students on high wooden clogs, girls in gaudy gala dress, fortune-tellers clad in the robes of Shinto priests—there were an endless number of them. Therein people of all descriptions, tortured by bullheaded hellhounds amidst blazing flames and raging smoke, were fleeing in all directions like so many autumn leaves scattered by a blast of wind. There were women apparently looking like shrine mediums, with their hair caught in forks and their limbs drawn in and bent like a spider's legs. There were men evidently looking like governors, suspended upside down with their hearts pierced with halberds. Some were being flogged with iron rods. Some were being crushed under living rocks. Some were being pecked by weird birds and others were having their throats torn out by poisonous dragons. There were so many varieties of torture suffered by sinners in numerous categories.

The most outstanding of all the horrors, however, was an ox carriage falling in midair grazing the tops of the sword trees that had branches pointed like animals' fangs, through which heaps of bodies of dead souls were spitted. In this carriage, with its bamboo blinds blown upward by the blast of Hell, a Court lady as gorgeously dressed as an empress or a princess was writhing in agony, her black hair streaming amidst flames and her white neck bent upward. This figure of the agonizing Court lady in the ox carriage consumed by flames was the most ghostly representation of the thousand and one tortures in the burning Hell. The multifarious horrors in the whole picture were focused on this one character. It was a masterwork of such divine inspiration that no one could have looked at her without hearing in his ears the agonizing outcries of the condemned souls in pandemonium.

It was for this reason, indeed, his consuming desire to paint this picture, that the terrible incident occurred. If it had not been for this event, how could even Yoshihide have succeeded in painting that graphic picture of the tortures and agonies in Hell? So he could complete the picture, his life had to come to a miserable end. Indeed, it was to this very Hell in his picture that Yoshihide, the greatest painter in Japan, had condemned himself.

I am afraid that in my hurry to tell you about this strange hell screen, I have reversed the order of my story. Now my story will return to Yoshihide who was commanded to paint a picture of Hell by the Grand Lord.

VII

For five or six months after that Yoshihide devoted himself to painting the picture on the screen without making even a single courtesy call at the mansion. Isn't it strange that, with all his indulgent love for his daughter, once he took to painting a picture, he had no thought of even seeing her. To borrow the words of his apprentices, he became like a man possessed of a fox. The rumor current at that time had it that he had been able to gain fame and reputation because he offered vows to Reynard the God of Good Fortune.

"For positive proof," some said, "steal a look at him when he is at work, and you can see the shady spirits of foxes thronging all around him."

Once he took up his brush, he forgot everything but his work. Night and day he confined himself to his studio, hardly coming out during daylight. His absorption in his work was most extraordinary when he was painting the hell screen.

Shut up in his studio with the shutters always drawn, he would mix his secret colors, and dressing up his apprentices in various gala costumes or in simple clothes, he would paint them with great care.

But these singular oddities were usual with him. It would not have taken the hell screen to drive him to such extreme eccentricities. While he was working on the painting of his "Five Phases of the Transmigration of Souls," he once came across rotting corpses in a street. Then calmly sitting down in front of the malodorous corpses, from which ordinary painters would have turned their eyes aside, he made accurate sketches, at his ease, of the rotting faces and limbs, exact to a single hair. I am afraid that what I have told you does not convey to you a clear idea of his extreme absorption. I cannot, at this time, tell you the particulars, but I will tell you some of the notable instances.

Once one of his boy apprentices had been mixing colors when he said abruptly, "Now I want to have a rest. For some days I've had some bad dreams."

"Indeed, sir?" the apprentice answered formally without interrupting his work. This was not unusual with his master.

"By the way," the artist said, making a rather modest request, "I want you to sit at my bedside while I'm resting."

"All right, sir," the apprentice replied, as he expected that it would be no trouble at all, although he thought it strange that his master should worry over his bad dreams.

"Come along with me into my inner room. Even if any other apprentice should come, don't let him come in," the master ordered hesitatingly, still looking worried. His inner room meant his studio.

On that occasion, as usual, his studio was closely shut up, dim lights burning as if it were night. Around the sides of the room was set up the screen, on which only the rough sketch was done in charcoal. Entering there, the artist went to sleep calmly as if he were dead tired. But he had not been asleep half an hour when an indescribably weird voice came to the apprentice's ears.

VIII

At first it was only a voice. But presently it turned gradually into disconnected words groaned out like a drowning man under water. "What? Do you tell me to come? . . . Where to? . . . Come where to? . . . Who is it that says, 'Come to Hell. Come to the burning Hell.' Whoever is this? Who could it be but . . . ?"

The apprentice forgot about mixing colors, and took a furtive look at his master's face. The wrinkled face had turned pale, oozing large drops of perspiration. His mouth was wide open as if gasping for breath, with his sparse teeth showing between dry lips. The thing, moving briskly in his mouth as if pulled by a string or a wire, was his tongue. Disconnected words, of course, came out of his mouth. "H'm, it's you. I expected it might be you . . . Have you come to meet me? . . . So, come. Come to Hell. In Hell my daughter is waiting for me."

The apprentice was petrified with fear, a chill running all over his whole frame, as his eyes seemed to catch sight of an obscure, weird phantom coming down close by the screen. He put his hand on Yoshihide at once, and with all his might tried to shake him out of the clutch of the nightmare. But, in a trance, his master continued to talk to himself and would not wake up. So the apprentice was bold enough to splash the water in the palette onto his master's face.

"I'll be waiting for you, so come by this carriage . . . Take this carriage to Hell." These words, strangled in his throat, had scarcely come out in the form of a groan when Yoshihide sprang up all of a sudden as though he had been stuck with a needle. The evil spirits in his nightmare must still have been hanging heavily upon his eyelids. For a moment he stared into space with his mouth still wide open. Then, returning to himself, he ordered curtly, "It's all right now. Go away, will you?"

If the apprentice had made any expostulation, he would surely have been sharply rebuked. So he hurriedly left his master's room. When he came out into the genial outdoor sunshine, he felt relieved as if he had awakened from his own nightmare.

But that was not the worst. A month later another apprentice was called into his studio. Yoshihide, who had been biting his brush, turned on him and said, "I must ask you to strip yourself bare." As the artist had given this kind of order once in a while, the apprentice immediately took off his clothes.

"I haven't seen anyone bound in chains and so, I'm sorry, but will you do as I tell you for a while?" Yoshihide said coldly, with a very strange frown on his face, without any air of being sorry for him. The apprentice was by nature a young man of such burly physique that he could have wielded a sword more adroitly than a brush. Nevertheless, he was astonished beyond measure, and in his later reference to the occasion, he repeatedly remarked, "Then I was afraid that the master had gone mad and that he was going to kill me." Yoshihide felt impatient at his hesitation. Producing iron chains from somewhere, he sprang on his back, and peremptorily wrenching his arms, he bound them tightly. Then he gave a sudden pull at one end of the chain with such cruel force that the apprentice was thrown plump on the floor by the sudden impact of the strong pull and the unendurable grip of the chain.

IX

The apprentice at that time looked just like a wine keg rolled over on its side. All his limbs were so cruelly bent and twisted that he could move nothing but his head. The arrest of the circulation of his blood under the tension of the chain turned the color of his skin, his face, chest, and limbs livid in no time. However, Yishihide gave no heed to his pain in the least, and walking about his chained body he made many sketches. It is quite needless to tell you what dreadful torture the apprentice suffered under the tight bondage.

If nothing had happened at the moment, his sufferings might have continued. Fortunately—it might rather be more appropriate to say unfortunately—after a while, a slender strip of something flowed gleaming up to the tip of the nose of the apprentice, who, overcome with fright, drew in his breath and screamed, "A snake! A snake!"

The apprentice told me that he had felt as if all the blood in his body would freeze at once. The snake was actually on the point of touching with its cold tongue the flesh of his neck into which the chain was biting. At this unexpected occurrence, the cold-blooded Yoshihide must have been startled. Hurriedly casting away his brush, he bent down, and catching the snake by the tail, he dangled it head downward. Suspended, the snake lifted its head and coiled itself around its own body, but could not reach Yoshihide's hand.

"Go to Hell, you damned snake! You've marred a good stroke." In exasperation, Yoshihide dropped the snake into the jar in the corner of the room, and reluctantly undid the chain that bound the apprentice's body. But he did nothing more than to unchain the poor apprentice without even offering a single word of apology or sympathy. For him, his failure in that one stroke must have been a matter of greater regret than to have his apprentice bitten by the snake. Later I was told that he kept the snake for the express purpose of making sketches of it.

To hear of these episodes, you will be able to form a good idea of Yoshihide's mad and sinister absorption. In conclusion let me tell you another story of how a thirteen- to fourteen-year-old apprentice met with such a dreadful experience that it nearly cost him his life during the painting of the hell screen. He was a fair-complexioned boy with a girlish face. One night he happened to be called to Yoshihide's room, when in the lamplight he saw his master feeding a strange bird a piece of raw meat which lay in the palm of his hand. The bird was the size of a house cat. It had big, round, amber-colored eyes and ear-shaped feathers jutting out from both sides of its head, and looked extraordinarily like a cat.

X

Yoshihide by nature hated any external interference in whatever he did. As was the case with the snake, he did not let his apprentices know what he planned to do. Sometimes on his desk were placed human skulls, and at other times silver bowls or lacquered tableware. The surprising things he set out on his desk varied according to what he was painting. Nobody could ever find out where he kept these things. For one thing, such circumstances must have lent force to the rumor widely afloat at that time that he was under the divine protection of the Great Goddess of Fortune. So when the apprentice caught sight of the strange creature, he thought that it must also be one of the models for his picture of Hell on the screen, and asked, "What do you wish, sir?" bowing respectfully before his master.

"Look, how tame it is!" the painter said, licking his red lips, as if he had not heard the question.

"What's the name of this creature, sir? I've never seen one like this." With these words, the apprentice stared at the cat-like bird with ears sticking out as if it were something sinister.

"What? Never seen anything like this? That's the trouble with town-bred folks. They ought to know better. It's a bird called a horned owl. A huntsman from Kurama[8] gave it to me a few days ago. I assure you there aren't many as tame as this."

So saying, he slowly raised his hand and stroked the feathers on the back of the horned owl which had just eaten up the good meat. Just at that moment the bird, with a shrill menacing screech, suddenly flew up from the desk, and with the talons of both feet outstretched, pounced upon the apprentice. At that instant had he not raised his sleeve and hid his face in it, he would have been badly wounded. Screaming in fright, he tried frantically to drive away the horned owl. But the big bird, taking advantage of his unguarded moments, continued to click its beak and peck at him. The boy, forgetting the

[8] Kurama is a village in the suburbs of Kyoto.

presence of his master, had to run up and down the room in confusion, standing up to defend himself, and sitting down to drive it away. The bird followed him closely and during unguarded moments would dart at his eyes. The fierce flapping of its wings brought on some mysterious effects, like the smell of fallen leaves, the spray of a waterfall, or the odor of soured monkey-wine.[9] The apprentice felt so helpless that the dim oil light looked like a misty moonlight, and his master's very room an ominous, ghastly valley in the depths of the remote mountains.

However, it was not only the horned owl's attacks that overwhelmed the apprentice with terror. What sent the horror of despair into his heart was the sight of Yoshihide. All this while his master had been coolly watching this tragic uproar and had been leisurely sketching, on a piece of paper which he had deliberately unrolled, this ghastly scene of the girlish boy tortured and disfigured by the sinister bird. When the poor boy out of the corner of his eye caught sight of what his master was doing, a shudder of deathly horror ran through his whole frame, and he expected every moment that he was going to be killed by him.

XI

As a matter of fact, it was possible that his master might have planned to kill him, for he deliberately called the apprentice that night to carry out his diabolical scheme to set the horned owl on the handsome boy and paint him running about in terror. So the instant the boy saw what his master's design was, he involuntarily hid his face in both his sleeves, and, after a wild, indescribable scream, he collapsed at the foot of the sliding door in the corner of the room. Just at that moment, something tumbled down with a loud crash. Then all of a sudden the horned owl's flapping of its wings became more violent than ever, and Yoshihide, giving a startled outcry, seemed to have risen to his feet. Terrified out of his wits, the apprentice raised his head to see what was the matter. The room had turned pitch dark, and out of the darkness his master's harsh irritated voice calling for his apprentice fell upon his ears.

[9] Monkey-wine is a wine produced by the natural fermentation of grapes collected by monkeys.

Presently there was a distant response by one of his apprentices, who hurriedly came in with a light. The sooty light showed that the rushlight stand had been knocked down and that a pool of the spilled oil had formed on the mats, where the horned owl was found tossing about in pain, flapping only one of its wings. Yoshihide, half raising himself, mumbled something understandable to no mortals—and with good reason. A black snake had coiled itself tightly around the body of the horned owl from its neck to one of its wings. This fierce fight had started, presumably because the apprentice overturned the jar as he suddenly crouched, and the cocky horned owl tried to clutch and peck at the snake which had slid out. The two apprentices, exchanging glances in openmouthed amazement, had been watching this thrilling battle for a while before they bowed humbly to their master and crept out of the room. No one knows what became of the horned owl and the snake after that.

There were many other instances of this kind. As I told you before, it was at the beginning of fall that he was ordered by the Grand Lord to paint the picture of Hell on the screen. From then on to the end of the winter, the apprentices were under constant danger from their master's mysterious behavior. Toward the end of the winter Yoshihide came to some deadlock in his work on the screen. He became gloomier than ever and noticeably harsher in speech. He could make no progress in the rough sketch, of which he had completed eighty percent. He appeared so dissatisfied that he might not have hesitated even to blot out the rough sketch.

No one could tell what the trouble was with the picture on the screen. Neither did anyone care to find out. The apprentices, who had learned at their bitter cost by past experience, took all possible means to keep away from their master as though they felt that they were in the same cage with a tiger or a wolf.

XII

Accordingly, for the time being there had been no occurrence worthy of a special mention. All that deserves some notice is that Yoshihide, the obstinate old man, somehow became so strangely maudlin that he was sometimes found weeping when there was no one near. One day when one of the apprentices went out into the garden, he found his master, with his eyes full of tears, looking vacantly into the sky, which indicated that spring was not a long while off. More ashamed and embarrassed than his master, the apprentice crept away from his presence without saying a word. Is it not strange that a stout-hearted old man who took up roadside corpses as models for his sketches should weep like a child because he could not find a suitable subject to paint on the screen?

While Yoshihide was so totally absorbed in painting the picture on the screen, somehow or other his daughter gradually became so gloomy that it became evident to us that she was trying to hold back her tears. As she was a modest fair-complexioned girl with a quiet composed face, she looked all the more lonely and disconsolate, with her tearful eyes overshadowed by her heavy eyelashes. At first various guesses were made, such as "She is always absorbed in her thoughts, missing her father and mother," "She is lovesick," and so on. However, in the course of time the rumor began to spread that the Grand Lord was trying to force his desire on her. From that time on, the people stopped talking about the girl as if they had completely forgotten about her affair.

It was just about this time that late one night I was passing by the corridor alone when suddenly the monkey Yoshihide came bounding up to me and persistently pulled me by the hem of my skirt. If I remember rightly, it was a mild night bathed in such mellow moonlight as one might have felt was laden with the fragrance of sweet plum blossoms. In the moonlight I could see the monkey baring his white teeth, with wrinkles on the tip of his nose, and screaming wildly as if it had gone mad. I felt thirty percent uncanny and seventy percent angry, and at first I wanted to give him a kick and pass by. But on reflection, I thought of the instance of the samurai who had incurred the displeasure of the young Lord by chastising the monkey. However, the monkey's behavior suggested that something out of the ordinary might have happened. So I walked aimlessly for a dozen yards toward the direction in which he pulled me.

I took a turn around the corridor and came as far as the side, which opened up, through the graceful branches of the pine tree, a fine vista of the broad expanse of the pond sparkling like crystals in the night. Then my ears were arrested by the sounds of a confused fight in the room near by. All around it was as still as a graveyard, and in a faint light that was half moonlight and half haze, nothing was to be heard but the splashing of the fish. Instinctively I stopped and went stealthily up to the outside of the sliding doors ready to deal them a blow if they proved to be rioters.

XIII

The monkey Yoshihide must have been impatient of my actions. Whining as pitifully as if his neck were being strangled, he scampered around my legs a couple of times and then suddenly bounded up on my shoulders. Instinctively I turned my head aside to dodge being clawed, while the monkey clung to the sleeve of my robe so as not to slip down. On the spur of the moment, I involuntarily staggered back a few steps and bumped against the sliding door. Then I had not a moment to hesitate. I abruptly threw open the door and was about to rush on into the inner part of the room outside the reach of the moonlight. Then to my alarm, my sight was barred by a young woman who came dashing out of the room as if projected by a spring. In her impetuosity she very nearly bumped into me and tumbled down outside the room. I could not tell why, but she knelt down there and looked up into my face, out of breath, shuddering all over as if she were still seeing something frightful.

I need not take the trouble to tell you that she was Yoshihide's daughter. But that night she looked so extraordinarily attractive that her image was indelibly branded upon my eyes as if she were a changed being. Her eyes were sparkling brightly, her cheeks in a rosy glow. Her disheveled skirt and undergarment added to her youthful bloom and irresistible charm quite unlike the innocent girl that she was. Was this really the painter's daughter who was so delicate and modest in every way? Supporting myself against the door, I watched the beautiful girl in the moonlight. Then suddenly aware of the flurried footsteps of a man receding into the dark, as if I could point him out, I asked, "Who is it?"

The girl, biting her lips, only shook her head silently. She appeared to feel deep chagrin.

So stooping down, I put my mouth to her ear and asked, "Who was it?" in a low voice. But still she shook her head again and made no answer. With the tips of her eyelashes full of tears, she was biting her lips harder than ever.

On account of my inborn stupidity, I can understand nothing but what is as clear as day. So not knowing what to say, I remained rooted to the spot, as if I were intent on listening to the thumping of the girl's heart. For one thing, I could not find it in my heart to question her any more.

I don't know how long I waited thus. However, shutting the door which I had left open, I looked back toward the girl who seemed to have recovered a little from her agitation, and as gently as possible said to her, "Now go back to your room."

Troubled with an uneasiness of mind for having seen something which I should not have, and feeling ashamed—of whom I did not know—I began to walk back to where I had come from. But I had not walked ten steps before someone behind me timidly pulled me by the hem of my skirt. In surprise, I looked back. Who do you think it was?

It was the monkey Yoshihide, repeatedly bowing his head to express his gratitude with his hands on the ground like a man, his gold bell tinkling.

XIV

One day two weeks later Yoshihide the painter presented himself at the Grand Lord's mansion and begged his personal audience. The Lord, to whom access was ordinarily difficult, was pleased to grant him an audience, and ordered him to be immediately brought before his presence, probably because the painter was in the Lord's good graces, although he was a man of humble station. The painter, as usual, was wearing a yellow robe and soft headgear. Wearing a more sullen look than usual, he respectfully prostrated himself in the Lord's presence. By and by, raising his head, he said in a hoarse voice:

"May it please your Lordship if I tell you about the picture of Hell on the screen which you were previously pleased to order me to paint. I have applied myself to the painting night and day, and have very nearly completed the work."

"Congratulations! I am pleased to hear it." However, the Grand Lord's voice was lacking in conviction.

"No, my Lord. Congratulations are not in order," Yoshihide said, lowering his voice, as if he were plagued with dissatisfaction. "It is mostly finished, but there is one thing I am unable to paint."

"What! Is there anything you can't paint?"

"Yes, my Lord. As a rule, I can't paint anything but what I have seen. Otherwise, however hard I try, I can't paint to my satisfaction. This amounts to the same thing as my being unable to paint it."

"Now that you are to paint Hell, you mean you must see it, eh?" 'A scornful smile crept across the Grand Lord's face.

"You are right, my Lord. A few years ago when there was a big fire, I could see with my own eyes a burning hell of raging flames. That was why I could paint the picture of the God of Twisting Flames. Your Lordship is also acquainted with that picture."

"How about criminals? You haven't yet seen prisoners, have you?" The Grand Lord followed with question upon question as if he had not heard what Yoshihide said.

"I have seen men bound in iron chains. I have made detailed sketches of those tormented by ominous birds. Nor would I say that I am not acquainted with criminals under tortures, and prisoners . . ." Here Yoshihide gave an uncanny grin. "Asleep or awake, they have appeared in my eyes ever so often. Almost every night and day bullheaded demons, horse-headed demons, or three-faced six-armed demons harrow and torment me, clapping their noiseless hands and opening their voiceless mouths. They are not those which I am neither anxious nor able to paint."

Yoshihide's words must have been a great surprise to the Grand Lord. After fixing his irritated glare into Yoshihide's face for a while, the Lord spat out, "Then what is it you can't paint?" with a disdainful look, knitting his eyebrows.

XV

"I am anxious to paint a nobleman's magnificent carriage falling in midair in the very center of the screen," Yoshihide said, and then for the first time fixed his sharp look full on the Lord's face.

I had once heard that when speaking about pictures, the

fellow would become as though insane. Certainly there was some such frightful look in his eyes when he spoke out.

"Allow me to describe the carriage," the painter went on. "In this vehicle, an elegant Court lady, amidst raging flames, writhes in the agony of pain, with her black hair hanging loose about her shoulders. Choked with a heavy black smoke, her face is turned up toward the roof of the carriage, with her brow tightly drawn. Around the carriage a score or more of ominous birds fly about, clicking their beaks . . . Oh, how can I ever paint such a Court lady in the burning carriage?"

"Hm . . . and what? . . ." Strangely enough, the Grand Lord urged Yoshihide to go on with his talk as if he were well pleased.

"Oh, I can't paint it," Yoshihide said once again in a dreary tone, his feverish red lips trembling. But suddenly he changed his attitude, and in dead earnest, made a bold and feverish request in a spirited and snappish tone, "Please, my Lord, burn a nobleman's carriage before my eyes, and if possible, . . ."

The Grand Lord darkened his face for an instant but suddenly burst into a peal of laughter.

"All your wishes shall be granted," the Grand Lord declared, his voice half choked with his laughter. "Don't take the trouble to inquire about the possibility."

His words struck horror into my heart. It may have been my presentiment. Anyway the Grand Lord's behavior on that occasion was most extraordinary, as though it had been infected with Yoshihide's madness. White froth was gathering at the corner of his mouth, and his eyebrows twitched violently.

"Yes, I will burn up a nobleman's carriage." As he paused, his incessant heavy laughter went on. "A charming woman dressed up like a Court lady shall ride in the carriage. Writhing amidst the deadly flames and black smoke, the lady in the carriage will die in agony. Your suggestion of finding such a model for your picture does you full credit as the greatest painter in the whole country. I praise you. I praise you highly."

At the Grand Lord's words, Yoshihide had turned pale and had been trying to move his lips for perhaps a minute when he put his hands on the matted floor as if all his muscles had relaxed, and said politely, "I am most grateful to you, my Lord," in a voice so low as to be hardly audible.

This was probably because, with the Grand Lord's words, the horror of the scheme which he had had in mind vividly flashed across his mind. Only this once in my life did I think of Yoshihide as a pitiful creature.

XVI

One night a few days later, according to his promise, the Grand Lord summoned Yoshihide to witness the burning of a nobleman's carriage right before his eyes. However, this did not take place on the grounds of the Grand Lord's mansion of Horikawa. It was burned at his villa in the hilly suburbs commonly called the mansion of Yuge (Snow-thaw) where his sister had once lived.

This residence had been uninhabited for a long time, and the spacious gardens had fallen into a state of dilapidation. In those days many uncanny rumors were going around about the late sister of the Grand Lord. Some said that on moonless nights her mysterious scarlet-colored skirts would be seen moving along the corridors without touching the floor. Without doubt, these rumors must have been wild guesses started by those who had seen the complete desertion of the mansion. But there is nothing to wonder at in the circulation of these rumors, for the whole neighborhood was so lonely and desolate even in the daytime that after dark even the murmuring of the water running through the gardens added all the more to the dismal gloom, and the herons flying about in the starlight might naturally have been taken for ominous birds.

On that night it was pitch dark with no moonlight. The rushlights showed that the Grand Lord, dressed in a bright-green garment and a dark-violet skirt, was seated near the veranda. He was sitting cross-legged on a rush mat hemmed with white brocade. Before and behind him and at the right and left of him, five or six samurai stood in respectful attendance upon him. One of them stood out with prominent conspicuousness. A few years before, during the campaign in the Tohoku district, he had eaten human flesh to allay his hunger. That gave him such herculean strength that he could tear the horn of a live deer apart. Clad in armor, he stood in full dignity beneath the veranda with the tip of his sheathed sword turned upward. The lurid ghastliness of the scene, turning bright and dark under the lights which flickered in the night wind, made me wonder whether I was dreaming or awake.

Presently when a magnificent carriage was drawn up into the garden to make its commanding appearance in the dark, with its long shafts placed on its chassis and its gold metalwork and fittings glittering like so many stars, we felt a chill come over us, although it was spring. The interior of the carriage was heavily enclosed with blue blinds, of which the hems were embroidered in relief, so we could not tell what was inside. Around the carriage a number of menials, each with a blazing torch in hand, waited attentively, worrying over the smoke which drifted toward the veranda.

Yoshihide was on his knees on the ground facing the veranda just in front of the Lord. Dressed in a cream-colored garment and soft headgear, he looked smaller and homelier than usual, as though he had been stunted under the oppressive atmosphere of the starry sky. The man squatting behind him, dressed in a similar garment, was presumably his apprentice. As they were some way off in the dark, even the colors of their garments were not clearly discernible.

XVII

The time was very near midnight. Darkness, enveloping the grove and stream, seemed to listen silently to the breathing of all those present. Meanwhile the passage of the gentle wind wafted the sooty smell of the torches toward us. The Grand Lord had been silently watching this extraordinary scene for a while when he stepped foward and called sharply, "Yoshihide."

Yoshihide seemed to say something in reply, but what my ears could catch sounded nothing more than a groan.

"Tonight I'm going to set fire to the carriage as you wish," the Grand Lord said, looking askance at his attendants. Then I saw the Grand Lord exchange a significant look with his attendants. But this might have been my fancy. Yoshihide seemed to have raised his head reverently, but did not say anything.

"I say, behold! That's the carriage in which I usually ride. Yoshihide, you know it, don't you? Now according to your wish, I am going to set fire to it and bring to life a blazing hell on earth before your very eyes."

The Lord paused again, and again exchanging significant looks with his attendants, he proceeded in a displeased tone.

"In the carriage is a woman criminal—bound in chains. If it is fired, I am sure that she will have her flesh roasted and her bones scorched, and that she will writhe in dire agony to death. No better model can you have for the completion of your picture. Don't miss seeing her snow-white skin burned and charred. Watch closely her black hair dance up in the infernal sparks of fire."

The Grand Lord closed his mouth for the third time. I do not know what came to his mind. Then shaking his shoulders in silent laughter, he said, "The sight will be handed down to posterity. I will also watch it here now. There, raise the blinds and let Yoshihide see the woman inside."

At his command, one of the menials, holding aloft a pine torch in one hand, strode up to the carriage, and stretching out his free hand, he quickly raised the blinds. The red blazing light from his torch waved wildly with a crackling noise, and suddenly lightened up the small interior with dazzling brightness, revealing a woman cruelly bound in chains on the seat. Oh, whoever could have mistaken her? Although she was dressed up in a gorgeously embroidered silken kimono with a cherry-blossom design, gold hairpins shining with a brilliant glitter in her hair which hung loose about her shoulders, the fact that she was Yoshihide's daughter was in unmistakable evidence in her trim, maidenly form, her lovely charming profile of graceful modesty. I very nearly gave an outcry.

At that moment the samurai who stood opposite me roused himself and cast a sharp glance at Yoshihide, with his hand on the hilt of his sword. In amazement, I looked toward Yoshihide, who seemed to have been startled out of his wits. Although he had been on his knees, he instantly sprang to his feet, and stretching out his arms, he unconsciously attempted to rush toward the carriage.

However, as he was off in the dark background, I could not discern his face clearly. But that was the matter of a passing moment. For all at once, his face which had turned sheet-white came vividly into view through the intervening shadow of the night, while his body seemed to have been lifted up into space by some invisible power. Just then at the Grand Lord's command, "Set fire!" a shower of torches thrown in by the menials bathed the carriage in a flood of lurid light and set it ablaze in a pillar of raging flames.

XVIII

The fire enveloped the whole chassis in no time. The instant the purple tassels on the roof, fanned by the sudden wind, waved upward, volumes of smoke spiraled up against the blackness of the night, and such furious sparks of fire danced up in midair that the bamboo blinds, the hangings on both sides, and the metal fittings on the roof, bursting into so many balls of fire, shot up skyward. The bright color of the tongues of the raging fire, which soared up far into the sky, looked like celestial flames spurting out of the orb of heaven which had fallen down to the earth. A moment before I had very nearly cried out, but now I was so completely stunned and dumbfounded with mouth agape I could do nothing but watch this terrible spectacle in a daze. But as for the father, Yoshihide. . . .

Still now I can remember how the painter Yoshihide looked at that moment. He attempted to rush toward the carriage in spite of himself. But the instant the fire blazed up, he stopped, and with his arms outstretched as if magnetized, he fastened such a sharp gaze upon the burning chassis as to penetrate the raging flames and heavy smoke which had enveloped the whole carriage. In the flood of light that had bathed his whole body, his ugly wrinkled face was brought into clear view even to the tip of his beard.

His wide-open eyes, his distorted lips, and the quivering of his cheeks which constantly twitched, all were tangible expressions of the mixture of dread, grief, and bewilderment which crowded upon his mind. Neither a robber who was about to be beheaded nor a heinous criminal who was dragged before the judgment seat of Yuma could have worn a more painful or agonized face. At the sight of him, even the samurai of herculean strength was greatly shocked and respectfully looked up into the Grand Lord's face.

The Grand Lord, however, tightly biting his lips, fixed his gaze upon the carriage, showing a sinister grin from time to time. Inside the carriage—oh, how could I ever have the heart or courage to convey to you a detailed description of the girl in the carriage who flashed into my sight. Her fair, charming face, which, choked with smoke, fell back, and her long alluring hair which came loose while she was trying to shake off the spreading fire, as well as her beautiful, gorgeous kimono with its cherry-blossom pattern which turned into a lambent flame in no time—what a cruel spectacle all this was! By and by a gust of night wind blew away the smoke toward the other side, and when the sparks of fire shot up like gold dust above the raging blaze, she fainted in such convulsive agonies that even the chains which bound her might have burst. Above all others, this atrocious torture of Hell itself brought into gruesome reality before our very eyes sent such a blood-curdling shudder through the hearts of all present including the samurai that our hair stood on end.

Then once again we thought that the midnight wind had moaned through the treetops. The sound of the wind had scarcely passed into the dark sky—no one knew where to—when something black bounded like a ball without either touching the ground or flying through the air, and plunged straight from the roof of the mansion into the furiously blazing carriage. Amidst the burned crimson-lacquered lattice which was crumbling in pieces, it put its hands on the warped shoulders of the girl, and gave, out of the screens of black smoke, a long and piercing shriek of intense grief like the tearing of silk, then again two or three successive screams.

Involuntarily we gave a unanimous outcry of surprise. What was holding fast to the shoulders of the dead girl, with the red curtain of blazing flames behind it, was the monkey, which went by the nickname of Yoshihide at the mansion of Horikawa.

XIX

But it was only for a few seconds that the monkey remained in our sight. The instant the sparks shot up like thousands of shooting stars into the night air, the girl together with the monkey sank to the bottom of the whirling black smoke. After that in the midst of the garden, nothing else was to be seen but the carriage of fire blazing up with a terrific noise. A pillar of fire might have been a more appropriate phrase to describe the turbulent, furious flames which shot up into the dark starry sky.

In front of the pillar of fire, Yoshihide stood still, rooted to the ground. What a wonderful transfiguration he had undergone! A mysterious radiance, a kind of blissful ecstasy showed on the wrinkled face of Yoshihide who had been agonized by the tortures of Hell until a minute before. His arms were tightly crossed on his chest as if he had forgotten that he was in the presence of the Grand Lord. No longer did his eyes seem to mirror the image of his daughter's agonized death. His eyes seemed to delight beyond measure in the beautiful color of the flame and the form of the woman writhing in her last infernal tortures.

The wonder was not limited to his ecstatic transport with which he was watching the death agony of his beloved daughter. Yoshihide at that moment revealed something that was not human, some such mysterious dignity as King Lion's wrath which you might see in your dreams. It may have been our imagination. But in our eyes, even the flocks of night birds, which, startled by the unexpected fire, screeched and clamored around, seemed to fly shy of the soft headgear of Yoshihide. Even the eyes of the soulless birds seemed to be aware of a mysterious dignity which shone over his head like a halo.

Even the birds appeared like that. Much more did we quake within, with bated breath, watching Yoshihide closely and intently, our hearts overwhelmed with such awe and reverence as if we looked up to a newly made Buddhist image at its unveiling ceremony. The fire and smoke of the carriage which had spread all around with a roaring sound and Yoshihide who stood captivated and petrified there by the spectacle inspired our horror-stricken hearts, for the moment, with a mysterious awe and solemnity beyond all description. However, the Grand Lord, harrowed by the very horror of the scene, appeared pale and livid as though he were a changed being. Foam gathering at his mouth, he gasped like a thirsty animal, grasping the knee of his purple-colored skirt tightly with both hands.

XX

The report of the Grand Lord's burning of the carriage spread far and wide—heaven only knows who started it. The first and foremost question that would naturally arise in your mind would be what led the Grand Lord to burn alive Yoshihide's daughter. A variety of guesses were made about the cause. Most people accepted the rumor that his motive was to carry out his vengeance against his thwarted love. But his real underlying intention must have been his design to chastise and correct the perversity of Yoshihide who was anxious to paint the screen even if it involved the burning of a magnificent carriage with the sacrifice of human life. That was what I heard from the Grand Lord's mouth.

Since Yoshihide was eager enough to paint the screen even at the very moment he saw his own daughter burned to death before his eyes, some reviled him as a devil in human shape, which felt no scruple about sacrificing his parental love for the sake of his art. The Abbot of Yokawa was one of the staunch supporters of this view, and used to say that, no matter how accomplished one might be in any branch of learning or art, one would have to be condemned to Hell, if one were not endowed with the five cardinal virtues of Confucius—benevolence, justice, courtesy, wisdom, and fidelity.

A month later when his hell screen was completed, Yoshihide took it immediately to the mansion, and presented it with great reverence to the Grand Lord. The abbot, who happened to be there at the time, had glared angrily at him from the first, showing a wry face. However, as the screen was unrolled, the high priest must have been struck by the truth of the infernal horrors, the storms of fire ranging from the firmament to the abyss of Hell.

"Wonderful!" the abbot exclaimed in spite of himself, giving an involuntary tap on his knee. Still now I remember how his ejaculation drew a forced smile from the Grand Lord.

From that time on hardly anyone, at least in the mansion, spoke ill of the painter, because, strangely enough, no one, including those who harbored the most intense hatred toward Yoshihide, could see the picture on the screen without being struck with its mysterious solemnity or being vividly impressed with its ghastly reality of the exquisite tortures in a burning hell.

However, by that time Yoshihide had already departed this life.

On the night of the day following the completion of his painting of the screen, he hanged himself by putting a rope over the beam of his room. Yoshihide, who survived the untimely death of his only beloved daughter, could no longer find it in his heart to live on in this world.

His body remains buried in the corner of the ruins of his house. However, with the passage of scores of years, wind and rain have worn out the tombstone marking his grave, and overgrowing moss has buried it into oblivion.

RIICHI YOKOMITSU
"Machine"
("Kikai," 1930)

Translated by Edward Seidensticker

Riichi Yokomitsu (1898–1947) was born in northern Japan but was raised in a village in the western part of the country by his mother's parents. Instead of remaining a student at Waseda University in Tokyo, Yokomitsu devoted himself to creative writing in the midst of his poverty. The most serious event that occurred in his life, he tells us, was the great earthquake of 1923, which devastated the Tokyo area. The citizens, including scientists and city planners, had all been well aware of possible disasters, and yet, he felt, they had been concerned only with their immediate self-interests and thus neglected their duties and preparations for such eventualities. For Yokomitsu, the earthquake was not merely a natural phenomenon; it became a symbol for the machine culture and modern utilitarianism. In 1924 he published "A Fly" ("Hae") and "Nichirin," both of which won him critical acclaim. In "A Fly" he describes an accident in which a wagon falls into a canyon while a horsefly easily escapes the mishap.

Yokomitsu was the founder of a new school of writing called "neo-perceptionists" (*shin kankaku ha*). His style, though at times marred by an excessive embellishment, may bear the mark of such European influences as dadaism, symbolism, expressionism, and surrealism. His startling images and sense impressions can be seen in his short story "The Head and the Belly" ("Atama narabini Hara," 1924). The opening of the story reads: "It is midday. The express train with its full passengers was galloping at a high speed. Little stations along the track were suppressed like little stones." However, the most eccentric of his stories are little read today. The better-known stories like "Spring Came on a Wagon" ("Haru wa Basha ni Notte," 1926) and Kawabata's "A Dancer of Izu"

("Izu no Odoriko," 1926) are least associated with the neo-perceptionists movement.

Yokomitsu's most successful works were two of the short stories written in the middle period of his career: "Machine" and "Time" ("Jikan," 1931). The problem of "self-consciousness" treated in these stories was soon popularized in "The Bed" ("Shinen," 1930) and "The Family Conference" ("Kazoku Kaigi," 1935), serialized in newspapers. His ambitious novel *A Memory of the Journey* (*Ryoshu*, 1937–39), based on his travel abroad, attempted to compare Eastern and Western cultures but ended in a relative failure.

At first I wondered sometimes if the master of the place was not insane. He would decide that his child, not yet three, did not like him. A child had no right to dislike its father, he would announce, frowning fiercely. Barely able to walk, the child would fall on its face. That gave the man cause to slap his wife—why had she let the child fall when she was supposed to be watching it? For the rest of us this was all fine comedy. The man was in dead earnest, however, and one did begin to wonder if he might not be insane.

A man of forty snatching his child up and marching about the room with it when for a moment it stopped crying! And it was not only with the child that he seemed strange. There was a suggestion of immaturity in everything he did. It was a home industry, and his wife naturally became its center, and it was natural too that her allies there gained strength from her position. Since my own ties were if anything with the husband, I was always left to do the work everyone most disliked. It was unpleasant work, really unpleasant work. Yet it was work that had to be done if the shop was not to come to a complete standstill. In this sense it was I and not the wife who was at the center of things; but I could only remain silent about the fact. I was among people who thought that the one given an unpleasant job was the one who was otherwise useless.

Still, the useless one can sometimes be strangely useful at a task that baffles others; and in all the many processes involving chemicals in this nameplate factory, the process entrusted to me was richest in violent poisons. My job was a slot made especially for dropping otherwise useless people into. Once in the slot, I found my skin and my clothes wearing out under the corrosive attacks of ferric chloride. Fumes tore at my throat; I was unable to sleep at night. Worse, my mind seemed to be affected, and my eyesight showed signs of failing. It was not likely that a useful person would have been put into such a slot. My employer had learned the same work in his youth, but no doubt because he too was a person who was considered otherwise useless.

Still, not even I meant to linger on there until in course of time I should become an invalid. I had come to Tokyo from a shipyard in Kyushu, and on the train I happened to meet a lady, a widow in her fifties, who had neither children nor home. She meant, after presuming upon the kindness of Tokyo relatives for a time, to open a rooming house or some such business. I said jokingly that when I found work I'd come and take one of her rooms. She replied that she'd take me to see the relatives she had mentioned. They would have work for me. I had no other prospects at the time, and something refined in her manner told me to trust her. So I trailed after her and arrived here.

At first the job seemed easy. Then, gradually, I saw that the chemicals were eating away my ability to work. I'll leave today, I'll leave tomorrow, I would tell myself. But having lasted so long, I decided I should at least wait until I had learned the secrets of the trade. I set about becoming interested in dangerous chemical processes.

My fellow worker, a man named Karube, promptly decided I was a spy who had crept in to steal trade secrets. Karube had lived next door to the wife's family, and, since that fact gave him certain liberties, he responded by putting the interests of the shop above everything, becoming the proverbial faithful servant. He would fix a burning gaze upon me whenever I took a poison down from the shelf. As I loitered before the darkroom he would come up with a great clattering to let me know he was there watching. I thought all this a trifle ridiculous, and yet his earnestness made me uncomfortable. He considered the movies the finest of textbooks and detective movies a mirror of life, and there was no doubt that I, who had wandered in unannounced, was good material for his fantasies. He had ambitions beyond spending the rest of his life here. He meant one day to set up a branch establishment, and he most certainly did not mean to let me learn the secret of making red plates, an invention of our employer, before he had learned it himself.

I was interested only in learning and had not a suggestion of a plan for making my living by what I learned. Karube was not one to understand such subtleties, however, and I could not in complete honesty deny that once I had learned the business I might consider making my living from it.

In any case, my conscience would be at rest if I could assure myself that it was good for him to be teased a little. Having reached this conclusion, I quite forgot about him.

His hostility grew, and even while I was calling him a fool I came to think that, precisely because he was a fool, perhaps he wasn't such a fool after all. It is rather fun to be made a gratuitous enemy, because you can make a fool of your adversary while the situation lasts; and it took me a long time to note that this pleasure left a crack in my own defenses. I would move a chair or turn an edging tool, and a hammer would fall on my head, or sheets of brass, ground down for plates, would come crashing at my feet. A harmless compound of varnish and ether would be changed for chromic acid. At first I thought I was being careless. When it came to me that Karube was responsible for all this, I concluded that if I wasn't careful, I'd find myself dead. This was a chilling thought. Karube, though a fool, was older than I, and adept at mixing poisons. He knew that if he put ammonium dichromate into a person's tea, the result could pass as suicide. I would see something yellow in my food, take it to be chromic acid, and have trouble making my hand move in its direction. Presently, however, this caution struck me as funny. Let him try killing me if it seemed so easy! And so I forgot him again.

One day I was at work in the shop when the wife came in to tell me that her husband was going out to buy sheet metal and that I was to go with him to carry the money. When he carried it himself, he invariably lost it. Her chief concern always was to keep him away from money. Indeed, most of our troubles could be traced to this particular failing of his. No one could understand how he always managed to drop whatever money he had. Lost money will not come back, however much one storms and scolds, but, on the other hand, one does want to protest when the money for which one has sweated disappears like foam upon water. If it had happened only once or twice, things would have been different; but it happened constantly. When the master had money, he lost it. Inevitably, then, the affairs of this house shaped up rather differently from the affairs of most other houses.

A man of forty taking money and promptly losing it—one wondered how it could happen! His wife would tie his wallet around his neck and drop it inside his shirt, but even when the wallet remained on him, the money would have quite disappeared. It seemed likely that he had dropped it when he took something from the wallet. Even so, one would think that as he took his wallet out or put it away again, he might occasionally have reminded himself to look and see if he had dropped anything. Perhaps he did in fact watch himself. If so, could one believe that he really lost all his money so often? Perhaps the story was a trick on the wife's part to delay paying our wages.

So I thought for a time, but finally his behavior was enough to convince me that the wife's reports were true. It is said of the rich that they do not know what money is; and in a somewhat different sense our employer was wholly indifferent both to the five-sen copper for the public bath and to the larger amount of money for sheet metal. There was a time in history when he would have been called a sage and a saint; but those who live with a saint must be alert. None of the shop work could be left to our master, and what he should perfectly well have been able to do by himself, two men had to go out to do. It is impossible to calculate the needless labor caused by that one man. All this was true; yet the place would have been far less popular had he not been there. The business may have had its detractors, but not because of him. Not everyone approved of his subservience to his wife, but he was so good-natured, so small and docile in his chains, that on the whole he pleased people. He was even more charming when, free for a moment from his wife's sharp eye, he scampered about like an uncaged rabbit and threw money in all directions.

I am therefore constrained to say that the heart of the

house was not the mistress, or Karube, or myself. Clearly I was an underling, with an underling's devotion to his master; but I liked the man and that was that. To imagine the sort of man he was, you must think of a child of, say, five who has become a man of forty. The very thought of such a person seems ridiculous. We wanted to feel superior to him, and yet we could not. The unsightliness of our own years was revealed to us paradoxically as something fresh and new. (These were not my thoughts alone. Much the same thoughts seemed to move Karube. It occurred to me afterward that his hostility came from a good-heartedness that made him want to protect our master.) The difficulty I found in deciding to leave the shop stemmed from the unique goodness of the master's heart; and the dropping of hammers on my head seemed to come from the same source. Goodness sometimes has strange manifestations.

Well, the master and I went out that day to buy sheet metal, and on the way he said that he'd had an interesting proposal that morning: someone wanted to buy the red-plating process for fifty thousand yen. Should he sell or shouldn't he? I could not answer, and he continued: no question would arise if the process could be kept secret forever, but his competitors were feverishly at work. If he was to sell at all, he should sell now.

That might be true, but I felt no right to discuss the process on which he had worked so long. Yet if I were to leave him to his own devices, he would do as his wife told him, and she was a woman who could think of nothing not immediately before her eyes.

I wanted to do what I could for him—indeed that wish became an obsession. When I was in the shop, it seemed that all the processes and all the materials were waiting for me to put them in order. I came to look upon Karube as a menial, and, worse than that, his somewhat histrionic manner annoyed me. But then my feelings began to move in another direction. I noted again how Karube's eyes were fixed on my smallest action. When I was at work his gaze almost never left me. It seemed clear that the wife had told him of her husband's latest research and of the red-plating process. Whether she had also told him to watch me, I could not be sure. I had begun to wonder if Karube and the wife would not one day steal the secret, and I was telling myself that it might be well to do a little watching myself. I was therefore under no illusion that the two of them did not have similar doubts about me. When I was the object of suspicious looks, I did, it is true, feel somewhat uncomfortable; but it amused me to think, perhaps impudently, that I was watching them in turn.

About this time the master told me of his new research: he had long been looking for a way to tarnish metal without using ferric chloride. So far he had found nothing satisfactory. He wondered if in my spare time I would help him. However good-natured he was, I thought he should not be giving out information on so important a matter. Still, I was touched that he should trust me. It did not occur to me that the trusted one is usually the loser, and that the master thus perpetually defeated us all. That infinite childishness was not something one could acquire; it gave him his worth. I thanked him from my heart and told him that I would do what I could to help him.

I thought that some time in my life I'd like to have someone thank *me* from his heart. But since the master had no petty thoughts about "doing and being done by," I could only bow lower before him. I was trapped as if hypnotized. Miracles, I found, are not worked from without; they are rather the result of one's own inadequacy. With me as with Karube, the master came first. I began to feel hostile toward the wife who controlled him, hostile toward everything she did. Not only did I wonder by what right such a woman monopolized such a man, I even thought occasionally of how I might free him from her. The motives that made Karube lash out at me became clear as day. When I saw him I saw myself, and the relevation fascinated me.

One day the master called me into the darkroom. He was holding a piece of aniline-coated brass over an alcohol burner, and he began to explain. In coloring a plate, one must pay the most careful attention to changes under heat. The sheet of brass was now purple, but presently it would be brownish black, and when, at length, it turned black, it promised in the next test to react to ferric chloride. The coloring process, he said, was a matter of catching a middle stage in a given transformation. The master then ordered me to make burning tests with as many chemicals as possible. I became fascinated with the organic relationships between compounds and elements, and as my interest grew I learned to see delicate organic movements in inorganic substances. The discovery that in the tiniest things a law, a machine, is at work came to me as the beginning of a spiritual awakening.

When Karube noticed that I had free entry to the darkroom (until then no one had been admitted), his attitude changed. He was thinking, no doubt, that the care with which he had watched me had been wasted, since what was not permitted to him—to him who thought only of the master—was now permitted to me, a newcomer. Still more, he was thinking that unless he was careful he might find himself completely in my power. I knew that I should be more circumspect, but who was Karube that I need worry about him at every move I made? I felt no sympathy for him, only a cool, detached interest in what the fool might be up to next, and I continued to treat him with lofty indifference.

He was infuriated. Once when I needed a punch he had been using, it disappeared. Hadn't he been using it until a minute ago, I asked. What had disappeared had disappeared, whether he had been using it or not, he answered, and I could go on hunting until I found it. That was true; but hunt as I would I could not find it. Then I happened to glance at his pocket and there it was. Silently, I reached for it. Who the devil did I think I was, reaching into a person's pocket without permission, he wanted to know. Another person's pocket indeed! I retorted; while we were here in the shop everyone's pocket was everyone else's. Because that was the way I felt, he said, I was the sort that would go around stealing secrets.

"When did I steal anything? If helping the master with his work means stealing, then you're stealing too," said I.

For a moment he was silent. Then, lips quivering, he stammered: "Get out of here! Get out of this shop!"

"All right, I'll go. But I owe it to the master not to leave until the research has gone a little farther."

"Then I'm going."

I tried to quiet him. "You'll only be causing trouble. Wait until I leave myself."

But he insisted he would go.

"All right. Go ahead. I'll take on the work of us both."

With that he snatched up the powdered calcium at his elbow and threw it into my face.

I knew that I was in the wrong, but wrongdoing could be interesting. I understood his impatience clearly, the fretful irritation in the man's good heart. I felt like relaxing to enjoy the sport, but at the same time I knew that would not do; so I sought to quiet him a bit. I had been wrong to ignore him. But it would have taken more of a man than I was to cower before each new wave of indignation. The smaller one is, the more one does to make people angry. As Karube grew progressively angrier, I recognized the measure of my own smallness. In the end, I no longer knew what to do, about myself or about Karube. Never before had I found myself so unmanageable. It has been well said that the spirit follows the body's dimensions. In silence I reflected that mine seemed to match exactly.

After a time I went into the darkroom and, to precipitate a bismuth dye, began heating potassium chromate in a test tube. That too was an unwise move. The fact that I had free entry into the darkroom had already aroused Karube's envy, and now here I was in there again. He exploded, of course. Flinging the door open, he pulled me out by the collar and threw me to the floor. I let him have his way; indeed, I almost threw myself down. Violence was the only thing that worked with a person like me. He looked into the darkroom to see whether the potassium chromate had spilled, and while he was about it he went in and made a hasty circuit of the room. Then he came back and stood over me, glaring—apparently the trip around the room had not calmed him. He seemed to be wondering what to do next; he might well decide to kick me if I moved. For a few tense moments I wondered what, exactly, I was doing; but soon I began to feel as if I were dreaming. I thought I must let him have a really good tantrum, and by the time I concluded that he was angry enough to be satisfied, I was quite at ease myself. I looked in to see how much damage he had done. The devastation, I decided, was worst on my own face. Calcium was gritty in my mouth and ears. Still not sure whether I should get up, I glanced at the shining pile of aluminum cuttings by my nose and felt astonished at the amount of work I had done in three days.

"Let's stop this foolishness and get to work," I said. "There's aluminum to be coated."

But Karube had no intention to work. "Suppose we coat your face instead!"

Shoving my head deep into the cuttings, he rubbed it back and forth as though the metal were a washcloth. I visualized my face being polished by a mountain of little plates from housedoors and thought how disturbing violence could be. The corners of the aluminum stabbed at the lines and hollows of my face. Worse, the half-dried lacquer stuck to my skin. Soon my face would start swelling. I concluded that I'd done my duty and started for the darkroom again. Thereupon he seized my arm, twisted it behind my back, and pushed my face against a window, thinking, apparently, to slash it with glass splinters.

The violence would not continue long, I was sure. But as a matter of fact, it did go on and on. Though much of the blame was no doubt mine, my feeling of contrition began to fade. My face, which I had hoped wore a diffident, conciliatory expression, was swelling more and more painfully, offering a pretext for new violence. I knew that Karube was no longer enjoying his anger, but it was now beyond his control.

As he pulled me toward a vat of the most poisonous corrosive, I turned on him: "It's your business, of course, if you want to torture me, but the experiments I've been working on in the darkroom are experiments no one else has done. If they're successful, there's no telling what profits they'll bring in. You won't let me work, and now you've upset the solution I spent all that time on. Clean it up!"

"Why don't you let me work with you, then?"

I could not tell him that the decision was out of my hands, that a person who could not even read a chemical equation would be less of a help than a hindrance. It may have been a little cruel of me, but I took him into the darkroom, showed him the closely written equations, and explained them to him.

"If you think you'd find it interesting, go ahead—mix and remix, using these figures. Go ahead! You can do it every day in my place, all day long." For the first time, I had the better of him.

With the fighting over, I found life easier for a time. Then, suddenly, Karube and I became extremely busy. An order arrived from a municipal office to make nameplates for a whole city, fifty thousand plates in ten days. The wife was delighted, but we knew it meant that we would have to go virtually without sleep. The master borrowed a craftsman from another nameplate shop. At first I was overwhelmed by the sheer volume of work; but soon I began to see something strange in the manner of the new man, Yashiki. Although his awkwardness and his sharp glance did suggest a craftsman, I suspected that he might perhaps have been sent to steal our secrets. If I were to speak of my suspicions, however, there would be no way of knowing what Karube might do to him, and I decided to keep quiet for a time and to observe. I noted that Yashiki's attention was always focused on the way Karube shook his vat. Karube's work was the second specialty of our shop, something no other shop could imitate. Yashiki put sheets of brass into a solution of caustic soda to wash away the varnish and glue that Karube used with corrosive ferric chloride. It was therefore natural that Yashiki should be interested. Still, given my doubts, the very naturalness of it was cause for further doubt.

But Karube, more and more pleased with himself now that he had an audience, was in great form as he shook his vat of ferric chloride. Since he had doubts about me, he should naturally have had even greater doubts about Yashiki. Quite the reverse was true: he explained the shaking of the vat in such esoteric terms that I wondered where he might have learned them. You always laid the inscription face down, it seemed, and let the weight of the metal do the work. The uninscribed surface corroded more rapidly—suppose Yashiki try for himself. At first I listened nervously to the chatter, but in the end I decided that it made no difference. One might as well teach the secrets to anyone who wanted them. I would no longer be on my guard against Yashiki.

My chief gain from this incident was the discovery that a secret leaks out because of the conceit of its possessor. But it was not only conceit that led Karube to tell everything. Without a doubt, Yashiki was an able seducer. Though the light in his eyes was sharp, it had a strange charm, when it softened, that had the effect of making one's caution melt away. That same charm affected me each time he spoke, but I was so busy with all the jobs I had to rush through that I paid little attention: from early in the morning I had to lacquer heated brass and dry it, put metal coated with ammonium dichromate out to react in the sun, add aniline, and then rush from burner to polisher to cutter. There was little time for Yashiki to charm me.

About five nights after he came, I awoke and saw Yashiki, who should have been doing night work, come from the darkroom and go into the wife's room. While I was wondering what could be taking him there at such an hour, I unfortunately fell asleep again. But the first thought that came into my mind next morning was of Yashiki. The trouble was that I gradually became less sure whether I had actually seen him or whether it had been a dream. I had had similar experiences from overwork before, and I suspected that I had only been dreaming. I could imagine what reason he might have for going into the darkroom, but I had no idea how to explain his entry into the other room. I could not believe that the wife and Yashiki were carrying on in secret. The easiest solution, then, was to dismiss it all as a dream.

At about noon, the master began laughing and asking his wife if there had been anything out of the ordinary on the previous evening.

"I may be a heavy sleeper," she answered quietly, "but I know who took the money. If you have to steal it, you might at least do it more cleverly."

He laughed still more delightedly.

Had it been not Yashiki but the master I had seen going into her room? I thought it odd that the latter should be sneaking into his own wife's room, chronically short of money though he was.

"It was you I saw coming from the darkroom?" I asked.

"The darkroom? I don't know anything about the darkroom."

The confusion deepened. Had it been Yashiki, after all, in the darkroom? It seemed certain that the man who had stolen into the wife's room was not Yashiki but the husband; yet I could not think I had only dreamed Yashiki's emergence from the darkroom. The suspicions that had for a time left me began to gather again. I saw, however, that doubting in solitude was like doubting oneself, and did no good. I'd better ask Yashiki directly. But if I did and it had in fact been he, then he would be upset, and to upset him would be no gain.

Still, the matter was of such interest that I thought it a pity not to push it further. For one thing, the secret formula for combining bismuth and zirconium silicate—the process on which I had been so hard at work—and the formula for the red amorphous selenium stain that was the master's specialty were both kept in the darkroom. Not only would their loss be a severe blow to the business, but the loss of my own secret would take all the zest from life. If Yashiki was trying to steal the formula, there was no reason that I shouldn't try to keep it hidden. I suspected him more intensely. When I thought how, after having been suspected by Karube, it had now become my turn to suspect Yashiki, I wondered if I'd be giving Yashiki the same prolonged pleasure I'd had in making a fool of Karube. But then I thought it over and decided it would do me good to let myself be made a fool of for once. So I turned my full attention to Yashiki.

Perhaps because he noticed how my eyes burned at him, Yashiki began to look exclusively in directions where his eyes would not meet mine. I was afraid that if I made him too uncomfortable he might take flight. I must be more circumspect. Eyes are strange things, however. When glances that have been wandering at the same level of consciousness meet, each seems to probe the other to its depths.

I would be at the polisher, talking of this and that, and my glance would ask him: "Have you stolen the formulas yet?"

"Not yet, not yet," that burning eye would seem to answer.

"Well, be quick about it."

"It takes a devil of a long time, now that you know what I'm after."

"My formula is full of mistakes anyway. It wouldn't do you much good to steal it now."

"I can correct it."

So the imaginary conversations went, while Yashiki and I worked together; and gradually I began to feel friendlier toward him than toward anyone else in the place. The Yashiki charm that had excited Karube and made him reveal all his secrets was now working on me. I would read the newspaper with Yashiki, and on subjects that interested us both our opinions always agreed, especially on technical matters. I'd speed up reading when he speeded up and slow down when he slowed down. Our views on politics and our plans for society were alike. The only question on which we disagreed was the propriety of trying to steal another person's invention. He had his own views, and thought there was nothing wrong with stealing if it contributed to the advance of civilization. In such a case, the person who tries to steal may, in fact, be better than the one who does not. Comparing his spy activities with my own attempts to hide inventions, I concluded that he was doing more for the world than I. So I thought—and so Yashiki made me think. He seemed to approach nearer and nearer; yet I wanted to keep at least the secret of the amorphous selenium stain from him. So, even while I became his closest friend, I was also the one who most got in his way.

I told him that Karube had suspected me of being a spy when I first came to work here, and had almost killed me. Karube had not done the same to him, laughed Yashiki, because Karube had learned a lesson with me.

"So that's why you found it so easy to be suspicious of me," he added mischievously.

"If you knew all along that I was suspicious, you must have come here prepared to be suspected."

"That's right," he said.

He was as good as admitting he had come to steal our secrets. I could not help being astonished at the openness with which he said so. Perhaps he had seen through me and was sure that in my surprise I would come to respect him. I glared at him for some seconds.

But Yashiki's expression had already changed. Somewhat loftily, he went on: "When you come to work in a shop like this, it's the usual thing to have people think you're up to something. But what could a person like me do? No—I won't begin apologizing now. Suppose we just work and let work. The worst thing," and he laughed, "is having someone like you look at me as if I ought to be doing something bad when I'm not."

He had touched a sensitive spot. I felt a certain sympathy for the man. I had borne the sort of treatment he was now getting.

"You can't be enjoying the work very much if it makes you say things like that," I said.

Yashiki pulled his shoulders back and shot a glance at me, then passed the moment off with a quick laugh.

I made it my policy to let him plot as he would. A person of his ability would no doubt have seen everything in a single trip into the darkroom, and, having let him see, one could do nothing, short of killing him, except take the consequences. Perhaps one should rather be grateful for having met such a remarkable person in such an unlikely place.

I went even further: I came to think that it would be a good thing if, in the course of time, he did succeed in taking advantage of the master and stealing our secrets.

One day I said to him: "I don't mean to stay here long myself. Do you know of any good openings?"

"I meant to ask you the same thing. If we're alike even in that, what right have you to be lecturing me?"

"I see what you mean. But don't misunderstand me. I don't mean to be lecturing and I don't mean to be prying. It's just that I respect you, and I thought you might let me be your pupil."

"Pupil?" He smiled wryly. Then, abruptly, he was sober again. "Go and have a look at a ferric chloride factory, where the trees and grass have died for a hundred yards around, and talk to me again afterward."

I had no idea what the "afterward" might mean, but I thought I caught a glimpse of his reasons for thinking me rather simple. But what were the limits to which he would go in making me look foolish? They seemed far out of sight. Gradually I lost interest, and as I did so I thought I would have a try at making *him* look foolish. I had been attracted to him, however, and the effort was abortive—in fact it was comical. These superior people put one through a harsh discipline!

One day when we were about to finish the rush order, Karube threw Yashiki on his face under the cutter. "Admit it, admit it!" he said.

Apparently he had caught Yashiki sneaking into the darkroom.

Astride Yashiki's back, Karube was pounding at his head when I came into the shop. So it's finally happened, I thought. But I felt no impulse to go to Yashiki's rescue. Indeed, I was rather a Judas, curious to see how the man I respected would respond to violence. I looked coolly into Yashiki's twisted face. He was struggling to get up, one side of his head in some varnish that was flowing across the floor, but each time Karube's knee hit him in the back he fell on his face again. His trousers were pushed up, and his stout legs were bare, threshing awkwardly at the floor. This rather spirited resistance struck me as utterly foolish, but revulsion was stronger than disdain, as if the face of the respected one, ugly from pain, showed an ugliness of spirit as well. I was troubled less by the violence itself than by the fact that Karube could force a person to wear such an ugly expression.

Karube had no eye for expressions, ugly or otherwise. He seized Yashiki's neck in both hands and pounded his head against the floor. I began to doubt whether my indifference to suffering was entirely proper, but I felt that if I were to make the slightest move to help one or the other, I would be guilty of still greater impropriety. I also began to wonder whether Yashiki, not prepared to confess in spite of the pain to which that ugly, twisted face testified, had actually stolen anything from the darkroom, and I turned to the task of reading his secret in the furrows of his distorted face. From time to time he glanced at me. To give him strength, I offered a contemptuous smile each time his eyes met mine. He made a really determined effort to overturn Karube. He was helpless, however, and there was a new rain of blows.

Starting up whenever I laughed at him, Yashiki was showing his true colors. The more he moved himself to action, it would seem, the more he gave himself away. Though I tried to continue laughing at him, I began to feel something more like contempt, until, as the moments passed, I was no longer able to laugh at all. Yashiki had a way of choosing the least likely moments for his struggles. A most ordinary human being he was, no different from the rest of us.

"Suppose you stop hitting him," I said to Karube. "Won't it do just to talk to him?"

"Stand up!" Karube gave his victim a kick and poured metal fragments over his head, much as he had buried my head in similar fragments.

Yashiki edged away and stood with his back to the wall. He explained rapidly that he had gone into the darkroom in search of ammonia. He had been unable to clean glue from sheet metal with caustic soda.

"If you needed ammonia, why didn't you ask for it?" said Karube, and hit him again. "Anyone ought to know that there's no place in a nameplate factory as important as the darkroom."

I knew that Yashiki's explanation was absurd, but the thunder of Karube's fists was too violent. "You ought at least to stop hitting him," I said.

With that Karube turned on me. "It's a plot between the two of you, is it?"

"You can answer that yourself if you give it a little thought," I was about to say; but it occurred to me that our actions not only could be thought a conspiracy; they might, in fact, be something very like one. I had calmly let Yashiki go into the darkroom, and even thought myself less of a person for *not* stealing the master's secrets. The result was, in effect, a conspiracy.

As my conscience began to trouble me, I assumed a confident manner. "Plot or no plot, I think you've hit him enough," I said.

With that Karube hit me on the jaw. "I suppose you let him into the darkroom."

I was less concerned about being struck than I was eager to show Yashiki, who had already been struck, how I was now being struck for taking his crime upon myself. I felt almost exhilarated. "Look at me now!" I wanted to cry. I had a strange feeling, however, that Karube and I must now seem the conspirators. Yashiki must think that I could so unconcernedly allow myself to be hit only because we had arranged this in advance. I glanced up at him—he seemed to have come to life now that there were two of us.

"Hit him!" he cried, flailing away at the back of Karube's head.

I was not particularly angry, but because of the pain I took a certain pleasure in the exercise of hitting back. I hit Karube in the face several times. Thus assaulted from before and behind, he turned his main attention to Yashiki. I tugged from behind, and Yashiki, still flailing away, took advantage of the opening to knock him down and sit on him. I was astonished at how lively Yashiki had become. Doubtless it was because he thought that I, angry at having been hit without reason, was with him in the attack.

But I had no need of further revenge. I stood silently by and watched. Effortlessly, Karube overturned Yashiki, and began pounding him more fiercely than before. Again Yashiki was helpless. After Karube had pounded Yashiki for a time, he suddenly stood up and came at me, perhaps thinking I might attack him from the rear. It was a foregone conclusion that I would lose in single combat with Karube. I kept my peace once more and waited for Yashiki to help me. But Yashiki began hitting not Karube but me. Unable to cope with even one adversary, I could do nothing against two. I lay there and let them hit.

Had I been so wrong? As I lay doubled up with my head in my arms, I wondered if I had so misbehaved that I must be hit by both of them. No doubt my conduct had been surprising, but had the other two not also chosen courses that could be called strange? At least, there was no reason for Yashiki to be hitting me. It was true that I had not joined him in the attack on Karube; but he had been a fool to expect me to.

In any event, the only one who had not been attacked by the other two simultaneously was Yashiki. The one who most deserved to be hit had most cleverly escaped.

By the time I began to think I'd like to give him a cuffing for his pains, we were all exhausted. The cause of the whole senseless fight had clearly been less that Yashiki had gone into the darkroom than that we were exhausted from having made fifty thousand nameplates in such a short time. Ferric chloride fumes wore on one's nerves and disordered one's reason, and instinct seemed to reveal itself from every pore. If a man chose to be angry at each small incident in a nameplate factory, there would be no end to anger.

I had, nonetheless, been hit by Yashiki, and the fact was not to be forgotten. What was he thinking? If his behavior gave me the occasion, I'd find ways to make him ashamed of himself.

When the incident stopped—though one could hardly have said that it had an ending—Yashiki turned to me. "It was wrong of me to hit you, but I had to finish the business. There was no telling how long Karube would go on hitting me. I'm sorry."

That was true, I had to agree. If I, the least guilty, had not been hit by both of them, the fighting would have gone on and on. I smiled wryly. I had, then, been protecting Yashiki in his thievery. And I must forgo the pleasure of making him ashamed of himself. The man was an astonishingly able plotter.

In some chagrin, I said to him: "If you've been so clever at using me, I'm sure you've been just as clever at getting secrets from the darkroom."

"If even you think that, it's only natural that Karube should have hit me." He laughed his practiced laugh. "Weren't you the one who turned him on me?"

I could offer no explanation if he chose to think that I had provoked the incident. Perhaps he had hit me because he suspected that I was in league with Karube. It was becoming harder and harder to know what these two thought of me.

In the midst of all this uncertainty, however, there was one clear thing: Karube and Yashiki, in their separate ways, were both suspicious of me. But however clear this fact might seem to me, was there any way for me to know how clear it *really* was? In any case, some invisible machine was constantly measuring us all, as if it understood everything that went on, and was pushing us according to the results of its measurements.

Even while we nursed our suspicions in this way, we were looking forward to the next day, when the job would finally be over and we could rest. Forgetting our exhaustion and enmity in pleasant thoughts of payment, we finished that day —and the next day a new blow hit.

On his way home, the master lost the whole of the money he had received for those fifty thousand nameplates. The labors that had not allowed us a decent night's sleep in ten days had come to precisely nothing.

The sister who had first introduced me had gone with her brother, foreseeing that he might drop the money—and at least that much had run true to form. He had said that for the first time in a very long while he would like to have the pleasure of holding the money we had earned, all of it. Quite understanding, his sister let him have it for a few minutes. And in those few minutes the flaw worked like an infallible machine.

Though we did report the loss to the police, naturally none of us thought the money would ever be seen again, and we just sat looking at each other. We could no longer expect to be paid, and exhaustion suddenly overtook us. For a time we lay motionless in the shop. Then, smashing some boards that lay at hand and flinging away the pieces, Karube turned on me.

"Why are you smiling?"

I did not mean to be smiling, but since he said I was, presumably I was. No doubt it was because the master was so comical—the comedy being probably a result of long years of exposure to ferric chloride fumes. I felt anew that few things were to be so feared as mental disorder. What a wondrous system it was whose workings made a man's defects draw others to him, leaving them unable to fear!

I did not answer. It would do no good to explain.

Then Karube stopped glaring at me. "We'll have a drink!" he said, clapping his hands.

He had spoken at a moment when one or another of us was to speak. Inevitably, our thoughts turned to liquor. At such times there is nothing for young men to do but drink. Not even Yashiki could have guessed that because of the liquor he would lose his life.

That night we sat drinking in the shop until after midnight. When I awoke I saw that Yashiki had mistaken leftover ammonium dichromate for water, had drunk from the jug, and had died. Even now I do not think, as the men from the shop that sent him here seem to, that Karube killed Yashiki. Althought it was I who had again that day done the gluing in which ammonium dichromate is used, Karube and not I had suggested that we drink, and it was natural that suspicion should fall more heavily on him. Still, it did not seem likely that Karube could have conceived the dark plot of getting him drunk and killing him unless we had thought of drinking much earlier in the evening. Karube was nonetheless suspected, probably because of the threatening manner that revealed him as one who liked violence.

I do not say with finality that Karube did not kill Yashiki. I can only say that my limited knowledge makes me able to conjecture that he did not. For I know he, like me, must have thought, upon seeing Yashiki go into the darkroom, that there was no way short of killing him to keep him from stealing the secrets. I had thought that the way to kill him would be to get him drunk and give him ammonium dichromate, and the same thought must have run through Karube's mind. Yet not only Yashiki and I were drunk. Karube was too. So it seems unlikely that Karube gave Yashiki the poison. And if the possibilities that had troubled Karube through recent days had worked in his drunken mind to make him offer Yashiki ammonium dichromate, then perhaps, by the same token, it was I who was the criminal.

Indeed how can I say absolutely that I did not kill him? Was it not I, rather than Karube, who feared him? All the time he was there, was it not I who was most on guard to see if he went into the darkroom? Was it not I who harbored the deepest resentment at the idea of his stealing the bismuth and zirconium silicate formula I was working on?

Perhaps I murdered him. I knew better than anyone where the ammonium dichromate was. Before drunkenness overtook me, I kept thinking about Yashiki and what he would be doing somewhere else the next day, when he would be free to leave. And if he had lived, would I not have lost more than Karube? And had not my head, like the master's, been attacked by ferric chloride?

I no longer understand myself. I only feel the sharp menace of an approaching machine, aimed at me. Someone must judge me. How can I know what I have done?

ANGO SAKAGUCHI
"The Idiot"
("Hakuchi," 1946)

Translated by George Saito

Ango Sakaguchi (1906–55) was born into a wealthy old family in the city of Niigata in northern Japan. His father was a member of the Diet and a classical Chinese poet. Since his childhood Sakaguchi had detested conventionality or established social institutions. At the age of seventeen he dropped out of a local middle school and went to Toyo. He studied Indian philosophy at Tokyo University, from which he was graduated in 1930. During his college days, he also studied French at Athénée Français.

In 1931 he published the group magazine *Blue Horse* (*Aoi Uma*) in collaboration with his friends at the French school. His earliest short stories "Dr. Kaze" ("Kaze Hakase," 1931) and "Kurotani Village" ("Kurotani Mura," 1931), published in that magazine, attracted the attention of critics. The thirties in Japan saw the rise of interest in an aesthetic movement as proletarian literature declined. Sakaguchi, joining the new movement, wrote a number of short stories and essays for such magazines as *Literary Season* (*Bungei Shunju*), *Action* (*Kodo*), and *Literary Circle* (*Bungaku Kai*), but failed to produce successful works. He lived the life of a hobo in various places until the war broke out.

"Pearl" ("Shinju," 1942) and "My Personal View of Japanese Culture" (Nippon Bunka Shikan," 1943) attracted attention even during the war. But his reputation was established after the war with the essay "A Theory of Degeneration" ("Daraku Ron," 1946) and the short story "The Idiot," published in *New Current* (*Shin Cho*). In the next ten years he enjoyed recognition as one of the most energetic writers to appear in the postwar era.

Sakaguchi was one of the few Japanese writers of fiction

who produced more essays and critical writings than stories. Some of his nonfiction works are accused of being pure journalism and hackwork. His writing is even said to have deteriorated in his later years because of alcohol, drugs, and parties. Unlike many established writers, Sakaguchi saw little value in the traditional beauties—classical literature, artifacts, and old temples. He was strongly opposed to nationalism as is indicated in "My Personal View of Japanese Culture." True art, he argued, is knowing how to live fully and passionately, and he kept his conviction till his death in poverty.

"The Idiot," Sakaguchi's greatest achievement, reflects both his view of life and his style of writing.

Various species lived in the house: human beings, a pig, a dog, a hen, a duck. But actually there was hardly any difference in their style of lodging or in the food they ate. It was a crooked building like a storehouse. The owner and his wife lived on the ground floor, while a mother and her daughter rented the attic. The daughter was pregnant, but no one knew who was responsible.

The room that Izawa rented was in a hut detached from the main house. It had formerly been occupied by the family's consumptive son, who had died. Even if it had been assigned to a consumptive pig, the hut could hardly have been considered extravagant. Nevertheless, it had drawers, shelves, and a lavatory.

The owner and his wife were tailors. They also gave sewing lessons to the neighbors, and this was the reason that the son had been placed in a separate hut. The owner was an official of the neighborhood association, in which the girl who lived in the attic had originally worked. It appeared that while she was living in the association's office, she had enjoyed sexual relations indiscriminately with all the officials of the association except the president and the tailor. She had thus had more than ten lovers and now she was with child by one of them. When this unfortunate fact became known, the officials collected a fund to take care of the child when it was born. In this world nothing goes to waste: among the officials was a bean-curd dealer who continued to visit the girl even after she had become pregnant and had taken refuge in the attic. In the end, the girl was virtually established as this man's mistress. When the other officials learned of the situation, they immediately withdrew their contributions and asserted that the bean-curd dealer ought to bear her living expenses. There were seven or eight of them who refused to pay, including the greengrocer, the watchmaker, and the landlord. Since they had been giving five yen each, the loss was considerable and there was no end to the girl's resentment.

She had a big mouth and two large eyes, yet she was fearfully thin. She disliked the duck and tried to give all the leftovers to the hen, but since the duck invariably butted in and snatched the food, she would chase it furiously round the room. The way she ran in a strangely erect posture, with her huge belly and her buttocks jutting out to the front and the rear, bore a striking resemblance to the duck's waddle.

At the entrance to the alley was a tobacconist, a thickly powdered woman of fifty-five. She had just got rid of her seventh or eighth lover, and rumor had it that she was now having trouble making up her mind about whether to choose in his stead a middle-aged Buddhist priest or a certain shopkeeper, also middle-aged. She was known to sell a couple of cigarettes (at the black-market price) to any young man who went to the back door of her shop. "Why don't you try buying some, sir?" the tailor had suggested to Izawa. Izawa, however, had no need to call on the old woman since he received a special ration at his office.

Behind the rice-supply office diagonally opposite the tobacconist's lived a widow who had accumulated some savings. She had two children: a son, who was a factory hand, and a younger daughter. Though really brother and sister, these two had lived as man and wife. The widow had connived at this, feeling that it would be cheaper in the long run. In the meantime, however, the son had acquired a mistress on the side. The need had therefore arisen to marry off the daughter, and it had been decided that she should become the bride of a man of fifty or sixty who was vaguely related. Thereupon the daughter had taken rat poison. After swallowing the poison, she had come to the tailor's (where Izawa lodged) for her sewing lesson. There she had begun to suffer the most atrocious agonies, and had finally died. The local doctor certified that she had died from a heart attack and this had been the end of the matter. "Eh?" Izawa had asked the tailor in surprise. "Where do you find doctors who'll issue such convenient certificates?" The tailor had been even more surprised. "D'you mean to say they don't do that sort of thing everywhere?" he said.

It was a neighborhood where tenements were clustered together. A considerable proportion of the rooms was occupied by kept women or prostitutes. Since these women had no children and since they were all inclined to keep their rooms neat, the caretakers of the buildings liked having them as tenants and did not mind about the disorderliness and immorality of their private lives. More than half of the apartments had become dormitories used by munitions factories and were occupied by groups of women volunteer-workers. Among the tenants were pregnant volunteers who continued receiving their salaries even though they never went to work; the girl friend of Mr. So-and-So in such-and-such a section of the government; the "wartime wife" of the section chief (which meant that the real wife had been evacuated from Tokyo); the official mistress of a company director.

One of the women was reported to be a five-hundred-yen mistress and was the object of general envy. Next door to the soldier of fortune from Manchuria, who proudly boasted that his profession used to be murder (his younger sister studied sewing with the tailor), lived a manual therapist; next to him lived a man who, it was rumored, belonged to one of the traditional schools that practiced the fine art of picking pockets. Behind him lived a naval sublieutenant who ate fish, drank coffee, feasted on tinned food, and had saké every day. Because of the subterranean water which one found on digging a foot or so below the surface, it was almost impossible to construct air-raid shelters in this neighborhood; the sublieutenant, however, had somehow contrived to build a concrete shelter which was even finer than his actual apartment.

The department store, a wooden, two-story building on the route that Izawa took on his way to work, was closed because of the wartime lack of commodities; but on the upper floor gambling was being carried on every day. The boss of the gambling gang also controlled a number of "people's bars." He got dead drunk every day of the week and used to glare fiercely at the people who stood in queues waiting to enter his bars.

On graduation from the university, Izawa had become a newspaper reporter; subsequently he had started working on educational films. This was his present job, but he was still an apprentice and had not yet directed anything independently. He was twenty-seven, an age at which one is likely to know something about the seamy side of society; and in fact he had managed to pick up a good deal of inside information about politicians, army officers, businessmen, geishas, and entertainers. Yet he had never imagined that life in a suburban shopping district surrounded by small factories and apartment buildings could be anything like this. It occurred to him that it might be due to the roughening effect of the war on people's characters, but when he asked the tailor about it one day, the man replied in a quiet, philosophical way: "No, to tell the truth, things have always been like this in our neighborhood."

But the outstanding character of them all was the man next door. This neighbor was mad. He was quite well off and one way in which his madness revealed itself was in an excessive fear of intrusion by burglars or other undesirable people. This had led him to choose for his house a place at the very end of the alley and to construct the entrance in such a way that one could not find it even if one went up to the house and past the gate. There was nothing to be seen from the front but a latticed window. The real entrance was at the opposite end of the house from the gate and one had to go around the entire building to reach it. The owner's plan was that an intruder would either give up and beat a hasty retreat, or else would be discovered as he roamed about the house looking for the elusive entrance. Izawa's mad neighbor had little liking for the common people of this floating world. His house was a two-story building with quite a large number of rooms, but even the well-informed tailor knew hardly anything about the interior design.

The madman was about thirty; he had a wife of about twenty-five, and a mother. People said that at least the mother should be classed as sane. She had an extremely hysterical nature, however, and was without doubt the most mettlesome woman in the neighborhood, so much so that when she was dissatisfied with her rational allocations she would rush out of the house barefoot to complain instantly to the town block-association.

The man's wife was an idiot. One lucky year he had undergone a religious awakening, clad himself in white, and set out on a pilgrimage to Shikoku. In the course of the trip he had become friendly with a feebleminded woman somewhere in Shikoku: he had brought her back as a sort of souvenir of his pilgrimage and had married her.

The madman was a handsome fellow. His feebleminded wife had an elegance becoming a daughter of a good family; her narrow-eyed, oval face had the prettiness of an old-fashioned doll or of a Noh mask. Outwardly the two were not only good-looking but appeared to be a well-matched couple of considerable breeding. The madman was extremely shortsighted and wore strong spectacles. As a rule he had a pensive air, as though tired from reading innumerable books.

One day when an air-raid drill was being held in the alley and the housewives were all bustling about efficiently, the madman had stood there in his everyday kimono, giggling inanely as he observed the scene. Then he had suddenly left and reappeared wearing an air-raid uniform. Grabbing a bucket from someone, he had started to draw water and to throw it about the place, uttering various curious exclamations all the while. After that he placed a ladder against the wall, climbed to the top, and began shouting orders from the roof, ending in a stirring admonitory speech. This was the first time that Izawa had actually realized that the man was mad. He had, it is true, already noticed certain eccentricities in his neighbor. For instance, the man would occasionally break through the fence into the tailor's garden and empty a bucket of leftovers into the pigpen; after this he would suddenly throw a stone at the duck or, with an air of perfect nonchalance, start feeding the hen and then abruptly give her a kick. But on the whole Izawa had taken the man to be compos mentis and he used to exchange silent greetings with him when they happened to meet.

What was the real difference, he wondered, between the

madman and normal people? The difference, if any, was that the madman was essentially more discreet. To be sure, he giggled when he wanted to, gave a speech when he felt like it, threw stones at the duck, and would spend a couple of hours poking a pig's head and rear if the spirit so moved him. Nevertheless, he was essentially far more apprehensive of public opinion than normal people and he took special care in trying to isolate the main part of his private life from others. This was another reason that he had placed the entrance to his house on exactly the opposite side from the gate. On the whole the madman's private life was devoid of noise, he did not go in for useless chatting, and he lived in a meditative way. On the opposite side of the alley was an apartment from which the sound of running water and of vulgar female voices constantly encroached upon Izawa's hut. The apartment was occupied by two sisters who were prostitutes. On nights when the elder sister had a customer, the younger one would pace the corridor; when the younger sister had a customer, the elder one would walk up and down deep into the night. And people considered the madman to be of a different race, thought Izawa, merely because he was in the habit of giggling.

The madman's feebleminded wife was a remarkably quiet and gentle woman. Her speech consisted of a timid mumble; even when one could make out the words, her meaning was usually obscure. She did not know how to prepare a meal or boil rice. She might have been able to cook if she had had to, but as soon as she made a mistake and was scolded, she became so nervous that she began to spill and drop everything. Even when she went to get rations she could do nothing herself; she merely stood there and let the neighbors manage for her. People said that since she was the wife of a madman it was quite appropriate that she should be an idiot and that the man's family could hardly expect anything better. The mother, however, was greatly dissatisfied and was constantly complaining about the misfortune of having a daughter-in-law who could not even boil rice. As a rule she was a modest and refined old woman, but owing to her hysteria she could become even fiercer than her mad son once she had been aroused. Among the three unbalanced occupants of the house it was the old mother who uttered the loudest screams. The idiot wife was so intimidated by this that she was in a perpetual state of nerves, even on peaceful days when nothing had gone wrong. The mere sound of footsteps would fill her with alarm. When Izawa greeted her on the street, she would stand there petrified, with a vacant look on her face.

The wife, too, occasionally came to the tailor's pigpen. Whereas the husband broke in openly, as if the house belonged to him, and threw stones at the duck or poked the pig's jowls, the feebleminded woman slipped in silently like a shadow and hid behind the pigpen. In a way this had become her sanctuary. After she had been there for a while, the old woman's croaking voice would usually come from the next door, shouting "Osayo, Osayo!" and the idiot's body would react to each call by crouching further in the corner or by bending over. Before reluctantly emerging from her hiding place, the wife would time after time repeat her impotent, wormlike movements of resistance.

Izawa's occupations of newspaper reporter and educational-film director were the meanest of the mean. The only thing such people seemed to understand was the current fashion, and their lives consisted of a constant effort not to be left behind by the times. In this world there was no room for personality, or the pursuit of the ego, or originality. Like office workers, civil servants, or school teachers, their daily conversation abounded with such words as ego, mankind, personality, originality. But all this was mere verbiage. What they meant by "human suffering" was some such nonsense as the discomfort of a hangover after a drunken night during which one has spent all one's money trying to seduce a woman. They absorbed themselves in making films or writing fanciful pieces of colored prose which had neither spiritual value nor any element of real feeling but made ample use of such clichés as "ah, how inspiring the sight of the Rising Sun flag!"; "all our thanks to you, brave soldiers!"; "despite oneself the hot tears well up"; "the thud-thud of bombs"; "frantically one hurls oneself to the ground"; "the chattering of machine-gun fire"; and they firmly believed that with this kind of drivel they were actually portraying war.

Some said they could not write because of military censorship, but the fact was that, war or no war, they had not the slightest idea how to write honestly on any subject. Truth or real feeling in writing has nothing to do with censorship. In whatever period these gentry had happened to live, their personalities would surely have displayed the same emptiness. They changed in accordance with the prevailing fashion, and took for their models expressions culled from popular novels of the day.

To be sure, the period itself was both crude and senseless. What relationship could there be between human honesty and the cataclysm of war and defeat in which Japan's two-thousand-year-old history was being submerged? The entire fate of the nation was being decided by the will of those men who had the feeblest power of introspection, and by the blind action of the ignorant mob that followed them. If you spoke about personality and originality in front of the city editor or the president, he would turn away as if to say that you were a fool. After all, a newspaper reporter was merely a machine whose function it was to spout forth "all our thanks to you, brave soldiers!"; "ah, how inspiring the sight of the Rising Sun flag!"; "despite oneself the hot tears well up." And so, indeed, was the entire period—it was all a mere machine. If you asked whether it was really necessary to give a full report of the speech by the divisional commander to his men, or whether you had to record every word of the weird Shinto prayer that the factory workers were obliged to recite each morning, the city editor would look away and click his tongue with annoyance; then he would suddenly turn round, crush his precious cigarette in the ash tray, and, glaring at you, shout: "Look here, what does beauty mean at a time like this? Art is powerless! Only news is real."

The directors, the members of the planning department, and the other groups had banded together to constitute their own private cabals, rather like the professional gambling societies of the Tokugawa period. Everything was based on group comradeship, and the individual talents of the members were used on a rotational basis with special emphasis on the traditional precepts of "duty" and "human feeling." The entire organization became more bureaucratic than the bureaucracy itself. Thus they managed to protect their respective mediocrities and to form a sort of mutual-aid relief organization founded on a hopeless dearth of talent. Any attempt to work one's way up by means of artistic individuality was regarded as a wicked violation of union rules. Internally the groups were relief organizations for the dearth of talent, but in their relations to the outside world they were alcohol-acquiring gangs whose members occupied the "people's bars" and argued drunkenly about art as they swilled their bottles of beer. Their berets, their long hair, their ties, and their blouses were those of artists; but in their souls they were more bureaucratic than the bureaucrats. Since Izawa believed in artistic creativeness and in individuality, he found it hard to breathe in the atmosphere of these cabals; their mediocrity, their vulgar and sordid spirit, were sheer anathema. He became an outcast: no one returned his greetings and some people in the office even glared at him when he made his appearance.

One day he strode resolutely into the president's office and asked whether there was any inevitable, logical link between the war and the current poverty of artistic output. Or was this poverty, he asked, the deliberate aim of the military, who insisted that all one needed to portray reality was a camera and a couple of fingers? Surely, said Izawa, the special duty of us artists is to decide on the particular angle from which we should portray reality so as to produce a work of art. While Izawa was still talking, the president turned aside and puffed at his cigarette with a look of disgust. Then he smiled sardonically as if to say "Why don't you leave our company if you don't like it here? Is it because you're afraid of being drafted for hard labor?" Gradually his expression changed to one of annoyance. "Why can't you fit in with our way of working?" he seemed to say. "Just do your daily stint like the other men and you'll collect your salary all the same! And stop thinking about what doesn't concern you. Damned impertinence!" Without a single word in reply to Izawa's questions, the president motioned for him to leave the room.

How could this job of his be anything but the meanest of the mean? Sometimes he felt that it would be best to be done with it all and to be called into the army. If only he could escape from the anguish of thinking, even bullets and starvation might seem a blessing.

While Izawa's company was working on films like *Don't Let Rabaul Fall to the Enemy!* and *More Planes for Rabaul!* the American forces had already passed Rabaul and landed on Saipan. Saipan fell before they had finished *The All-Out Fight for Saipan;* and soon American planes based on Saipan were flying overhead in Japan. Strange was the enthusiasm with which Izawa's colleagues planned their films. *How to Extinguish Incendiary Bombs; Bodies that Crash in Midair; How to Grow Potatoes; Let Not a Single Enemy Plane Survive!; Power Saving and Airplanes*—one after another they turned out their infinitely boring lengths of celluloid.

Soon they began to run out of film stock, and usable cameras also grew scarce. The artists' enthusiasm reached new heights, as though they were possessed by some lyrical frenzy. Their films now bore such titles as *The Kamikaze Suicide Pilots; The Decisive Battle for the Mainland; The Cherry Blossoms Have Fallen.* Infinitely boring films, films like pieces of pale paper. And Tokyo was about to turn into ruins.

Izawa's enthusiasm was dead. When he woke up in the morning and realized that he had to go to work again, he immediately became sleepy. Just as he was dozing off, the air-raid warning sounded. He got up and put on his leggings. Then he took out a cigarette and lit it. It occurred to him that if he missed work he would run out of cigarettes.

One night Izawa was late and barely managed to catch the last tram. The private electric line had already closed down and to get home he had to walk a considerable distance through the dark streets. When he turned on the light he was surprised to find that his bedding, which he always left spread out on the floor, had disappeared. This was strange since no one ever came into his room when he was out. He opened the closet. There, next to the heaps of his bedding, crouched the idiot woman from next door.

She glanced uneasily at Izawa and buried her face in the bedding. But when she discovered that he was not going to be angry, her relief gave rise to a great deluge of friendliness. She became remarkably composed. Yet she was still unable to talk coherently. All she could produce was a series of mumblings, and even when Izawa could make out what she was saying, it had no connection with what he was asking her. In a vague, fragmentary manner she voiced the confused scraps of thought in her head. Izawa surmised that she had been thoroughly scolded at home and that when it had become too much for her she had taken refuge in his hut. Since questions only seemed to frighten her, he limited himself to asking when and how she had arrived. After a spate of unintelligible mumblings, the woman rolled up her sleeve and rubbed a bruise on her arm.

"It hurts," she said. "It still hurts . . . it's been hurting for some time now." From her stumbling efforts to point out the time sequence—the distinction between past pain and present pain—Izawa finally gathered that she had climbed into his room through the window after it had become dark. She also mumbled something to the effect that she had been walking about barefoot outside and that she was sorry for having muddied the floor. But since Izawa had to extricate her meaning from among a confusion of mutterings that meandered up one blind alley after another, he was quite unable to tell the direction in which this particular apology was aimed.

It seemed difficult to rouse his neighbor in the dead of night to return this thoroughly frightened woman to her house. At the same time, if he brought her back in the morning, there was no telling what misunderstanding might arise from his having let her stay the night, especially since her husband was a madman.

"I don't care," he thought, suddenly imbued with a peculiar form of courage. "I'll let her stay."

The substance of his courage was simply this: the loss of emotion in his life had provoked in him a certain curiosity; he felt it did not matter what happened and that it was essential for his own way of life that he should regard the present reality as a sort of test. He told himself that there was no need to think about anything other than his duty to protect this feebleminded woman for a night. He told himself that there was nothing to be ashamed of in the fact that he was so strangely moved by this unexpected turn of events.

Izawa made up two sets of bedding on the floor and told the woman to lie down. Then he switched off the light. A couple of minutes later he heard her crawling out of bed. She went to the corner of the room and crouched down. If it had not been the middle of winter, Izawa would probably have gone to sleep without troubling about her. But it was a bitterly cold night—so cold that he could not stop shivering. Since he had sacrificed one half of his bedding to his guest, the icy air seemed to impinge directly on his skin. He got up and turned on the light. The woman was crouching by the door, holding the front of her dress tightly about her body. Her eyes were those of a creature who has lost its hiding place and is driven to bay.

"What's the matter?" he said. "Go to bed."

The woman nodded—almost too readily—and crawled back into the bed. Izawa turned out the light. A moment later he heard her getting up as before. When he took the woman back to her bed this time, he tried to reassure her. "Don't worry," he said. "I'm not going to touch you." With a startled expression the woman muttered something that sounded vaguely like an excuse. The third time that he turned out the light, she got up without a moment's delay, opened the closet door, stepped inside, and shut herself in.

The woman's persistence had begun to annoy Izawa. He opened the closet roughly. "I don't know what you think you're doing," he said crossly, "but you seem to have got the wrong idea about me. Why on earth do you have to hide in the closet like that when I've told you I don't have the slightest intention of touching you? It's damned insulting. If you can't trust me, why come here in the first place? You've humiliated me, made a fool of me. What right have you to act as if you were being victimized in this place? I've had quite enough of your nonsense for one night."

Then it occurred to him that the woman could not possibly understand a word he was saying. What could be more futile than to remonstrate with a half-wit? Probably the best thing would be to give her a good slap on the cheek and then go to sleep without bothering any more about her. He noticed that the woman was muttering away with an inscrutable look on her face. Apparently she was stuttering out something to the effect that she wanted to go home and that it would have been better if she had never come.

"But now I have nowhere to go home to," she added.

Izawa could not help being touched. "Then why not spend the night here quietly?" he said. "There's really nothing to worry about, you know. The only reason I got a bit angry just now is that you started setting yourself up in the role of a victim when I didn't have the slightest intention of harming you. Now then, stay out of that closet and get into bed and have a good night's sleep!"

The woman stared at Izawa and launched into some more rapid mumbling.

"What?" he asked.

Then Izawa had the shock of his life. For out of her confused mumblings he clearly caught the words "I see you don't like me."

"Eh?" said Izawa, gazing at her with open-eyed amazement. "What's that you said?"

With a dejected expression, the woman began to explain herself, repeating over and over: "I shouldn't have come"; "You don't really like me"; "I thought you liked me, but you don't." Finally she lapsed into silence and gazed vacantly at a spot in the air.

Now Izawa understood for the first time. The woman had not been afraid of him. The situation was exactly the reverse. The woman had not come just because she had been scolded at home and didn't have anywhere else to hide. She had been counting on Izawa's imagined love for her. But what on earth could have made the woman believe that Izawa loved her? He had only exchanged the briefest possible greetings with her a few times near the pigpen or in the alley or on the road. The situation could hardly have been more absurd. Here he was being coerced by an idiot's will, by an idiot's susceptibility—forces that must be completely different from those of normal people. It was not clear to Izawa whether what had happened to the woman that evening was, in her idiot mind, a truly painful experience. Having lain in bed for a few minutes without Izawa's so much as touching her, the woman had come to the conclusion that she was unloved; this had filled her with shame and she had got out of bed. Finally she had shut herself in the closet. How could one interpret this peculiar action? As an expression of an idiot's shame and self-abasement? The trouble was that in the language of normal people there did not even exist the proper words in which to phrase a conclusion. In such a situation the only way was to lower oneself to the same level as the idiot's mentality. And after all, thought Izawa, what need was there for normal human wisdom? Would it be all that shameful if he himself adopted the frank simplicity of an idiot's mind? Perhaps that was what he needed more than anything else—the childlike, candid mind of an idiot. He had mislaid it somewhere, and in the meantime he had become bedraggled with thoughts of the workaday people who surrounded him; he had pursued false shadows and had nothing to show for it all but exhaustion.

He tucked the woman in bed and, sitting by the pillow, stroked her forelocks as if he were stroking a little girl—his own child perhaps—and trying to put her to sleep. Her eyes stayed open with a vacant look. There was an innocence about her, exactly like that of a little child's.

"I do not dislike you," Izawa began solemnly. "There are other ways, you know, of expressing love than by simple physical contact. The ultimate abode for us human beings is our birthplace, and in a strange way you seem to be living permanently in such a birthplace."

Of course there was no possibility of her understanding what he said. But what, after all, were words? What real value did they have? And where did reality reside? There was no evidence that it could be found even in human love. Where, if anywhere, could there be anything so real that it warranted a man's devoting his entire passion to it? Everything was merely a false shadow. But as he stroked the woman's hair, he felt like bursting into tears. He was overcome by the heartrending idea that this small, elusive, utterly uncertain love was the very haven of his life, that involuntarily he was stroking the hair of his own fate.

How was the war going to turn out? No doubt Japan would be defeated, the Americans would land on the mainland, and the greater part of the Japanese people would be annihilated. But all this could be conceived only as part of a supernatural destiny—the decree of Heaven, so to speak. What really bothered Izawa was a far more trivial problem—a surprisingly trivial problem, yet one that always flickered exigently before his eyes. It was the question of the two-hundred-yen wage he received every month from his company. How long would he continue to receive this salary? He never knew from one day to another when he would be dismissed and reduced to utter destitution. Each time he went to collect his salary he was terrified that he would also be given his dismissal notice. And when he actually held his pay envelope in his hand he was invariably overcome by intense joy at having survived for another month. He always felt like crying at the thought of how trivial it all was. Here he was—a man who dreamed about the great ideals of art—yet a wage of two hundred yen, which in the presence of art was less than the smallest speck of dust, could become a source of such agony that it penetrated to his marrow and shook the entire foundation of his existence. It was not merely his external life that was circumscribed by the two hundred yen; his very mind and soul were absorbed by it. And the fact that he could gaze calmly, steadily, at this triviality and retain his sanity made him even more wretched.

The editor's loud, stupid voice, shouting "What does beauty mean at a time like this? Art is powerless!" filled Izawa's mind with a completely different sort of reality and ate into him with a great, biting force. Ah yes, he thought, Japan would lose. His countrymen would fall one after another like so many clay dolls, innumerable legs and heads and arms would fly skyward mixed with the debris of bricks and concrete, and the land would become a flat graveyard devoid of trees, buildings, everything. Where would he seek refuge? Which hole would he be driven into? Where would he be when finally he was blown up, hole and all?

Yet sometimes he dreamed of how things would be if, by some peculiar chance, he survived. What he felt chiefly at such moments was curiosity—curiosity about life in an unpredictable new world, life in rubble-buried fields, curiosity also about the regeneration that would come. It was bound to happen, in six months or perhaps a year; yet he could only imagine it as some remote fancy, like a world of dreams. Meanwhile the decisive force of a mere two hundred yen blocked off everything else and swept away all hope from his life; even in his dreams it choked and haunted him; it bleached every emotion of his youth, so that although he was still only twenty-seven years old, he already found himself wandering aimlessly over a dark moorland.

Izawa wanted a woman; this was what he longed for most of all. Yet life with any woman would ineluctably be limited by the two hundred yen. His saucepan, his cooking pot, his bean paste, his rice—everything bore this curse. When his child was born, it too would be haunted by the curse, and the woman herself would turn into a demon obsessed by the same curse and would be grumbling from morning until night. His enthusiasm and his art and the light of his hopes were all dead; his very life was being trampled on like horse dung by the wayside, drying up and being blown away by the wind to disappear without a trace, without so much as the slightest nail mark. Such a curse it was that would cling to the woman's back.

His way of living was unbearably trivial and he himself lacked the power to resolve this triviality. War—this vast destructive force in which everyone was being judged with fantastic impartiality, in which all Japan was becoming a rubble-covered wasteland and the people were collapsing like clay dolls—what a heartrending, what a gigantic love it represented on the part of nothingness! Izawa felt a desire to sleep soundly in the arms of the god of destruction. This resignation to the force of nothingness had the effect of making him rather more active than before, and when the air-raid alarm sounded he would briskly put on his leggings. The only thing that made life worth living each day was to toy with the uneasiness of life. When the all clear sounded, he would be thoroughly dispirited and once more would be overcome by the despair of having lost all emotion.

This feebleminded woman did not know how to boil rice or to make bean-paste soup. She had trouble in expressing the simplest thought and the most she could do was to stand in line to get the rations. Like a thin sheet of glass, she reacted to the slightest suggestion of joy or anger; between the furrows of her fear and her abstractedness she simply received the will of others and passed it on. Even the evil spirit of the two hundred yen could not haunt such a soul. This woman, thought Izawa, was a forlorn puppet made for him. In his mind's eye he pictured an endless journey in which he would roam over the dark moorland with this woman in his arms and the wind blowing about him.

Yet he felt that there was something rather fantastic and ludicrous about the whole idea. This was probably because his external triviality had by now begun to erode his very heart in such a way that the frank feeling of love that was gushing up within him seemed entirely false. But why should it be false? Was there some intrinsic rule which said that the prostitutes in their apartments and the society ladies in their houses were more human than this feebleminded woman? Yes, absurdly enough, it looked as if there really was such a rule.

What am I afraid of? It all comes from the evil spirit of those two hundred yen. Yes, now when I am on the point of freeing myself from the evil spirit by means of this woman, I find that I am still bound by its curse. The only thing I am really afraid of is worldly appearances. And what I mean by "world" is merely the collection of women who live here in the apartments—the prostitutes and the kept women and the pregnant volunteer-workers and the housewives who cackle away in their nasal voices like so many geese. I know that there is no other world. Yet, indisputable as this fact is, I am completely unable to *believe* it. For I live in fear of some strange rule.

It was a surprisingly short (yet at the same time an endlessly long) night. Dawn broke before he knew it and the chill of daybreak numbed his body into an unfeeling block of stone. All night long he had simply stayed by the woman's pillow, stroking her hair.

From that day a new life began for Izawa.

Yet, aside from the fact that a woman's body had been added to a house, there was nothing peculiar or even different. Unbelievable though it might seem, not a single new bud appeared to sprout forth round him or within him. His reason perceived what an extraordinary event it was; but apart from that, there was not the slightest alteration in his life—not so much as the position of his desk was changed. He went to work each morning, and while he was out a feebleminded woman stayed in the closet awaiting his return. Once he had stepped outside, he forgot entirely about the woman, and if he thought at all about the event, it seemed like something that had happened in the indefinite past, ten or even twenty years before.

War produced a strangely wholesome kind of amnesia. Its fantastic destructive power caused a century of change to take place in a single day, made last week's events seem as if they had happened several years before and submerged the events of the previous year at the very bottom of one's memory. It was only recently that the buildings surrounding the factories near where Izawa lived had been torn down in a frenzy of "planned evacuation," which had turned the entire neighborhood into a whirling mass of dust; yet, though the debris had still not been cleared away, the demolition had already receded into the past as if it were something that had taken place over a year before. Immense changes that completely transformed the city were taken for granted when one saw them for the second time.

The feebleminded woman too had become one of the multifarious blurred fragments belonging to this wholesome amnesia. Her face lay among the various other fragments: among the sticks and splinters on the site of the evacuated "people's bar" in front of the railway station where, until a couple of days before, people had been waiting in queues, among the holes in the nearby building that had been wrecked by a bomb, among the fire-ravaged ruins of the city.

Every day the siren rang out. Sometimes it was an air-raid warning. At its sound Izawa would be plunged into deep disquiet. What worried him was that there might be an air raid near where he lived and that even now, while he sat in his office, some unknown change might be taking place at home. If there was an air raid, the feebleminded woman might well become excited and rush out of the house, thus exposing their secret to the entire neighborhood. Fear about an unknown change concerned Izawa more than anything else and made it impossible for him to return home while it was still light. Many were the times that he vainly struggled against this pitiful condition in which he was dominated by vulgar worries. If nothing else, he would have liked to be able to confide everything to the tailor; but this struck him as a hopelessly mean action, for it would simply have meant getting rid of his worries by the least damaging possible form of confession. So he remained silent and angrily cursed himself for being no better in his true nature than the common run of men whom he despised.

For Izawa the feebleminded woman had two unforgettable faces. When turning a street corner, when walking up the stairs in his office building, when detaching himself from the crowd of people in front of a tram—at these and other unexpected moments he would suddenly recall the two faces. His thoughts would freeze up and he would be congealed in a momentary frenzy.

One face was that which he had seen when he first touched her body. The occurrence itself had on the very next day receded into the memories of a year before; only the face would come back to him, detached from the surrounding events.

From that day the feebleminded woman had been no more than a waiting body with no other life, with not so much as a scrap of thought. She was always waiting. Merely from the fact that Izawa's hands had touched a part of her body, the woman's entire consciousness was absorbed by the sexual act; her body, her face, were simply waiting for it. Even in the middle of the night, if Izawa's hand happened to touch her, the woman's sleep-drugged body would show exactly the same reaction. Her body alone was alive, always waiting. Yes, even while asleep.

When it came to the question of what the woman was thinking about when awake, Izawa realized that her mind was a void. A coma of the mind combined with a vitality of the flesh—that was the sum and total of this woman. Even when she was awake, her mind slept; and even when she was asleep, her body was awake. Nothing existed in her but a sort of unconscious lust. The woman's body was constantly awake and reacted to outer stimuli by a tireless, wormlike wriggling.

But she had another face as well. There happened to be a daytime air raid on Izawa's day off and for two solid hours the bombers had concentrated on a nearby part of the city. Since Izawa had no air-raid shelter, he hid in the closet with the woman, barricading their bodies with the thick bedding. The center of the bombing was about five hundred yards away, but the houses in Izawa's neighborhood trembled as the earth shook; with each great thud of the bombs Izawa's breath and thoughts stood still.

Although both incendiary and demolition bombs were dropped alike from the planes, they had all the difference in degree of horror that exists between a common grass snake and a viper. Incendiary bombs were equipped with a mechanism that produced a ghastly, rattling sound, but they did not explode on reaching the ground and the noise fizzled out above one's head. "A dragon's head and a serpent's tail,"[1] people used to say. In fact there was no tail at all, serpentine or otherwise, and one was spared the culminating terror. In the case of TNT bombs, however, the sound as they fell was like the subdued swishing of rain, but this ended in a fabulous explosion that seemed to shatter the very axis of the earth. The horror of the rainlike warning, the hopeless terror as the thud of the explosions approached, made one feel more dead than alive. Worse still, since the American planes flew at a high altitude, the sound of their passage overhead was extremely faint, and they gave the impression of being totally unconcerned with what was happening below. Accordingly, when the bombs fell, it was exactly like being struck by a huge ax wielded by a monster who is looking the other way. Because one could have no idea what the enemy planes were going to do, the strange buzzing of their motors in the distance filled one with a peculiar sense of uneasiness; then on top of this would come the swish of the falling bomb. The terror one felt while waiting for the explosion was really enough to stop every word and breath and thought. The only thing in one's mind was the despair that flashed through one, icy like impending madness—despair at the idea that this was assuredly one's final moment on earth.

Izawa's hut was fortunately surrounded on all sides by two-story buildings (apartments, the madman's house, the tailor's house) and it alone escaped without so much as a cracked windowpane, whereas the windows in the neighboring houses

[1] Proverbial expression, roughly corresponding to "Up like a rocket and down like a stick."

were shattered and, in some cases, the roofs badly damaged. The only untoward incident was that a blood-drenched hood, of the type people wore in air raids, fell on the field in front of the pigpen. In the darkness of the closet Izawa's eyes glittered. Then he saw it—he saw the idiot's face and its writhing agony of despair.

Ah, yes, he thought, most people have intellect and even at the worst of times they retain control and resistance. How appalling it was to see someone who was entirely bereft of intellect and restraint and resistance! To the woman's face and body, as she gazed into the window of death, nothing adhered but anguish. Her anguish moved, it writhed, it shed a tear. If a dog's eyes were to shed tears, it would probably be infinitely ugly, just as if he were to laugh. Izawa was shocked to see how ugly tears could be when there was no trace of intellect behind them. Strangely enough, children of five or six rarely cry in the middle of a bombing. Their hearts beat like hammers, they become speechless, and they stare ahead with wide-open eyes. Only their eyes are alive; but apparently they are just kept wide open and they fail to show any direct or dramatic fear. The fact is that children calmly subdue their emotions to the extent that they appear more intelligent than under normal circumstances. At the instant of danger, they are the equal of adults. One might even say that they are superior, for adults plainly manifest their fears of death. Yes, children actually appear more intelligent at such times than adults.

But the idiot's anguish did not bear the slightest resemblance to the wide-eyed reaction that children show at times of danger. It was merely an instinctive fear of death, a single ugly movement. Her reaction was not that of a human being or even of an insect. If it could be said to resemble anything, it was like the writhings of a small three-inch caterpillar that has swollen to about six feet—and that has a teardrop in its eye.

There were no words, no screams, no groans; nor was there any expression. She was not even aware of Izawa's existence. If she were human, she would be incapable of such solitude. It was impossible that a man and a woman could be together in a closet with one of them entirely forgetting about the other. People talk of absolute solitude, but absolute solitude can exist only by one's being aware of the existence of others. Absolute solitude could never be such a blind and unconscious thing as what Izawa was now witnessing. This woman's solitude was like a caterpillar's—the ultimate in wretchedness. How unbearable it was—this anguish entirely devoid of any thought!

The bombing ended. Izawa raised the crouching woman in his arms. As a rule she reacted amorously if Izawa's finger so much as brushed against her breast, but now she appeared to have lost even her sense of lust. He was falling through space with a corpse in his arms. Nothing existed but the dark, dark, endless fall.

Immediately after the bombing Izawa took a walk past the houses that had just been mowed down. In the ruins he saw a woman's leg that had been torn from her body, a woman's trunk with the intestines protruding, and a woman's severed head.

Among the ruins of the great air raid of March tenth, Izawa also wandered aimlessly through the still rising smoke. On all sides people lay dead like so many roast fowl. They lay dead in great clusters. Yes, they were exactly like roast fowl. They were neither gruesome nor dirty. Some of the corpses lay next to the bodies of dogs and were burned in exactly the same manner, as if to emphasize how utterly useless their deaths had been. Yet these bodies lacked even the pathos implied in the expression "a dog's death." [2] It was a case, not of people's having died like dogs, but of dogs lying there in the ruins next to other objects, as though they were all pieces of roast fowl neatly arranged on a platter. Those four-legged things were not really dogs; still less were those two-legged objects human beings.

If the idiot woman should be burned to death, would it not simply mean that a clay doll had returned to the earth whence it came? Izawa imagined the night that might come at any time when incendiary bombs would rain down on his street, and he could not help being conscious of his own form, his face, his eyes, as he lay there strangely calm, sunk in thought.

[2] To "die like a dog" (*inujini suru*) means to die in vain.

I am calm, he thought. And I am waiting for an air raid. That's all right. He smiled scornfully. It's merely that I dislike ugly things. Is it not natural that a body which has no mind should burn and die? I shan't kill the woman. I am a cowardly and vulgar man. I don't have the courage for that. But the war will probably kill her. All that is necessary is to grasp the first opportunity to direct the unfeeling hand of war toward this woman's head. I shall not really be concerned. It will probably be a matter of having everything automatically settled by some crucial instant. Very calmly, Izawa awaited the next air raid.

It was April fifteenth. Two days before, on the thirteenth, the second great night-bombing had taken place, inflicting immense damage on Ikebukuro, Sugamo, and other residential districts in Tokyo. As a result of that raid, Izawa had managed to obtain a calamity certificate. This enabled him to take a train to Saitama Prefecture and to return with some rice in his rucksack. The air-raid alarm had started the moment he reached home.

By examining the areas of Tokyo that still remained unburned, anyone could surmise that the next raid would be directed at Izawa's neighborhood. Izawa knew that the fatal moment was near; at the earliest it would come on the following day, at the latest within a month. The reason Izawa thought it would not happen before the following day was that the tempo of raids until then indicated that at least another twenty-four hours would be necessary to complete preparations for a night attack. It never occurred to him that this might be the day of doom. That is why he had gone food-hunting. The main purpose of his trip, however, was not to buy food. Since his school days he had had connections with a certain farm in Saitama, and his principal objective in going to the country had been to deposit his belongings, which he had packed in a couple of trunks and a rucksack.

Izawa was tired out. He had made the trip in his air-raid uniform and when he reached his room he lay down as he was, using his rucksack as a pillow. When the crucial moment came, he had actually dozed off. He awoke to the blaring of radios. At that moment the front of the attacking squadron was approaching the southern tip of Izu Peninsula. A moment later, the bombers were over the mainland and the sirens started to shriek out their warning. Instinctively Izawa knew that the final day for his neighborhood had come. He put the feebleminded woman in the closet and went outside to the well with a towel in his hand and a toothbrush in his mouth. A few days before, Izawa had managed to obtain a tube of Lion toothpaste and he had been enjoying the astringent taste that had been denied him for such a long time. When it dawned on him that the fatal moment had come, he was for some reason inspired to brush his teeth and wash his face. But first it took him a while—it seemed like ages—to find the tube, which had been moved a small distance from where he remembered having put it; then he had trouble finding the soap (it was a perfumed cake of a type that was no longer obtainable in the shops) because it too had been slightly misplaced. "I'm getting rattled," he told himself. "Calm down, Izawa, calm down!" Thereupon he struck his head against the closet and stumbled over the desk.

For a while he tried to gather his wits by suspending all movement and thought; but his entire body was flustered and refused to respond to orderly control.

Finally he found the soap and went to the well. The tailor and his wife were throwing their belongings into the shelter that they had dug in the corner of the field, and the ducklike girl from the attic was bustling about with a suitcase in her hand. Izawa congratulated himself for his persistence in having found the toothpaste and the soap, and wondered what fate really had in store for him that night.

While he was still wiping his face, the antiaircraft guns started banging away. When he looked up, he saw that a dozen or more searchlights were already crisscrossing overhead. In the very center of their beams an American plane showed up clearly. Then another plane and yet another. When he happened to glance in the direction of the station, he saw that the whole area was a sea of flames.

The time had finally come. Now that the situation was clear, Izawa calmed down. He put on his air-raid hood and covered himself in his bedding. Standing outside his hut, he counted up to twenty-four planes. They all flew overhead, clearly exposed in the beams of the searchlights.

The antiaircraft guns boomed crazily, but there was still no sound of bombing. When he had counted the twenty-fifth plane, he heard the familiar rattling sound of incendiary bombs, like a freight train crossing a bridge. Apparently the planes were passing over Izawa's head and concentrating their attack on the factory area behind. Since he could not see from where he was standing, he went to the pigpen and looked back. The factory area was bathed in flames, and to his amazement Izawa saw that, apart from the bombers which had just passed overhead, planes were approaching in quick succession from the exact opposite direction and were bombing the entire area to the rear. Then the radios stopped. The whole sky was hidden by a thick, red curtain of smoke, which blotted out the American planes and the beams of the searchlights.

The tailor and his wife were a prudent couple. Some time before, they had made the shelter for their belongings and had even provided mud to seal up the entrance. Now they briskly stored everything in the shelter as planned, sealed it, and covered it with earth from the rice field.

"With a fire like this," said the tailor, "it's absolutely hopeless." He stood there in his old fireman's clothes, with his arms folded, and gazed at the flames. "It's all very well their telling us to put it out," he continued, "but when the fire gets as bad as this there's nothing to be done. I'm going to run for it. What's the use of staying here and being choked to death by the smoke?"

The tailor heaped his remaining belongings onto a bicycle-drawn cart. "Why don't you come along with me, sir?" he said to Izawa.

Izawa was seized with a complex form of terror. His body was on the verge of running away with the tailor, but he was checked by a strong internal resistance. As he stood there immobile, he felt that a splitting shriek was rising in his heart: because of this moment's delay I'm going to be burned to death! His terror almost benumbed his mind, yet somehow he managed to withstand the urgings of his body as it staggered into the motions of flight.

"I'll stay a little longer," he said. "I've got a job to do, you see. After all, I'm an entertainer and when I have an opportunity to study myself in the face of death I've got to carry on to the very end. I'd like to escape, but I can't. I can't miss this opportunity. You'd better run for it now. Hurry, hurry! In a minute it'll all be too late."

Hurry, hurry! In a minute it'll all be too late. In saying "all," Izawa was, of course, referring to his own life. "Hurry, hurry" was not aimed at urging the tailor to escape, but came from his own desire to get away as soon as possible. For him to get away, it was essential that everyone in the neighborhood should leave ahead of him. If not, people might find out about his feebleminded woman.

"Very well, then," said the tailor, "but be careful." He started to pull his cart. But he too was thoroughly flustered and as he hurried along the alley he kept bumping into things. That was Izawa's last picture of his neighbors as they fled from their dwellings.

A ghastly rustling continued without pause or modulation. It sounded like the roaring of waves as they beat against the rocks, or like the endless pattering on rooftops of splinters from antiaircraft guns; but it was the footsteps of a mass of evacuees scurrying along the main road. The sound of the antiaircraft guns now seemed out of place, and the flow of footsteps had a strange vitality. Who in the world could possibly have imagined that the endless flow of this uncanny sound—this sound without pause or modulation—was produced by human footsteps? The sky and the earth were filled with countless sounds: the whirring of American planes, the antiaircraft guns, the downpour, the roar of explosions, the sound of feet, the splinters striking the roofs. But the area immediately surrounding Izawa formed a quiet little realm of darkness in the midst of the red sky and earth. The walls of a strange silence, the walls of a maddening solitude, surrounded Izawa on all sides.

"Wait another thirty seconds. . . . Now just ten more." He did not know who was ordering him or why; nor did he know what made him obey. He felt that he was going insane. He felt that at any moment he would start running along blindly, screaming in agony.

At that moment something started to fall immediately above his head and seemed to churn the insides of his eardrums. Frantically, he threw himself to the ground. The sound abruptly vanished and an incredible quiet once more descended on the surroundings. "Well, that gave me quite a fright," thought Izawa. He arose slowly and brushed the earth from his clothes. When he looked up, he found the madman's house in flames. "Oh, so it's finally been hit." He was strangely calm. Then he realized that the houses on both sides and the apartments opposite were also in flames.

Izawa rushed into his hut. He sent the door of the closet flying (it slipped from its groove and fell with a clatter) and rushed out covered with his bedding and holding the feebleminded woman in his arms. For the next minute or so he was in a daze and had no idea what he was doing. As he reached the entrance to the alley, he once more heard the falling sound overhead. He threw himself down. When he stood up, he saw that the tobacco shop was burning, and that in the house opposite, violent flames were gushing from the family Buddhist altar. Looking back as he left the alley, he noticed that the tailor's house had also caught fire; no doubt his own hut was already in flames.

The entire neighborhood was burning and sparks of fire were swirling all about. Izawa felt that the situation was hopeless. When he reached the crossroads, he found that all was in utter confusion. Everybody was pressing forward in a single direction—the direction furthest from the flames. It was no longer a road but just a deluge of people, baggage, and screams, a deluge of hustling and jostling, shoving and pushing, stumbling and staggering forward. As people heard the swishing sound of bombs overhead, they would fall to the ground at once and the deluge would come to a complete standstill. A few people would run on, trampling over the others. But the majority had their personal belongings and were accompanied by children, women, and aged people. They were calling out to the members of their party, halting, turning back, bumping into one another.

The flames drew close on both sides of the road. Izawa reached a small intersection. Here, too, the entire deluge was pressing forward in one direction, again because it was farthest from the flames. Izawa, however, knew that in that direction there were neither open spaces nor fields: if the next batch of incendiary bombs from the American planes were to block the way, that particular road would lead to certain death. The houses on both sides of the other road were already burning, but Izawa remembered that some way ahead there was a river, and that a few hundred yards farther upstream one came to a wheat field. Not a single person seemed to have chosen that road, however, and for a moment Izawa hesitated. Then he noticed that about a hundred and fifty yards up the road a man was standing by himself, throwing water on the raging flames. Though he was throwing water on the flames, he certainly did not cut a valiant figure. He was merely a man with a bucket; occasionally he would throw some water about, but most of the time he stood there vacantly or wandered up and down. His movements were curiously sluggish and Izawa wondered whether he was not deranged. At any rate, thought Izawa, a man can stand there without burning to death. I'll try my luck. Luck, one thread of luck and the resolve to try it—that was all that remained.

At the crossroads was a ditch, and Izawa soaked his bedding in the muddy water. Then he pulled the woman close to him and, covering both their bodies with the bedding, left the mass of people with whom they had been walking. But as they approached the road that was lined with raging flames, the woman instinctively stopped and falteringly tried to return toward the human deluge as if she were being sucked back into a whirlpool.

"You fool!" cried Izawa, pulling the woman with all his might. He hugged her shoulders and held her close to his breast. "You'll only die if you go that way," he whispered. "When we die, we'll be together—just like this. Don't be frightened! And don't leave my side whatever you do! Forget about those flames and those bombs! The road of our two lives will always be this road. You just look straight ahead along this road and rely on me! Do you understand?"

The woman nodded. It was a childish nod, but Izawa was overwhelmed with emotion. For this was the first sign of volition, the first answer, that the woman had shown in these long, repeated hours of terror during the day and night bombings. It was so touching that Izawa felt quite dizzy.

Now at last he was embracing a human being, and he was filled with immeasurable pride about that human being.

The two of them rushed through the wild flames. When they emerged from under the mass of hot air, both sides of the road were still a sea of flame; but the houses had already collapsed in the fire and as a result the force of the conflagration had decreased and the heat was less intense. Here again there was a ditch full of water. Izawa doused the woman from head to toe, soaked the bedding, and covered her and himself with it once again. Burned belongings and bedding lay strewn on the road, and two dead bodies also lay there. They were a middle-aged man and woman.

Izawa again put his arm around the woman and the two dashed through the flames. At last they reached the stream. The factories on both sides were sending up furious jets of flame. Retreat and advance were equally impossible, nor could they stay where they were. Looking around, Izawa noticed a ladder leading down to the stream. He covered the woman with the bedding and had her walk down, while he himself jumped for it.

People were walking along by the stream in little groups. Now and then the woman dipped herself in the water of her own accord. The situation was such that even a dog would have had to do so, but Izawa was wide-eyed at the sight of the birth of a new and lovable woman, and he watched her figure greedily as she immersed herself.

The stream emerged from beneath the flames and flowed beneath the darkness. It was not really dark because of the glow of the fire that covered the sky; but this semidarkness, which he could see once again inasmuch as he was still alive, filled Izawa with a sense of vacancy—vacancy that came from a vast, ineffable weariness, from a boundless feeling of nothingness. At the bottom of it all lay a small sense of relief, but that struck him as strangely insignificant and absurd. He felt that everything was absurd.

Upstream they came to the wheat field. It was a large field enclosed on three sides by hills; a highway ran across the middle, cutting through the hills. The houses on the hills were all burning; and the buildings around the field—the

Buddhist temple, the factory, the bathhouse—were also burning. The flames of each fire were a different color—white, red, orange, blue. A sudden wind sprang up and filled the air with a great roar, while minute, misty drops of water showered all around.

The crowd was still meandering down the highway. There were only a few hundred people resting in the wheat field— nothing in comparison with the crowds that stretched along the road. Next to the field was a little thicket-covered hill. There were hardly any people in this grove. Izawa and the woman spread their bedding under a tree and lay down. At the side of the field below the hill a farmhouse was burning. A few people could be seen throwing water on the flames. At the rear was a well where a man was working the pump handle and was drinking water. Seeing this, about twenty men and women rushed toward the well from all directions. They took turns in working the pump handle and drinking. Then they crowded about the burning house and stretched their hands toward the flames to warm themselves. As burning fragments fell from the house they sprang back and turned away from the smoke. Then they went on talking. Nobody lent a hand to try to put out the fire.

The woman said that she was sleepy. She also muttered that her feet ached, that her eyes smarted; but her main complaint was that she was sleepy.

"All right, then," said Izawa, "sleep for a while." He wrapped her in the bedding and lit a cigarette for himself. When he had smoked a number of cigarettes and was about to light another, the all-clear signal sounded in the distance and several policemen came running through the wheat field to announce that the alarm had been lifted. Their voices were hoarse, not like the voices of human beings at all.

"The raid is over," they shouted. "Everyone living in the area of the Kamata Police Station is to assemble at the Yaguchi Elementary School. The school building is still standing."

The people rose from the ridges in the field and walked down to the highway. But Izawa did not move. A policeman came up to him.

"What's the matter with that woman? Is she hurt?"

"No," said Izawa, "she's tired and sleeping."

"Do you know the Yaguchi Elementary School?"

"Yes. We'll have a rest here for a while and then we'll come along."

"Brace up, man! You mustn't let a little raid get you down."

The policeman's voice trailed off as he disappeared down the hill. Only two people were left in the grove. Two people? But wasn't the woman in fact a mere lump of flesh? Now she lay there sound asleep. Everyone else was walking through the smoke of the fire-ravaged ruins. They had all lost their homes and they were all walking. Certainly none of them was thinking about sleep. The only ones who could sleep now were the dead and this woman. The dead would never wake again, but this woman would eventually wake up. Yet even when she awoke nothing would be added to this sleeping lump of flesh.

She was snoring faintly. It was the first time that he had heard her snore. It sounded like the grunting of a little pig. Yes, thought Izawa, everything about her is porcine. And abruptly a fragmentary memory from his childhood came back to him. A group of about a dozen urchins had been chasing a baby pig at the command of their gang leader. When they cornered the animal, the leader took out his jackknife and sliced a piece of flesh off its thigh. Izawa recalled that the pig's face had showed no sign of pain and that it had not even squealed very loudly. It simply ran away, evidently unaware that some flesh had been sliced off its thigh.

Now Izawa's mind conjured up a picture of himself and the woman as they would run away, stumbling among the clouds of dust, the crumbled buildings, the gaping holes. The American forces would have landed; the heavy artillery shells would be roaring on all sides, huge concrete buildings would be blown sky-high, enemy planes would be diving and spraying them with machine-gun fire. Behind a pile of rubble a woman would be held down by a man; he would overpower her and, while indulging in the sexual act, would be tearing off the flesh from her buttocks and devouring it. The flesh on the woman's buttocks would gradually diminish, but the woman would be so preoccupied with her carnal enjoyment that she would not even notice the depredations from behind.

As dawn approached, it began to grow cold. Izawa was wearing his winter overcoat and also had on a thick jacket, yet the cold was quite unbearable. The field below was still burning in places. Izawa wanted to go and warm himself, but he was unable to move because he was afraid of waking the woman. Somehow the thought of the woman waking up seemed intolerable.

He wanted to go away and leave her as she slept, but even that seemed too much trouble. When a person discards something, even a piece of waste paper, it means that he still possesses the necessary initiative and fastidiousness. But Izawa did not even have enough initiative or fastidiousness left to abandon this woman of his. He did not have the slightest affection for her now, not the slightest lingering attachment; yet neither did he have sufficient incentive to discard her. For he was devoid of any hopes for the future. Even if he were to get rid of the woman without delay, where would there be any hope for him? What was there to lean on in life? He did not even know where he would find a house to live in, a hole to sleep in. The Americans would land, and there would be all kinds of destruction in the heavens and on earth; and the gigantic love extended by the destructiveness of war would pass impartial judgment upon everything. There was no longer any need even to think.

Izawa decided that at daybreak he would wake the woman and that, without even a glance in the direction of the devastated area, they would set out for the most distant possible railway station in search of a roost. He wondered whether the trams and trains would be running. He wondered whether there would be a clear sky and whether the sun would pour down on his back and on the back of the pig that lay beside him. For it was a very cold morning.

OSAMU DAZAI

"The Courtesy Call"
("Shinyu Kokan," 1946)

Translated by Ivan Morris

Osamu Dazai (1909–1948), whose real name was Shuji Shimazu, was the sixth son of a wealthy landlord in Aomori Prefecture. He developed a passion for literature in middle school. While still in high school he tried his hand at fiction; many of his stories then appeared in a group magazine and alumni bulletin. He obtained contributions for the same group magazine from some established writers including Masuji Ibuse (1868–), mentioned in "The Courtesy Call" as his close friend. After he entered Tokyo University in 1930, he became involved in a leftist student movement. In a suicide attempt with a barmaid, only Dazai survived, and he later married a geisha he had befriended since his high-school days. After this he attempted suicide again, and from time to time he was hospitalized for drug addiction.

Meanwhile, he turned out a number of works based on such experiences. In 1935 "Counteraction" ("Gyakko") and "The Flower of Clowning" ("Doke no Hana") were nominated for the first Akutagawa Prize, and his originality came to be recognized in literary circles. By 1937, Dazai had begun to lead a normal life now that he was married to the daughter of a good family after his divorce from the geisha. Shortly before and during the war his steady literary production continued in the atmosphere of a quiet family life and in his effort to be a good citizen. But he was deeply troubled by the war, particularly by the loss of individual freedom under a military state. A victim of an air raid, he is said to have cried and remarked that he had been deceived by the Emperor.

Dazai's most significant work was accomplished during the two short years between the resumption of literary activities in Japan after the war and his suicide by casting himself into a reservoir in Tokyo. His gloom from the preceding years still persisted under the chaotic conditions of the postwar era. His nihilistic mood and sense of great despair were reflected in all of his novels and stories written in this period: *The Setting Sun* (*Shayo*, 1947), "Villon's Wife" ("Villon no Tsuma," 1947), *No Longer Human* (*Ningen Shikkaku*, 1948), and "Cherries and Peaches" ("Oto," 1948). His version of existentialism, a philosophy popularized by translations of Jean Paul Sartre and Albert Camus, not only appealed to the young generation but also attracted critics' attention.

"The Courtesy Call" (translated in England as "A Visitor") is largely autobiographical as are all Dazai's works. It reflects the dark mood that prevailed in much of his later period, but it also contains a sense of dry humor—another aspect of Dazai's personality that is often disregarded.

Until the day of my death I shall not forget the man who came to my house that afternoon last September. Although on the surface there may have been nothing very spectacular about his visit, I am convinced that it was a momentous event in my life. For to me this man foretold a new species of humanity. During my years in Tokyo, I had frequented the lowest class of drinking house and mixed with some quite appalling rogues. But this man was in a category all his own: he was far and away the most disagreeable, the most loathsome, person I had ever met; there was not a jot of goodness in him.

After my house in Tokyo was bombed, I moved with my family to a cottage in a remote country district where I had lived as a child and where my brother had recently stood for election. Here it was after lunch one day, as I sat smoking dreamily by myself in the living room, that a tall, corpulent man appeared, dressed in a farmer's smock.

"I'll be damned," he said, when I opened the door. "If it isn't old Osamu himself!"

I looked at him blankly.

"Come, come," he said, laughing and showing a set of

sharp, white teeth, "don't say you've forgotten me! I'm Hirata, your old friend from primary school."

From the dim recess of my memory there emerged some vague recollection of the face. We may indeed have known each other in school, but as for being old friends, I was not so sure.

"Of course I remember you," I said with a great show of urbanity. "Do come in, Mr. Hirata."

He removed his clogs and strode into the living room.

"Well, well," he said loudly, "it's been a long time, hasn't it?"

"Yes, years and years."

"Years?" he shouted. "Decades, you mean! It must be over twenty years since I saw you. I heard some time ago that you'd moved to our village but I've been far too busy on the farm to call. By the way, they tell me you've become quite a tippler. Spend most of your time at the bottle, eh? Ha, ha, ha!"

I forced a smile and puffed at my cigarette.

"D'you remember how we used to fight at school?" he said, starting on a new tack. "We were always fighting, you and me."

"Were we really?"

"Were we really, indeed!" he said, mimicking my intonation. "Of course we were! I've got a scar here on the back of my hand to remind me. You gave me this scar."

He held out his hand for me to examine, but I could see nothing that even vaguely resembled a scar.

"And what about that one on your left shin? You remember where I hit you with a stone. I bet you've still got a nasty scar to show for it."

I did not have the slightest mark on either of my shins. I smiled vaguely and looked at his large face with its shrewd eyes and fleshy lips.

"Well, so much for all that," he said. "Now I'll tell you why I've come. I want you and me to organize a class reunion. I'll get together about twenty of the lads and we'll have ten gallons of saké. It'll be a real drinking bout. Not such a bad idea, eh?"

"No," I said dubiously. "But isn't ten gallons rather a lot?"

"Of course not," he said. "To have a good time, you want at least eight pints a head."

"Where are you going to buy ten gallons of saké these days?" I said. "One's lucky to find a single bottle."

"Don't worry about that," he said. "I know where I can lay my hands on the stuff. But it's expensive, you know, even here in the country. That's where I want you to help out."

I stood up with a knowing smile. So it was as simple as all that, I thought almost with relief. I went to the back room and returned with a couple of bank notes.

"Here you are," I said.

"Oh no," he said, "I didn't come here today to get money. I came to discuss the class reunion. I wanted to hear your ideas. Besides, I wanted to see my old pal again after all these years. . . . Anyhow that won't be nearly enough. We'll need at least a thousand yen. You can put those notes away."

"Really?" I said, replacing the money in my wallet.

"What about something to drink?" he said all of a sudden.

I looked at him coldly, but he stood his ground.

"Come on," he said, "you needn't look as if you'd never heard of the stuff! They tell me you've always got a good supply put away. Let's have a little drink together! Call the missus! She can pour for us."

"All right," I said, standing up, "come with me." From that moment I was lost.

I led him to the back room, which I used as my study.

"I'm afraid it's in a bit of a mess," I said.

"It doesn't matter," he answered tolerantly. "Scholars' rooms are always like pigsties. I used to know quite a few of you bookworms in my Tokyo days."

I glanced at him suspiciously; his "Tokyo days" were, without doubt, another figment of his imagination.

"It's not a bad little room, all the same," he said. "You've got a nice view of the garden, haven't you? Ah, I see you have some *hiiragi* holly trees out there. Now tell me: do you know what the word '*hiiragi*' comes from?"

"No," I replied.

"Ha, ha! You're a fine scholar, aren't you?" he said. "Don't you really know? Well, I'll give you a hint. The whole word has a universal meaning and part of the word means something that you bookworms use for your scribbling."

He seemed to be talking gibberish and I began to wonder if he was not mentally deficient. By the end of the afternoon I was to realize how far from deficient he really was.

"Well, have you figured it out?"

"No, I'm afraid not," I said. "I give up. What's the answer?"

"I'll tell you some other time," he said, smiling self-importantly.

I went to the cupboard and took out a bottle of good whiskey, which was about half full.

"I don't have any saké," I said. "I hope you won't mind some whiskey."

"It'll do," he said. "But I want your little woman to pour the stuff."

"I'm sorry but my wife isn't at home," I said.

In fact she was in the bedroom, but I was determined to spare her this ordeal. Besides, I felt sure that the farmer would be disappointed in her. He would no doubt expect a smart, sophisticated woman from the city and, although my wife was born and bred in Tokyo, she had about her something rustic, almost gauche.

But the deception did not escape my visitor.

"Of course she's at home," he said. "Tell her to come and do the pouring."

I decided simply to ignore his request and, filling a teacup with whiskey, handed it to him.

"I'm afraid it's not quite up to prewar quality," I said.

He tossed it off at a single draught, smacked his lips loudly and said: "It's pretty cheap stuff, isn't it?"

"I'm sorry, but it's the best I can get.... I wouldn't drink it down too quickly if I were you," I added.

"Ha, ha!" he said, putting the cup to his lips. "I can see you don't know who you're dealing with. I used to polish off two bottles an evening just by myself. And that was real Suntory whiskey, not this watered-down stuff. I shouldn't think this is more than sixty percent, is it?"

"I really don't know."

He took the bottle and poured a cup for me. Then he filled his own cup to the brim.

"The bottle's almost empty," he announced.

"Oh, really?" I said, assuming a nonchalance that I was

far from feeling. I took another bottle out of the cupboard.

The man continued drinking and as the level of the whiskey in the second bottle began to sink, I finally felt anger rise within me. It was not that I was usually jealous about my property. Far from it. Having lost almost all my possessions in the bombings, what was left meant hardly anything to me. But this whiskey was an exception. I had obtained it some time before at immense difficulty and expense, and had rationed myself severely, only now and then sipping a small glass after dinner. At the beginning of that afternoon two and a half bottles remained, and I had looked forward to offering some to my friend Mr. Ibuse Masuji when he came to visit, for I knew that he was partial to an occasional glass. When this terrible farmer appeared after lunch, I brought out the whiskey, never for a moment dreaming that he would take more than one cup. Now as I watched in impotent fury while he gulped the contents of the second bottle, I almost felt that the whiskey was my lifeblood being poured down his insensitive gullet.

"I hear you got into plenty of trouble over women in Tokyo," he said, filling his cup once more. "Well, to tell you the truth, I got into trouble myself during my Tokyo period. But I got myself out of it all right. Yes, it takes more than a woman to hold me. Of course, once they've set their hearts on you, they don't let go easy. Mine still writes me every now and then. Why, only the other day she sent me a packet of rice cakes. Women are fools, aren't they, damned fools! When they're in love with you, they don't care about your looks or even about how much money you've got. All they think about is feelings and heart and all that claptrap." He laughed raucously. "Yes, I had quite a wild time in my Tokyo period. Come to think of it, I must have been in Tokyo about the same time that you were there, breaking the hearts of your geisha girls. You made quite a name for yourself, didn't you? Ha, ha! Funny we never bumped into each other. Where did you hang out in those days?"

I had no idea to which days he was referring, nor did I remember breaking the hearts of any geisha. To be sure, I had had various emotional complications when I lived in Tokyo. For this I had been amply abused by my literary acquaintances and even by so-called friends, until their criticisms had now ceased utterly to affect me. Yet something about this man's tone made me feel, for the first time in years, that I had to defend myself from the charge of being a callous libertine.

"You know," I said, looking straight at him, "I've never set myself up as a lady-killer. And I don't get any pleasure from going around seducing women indiscriminately."

"I know all about you," he said, looking at me with a snigger, and I realized that he did not believe a word I had said. An unpleasant feeling of cheapness came over me. This man with his ugly mind seemed to see right through me—into the ugliest recesses of my being.

I suddenly wanted to ask him to leave. Yet the fact was that I did not dare to. Our position in this village was far from secure and I could not risk offending someone who appeared to be an old and well-established inhabitant. Besides, I was afraid that if I asked him to go, he might think that I looked down on him for being an uneducated farmer. I went into the living room and came back with a plate of fruit.

"Have a pear," I said. "It'll do you good."

I was terrified that the man would soon become roaring drunk and it occurred to me that some fruit might avert this calamity. He looked blankly at the plate and reached for his cup of whiskey.

"I hate politics," he said abruptly. "In fact we farmers all hate politics. What good have those politicians ever done us? If they helped us in any way, we'd support them. We're grateful folk, you know, us country people, and we always return favors. But all those politicians can do is jabber away, while we get on with the real work. Socialists, Progressives, Liberals—bah! They're all the same to us!"

For a moment I wondered where this new line was leading.

"Your brother was campaigning in the last elections, wasn't he?" continued the farmer.

"Yes," I said, "this was his district. He lost."

"I suppose you did quite a bit of campaigning yourself?"

"No, I didn't even bother to vote. I stayed at home and worked."

"Nonsense," he said, "of course you campaigned for your

own brother! It's just a simple matter of humanity. I may not be a great scholar like you, but at least I know what humanity is. That's one thing we farmers understand. I hate politics, but when I heard that the brother of my old school pal was a candidate, I went right out and voted for him without even waiting for anyone to ask me. That's humanity for you! As long as we don't lose that quality, we farmers are going to be all right."

His object was now transparent: his vote—if, indeed, he had ever cast it—was to be a passport for an indefinite amount of whiskey.

"It was very good of you to support my brother," I said with a sardonic smile.

"Don't get me wrong," he said. "I did it out of common humanity—not because I thought he was any good. Your family may have got ahead in the world now, but a couple of generations ago they were just common oil-sellers. Did you know that? I've been doing a bit of research. Your family used to sell cans of oil and if anyone bought half a pint or more, they gave him a piece of toffee as a premium. That's how they made their money. It's the same with almost all the so-called good families. Take the Oike family, for instance, who own half the land around here and go about lording it over us all. It's not so long ago that their ancestors were putting buckets by the roadside for the passersby to piss in. As soon as the buckets were full, they sold them to the farmers to mix with their fertilizer. That's how they started their fortune. You can't fool me!"

"I'm sure I can't," I said, wondering whether he was inventing all this on the spur of the moment or whether he had come fully prepared.

"I myself come from a really old family, though," he continued. "My ancestors moved to this village hundreds of years ago from Kyoto."

"Really? In that case, I expect you are of noble lineage."

"You may not be far wrong," he said with a nasal laugh. "Of course, you wouldn't think it to see me in these clothes. But both my brothers went to university. The older one's made quite a name for himself in the government. You've probably seen his name in the papers."

"Yes, of course," I said.

"Well, I didn't bother to go to university myself. I decided to stay in the country and do some really useful work. And now, of course, I'm the one who's got ahead and they have to come begging me for rice and all the things they can't get in Tokyo. Not that I begrudge them anything. And look here," he said, sticking his finger almost into my face, "if you're ever short of food, you can come to my farm too and I'll give you whatever you need. I'm not the sort of fellow who'd drink a man's liquor for nothing. I'll repay you—down to the last penny. We farmers are grateful folk."

He examined his empty cup pensively and then all of a sudden shouted: "Call in the little woman! I won't drink another drop unless she pours it for me herself. Not another drop, d'you hear?" He staggered to his feet. "Where is the little woman, anyway? In the bedroom, I expect, snug in bed, eh? D'you know who I am? I'm Hirata, I'm a lord among farmers! Haven't you heard of the great Hirata family?"

My worst fears were being realized and I saw that there was nothing for it but to fetch my wife.

"Do sit down, Mr. Hirata," I said calmly. "I'll call her right away, if it means all that much to you."

I went into the bedroom, where my wife was busy darning some socks.

"Would you mind coming in for a minute?" I asked her casually. "An old school friend has come to see me." I said no more, as I did not want my wife to be prejudiced in advance against the visitor. In particular I did not want her to think that I considered him in any way inferior to us. She nodded and followed me into the back room.

"Let me introduce Mr. Hirata," I said, "my old friend from primary school. We were always fighting when we were kids. He's got a mark on the back of his hand where I scratched him. Today he's come to get his revenge."

"How terrifying!" she said, laughing. "Anyhow, I'm glad to meet you." She bowed in his direction.

Our visitor seemed to relish these courtesies.

"Glad to meet you, madam," he said. "But you needn't stand on ceremony with me. By the way, I'd very much appreciate it if you'd pour me some whiskey."

I noticed that he was sober enough to address my wife politely, although a few moments before he had been referring to her as "the little woman."

"You know, madam," he said, when my wife had filled his cup, "I was just telling Osamu here that if you ever need any food, be sure to come round to my place. I've got plenty of everything: potatoes, vegetables, rice, eggs, chickens. What about some horsemeat? Would you like a nice hunk of horsemeat? I'm a great expert at stripping horsehides, you know. Come along tomorrow and I'll give you a whole horse's leg to take home. Do you like pheasant? Of course you do! Well, I'm the most famous shot in these parts. Just tell me what you want and I'll shoot it. Maybe madam would fancy some nice wild duck. Right, I'll go out tomorrow morning and shoot a dozen for you. That's nothing—a dozen. I've shot five dozen before breakfast in my day. If you don't believe me, ask anyone round here. I'm the greatest marksman in the district. The young people are all scared stiff of me. That's right—they know I can show them a thing or two. Hey, you there, bookworm!" he shouted at me. "Why don't you come along to the Shinto gate one of these evenings? There's usually a good fight going on down there—a lot of rowdy youngsters slugging at each other. Well, as soon as I get there, I throw myself right into the middle of them all and make them stop fighting. Of course, I'm risking my life every time I go there, but what does that matter? I've got a bit of money put aside for my wife and little ones. They'll be all right even when I'm gone."

For a moment his tone was maudlin. Then, suddenly turning to me again, he shouted almost ferociously: "Hey you, Mr. Bookworm! I'll call for you tomorrow evening and we'll go down to the gate together. I'll show you what life is really like. You won't be able to write anything good just sitting here on your backside all day long. What you need is a little experience. What sort of books do you write anyway? Books about geisha girls, I suppose. Ha, ha, ha! The trouble is, you don't know what life's all about. Now take me. I've had three wives already. But I always like the present one best. How many wives have you had? Two? Three? What about it, madam? Does he know how to make love to you right?"

"Please go and fetch some cakes," I said to my wife, with a sigh.

"I imagine you're going back to Tokyo pretty soon," said Mr. Hirata, as my wife left the room. "You'll be playing around with those girls again. Ha, ha! Where do you live in Tokyo?"

"I lost my house in the war."

"So you were bombed out, were you? That's the first I've heard of it. Well, in that case you must have got that special allocation of a blanket that they gave each family of evacuees. Would you mind letting me have it?"

I looked at him with renewed amazement.

"That's right," he said, calmly refilling his cup, "give me the blanket. It's meant to be quite good wool. My wife can make me a jumper with it. . . . I suppose you think it's funny of me to ask you for the blanket like this. But that's the way I do things. If I want something, I just ask for it. And when you come to my place, you can do the same. I'll give you whatever you like. What's the use of standing on ceremony with each other? Well, what about it? Are you going to let me have that blanket?"

I still stared at him blankly. This wool blanket, which we had been given as a sort of consolation prize, seemed to be my wife's most treasured possession. When our house was bombed and we moved to the country with our children, like a family of crabs whose shells have been smashed and who crawl naked and helpless across a hostile beach, she had kept the blanket constantly in sight, as though it were some sort of talisman. The man who now faced me could never know how a family felt who had lost their house in the war, or how close to committing mass suicide such families often were.

"I'm afraid you'll have to forget about the blanket," I said firmly.

"You stingy devil!" he said. "Why can't I have it?"

At this moment I was delighted to see my wife reappear with a tray of cakes. As I expected, our visitor instantly forgot about the blanket.

"Good gracious, madam," he said, "you shouldn't have gone to all that trouble. I don't want anything to eat. I came here to drink. But I want you to do the pouring from now on. This husband of yours is too damned stingy for my liking." He glared at me. "What about it, madam? Shall I give him a good beating? I used to be quite a fighter in my Tokyo days. I know a bit of jujitsu too. He'll be an easy match, even though he may be a few years younger than me. Well, madam, if he ever gives you any trouble, just tell me and I'll let him have a thrashing he won't forget in a hurry. You see, I've known him since we were boys together at school and he doesn't dare put on any of his airs with me."

It was then that the various stories which I had read years ago in textbooks on moral training came back to me—stories about great men like Kimura Shigenari, Kanzaki Yogoro, and Kanshin, who, on being abused by unmannerly rogues like this, did not answer in kind, but instead displayed their true moral superiority, as well as their fathomless contempt for these ruffians, by forthrightly asking them for forgiveness, when by all rights it was they who deserved apology. I remembered how, in the case of Kanzaki Yogoro, his assailant, who was a packhorse driver, had been so impressed by the great man's humility and forbearance that he had spent days trying to compose an adequate letter of apology and had thereafter fallen into a decline and taken to drink. Until now, rather than admire the much-vaunted patience of these men, I had always tended to despise it as concealing an arrogant sense of superiority; my sympathy had, in fact, been on the side of the so-called rogues, whose behavior was at least natural and unpretentious. But now unexpectedly I found myself in the role of Kimura, Kanzaki, and Kanshin. All of a sudden I knew the sense of isolation which they too must have felt when being attacked. It occurred to me that these didactic stories should be classified, not under the usual headings of "Forbearance" or "Great Men and Little Men," but, rather, under "Loneliness." At the same time I perceived that forbearance really had very little to do with the matter. It was simply that these "great men" were weaker than their assailants and knew that they would not stand a chance if it came to a fight.

"Always fly a wild horse!"—that simple maxim explained their conduct, as well as my own behavior in face of this "old friend." I had a horrible vision of our visitor suddenly running amok and smashing the screens, sliding doors, and furniture. Since none of the property belonged to me, I lived in a constant state of apprehension that the children might scribble on the walls or push the doors too roughly; the idea of the terrible ravages that this farmer might now perpetrate made cold shivers run down my spine. At all cost, I thought in my lonely cowardice, I must avoid offending him.

Suddenly I heard him roaring at the top of his lungs; "Ho, ho!" I looked up aghast. "Good lord, I'm drunk!" he shouted. "Yes, damn it, I'm drunk!"

Then he gave a groan, closed his eyes tightly, and planting both elbows on his knees, sat there with a look of complete concentration, as if desperately fighting his drunkenness. The perspiration glistened on his forehead and his face was almost purple. He looked like some great struggling behemoth. He certainly must have been drunk: he had finished over half of the second bottle of whiskey. My wife and I looked at each other uneasily. Then, to our amazement, he opened his eyes and said calmly, as if nothing whatever had happened: "When all's said and done, I like an occasional nip of whiskey. It makes me feel good. Come over here, madam, and pour me another cup. Don't worry, us farmers can drink as much as we like without getting tipsy."

Seeing that my wife made no move, he reached for the bottle himself, filled his cup, and drained it at a single draught.

"Well, you've both been very civil," he said, smacking his lips. "Next time you must be my guests. The trouble is, though, I really don't know what I'd give you if you did come to my place. I have a few birds, of course, but I'm keeping them for the cockfights in November. You'll have to wait till November. I suppose I could let you have a couple of pickled radishes. . . ." His words trailed off into murmur and for a while he was silent.

"I've really got nothing in my place," he continued, "nothing at all. That's why I came here today for a drink. Of course, I could try to shoot a wild duck. We'd eat it together —just the three of us—and Osamu here would provide the whiskey. But I'll do it only on one condition: while you're eating it you've got to keep saying: 'How delicious! What a splendid duck!' If you don't, I'll be furious. In fact I'll never forgive you. Ha, ha, ha! Yes, madam, that's the way we farmers are. Treat us right and there's nothing in the world we won't do for you. But if you're snooty and standoffish, we won't give you as much as a piece of string. No use putting on airs with me, madam. You look pretty cool and haughty right now, don't you, but I bet when you're in bed you let yourself go—just like other women."

My wife laughed good-naturedly and stood up. "I'm afraid I'll have to leave you," she said. "I hear the baby crying."

"She's no good!" he shouted, as soon as my wife had left the room. "Your missus is no damned good, I tell you! Now take my old woman, for instance. There's a real wife for you! We've got six lovely kids and we're as happy a family as you'll find anywhere in these parts. Ask anyone in the village if you don't believe me." He glared at me defiantly. "Your missus thinks she can make a fool of me by walking out like that. Well, I'm going to bring her right back to say she's sorry. Where is she? In the bedroom, I expect. I'll go and drag her out of her bedroom."

He staggered to his feet. I immediately got up and took him by the hand.

"Forget about her." I said. "Sit down and have another drink." He flopped heavily into the chair. I tried to smile, but my face was frozen.

"I knew it all along," he said. "You're having trouble with your wife. You're unhappily married, aren't you? I felt it right away."

I did not bother to contradict him.

"Well, it's none of my business," he said, filling his cup. "What about a poem to make you forget your troubles? Shall I recite you a poem?"

This was a welcome departure. Not only would it take his mind off my wife and her imagined insult, but to hear him recite a poem—perhaps some ancient melancholy verses handed down from generation to generation in this remote little village—might mitigate the picture of unrelieved loathsomeness that I had by now formed of my "old friend," a picture that I feared would pursue me to the end of my days.

"Yes, do let me hear your poem," I said warmly. For the first time that afternoon, I was sincere.

He took a drink, hiccuped loudly, and started to recite:

> O'er mountains, rivers, plants, and trees
> The dreary air of desolation grows.
> Mile after mile stretches the fearful battlefield
> Reeking of new-spilled blood.

He hiccuped again. "I've forgotten the second verse," he said. "It's something I read in a magazine."

"I see."

"Well, I'm off," he said, getting slowly to his feet. "Your missus has left and I don't enjoy drinking the whiskey when you pour it."

I did not try to detain him.

"We'll discuss the class reunion when I have more time," he said. "I'll have to leave most of the arrangements to you. In the meantime you can let me have a little of your whiskey to take home."

I was prepared for this and immediately started to pour the whiskey that remained in his cup into the bottle, which was still about a quarter full.

"You can have this bottle," I said, handing it to him.

"Hey, hey," he said, "none of that!" I've had enough of your stinginess for one day. You've still got another full bottle stored away in that cupboard, haven't you? Let me have it!"

"All right," I said.

There was nothing for it but to hand over my final bottle of whiskey. At least this put the proper finishing touch to the afternoon, I thought with a bitter smile. Now if Mr. Ibuse or any other friend came to visit, we would no longer be able to enjoy a convivial drink. For a moment I thought of mentioning the cost of whiskey, just to see what reaction it would bring, but even now I could not bring myself to violate the code of a host. Instead I heard myself asking ignominiously: "What about cigarettes? Do you need any cigarettes?"

"I'll get those next time," he said, picking up a whiskey bottle in each hand.

I followed him to the front door and here it was that the climax of the visit came. As he was about to step out of the door, he hiccuped loudly, turned round, and hissed into my ear: "You shouldn't be so damned stuck-up!"

Yes, he was a man of truly epic proportions.

YASUNARI KAWABATA

"The Moon on the Water" ("Suigetsu," 1953)

Translated by George Saito

Yasunari Kawabata (1899–1972) was born in Osaka and soon orphaned. He was enrolled in the English Literature Department of Tokyo University in 1920 and was graduated three years later. In 1948 he became president of the Japanese P.E.N. Club. Kawabata is known for his magnanimity and warmheartedness; he made many friends including Yokomitsu and was also instrumental in discovering a number of young writers, Yukio Mishima among them. In 1968 he was awarded the Nobel Prize. In ill health for several years, he committed suicide in the spring of 1972.

While in college he published his first piece of fiction "A View of the Memorial Day Festival" ("Shokonsai Ikkei") in *New Current of Thought*. His talent was recognized when "A Dancer of Izu" ("Izu no Odoriko," 1926) appeared in the neo-perceptionist magazine *The Generation of Literature and Art*. (*Bungei Jidai*). *The Kurenaidan of Asakusa* (*Asakusa Kurenaidan*, 1929–30), "Rainbow" ("Niji," 1934–35), and "Flower Waltz" ("Hana no Warutsu," 1936–37), all dealing with the lives of cabaret dancers, created a unique world of fiction and became very popular with general readers. His masterpiece is *Snow Country* (*Yukiguni*), begun in 1934, published piecemeal between 1935 and 1937, and finally completed in 1947. Two years later another major work appeared, *Thousand Cranes* (*Senbazuru*), which was made into a very successful play. He also wrote *The Sound of the Mountain* (*Yama no Oto*, 1949), *People of Tokyo* (*Tokyo no Hito*, 1954–55), and *Sleeping Beauties* (*Nemureru Bijo*, 1961). *People of Tokyo*, reissued later in three volumes, was serialized in a well-known local paper and became popular at the time.

Many of Kawabata's later works are marked by a loosely knit plot structure unlike a well-made Western novel. His writing lacks the mechanical contrivance often seen in modern novels and short stories. Commenting on his own work, he once said, "My novel has an ending anywhere in it and yet it does not seem to end." When he heard with surprise that he was given the Nobel Prize, he said to the newsmen, "My writing lacks a sense of power and strength." His qualities are unique among contemporary Japanese novelists. His prose, at times almost elegiac, is shown at its best in "The Moon on the Water," which seems permeated with the subtle and elegant beauties of classical Japanese literature.

It occurred to Kyoko one day to let her husband, in bed upstairs, see her vegetable garden by reflecting it in her hand mirror. To one who had been so long confined, this opened a new life. The hand mirror was part of a set in Kyoko's trousseau. The mirror stand was not very big. It was made of mulberry wood, as was the frame of the mirror itself. It was the hand mirror that still reminded her of the bashfulness of her early married years when, as she was looking into it at the reflection of her back hair in the stand mirror, her sleeve would slip and expose her elbow.

When she came from the bath, her husband seemed to enjoy reflecting the nape of her neck from all angles in the hand mirror. Taking the mirror from her, he would say: "How clumsy you are! Here, let me hold it." Maybe he found something new in the mirror. It was not that Kyoko was clumsy, but that she became nervous at being looked at from behind.

Not enough time had passed for the color of the mulberry-wood frame to change. It lay in a drawer. War came, followed by flight from the city and her husband's becoming seriously ill; by the time it first occurred to Kyoko to have her husband see the garden through the mirror, its surface had become cloudy and the rim had been smeared with face powder and dirt. Since it still reflected well enough, Kyoko did not worry about this cloudiness—indeed she scarcely noticed it. Her husband, however, would not let the mirror go from his bedside and polished it and its frame in his idleness with the peculiar nervousness of an invalid. Kyoko sometimes imagined that tuberculosis germs had found their way into the imperceptible cracks in the frame. After she had combed her husband's hair with a little camellia oil, he sometimes ran the palm of his hand through his hair and then rubbed the mirror. The wood of the mirror stand remained dull, but that of the mirror grew lustrous.

When Kyoko married again, she took the same mirror stand with her. The hand mirror, however, had been burned in the coffin of her dead husband. A hand mirror with a carved design had now taken its place. She never told her second husband about this.

According to custom, the hands of her dead husband had been clasped and his fingers crossed, so that it was impossible to make them hold the hand mirror after he had been put into the coffin. She laid the mirror on his chest.

"Your chest hurt you so. Even this must be heavy."

Kyoko moved the mirror down to his stomach. Because she thought of the important role that the mirror had played in their marital life, Kyoko had first laid it on his chest. She wanted to keep this little act as much as possible from the eyes even of her husband's family. She had piled white chrysanthemums on the mirror. No one had noticed it. When the ashes were being gathered after the cremation, people noticed the glass which had been melted into a shapeless mass, partly sooty and partly yellowish. Someone said: "It's glass. What is it, I wonder?" She had in fact placed a still smaller mirror on the hand mirror. It was the sort of mirror usually carried in a toilet case, a long, narrow, double-faced mirror. Kyoko had dreamed of using it on her honeymoon trip. The war had made it impossible for them to go on a honeymoon. During her husband's lifetime she never was able to use it on a trip.

With her second husband, however, she went on a honeymoon. Since her leather toilet case was now very musty, she bought a new one—with a mirror in it too.

On the very first day of their trip, her husband touched Kyoko and said: "You are like a little girl. Poor thing!" His tone was not in the least sarcastic. Rather it suggested unexpected joy. Possibly it was good for him that Kyoko was like a little girl. At this remark, Kyoko was assailed by an intense sorrow. Her eyes filled with tears and she shrank away. He might have taken that to be girlish too.

Kyoko did not know whether she had wept for her own sake or for the sake of her dead husband. Nor was it possible to know. The moment this idea came to her, she felt very sorry for her second husband and thought she had to be coquettish.

"Am I so different?" No sooner had she spoken than she felt very awkward, and shyness came over her.

He looked satisfied and said: "You never had a child . . ."

His remark pierced her heart. Before a male force other than her former husband Kyoko felt humiliated. She was being made sport of.

"But it was like looking after a child all the time."

This was all she said by way of protest. It was as if her first husband, who had died after a long illness, had been a child inside her. But if he was to die in any case, what good had her continence done?

"I've only seen Mori from the train window." Her second husband drew her to him as he mentioned the name of her hometown. "From its name [1] it sounds like a pretty town in the woods. How long did you live there?"

"Until I graduated from high school. Then I was drafted to work in a munitions factory in Sanjo."

"Is Sanjo near, then? I've heard a great deal about Sanjo beauties. I see why you're so beautiful."

"No, I'm not." Kyoko brought her hand to her throat.

"Your hands are beautiful, and I thought your body should be beautiful too."

"Oh no."

Finding her hands in the way, Kyoko quietly drew them back.

"I'm sure I'd have married you even if you had had a child. I could have adopted the child and looked after it. A girl would have been better," he whispered in Kyoko's ear. Maybe it was because he had a boy, but his remark seemed odd even as an expression of love. Possibly he had planned

[1] "Mori" means "grove."

the long, ten-day honeymoon so that she would not have to face the stepson quite so soon.

Her husband had a toilet case for traveling, made of what seemed to be good leather. Kyoko's did not compare with it. His was large and strong, but it was not new. Maybe because he often traveled or because he took good care of it, the case had a mellow luster. Kyoko thought of the old case, never used, which she had left to mildew. Only its small mirror had been used by her first husband, and she had sent it with him in death.

The small glass had melted into the hand mirror, so that no one except Kyoko could tell that they had been separate before. Since Kyoko had not said that the curious mass had been mirrors, her relatives had no way of knowing.

Kyoko felt as if the numerous worlds reflected in the two mirrors had vanished in the fire. She felt the same kind of loss when her husband's body was reduced to ashes. It had been with the hand mirror that came with the mirror stand that Kyoko first reflected the vegetable garden. Her husband always kept that mirror beside his pillow. Even the hand mirror seemed to be too heavy for the invalid, and Kyoko, worried about his arms and shoulders, gave him a lighter and smaller one.

It was not only Kyoko's vegetable garden that her husband had observed through the two mirrors. He had seen the sky, clouds, snow, distant mountains, and nearby woods. He had seen the moon. He had seen wild flowers, and birds of passage had made their way through the mirror. Men walked down the road in the mirror and children played in the garden.

Kyoko was amazed at the richness of the world in the mirror. A mirror which had until then been regarded only as a toilet article, a hand mirror which had served only to show the back of one's neck, had created for the invalid a new life. Kyoko used to sit beside his bed and talk about the world in the mirror. They looked into it together. In the course of time it became impossible for Kyoko to distinguish between the world that she saw directly and the world in the mirror. Two separate worlds came to exist. A new world was created in the mirror and it came to seem like the real world.

"The sky shines silver in the mirror," Kyoko said. Looking up through the window, she added: "When the sky itself is grayish." The sky in the mirror lacked the leaden and heavy quality of the actual sky. It was shining.

"Is it because you are always polishing the mirror?"

Though he was lying down, her husband could see the sky by turning his head.

"Yes, it's a dull gray. But the color of the sky is not necessarily the same to dogs' eyes and sparrows' eyes as it is to human eyes. You can't tell which eyes see the real color."

"What we see in the mirror—is that what the mirror eye sees?"

Kyoko wanted to call it the eye of their love. The trees in the mirror were a fresher green than real trees, and the lilies a purer white.

"This is the print of your thumb, Kyoko. Your right thumb."

He pointed to the edge of the mirror. Kyoko was somehow startled. She breathed on the mirror and erased the fingerprint.

"That's all right, Kyoko. Your fingerprint stayed on the mirror when you first showed me the vegetable garden."

"I didn't notice it."

"You may not have noticed it. Thanks to this mirror, I've memorized the prints of your thumbs and index fingers. Only an invalid could memorize his wife's fingerprints."

Her husband had done almost nothing but lie in bed since their marriage. He had not gone to war. Toward the end of the war he had been drafted, but he fell ill after several days of labor at an airfield and came home at the end of the war. Since he was unable to walk, Kyoko went with his elder brother to meet him. After her husband had been drafted, she stayed with her parents. They had left the city to avoid the bombings. Their household goods had long since been sent away. As the house where their married life began had been burned down, they had rented a room in the home of a friend of Kyoko's. From there her husband commuted to his office. A month in their honeymoon house and two months at the house of a friend—that was all the time Kyoko spent with her husband before he fell ill.

It was then decided that her husband should rent a small

house in the mountains and convalesce there. Other families had been in the house, also fugitives from the city, but they had gone back to Tokyo after the war ended. Kyoko took over their vegetable garden. It was only some six yards square, a clearing in the weeds. They could easily have bought vegetables, but Kyoko worked in the garden. She became interested in vegetables grown by her own hand. It was not that she wanted to stay away from her sick husband, but such things as sewing and knitting made her gloomy. Even though she thought of him always, she had brighter hopes when she was out in the garden. There she could indulge her love for her husband. As for reading, it was all she could do to read aloud at his bedside. Then Kyoko thought that by working in the garden she might regain that part of herself which it seemed she was losing in the fatigue of the long nursing.

It was in the middle of September that they moved to the mountains. The summer visitors had almost all gone and a long spell of early autumn rains came, chilly and damp.

One afternoon the sun came out to the clear song of a bird. When she went into the garden, she found the green vegetables shining. She was enraptured by the rosy clouds on the mountaintops. Startled by her husband's voice calling her, she hurried upstairs, her hands covered with mud, and found him breathing painfully.

"I called and called. Couldn't you hear me?"

"I'm sorry. I couldn't."

"Stop working in the garden. I'd be dead in no time if I had to keep calling you like that. In the first place, I can't see where you are and what you're doing."

"I was in the garden. But I'll stop."

He was calmer.

"Did you hear the lark?"

That was all he had wanted to tell her. The lark sang in the nearby woods again. The woods were clear against the evening glow. Thus Kyoko learned to know the song of the lark.

"A bell will help you, won't it? How about having something you can throw until I get a bell for you?"

"Shall I throw a cup from here? That would be fun."

It was settled that Kyoko might continue her gardening; but it was after spring had come to end the long, harsh mountain winter that Kyoko thought of showing him the garden in the mirror.

The single mirror gave him inexhaustible joy, as if a lost world of fresh green had come back. It was impossible for him to see the worms she picked from the vegetables. She had to come upstairs to show him. "I can see the earthworms from here, though," he used to say as he watched her digging in the earth.

When the sun was shining into the house, Kyoko sometimes noticed a light and, looking up, discovered that her husband was reflecting the sun in the mirror. He insisted that Kyoko remake the dark-blue kimono he had used during his student days into pantaloons for herself. He seemed to enjoy the sight of Kyoko in the mirror as she worked in the garden, wearing the dark blue with its white splashes.

Kyoko worked in the garden half-conscious and half-unconscious of the fact that she was being seen. Her heart warmed to see how different her feelings were now from the very early days of her marriage. Then she had blushed even at showing her elbow when she held the smaller glass behind her head. It was, however, only when she remarried that she started making up as she pleased, released from the long years of nursing and the mourning that had followed. She saw that she was becoming remarkably beautiful. It now seemed that her husband had really meant it when he said that her body was beautiful.

Kyoko was no longer ashamed of her reflection in the mirror—after she had had a bath, for instance. She had discovered her own beauty. But she had not lost that unique feeling that her former husband had planted in her toward the beauty in the mirror. She did not doubt the beauty she saw in the mirror. Quite the reverse: she could not doubt the reality of that other world. But between her skin as she saw it and her skin as reflected in the mirror she could not find the difference that she had found between that leaden sky and the silver sky in the mirror. It may not have been only the difference in distance. Maybe the longing of her first husband confined to his bed had acted upon her. But then, there was now no way of knowing how beautiful she had looked to him in the mirror as she worked in the garden. Even before his death, Kyoko herself had not been able to tell.

Kyoko thought of, indeed longed for, the image of herself working in the garden, seen through the mirror in her husband's hand, and for the white of the lilies, the crowd of village children playing in the field, and the morning sun rising above the far-off snowy mountains—for that separate world she had shared with him. For the sake of her present husband, Kyoko suppressed this feeling, which seemed about to become an almost physical yearning, and tried to take it for something like a distant view of the celestial world.

One morning in May, Kyoko heard the singing of wild birds over the radio. It was a broadcast from a mountain near the heights where she had stayed with her first husband until his death. As had become her custom, after seeing her present husband off to work, Kyoko took the hand mirror from the drawer of the stand and reflected the clear sky. Then she gazed at her face in the mirror. She was astonished by a new discovery. She could not see her own face unless she reflected it in the mirror. One could not see one's own face. One felt one's own face, wondering if the face in the mirror was one's actual face. Kyoko was lost in thought for some time. Why had God created man's face so that he might not see it himself?

"Suppose you could see your own face, would you lose your mind? Would you become incapable of acting?"

Most probably man had evolved in such a way that he could not see his own face. Maybe dragonflies and praying mantises could see their own faces.

But then perhaps one's own face was for others to see. Did it not resemble love? As she was putting the hand mirror back in the drawer, Kyoko could not even now help noticing the odd combination of carved design and mulberry. Since the former mirror had burned with her first husband, the mirror stand might well be compared to a widow. But the hand mirror had had its advantages and disadvantages. Her husband was constantly seeing his face in it. Perhaps it was more like seeing death itself. If his death was a psychological suicide by means of a mirror, then Kyoko was the psychological murderer. Kyoko had once thought of the disadvantages of the mirror, and tried to take it from him. But he would not let her.

"Do you intend to have me see nothing? As long as I live, I want to keep loving something I can see," her husband said. He would have sacrificed his life to keep the world in the mirror. After heavy rains they would gaze at the moon through the mirror, the reflection of the moon from the pool in the garden. A moon which could hardly be called even the reflection of a reflection still lingered in Kyoko's heart.

"A sound love dwells only in a sound person." When her second husband said this, Kyoko nodded shyly, but she could not entirely agree with him. When her first husband died, Kyoko wondered what good her continence had done; but soon the continence became a poignant memory of love, a memory of days brimming with love, and her regrets quite disappeared. Probably her second husband regarded woman's love too lightly. "Why did you leave your wife, when you are such a tenderhearted man?" Kyoko would ask him. He never answered. Kyoko had married him because the elder brother of her dead husband had insisted. After four months as friends they were married. He was fifteen years older.

When she became pregnant, Kyoko was so terrified that her very face changed.

"I'm afraid. I'm afraid." She clung to her husband. She suffered intensely from morning sickness and she even became deranged. She crawled into the garden barefooted and gathered pine needles. She had her stepson carry two lunch boxes to school, both boxes filled with rice. She sat staring blankly into the mirror, thinking that she saw straight through it. She rose in the middle of night, sat on the bed, and looked into her husband's sleeping face. Assailed by terror at the knowledge that man's life is a trifle, she found herself loosening the sash of her night robe. She made as if to strangle him. The next moment she was sobbing hysterically. Her husband awoke and retied her sash gently. She shivered in the summer night.

"Trust the child in you, Kyoko." Her husband rocked her in his arms.

The doctor suggested that she be hospitalized. Kyoko resisted, but was finally persuaded.

"I will go to the hospital. Please let me go first to visit my family for a few days."

Some time later her husband took her to her parents' home.

The next day Kyoko slipped out of the house and went to the heights where she had lived with her first husband. It was early in September, ten days earlier than when she had moved there with him. Kyoko felt like vomiting. She was dizzy in the train and obsessed by an impulse to jump off. As the train passed the station on the heights, the crisp air brought her relief. She regained control of herself, as if the devil possessing her had gone. She stopped, bewildered, and looked at the mountains surrounding the high plateau. The outline of the blue mountains where the color was now growing darker was vivid against the sky, and she felt in them a living world. Wiping her eyes, moist with warm tears, she walked toward the house where he and she had lived. From the woods which had loomed against the rosy evening glow that day there came again the song of a lark. Someone was living in the house and a white lace curtain hung at the window upstairs. Not going too near, she gazed at the house.

"What if the child should look like you?" Startled at her own words, she turned back, warm and at peace.

YUKIO MISHIMA

"The Priest of Shiga Temple and His Love"
("Shigadera Shonin no Koi," 1954)

Translated by Ivan Morris

Yukio Mishima (1925–1970), whose real name was Kimitake Hiraoka, was born of a high government official living in Tokyo. From the Peers' School he entered the Tokyo University Law School, from which he was graduated with an excellent record in 1947. He immediately obtained a position in the Finance Ministry, but resigned a few months later to become a writer. His earliest work, however, dates back to "The Grove in Bloom" ("Hana Zakari no Mori"), completed at the age of sixteen and published three years later in a collection of short stories under the same title. At the end of the war Mishima was writing a play while away from the university as a volunteer worker. By the time he joined the Finance Ministry, he had already made his name in literary circles with "Tobacco" ("Tabako" 1946), published with the recommendation of Yasunari Kawabata.

His first novel *Confessions of a Mask* (*Kamen no Kokuhaku*, 1949) established his reputation as one of the most gifted young writers to appear since the war. Then followed his other major novels: *The Thirst for Love* (*Ai no Kawaki*, 1950); *Forbidden Colors* (*Kinjiki*, 1952); *The Sound of Waves* (*Shiosai*, 1954); *The Temple of the Golden Pavilion* (*Kinkuji*, 1956); *The Fall of a Virtue* (*Bitoku no Yoromeki*, 1957); *The House of Kyoko* (*Kyoko no Ie*, 1959); *After the Banquet* (*Utage no Ato*, 1960); *The Sailor Who Fell from Grace with the Sea* (*Gogo no Eiko*, 1963); *Madame de Sade* (*Sado Koshaku Fujin*, 1965); and finally a tetralogy, *The Sea of Fertility* (*Hojo no Umi*), consisting of *Spring Snow* (*Haru no Yuki*, 1969), *Galloping Horse* (*Honba*, 1969), *The Temple of the Dawn* (*Akatsuki no Tera*, 1970), and *The Divinity's Five Omens* (*Tennin Gosui*, 1971).

Apart from these well-known novels, his total output consists of well over fifty volumes of short stories, poems, essays, and plays. He traveled in Europe and Asia, and also held a visiting lectureship at American universities. His fascination with the past glory of Japan expressed in the samurai code of honor led him to his version of conservatism. In the sixties he became deeply involved in a right-wing movement, even forming his own private army. All his life Mishima was a controversial figure as a writer and as a man of action. As the latter, his contemporaries never took him seriously. Mishima must have been aware that his political philosophy was an anachronism, but could not alter his conviction. He killed himself by *seppuku*, in the manner prescribed in his short story "Grief over the Nation" ("Yukoku," 1960).

According to Eshin's "Essentials of Salvation," the Ten Pleasures are but a drop in the ocean when compared to the joys of the Pure Land. In that land the earth is made of emerald and the roads that lead across it are lined by cordons of gold rope. The surface is endlessly level and there are no boundaries. Within each of the sacred precincts are fifty thousand million halls and towers wrought of gold, silver, lapis lazuli, crystal, coral, agate, and pearls; and wondrous garments are spread out on all the jeweled daises. Within the halls and above the towers a multitude of angels is forever playing sacred music and singing paeans of praise to the Tathagata Buddha. In the gardens that surround the halls and the towers and the cloisters are great gold and emerald ponds where the faithful may perform their ablutions; the gold ponds are lined with silver sand, and the emerald ponds are lined with crystal sand. The ponds are covered with lotus plants which sparkle in variegated colors and, as the breeze wafts over the surface of the water, magnificent lights crisscross in all directions. Both day and night the air is filled with the songs of cranes, geese, mandarin ducks, peacocks, parrots, and sweet-voiced Kalavinkas, who have the faces of beautiful women. All these and the myriad other hundred-jeweled birds are raising their melodious voices in praise of the Buddha. (However sweet their voices may sound, so immense a collection of birds must be extremely noisy.)

The borders of the ponds and the banks of the rivers are lined with groves of sacred treasure trees. These trees have golden stems and silver branches and coral blossoms, and their beauty is mirrored in the waters. The air is full of jeweled cords, and from these cords hang the myriad treasure bells which forever ring out the Supreme Law of Buddha; and strange musical instruments, which play by themselves without ever being touched, also stretch far into the pellucid sky.

If one feels like having something to eat, there automatically appears before one's eyes a seven-jeweled table on whose shining surface rest seven-jeweled bowls heaped high with the choicest delicacies. But there is no need to pick up these viands and put them in one's mouth. All that is necessary is to look at their inviting colors and to enjoy their aroma; thereby the stomach is filled and the body nourished, while one remains oneself spiritually and physically pure. When one has thus finished one's meal without any eating, the bowls and the table are instantly wafed off.

Likewise, one's body is automatically arrayed in clothes, without any need for sewing, laundering, dyeing, or repairing. Lamps, too, are unnecessary, for the sky is illumined by an omnipresent light. Furthermore, the Pure Land enjoys a moderate temperature all year round, so that neither heating nor cooling is required. A hundred thousand subtle scents perfume the air, and lotus petals rain down constantly.

In the chapter on the Inspection Gate we are told that, since uninitiated sightseers cannot hope to penetrate deep into the Pure Land, they must concentrate, first, on awakening their powers of "external imagination" and, thereafter, on steadily expanding these powers. Imaginative power can provide a shortcut for escaping from the trammels of our mundane life and for seeing the Buddha. If we are endowed with a rich, turbulent imagination, we can focus our attention on a single lotus flower and from there can spread out to infinite horizons.

By means of microscopic observation and astronomical projection the lotus flower can become the foundation for an entire theory of the universe and an agent whereby we may perceive Truth. And first we must know that each of the petals has eighty-four thousand veins and that each vein gives off eighty-four thousand lights. Furthermore, the smallest of these flowers has a diameter of two hundred and fifty yojana. Thus, assuming that the yojana of which we read in the Holy Writings correspond to seventy-five miles each, we may conclude that a lotus flower with a diameter of nineteen thousand miles is on the small side.

Now such a flower has eighty-four thousand petals and between each of the petals there are one million jewels, each emitting one thousand lights. Above the beautifully adorned calyx of the flower rise four bejeweled pillars and each of these pillars is one hundred billion times as great as Mount Sumeru, which towers in the center of the Buddhist universe. From the pillars hang great draperies and each drapery is adorned with fifty thousand million jewels, and each jewel emits eighty-four thousand lights, and each light is composed of eighty-four thousand different golden colors, and each of those golden colors in its turn is variously transmogrified.

To concentrate on such images is known as "thinking of the Lotus Seat on which Lord Buddha sits"; and the conceptual world that hovers in the background of our story is a world imagined on such a scale.

The Great Priest of Shiga Temple was a man of the most eminent virtue. His eyebrows were white, and it was as much as he could do to move his old bones along as he hobbled on his stick from one part of the temple to another.

In the eyes of this learned ascetic, the world was a mere pile of rubbish. He had lived away from it for many a long year, and the little pine sapling that he had planted with his own hands on moving into his present cell had grown into a great tree whose branches swelled in the wind. A monk who had succeeded in abandoning the Floating World for so long a time must feel secure about his afterlife.

When the Great Priest saw the rich and the noble, he smiled with compassion and wondered how it was that these people did not recognize their pleasures for the empty dreams that they were. When he noticed beautiful women, his only reaction was to be moved with pity for men who still inhabited the world of delusion and who were tossed about on the waves of carnal pleasure.

From the moment that a man no longer responds in the slightest to the motives that regulate the material world, that world appears to be at complete repose. In the eyes of the Great Priest the world showed only repose; it had become a mere picture drawn on a piece of paper, a map of some foreign land. When one has attained a state of mind from which the evil passions of the present world have been so utterly winnowed, fear too is forgotten. Thus it was that the priest no longer could understand why Hell should exist. He knew beyond all peradventure that the present world no longer had any power left over him; but, as he was completely devoid of conceit, it did not occur to him that this was the effect of his own eminent virtue.

So far as his body was concerned, one might say that the priest had well-nigh been deserted by his own flesh. On such occasions as he observed it—when taking a bath, for instance —he would rejoice to see how his protruding bones were precariously covered by his withered skin. Now that his body had reached this stage, he felt that he could come to terms with it, as if it belonged to someone else. Such a body, it seemed, was already more suited for the nourishment of the Pure Land than for terrestrial food and drink.

In his dreams he lived nightly in the Pure Land, and when he awoke he knew that to subsist in the present world was to be tied to a sad and evanescent dream.

In the flower-viewing season large numbers of people came from the capital to visit the village of Shiga. This did not trouble the priest in the slightest, for he had long since transcended that state in which the clamors of the world can irritate the mind. One spring evening he left his cell, leaning on his stick, and walked down to the lake. It was the hour when dusky shadows slowly begin to thrust their way into the bright light of the afternoon. There was not the slightest ripple to disturb the surface of the water. The priest stood by himself at the edge of the lake and began to perform the holy rite of Water Contemplation.

At that moment an ox-drawn carriage, clearly belonging to a person of high rank, came around the lake and stopped close to where the priest was standing. The owner was a Court lady from the Kyogoku district of the capital who held the exalted title of Great Imperial Concubine. This lady had come to view the springtime scenery in Shiga and now on her return she stopped the carriage and raised the blind in order to have a final look at the lake.

Unwittingly the Great Priest glanced in her direction and at once he was overwhelmed by her beauty. His eyes met hers and, as he did nothing to avert his gaze, she did not take it upon herself to turn away. It was not that her liberality of spirit was such as to allow men to gaze on her with brazen looks; but the motives of this austere old ascetic could hardly, she felt, be those of ordinary men.

After a few moments the lady pulled down the blind. Her carriage started to move and, having gone through the Shiga Pass, rolled slowly down the road that led to the capital. Night fell and the carriage made its way toward the city along the Road of the Silver Temple. Until the carriage had become a pinprick that disappeared between the distant trees, the Great Priest stood rooted to the spot.

In the twinkling of an eye the present world had wreaked its revenge with terrible force on the priest. What he had imagined to be completely safe had collapsed in ruins.

He returned to the temple, faced the main image of Buddha, and invoked the Sacred Name. But impure thoughts now cast their opaque shadows about him. A woman's beauty, he told himself, was but a fleeting apparition, a temporary phenomenon composed of flesh—of flesh that was soon to be destroyed. Yet, try as he might to ward it off, the ineffable beauty which had overpowered him at that instant by the lake now pressed on his heart with the force of something that had come from an infinite distance. The Great Priest was not young enough, either spiritually or physically, to believe that this new feeling was simply a trick that his flesh had played on him. A man's flesh, he knew full well, could not alter so rapidly. Rather, he seemed to have been immersed in some swift, subtle poison which had abruptly transmuted his spirit.

The Great Priest had never broken his vow of chastity. The inner fight that he had waged in his youth against the demands of the flesh had made him think of women as mere carnal beings. The only real flesh was the flesh that existed in his imagination. Since, therefore, he regarded the flesh as an ideal abstraction rather than as a physical fact, he had relied on his spiritual strength to subjugate it. In this effort the priest had achieved success—success, indeed, that no one who knew him could possibly doubt.

Yet the face of the woman who had raised the carriage blind and gazed across the lake was too harmonious, too refulgent, to be designated as a mere object of flesh, and the priest did not know what name to give it. He could only think that, in order to bring about that wondrous moment, something which had for a long time lurked deceptively within him had finally revealed itself. That thing was nothing other than the present world, which until then had been at repose, but which had now suddenly lifted itself out of the darkness and begun to stir.

It was as if he had been standing by the highway that led to the capital, with his hands firmly covering both ears, and had watched two great oxcarts rumble past each other. All of a sudden he had removed his hands and the noise from outside had surged all about him.

To perceive the ebb and flow of passing phenomena, to have their noise roaring in one's ears, was to enter into the circle of the present world. For a man like the Great Priest who had severed his relations with all outside things, this was to place himself once again into a state of relationship.

Even as he read the sutras he would time after time hear himself heaving great sighs of anguish. Perhaps nature, he thought, might serve to distract his spirit, and he gazed out the window of his cell at the mountains that towered in the distance under the evening sky. Yet his thoughts, instead of concentrating on the beauty, broke up like tufts of cloud and drifted away. He fixed his gaze on the moon, but his thoughts continued to wander as before; and when once again he went and stood before the main image in a desperate effort to regain his purity of mind, the countenance of the Buddha was transformed and looked like the face of the lady in the carriage. His universe had been imprisoned within the confines of a small circle: at one point was the Great Priest and opposite him was the Great Imperial Concubine.

The Great Imperial Concubine of Kyogoku had soon forgotten about the old priest whom she had noticed gazing so intently at her by the lake at Shiga. After some time, however, a rumor came to her ears and she was reminded of the incident. One of the villagers happened to have caught sight of the Great Priest as he had stood watching the lady's carriage disappear into the distance. He had mentioned the matter to a Court gentleman who had come to Shiga for flower-viewing, and had added that since that day the priest had behaved like one crazed.

The Imperial Concubine pretended to disbelieve the rumor. The virtue of this particular priest, however, was noted throughout the capital, and the incident was bound to feed the lady's vanity.

For she was utterly weary of the love that she received from the men of this world. The Imperial Concubine was fully aware of her own beauty, and she tended to be attracted by any force, such as religion, that treated her beauty and her high rank as things of no value. Being exceedingly bored with the present world, she believed in the Pure Land. It was inevitable that Jodo Buddhism, which rejected all the beauty and brilliance of the visual world as being mere filth and defilement, should have a particular appeal for someone like the Imperial Concubine who was thoroughly disillusioned with the superficial elegance of Court life—an elegance that seemed unmistakably to bespeak the Latter Days of the Law and their degeneracy.

Among those whose special interest was love, the Great Imperial Concubine was held in honor as the very personification of courtly refinement. The fact that she was known never to have given her love to any man added to this reputation. Though she performed her duties toward the Emperor with the most perfect decorum, no one for a moment believed that she loved him from her heart. The Great Imperial Concubine dreamed of a passion that lay on the boundary of the impossible.

The Great Priest of Shiga Temple was famous for his virtue, and everyone in the capital knew how this aged prelate had totally abandoned the present world. All the more startling, then, was the rumor that he had been dazzled by the charms of the Imperial Concubine and that for her sake he had sacrificed the future world. To give up the joys of the Pure Land which were so close at hand—there could be no greater sacrifice than this, no greater gift.

The Great Imperial Concubine was utterly indifferent to the charms of the young rakes who flocked about the Court and of the handsome noblemen who came her way. The physical attributes of men no longer meant anything to her. Her only concern was to find a man who could give her the strongest and deepest possible love. A woman with such aspirations is a truly terrifying creature. If she is a mere courtesan, she will no doubt be satisfied with wordly wealth. The Great Imperial Concubine, however, already enjoyed all those things that the wealth of the world can provide. The man whom she awaited must offer her the wealth of the future world.

The rumors of the Great Priest's infatuation spread throughout the Court. In the end the story was even told half-jokingly to the Emperor himself. The Great Concubine took no pleasure in this bantering gossip and preserved a cool, indifferent mien. As she was well aware, there were two reasons that the people of the Court could joke freely about a matter which would normally have been forbidden: first, by referring to the Great Priest's love they were paying a compliment to the beauty of the woman who could inspire even an ecclesiastic of such great virtue to forsake his meditations; secondly, everyone fully realized that the old man's love for the noblewoman could never possibly be requited.

The Great Imperial Concubine called to mind the face of the old priest whom she had seen through her carriage window. It did not bear the remotest resemblance to the face of any of the men who had loved her until then. Strange it was that love should spring up in the heart of a man who did not have the slightest qualification for being loved. The lady recalled such phrases as "my love forlorn and without hope" that were widely used by poetasters in the palace when they wished to awaken some sympathy in the hearts of their indifferent paramours. Compared to the hopeless situation in which the Great Priest now found himself, the state of the least fortunate of these elegant lovers was almost enviable, and their poetic tags struck her now as mere trappings of worldly dalliance, inspired by vanity and utterly devoid of pathos.

At this point it will be clear to the reader that the Great

Imperial Concubine was not, as was so widely believed, the personification of courtly elegance, but, rather, a person who found the real relish of life in the knowledge of being loved. Despite her high rank, she was first of all a woman; and all the power and authority in the world seemed to her empty things if they were bereft of this knowledge. The men about her might devote themselves to struggles for political power; but she dreamed of subduing the world by different means, by purely feminine means. Many of the women whom she had known had taken the tonsure and retired from the world. Such women struck her as laughable. For, whatever a woman may say about abandoning the world, it is almost impossible for her to give up the things that she possesses. Only men are really capable of giving up what they possess.

That old priest by the lake had at a certain stage in his life given up the Floating World and all its pleasures. In the eyes of the Imperial Concubine he was far more of a man than all the nobles whom she knew at Court. And, just as he had once abandoned this present Floating World, so now on her behalf he was about to give up the future world as well.

The Imperial Concubine recalled the notion of the sacred lotus flower, which her own deep faith had vividly imprinted upon her mind. She thought of the huge lotus with its width of two hundred and fifty yojana. That preposterous plant was far more fitted to her tastes than those puny lotus flowers which floated on the ponds of the capital. At night when she listened to the wind soughing through the trees in her garden, the sound seemed to her extremely insipid when compared to the delicate music in the Pure Land when the wind blew through the sacred treasure trees. When she thought of the strange instruments that hung in the sky and that played by themselves without ever being touched, the sound of the harp that echoed through the palace halls seemed to her a paltry imitation.

The Great Priest of Shiga Temple was fighting. In the fight that he had waged against the flesh in his youth he had always been buoyed up by the hope of inheriting the future world. But this desperate fight of his old age was linked with a sense of irreparable loss.

The impossibility of consummating his love for the Great Imperial Concubine was as clear to him as the sun in the sky. At the same time he was fully aware of the impossibility of advancing toward the Pure Land so long as he remained in the thralls of this love. The Great Priest, who had lived in an incomparably free state of mind, had in a twinkling been enclosed in darkness, and the future was totally obscure. It may have been that the courage which had seen him through his youthful struggles had grown out of self-confidence and pride in the fact that he was voluntarily depriving himself of pleasure that could have been his for the asking.

The Great Priest once more possessed himself of fear. Until that noble carriage had approached the side of Lake Shiga, he had believed that what lay in wait for him, close at hand, was nothing less than the final release of Nirvana. But now he had awakened into the darkness of the present world, where it is impossible to see what lurks a single step ahead.

The various forms of religious meditation were all in vain. He tried the Contemplation of the Chrysanthemum, the Contemplation of the Total Aspect, and the Contemplation of the Parts; but each time that he started to concentrate, the beautiful visage of the concubine appeared before his eyes. Water Contemplation, too, was useless, for invariably her lovely face would float up shimmering from beneath the ripples of the lake.

This, no doubt, was a natural consequence of his infatuation. Concentration, the priest soon realized, did more harm than good, and next he tried to dull his spirit by dispersal. It astonished him that spiritual concentration should have the paradoxical effect of leading him still deeper into his delusions; but he soon realized that to try the contrary method by dispersing his thoughts meant that he was, in effect, admitting these very delusions. As his spirit began to yield under the weight, the priest decided that, rather than pursue a futile struggle, it were better to escape from the effort of escaping by deliberately concentrating his thoughts on the figure of the Great Imperial Concubine.

The Great Priest found a new pleasure in adorning his vision of the lady in various ways, just as though he were adorning a Buddhist statue with diadems and baldachins. In so doing, he turned the object of his love into an increasingly resplendent, distant, impossible being; and this afforded him particular joy. But why? Surely it would be more natural for him to envisage the Great Imperial Concubine as an ordinary female, close at hand and possessing normal human frailties. Thus he could better turn her to advantage, at least in his imagination.

As he pondered this question, the truth dawned on him. What he was depicting in the Great Imperial Concubine was not a creature of flesh, nor was it a mere vision; rather, it was a symbol of reality, a symbol of the essence of things. It was strange, indeed, to pursue that essence in the figure of a woman. Yet the reason was not far to seek. Even when falling in love, the Great Priest of Shiga had not discarded the habit, to which he had trained himself during his long years of contemplation, of striving to approach the essence of things by means of constant abstraction. The Great Imperial Concubine of Kyogoku had now become uniform with his vision of the immense lotus of two hundred and fifty yojana. As she reclined on the water supported by all the lotus flowers, she had become vaster than Mount Sumeru, vaster than an entire realm.

The more the Great Priest turned his love into something impossible, the more deeply was he betraying the Buddha. For the impossibility of this love had become bound up with the impossibility of attaining enlightenment. The more he thought of his love as hopeless, the firmer grew the fantasy that supported it and the deeper rooted became his impure thoughts. So long as he regarded his love as being even remotely feasible, it was paradoxically possible for him to resign himself; but now that the Great Concubine had grown into a fabulous and utterly unattainable creature, the priest's love became motionless like a great, stagnant lake which firmly, obdurately, covers the earth's surface.

He hoped that somehow he might see the lady's face once more, yet he feared that when he met her that figure, which had now become like a giant lotus, would crumble away without a trace. If that were to happen, he would without doubt be saved. Yes, this time he was bound to attain enlightenment. And the very prospect filled the Great Priest with fear and awe.

The priest's lonely love had begun to devise strange, self-deceiving guiles, and when at length he reached the decision to go and see the lady, he was under the delusion that he had almost recovered from the illness that was searing his body. The bemused priest even mistook the joy that accompanied his decision for relief at having finally escaped from the trammels of his love.

None of the Great Concubine's people found anything especially strange in the sight of an old priest standing silently in the corner of the garden, leaning on a stick and gazing somberly at the residence. Ascetics and beggars frequently stood outside the great houses of the capital and waited for alms. One of the ladies in attendance mentioned the matter to her mistress. The Great Imperial Concubine casually glanced through the blind that separated her from the garden. There in the shadow of the fresh green foliage stood a withered old priest with faded black robes and bowed head. For some time the lady looked at him. When she realized that this was without any question the priest whom she had seen by the lake at Shiga, her pale face turned paler still.

After a few moments of indecision, she gave orders that the priest's presence in her garden should be ignored. Her attendants bowed and withdrew.

Now for the first time the lady fell prey to uneasiness. In her lifetime she had seen many people who had abandoned the world, but never before had she laid eyes on someone who had abandoned the future world. The sight was ominous and inexpressibly fearful. All the pleasure that her imagination had conjured up from the idea of the priest's love disappeared in a flash. Much as he might have surrendered the future world on her behalf, that world, she now realized, would never pass into her own hands.

The Great Imperial Concubine looked down at her elegant clothes and at her beautiful hands, and then she looked across the garden at the uncomely features of the old priest and at his shabby robes. There was a horrible fascination in the fact that a connection should exist between them.

How different it all was from the splendid vision! The Great Priest seemed now like a person who had hobbled out of Hell itself. Nothing remained of the man of virtuous presence who had trailed the brightness of the Pure Land behind him. The brilliance which had resided within him and which had called to mind the glory of the Pure Land had vanished utterly. Though this was certainly the man who had stood by Shiga Lake, it was at the same time a totally different person.

Like most people of the Court, the Great Imperial Concubine tended to be on her guard against her own emotions, especially when she was confronted with something that could be expected to affect her deeply. Now on seeing this evidence of the Great Priest's love, she felt disheartened at the thought that the consummate passion of which she had dreamed during all these years should assume so colorless a form.

When the priest had finally limped into the capital leaning on his stick, he had almost forgotten his exhaustion. Secretly he made his way into the grounds of the Great Imperial Concubine's residence at Kyogoku and looked across the garden. Behind those blinds, he thought, was sitting none other than the lady whom he loved.

Now that his adoration had assumed an immaculate form, the future world once again began to exert its charm on the Great Priest. Never before had he envisaged the Pure Land in so immaculate, so poignant an aspect. His yearning for it became almost sensual. Nothing remained for him but the formality of meeting the Great Concubine, of declaring his love, and of thus ridding himself once for all of the impure thoughts that tied him to this world and prevented him from attaining the Pure Land. That was all that remained to be done.

It was painful for him to stand there supporting his old body on his stick. The bright rays of the May sun poured through the leaves and beat down on his shaven head. Time after time he felt himself losing consciousness and without his stick he would certainly have collapsed. If only the lady would realize the situation and invite him into her presence, so that the formality might be over with! The Great Priest waited. He waited and supported his ever-growing weariness on his stick. At length the sun was covered with the evening clouds. Dusk gathered. Yet still no word came from the Great Imperial Concubine.

The Priest of Shiga Temple and His Love   305

She, of course, had no way of knowing that the priest was looking through her, beyond her, into the Pure Land. Time after time she glanced out through the blinds. He was standing there immobile. The evening light thrust its way into the garden. Still he continued standing there.

The Great Imperial Concubine became frightened. She felt that what she saw in the garden was an incarnation of that "deep-rooted delusion" of which she had read in the sutras. She was overcome by the fear of tumbling into Hell. Now that she had led astray a priest of such high virtue, it was not the Pure Land to which she could look forward, but Hell itself, whose terrors she and those about her knew in such detail. The supreme love of which she had dreamed had already been shattered. To be loved as she was—that in itself represented damnation. Whereas the Great Priest looked beyond her into the Pure Land, she now looked beyond the priest into the horrid realms of Hell.

Yet this haughty noblewoman of Kyogoku was too proud to succumb to her fears without a fight, and she now summoned forth all the resources of her inbred ruthlessness. The Great Priest, she told herself, was bound to collapse sooner or later. She looked through the blind, thinking that by now he must be lying on the ground. To her annoyance, the silent figure stood there motionless.

Night fell and in the moonlight the figure of the priest looked like a pile of chalk-white bones.

The lady could not sleep for fear. She no longer looked through the blind and she turned her back to the garden. Yet all the time she seemed to feel the piercing gaze of the Great Priest on her back.

This, she knew, was no commonplace love. From fear of being loved, from fear of falling into Hell, the Great Imperial Concubine prayed more earnestly than ever for the Pure Land. It was for her own private Pure Land that she prayed —a Pure Land which she tried to preserve invulnerable within her heart. This was a different Pure Land from the priest's and it had no connection with his love. She felt sure that if she were ever to mention it to him, it would instantly disintegrate.

The priest's love, she told herself, had nothing to do with her. It was a one-sided affair, in which her own feelings had no part, and there was no reason that it should disqualify her from being received into her Pure Land. Even if the Great Priest were to collapse and die, she would remain unscathed. Yet, as the night advanced and the air became colder, this confidence began to desert her.

The priest remained standing in the garden. When the moon was hidden by the clouds, he looked like a strange, gnarled old tree.

"That form out there has nothing to do with me," thought the lady, almost beside herself with anguish, and the words seemed to boom within her heart. "Why in Heaven's name should this have happened?"

At that moment, strangely, the Great Imperial Concubine completely forgot her own beauty. Or perhaps it would be more correct to say that she had made herself forget it.

Finally, faint traces of white began to break through the dark sky and the priest's figure emerged in the dawn twilight. He was still standing. The Great Imperial Concubine had been defeated. She summoned a maid and told her to invite the priest to come in from the garden and to kneel outside her blind.

The Great Priest was at the very boundary of oblivion when the flesh is on the verge of crumbling away. He no longer knew whether it was for the Great Imperial Concubine that he was waiting or for the future world. Though he saw the figure of the maid approaching from the residence into the dusky garden, it did not occur to him that what he had been awaiting was finally at hand.

The maid delivered her mistress' message. When she had finished, the priest uttered a dreadful, almost inhuman, cry. The maid tried to lead him by the hand, but he pulled away and walked by himself toward the house with fantastically swift, firm steps.

It was dark on the other side of the blind and from outside it was impossible to see the lady's form. The priest knelt down and, covering his face with his hands, he wept. For a long time he stayed there without a word and his body shook convulsively.

Then in the dawn darkness a white hand gently emerged from behind the lowered blind. The priest of the Shiga Temple took it in his own hands and pressed it to his forehead and cheek.

The Great Imperial Concubine of Kyogoku felt a strange, cold hand touching her hand. At the same time she was aware of a warm moisture. Her hand was being bedewed by someone else's tears. Yet when the pallid shafts of morning light began to reach her through the blind, the lady's fervent faith imbued her with a wonderful inspiration: she became convinced that the unknown hand which touched hers belonged to none other than the Buddha.

Then the great vision sprang up anew in the lady's heart: the emerald earth of the Pure Land, the millions of seven-jeweled towers, the angels playing music, the golden ponds strewn with silver sand, the resplendent lotus, and the sweet voices of the Kalavinkas—all this was born afresh. If this was the Pure Land that she was to inherit—and so she now believed—why should she not accept the Great Priest's love?

She waited for the man with the hands of Buddha to ask her to raise the blind that separated her from him. Presently he would ask her; and then she would remove the barrier and her incomparably beautiful body would appear before him as it had on that day by the edge of the lake at Shiga; and she would invite him to come in.

The Great Imperial Concubine waited.

But the priest of Shiga Temple did not utter a word. He asked her for nothing. After a while his old hands relaxed their grip and the lady's snow-white hand was left alone in the dawn light. The priest departed. The heart of the Great Imperial Concubine turned cold.

A few days later a rumor reached the Court that the Great Priest's spirit had achieved its final liberation in his cell at Shiga. At this news the lady of Kyogoku set to copying the sutras in roll after roll of beautiful writing.

JUNICHIRO TANIZAKI

"The Bridge of Dreams"
("Yume no Ukihashi," 1959)

Translated by Howard Hibbett

Junichiro Tanizaki (1886–1965) was born in Tokyo, and attended Tokyo University to study Japanese literature but did not graduate. Instead, he became a disciple of Kafu Nagai (1879–1959), then regarded as one of the masters of modern fiction for his works *Tales of America* (*Amerika Monogatari*, 1908) and *Tales of France* (*Fransu Monogatari*, 1909). Tanizaki was recognized by such established writers as Ogai Mori when he published his earliest short stories, including "Tattoo" ("Irezumi," 1910), in *New Current of Thought*. Under the influences of Oscar Wilde, Charles Baudelaire, and Anatole France, he developed an interest in sensual aestheticism. His version of fetishism can be seen in many of his early works such as "Demon" ("Akuma," 1912) and "The Feet of Fumiko" ("Fumiko no Ashi," 1919). In "Demon," for example, he gave a detailed description of a young man licking the soiled handkerchief of his girl friend, and this abnormality became a topic of conversation for the public.

After the great earthquake of 1923 in the Tokyo area, Tanizaki moved to the Kansai (western) district. His continued interest in sensualism is demonstrated in his first novel *A Fool's Love* (*Chijin no Ai*, 1924–25) and another masterpiece, *A Portrait of Shunkin* (*Shunkinsho*, 1933). Living close to the center of old culture, he also made new discoveries in the traditional beauty of Japan; his ambivalent feelings about the West and the Japanese past are sensitively treated in *Some Prefer Nettles* (*Tade Kuu Mushi*, 1929). His most ambitious work, *The Makioka Sisters* (*Sasame Yuki*, 1943–48), written during and after World War II, made Tanizaki a giant among twentieth-century Japanese novelists. This novel, said to have been based on the relatives of his third wife, delineates thoroughly the inner life of a family against the background of Osaka.

His later works include *The Mother of General Shigemoto* (*Shosho Shigemoto no Haha*, 1949–50), *The Key* (*Kagi*, 1956), *Diary of a Mad Old Man* (*Futen Rojin Nikki*, 1961–62), and *Spring of My Seventy-ninth Year* (*Nanajukyu Sai no Haru*, 1965). "The Bridge of Dreams," written in his later period, is perhaps a work most representative of his theme and technique.

Tanizaki is also known for his refined prose style reminiscent of classical Japanese literature. His lifelong fascination with *The Tale of Genji* must have developed a keen sense of the need for the purification and further enrichment of modern Japanese prose.

On reading the last chapter of *The Tale of Genji*:

> Today when the summer thrush
> Came to sing at Heron's Nest
> I crossed the Bridge of Dreams.

This poem was written by my mother. But I have had two mothers—the second was a stepmother—and although I am inclined to think my real mother wrote it, I cannot be sure. The reasons for this uncertainty will become clear later: one of them is that both women went by the name of Chinu, I remember hearing as a child that mother was named after the Bay of Chinu, since she was born nearby at Hamadera, where her family, who were Kyoto people, had a seaside villa. She is listed as Chinu in the official city records. My second mother was also called Chinu from the time she came to our house. She never used her real name, Tsuneko, again. Even my father's letters to her were invariably addressed to "Chinu"; you can't tell by the name which of the two he meant. And the "Bridge of Dreams" poem is simply signed "Chinu."

Anyway, I know of no other poems by either woman. I happen to be acquainted with this one because the square slip of wave-patterned paper on which it is written was reverently mounted in a hanging scroll to be kept as a family heirloom. According to my old nurse, who is now in her sixties, this kind of handmade paper was decorated by the ancient "flowing ink" process (that is, by dipping it in water and letting it absorb a swirl of ink) and had to be ordered all the way from Echizen. My mother must have gone to a great deal of trouble to get it. For years I puzzled over the Konoe-style calligraphy of the poem, and the many unusual Chinese characters that even an adult—let alone a child—would find hard to read. No one uses such characters nowadays. I am reminded that we have a set of poem cards which seem to have been written by one of my mothers in that same esoteric style.

As for the quality of the hand, I am not really able to judge. "They tell me nobody else wrote such a beautiful Konoe style," my nurse used to say; and to my own amateur taste, for whatever that is worth, it appears to be the work of quite an accomplished calligrapher. But you would expect a woman to choose the slender, graceful style of the Kozei school. It seems odd that she preferred the thick, fleshy Konoe line, with its heavy sprinkling of Chinese characters. Probably that reveals something of her personality.

When it comes to poetry I am even less qualified to speak, but I hardly think this verse has any special merit. The line "I crossed the Bridge of Dreams" must mean "Today I read 'The Bridge of Dreams'—the last chapter of *The Tale of Genji*." Since that is only a short chapter, one that would take very little time to read, no doubt she is saying that today she at last finished the whole of *Genji*. "Heron's Nest" is the name by which our house has been known ever since my grandfather's time, a name given to it because night herons often alighted in its garden. Even now, herons occasionally come swooping down. Although I have seldom actually seen them, I have often heard their long, strident cry.

Heron's Nest is on a lane running eastward through the woods below the Shimogamo Shrine in Kyoto. When you go into the woods a little way, with the main building of the shrine on your left, you come to a narrow stone bridge over a stream: our gate is just beyond it. People who live in the neighborhood say that the stream flowing under this bridge is the subject of the famous poem by Chomei:

> The stony Shallow Stream—
> So pure that even the moon
> Seeks it out to dwell in it.

But this seems doubtful. Yoshida Togo's gazetteer describes our "Shallow Stream" as "the brook that flows southward, east of the Shimogamo Shrine, into the Kamo River." Then it adds: "However, the 'Shallow Stream' mentioned in ancient topographical writings was the Kamo River itself, of which the brook in question is merely a tributary having its source in Matsugasaki." That is probably right, since Chomei is quoted elsewhere as saying that "Shallow Stream" is the old name of the Kamo River. The Kamo is also mentioned by that name in a poem by Jozan, which I will cite later, and the poet's prefatory note explains: "On refusing to cross the Kamo River into Kyoto." Of course our little stream is no longer especially pure and limpid, but until my childhood it was as clear as Chomei's poem might suggest. I remember that in mid-June, during the ceremony of purification, people bathed in its shallow waters.

The garden pond at Heron's Nest was linked to this stream by earthen drainage pipes to prevent it from overflowing. Once inside our main gate, with its two thick cedar pillars, you went down a flagstone walk to an inner gate. Dwarf bamboo were planted along both sides of the walk, and a pair of stone figures of Korean Court officials (apparently of the Yi Dynasty) stood face to face on either side of it. The inner gate, which was always kept closed, had a roof thatched with cypress bark in an elegant rustic style. Each gate pillar bore a narrow bamboo tablet inscribed with one line of a Chinese couplet:

> Deep in the grove the many birds are gay.
> Far from the dust the pine and bamboo are clean.

But my father said he had no idea whose poem or whose calligraphy it was.

When you rang the doorbell (the button was beside one of the poem tablets) someone came out to open the gate for you.

Then you went along under the shade of a large chestnut tree to the front door; in the main entrance hall, you saw mounted over the transom a piece of calligraphy from the brush of the scholar-poet Rai Sanyo:

> The hawk soars, the fish dives.

What gave Heron's Nest its value was its landscape garden of almost an acre; the house itself was low and rambling but not particularly large. There were only some eight rooms, including the maids' room and the smaller entrance hall; but the kitchen was a spacious one, big enough for an average restaurant, and there was an artesian well next to the sink. Originally my grandfather lived on Muromachi Street near the Bukko Temple, and used Heron's Nest as his villa. Later, though, he sold the Muromachi Street house and made this his home, adding a sizable storehouse at its northwest corner. Going back and forth to the storehouse for a scroll or vase was quite inconvenient, since you had to go through the kitchen.

Our household consisted of seven persons—my parents and me, my nurse Okane, and three maids—and we found the house comfortable enough. Father liked a quiet life. He put in an appearance at his bank now and then, but spent most of his time at home, seldom inviting guests. It seems that my grandfather enjoyed the tea ceremony and led an active social life: he had a fine old teahouse brought in by the side of the pond, and built another small place for entertaining, which he called the Silk-Tree Pavilion, in the southeast corner of the garden. But after his death his prized teahouse and pavilion were no longer used, except as a place to take an afternoon nap or read or practice calligraphy.

All of my father's love was concentrated on my mother. With this house, this garden, and this wife, he seemed perfectly happy. Sometimes he would have her play the koto for him, and he would listen intently, but that was almost his only amusement at home. A garden of less than an acre seems a little cramped to be called a true landscape garden, but it had been laid out with the greatest care and gave the impression of being far deeper and more secluded than it actually was.

When you went through the sliding doors on the other side

of the main entrance hall you found yourself in an average-sized room of eight mats, beyond which was a wide, twelve-mat chamber, the largest room in the house. The twelve-mat room was somewhat after the fashion of the palace-style, with a veranda along the eastern and southern sides, enclosed by a formal balustrade. On the south, in order to screen out the sun, the wide eaves were extended by latticework with a luxuriant growth of wild akebia vine hanging out over the pond; the water came lapping up under the vine leaves to the edge of the veranda. If you leaned on the rail and gazed across the pond you saw a waterfall plunging out of a densely wooded hill, its waters flowing under double globeflowers in the spring or begonias in autumn, emerging as a rippling stream for a little way, and then dropping into the pond. Just at the point where the stream entered the pond a bamboo device called a "water mortar" was set up: as soon as the water filled its bamboo tube, which was pivoted off-center, the tube would drop with a hollow clack against a block of wood set below it and the water would run out. Since the tube was supposed to be of fresh green bamboo, with a cleanly cut open end, the gardener had to replace it often. This sort of device is mentioned in a fourteenth-century poem:

> Has the water upstream
> Become a lazy current?
> The sound of the mortar is rarely heard.

Even today, the sound of a water mortar echoes through the garden of the well-known Hall of Poets, the home of the early Edo poet Ishikawa Jozan in the northern suburbs of Kyoto. There, too, is displayed an explanatory text written in Chinese by Jozan. I suppose the reason that we had a water mortar is that my grandfather went there, read the description, and got the impulse to copy the device for his own house. It is said that Jozan's poem about not wishing to cross the Kamo River was written as a polite way of declining an invitation from the Emperor:

> Alas, I am ashamed to cross it—
> Though only a Shallow Stream
> It would mirror my wrinkled age.

A rubbing of the poem hangs in an alcove in the Hall of Poets, and we had one at our house too.

When I was about three or four, I was enchanted by the clack, clack of our water mortar.

"Tadasu!" mother would call. "Don't go over there or you'll fall in the pond!" But no matter how often she stopped me, I would run out into the garden and make my way through the tall bamboo grass of the artificial hill, trying to get to the edge of the stream.

"Wait! It's dangerous! You mustn't go there alone!" Mother or Okane would hurry after me in alarm and seize me by the back of my sash. Squirming forward while one of them held fast to me, I would peer down into the stream. As I watched, the green bamboo tube of the mortar slowly filled, dropped with a sharp rap against the block of wood, spilling its water into the pond, and then sprang back into place. After a few minutes it was full again, repeating the process. I suppose this clacking noise is my earliest memory of our house. Day and night it echoed in my ears, all the while that I was growing up.

Okane was always on her guard with me, hardly daring to let me out of her sight. Yet my mother often scolded her. "Do be careful, Okane!" she would say. There was an earth-covered footbridge over the pond, and whenever I tried to cross it Okane was sure to stop me. Sometimes mother came running after me too. Most of the pond was shallow, but it was over six feet deep at one place, where a hole had been sunk so that the fish could survive if the rest of the water dried up. The hole was near the bridge, and mother warned me about it time and again. "It would be dreadful if you fell in there," she used to say. "Even a grownup couldn't get out."

On the other side of the bridge was an arbor, and next to it the teahouse, my favorite playroom.

"Wait outside, Okane!" I would tell my nurse. "You mustn't come in after me." I was delighted with the low-roofed, narrow little building because it seemed exactly like a toy house for a child. I would play there for hours: sprawling out on its straw-matted floor, going through the tiny doorways, turning the water on and off in the pantry, untying the braided cords of the wooden boxes I found and taking out the tea objects, or putting on one of the wide rush hats the guests wore when coming to the tea ceremony in the rain.

Okane, who was standing outside, would begin to worry. "Tadasu!" she would call. "Don't stay any longer—your mother won't like it." Or again: "Look! There's a great big centipede here! It's terrible if a centipede bites you!" I actually did see large centipedes in the teahouse a few times, but I was never bitten.

I was far more afraid of the half dozen stone figures of Buddhist saints which stood here and there on the hill and around the pond. These were only three or four feet high, considerably smaller than the Korean statues before the inner gate, but their ugly, grotesque faces seemed somehow very Japanese. Some of them had hideously distorted noses and seemed to be staring at you out of the corners of their eyes; others seemed on the verge of a sly, malicious laugh. I never went near them after sunset.

Now and then mother called me over to the veranda when she fed crumbs to the fish.

"Here, little fish," she said, scattering crumbs out into the pond as the carp and crucian came swimming up from their hiding place in that deep hollow. Sometimes I sat close to her on the edge of the veranda, leaning against the low rail and tossing crumbs to them too; or else I sat on her lap, feeling the warm, resilient touch of her rather full thighs as she held me snugly in her embrace.

In the summer my parents and I used to have supper by the pond, and sit there to enjoy the cool of evening. Occasionally we ordered food from a restaurant or had a man come in from a caterer, bringing all the ingredients and cooking them in our huge kitchen. Father would put a bottle of beer under the spout of the bamboo mortar. Mother would sit at the edge of the pond and dangle her feet in the water, where they looked more beautiful than ever. She was a small, delicately built woman, with plump, white, little dumpling-like feet which she held quite motionless as she soaked them in the water, letting the coolness seep through her body. Years later, after I was grown up, I came across this line of Chinese verse:

> When she washes the inkstone,
> the fish come to swallow ink.

Even as a young child I thought how pleasant it would be if the fish in our pond came gliding playfully around her beautiful feet, instead of coming only when we fed them.

I remember that on one of those summer evenings I noticed some long, thin, slippery-looking leaves in my soup, and asked mother what they were.

"That's called *nenunawa*," she said.

"Oh? What's *that*?"

"A kind of water plant, like a lotus—they gather it at Mizoro Pond," she explained in her soft, well-bred voice.

Father laughed. "If you say it's *nenunawa* people won't know what you're talking about," he told her. "They call it *junsai* nowadays."

"But doesn't *nenunawa* sound long and slippery, just the way it is? That's the name for it in all the old poems, you know." And she began reciting one of them. From that time on it was always called *nenunawa* at our house, even by the maids and by the men who came to cook for us.

At nine o'clock I would be told that it was bedtime, and be taken away by my nurse. I don't know how late my parents stayed up; they slept in the room with the veranda around it, while Okane and I were in a small room of six mats on the north side, across the corridor from them. Sometimes I fretted and lay awake a long time, pleading: "Let me sleep with mama!"

Then mother would come to look in at me. "My, what a little baby I have tonight," she would say, taking me up in her arms and carrying me to her bedroom. Even though the bed had already been prepared for sleeping, father would not be in it—perhaps he was still out in the pavilion. Mother herself had yet to dress for bed. She lay down beside me just as she was, not taking off her sash, and held me so that my head nestled under her chin. The light was on, but I buried my face inside the neck opening of her kimono and had a blurred impression of being swathed in darkness. The faint scent of her hair, which was done up in a chignon, wafted into my nostrils. Seeking out her nipples with my mouth, I played with them like an infant, took them between my lips, ran my tongue over them. She always let me do that as long as I wanted, without a word of reproach. I believe I used to suckle at her breasts until I was a fairly large child, perhaps because in those days people were not at all strict about weaning their children. When I used my tongue as hard as I could, licking her nipples and pressing around them, the milk flowed out nicely. The mingled scents of her hair and milk hovered there in her bosom, around my face. As dark as it was, I could still dimly see her white breasts.

"Go to sleep now," she would murmur; and as she comforted me, patting me on the head and stroking my back, she began to sing her usual lullaby:

> Go to sleep, go to sleep.
> Don't cry, there's a good child, go to sleep.
> It's Mother cuddling you,
> Mother cradling you,
> Don't cry, there's a good child, go to sleep.

She would sing it over and over while I drifted off into a peaceful sleep, still clutching her breasts and running my tongue around her nipples. Often my dreams were penetrated by the distant clack of the water mortar, far beyond my shuttered windows.

Okane also knew a number of lullabies, such as this one:

> When I asked the pillow, "Is he asleep?"
> The honest pillow said, "He is!"

She sang many others for me too, but I was never easily lulled asleep by her songs. (Nor, in the room I shared with her, could I hear the sound of the water mortar.) Mother's voice had a seductive rhythm all its own, a rhythm that filled my mind with pleasant fancies and quickly put me to sleep.

Although I have thus far written "mother" without specifying which of the two I meant, my intention has been to relate only memories of my true mother. Yet it occurs to me that these recollections seem a little too detailed for a child of three or four. Seeing her dangle her feet in the pond, or hearing her talk about *nenunawa*, for instance—would such things, if they had really happened when I was a child of that age, have left any impression whatever? Possibly impressions of the first mother were overlaid by those of the second, confusing my memory. For early one autumn, just as the chestnut tree at our doorway was beginning to shed its leaves, my twenty-two-year-old mother, who was with child, contracted an infection of the womb and died. I was five at the time. A few years later I had a stepmother.

I cannot recall my first mother's features distinctly. According to Okane, she was very beautiful, but all that I can summon to my mind's eye is the vague image of a full, round face. Since I often looked up at her as she held me in her arms, I could see her nostrils clearly. The lamplight gave a pink luminosity to her lovely nose: seen from that angle, it appeared to be all the more exquisitely proportioned—not in the least like Okane's nose, or anyone else's. But when I try to remember her other features—her eyes, her mouth—I can only visualize them in a very general way. Here too I am perhaps being misled by the superimposed image of my second mother. After my real mother's death father used to read the sutras and say prayers for her every morning and evening before her memorial tablet, and I often sat beside him praying too. But as hard as I stared at her photograph, which stood beside the tablet on our Buddhist altar, I never had the sudden poignant feeling that this was my own mother—the woman who had suckled me at her breasts.

All I could tell from the picture was that she wore her hair in an old-fashioned style, and that she seemed even plumper than I had remembered. It was too faded to re-create in my mind the way she actually looked.

"Papa," I asked, "is that really mama's picture?"

"Yes, of course it is," he said. "It was taken before we were married, when she was about sixteen."

"But it doesn't look like her, does it? Why don't you put up something better? Don't you have another one?"

"Your mother didn't like to be photographed, so this is the only one I could find of her by herself. After we were married we had some pictures taken together, but the man did such a bad job retouching them that she thought they spoiled her face. Now this one shows her when she was a very young girl, and she may seem different from the way you remember her. But that was how she really looked at the time."

I could see then that it did bear a certain resemblance to her, though by no means enough to bring the forgotten image of my mother back to life.

I would think of her wistfully as I leaned on the balustrade and watched the carp swimming in the pond, yearn for her as I listened to the clack of the bamboo mortar. But it was especially at night, when I was lying in bed in my nurse's arms, that I felt an indescribable longing for my dead mother. That sweet, dimly white dream world there in her warm bosom among the mingled scents of her hair and her milk—why had it disappeared? Was this what "death" meant? Where could she have gone? Okane tried to console me by singing mother's lullabies, but that made my grief all the worse. "No, no!" I cried, thrashing about in bed. "I don't like you to sing for me! I want mama!" Kicking off the covers, I howled and wept.

At last my father would come in to say: "Tadasu, you mustn't give Okane so much trouble. Now be a good boy and go to sleep." But I cried even harder.

"Your mother has died," he would tell me, his voice thickening and faltering. "It doesn't do any good to cry about it. I feel as much like crying as you do—maybe more—but I'm being brave. You try to be brave too."

Then Okane would say: "If you want to see your mama, you ought to pray as hard as you can. If you do, she'll come to you in a dream, and say: "Tadasu, you're such a good little boy!' But if you cry she won't come!"

Sometimes father would give up in despair at my incessant wailing and screaming, and say: "All right then, come sleep with me." Taking me along to his room, he would lie down with me in his arms. But I found his masculine smell so different from my mother's fragrance that I was inconsolable. Rather than sleep with him, I preferred to sleep with my nurse.

"Papa, you make me feel sick. I want to go back to Okane."

"Well, go sleep in the other room then."

But Okane would scold me for it when I got back into bed with her. "Even if your father *does* make you feel sick, why do you have to say such an awful thing?" She used to say I looked exactly like him, not like my mother. That made me unhappy too.

Father always spent an hour morning and evening reading aloud from the sutras before the memorial tablet. As soon as I thought he was going to stop I would steal up to the altar and sit beside him for the few remaining minutes, running my little string of prayer beads through my fingers. But sometimes he led me there by the hand, saying: "Come to pray for your mother"; and I had to sit still beside him for the whole hour.

The next spring, when I was six, I entered elementary school, and from that time on I seldom made a nuisance of myself at night. But I longed for mother all the more. Even my unsociable father, who had never cared for any company except my mother's, seemed to feel lonely, and began going out occasionally for diversion. On Sundays he often took Okane and me along to dine at a riverside restaurant in Yamabana, or on an excursion to the hills west of the city.

One day he said to me: "When your mother was alive we often used to go out to Yamabana for dinner. Do you remember that, Tadasu?"

"I only remember once. Weren't some frogs croaking in the river behind us?"

"That's right. Do you remember hearing your mother sing a song there one evening?"

"I don't think so."

Then, as if it had suddenly occurred to him. "Tadasu, suppose there was someone just like your mother, and suppose she was willing to come and *be* your mother—how would you feel about that?"

"Do you really think there *is* such a person?" I asked dubiously. "Do you know anyone, papa?"

"No," he replied hastily, "I only said 'suppose.'" He seemed anxious to drop the subject.

I am not sure exactly how old I was when father and I had that conversation. Nor have I any way of knowing whether he already had someone in mind, or whether it was simply a chance remark. But when I was in the second grade—in the spring, when the double globeflowers at the mouth of the waterfall were in full bloom—I came home from school one day and was startled to hear the sound of a koto from the inner room. Who could be playing? My mother had been an accomplished musician of the Ikuta school, and I had often seen father sitting beside her on the veranda, listening absorbedly as she played for him on her six-foot-long koto, which was decorated with a pine-tree pattern worked in gold lacquer. After her death, her beloved koto was wrapped in a cloth dyed with our family crest of Paulownia leaves and flowers, placed in a black-lacquered box, and put away in the storehouse, where it had remained undisturbed ever since. Could that be her koto? I wondered, as I came in through the side entrance. Just then Okane appeared, and whispered into my ear. "Tadasu, be very quiet and peek in the other room. There's a pretty young lady here today!"

When I went through the eight-mat room to the other side, pushed open the sliding doors a little, and peered in, father noticed me at once and beckoned. The strange lady was engrossed in her koto; even after I came up beside her she kept on playing without so much as turning her head. She sat where my mother used to sit, and in the very same pose, her instrument laid out at the same angle, her left hand stretched out in the same way as she pressed the strings. The koto was not mother's—it was a plain one, completely unadorned. But father's position and attitude as he sat there listening so attentively were exactly the same as in my mother's time. It was only after she finished and took off the ivory finger picks that the strange lady turned to smile at me.

"Are you Tadasu?" she inquired politely, in a well-bred Kyoto accent. "You look just like your father."

"Make a nice bow," father said, putting his hand on my head.

"Did you just come home from school?" she asked. Then she slipped the picks back on her fingers and began to play again. I didn't recognize the piece, but it sounded extremely difficult. Meanwhile I sat obediently beside my father and watched her every movement, hardly daring to breathe. Even after she stopped playing for us, she made no attempt to shower me with compliments—all she did was smile when our eyes met. She talked to father in a calm, relaxed way, and seemed to have an air of composure. Soon a ricksha came for her; she was gone before dusk. But she left her koto with us. We stood it up against the wall in the alcove of the eight-mat room.

I was sure that father would ask me what I thought of her, whether I didn't agree that she looked like my mother. But he said nothing, nor did I try to find out how they happened to become acquainted. Somehow I hesitated to bring the matter up. To tell the truth, if I'd been asked whether or not she looked like my mother I would scarcely have known what to say. At least, my first glimpse of her had not given me the impression that here indeed was the reincarnation of my mother. And yet her soft, round face, her delicate body, her calm, unhurried speech, in particular her polite reserve and utter lack of flattery when we met, together with her indefinable attractiveness and charm—in all this she seemed to resemble my mother, and I felt friendly toward her.

"Who was that?" I asked Okane later.

"I really don't know," she said. Possibly she had been warned not to tell me.

"Is this the first time she's come here?"

"No, she was here about twice before. . . . It's the first time she's played the koto, though."

I saw the woman once more that summer, around the season when you begin to hear the song of the thrush. That time she seemed even more at ease, staying to feed crumbs to the fish with father and me after playing the koto. But she left before supper. Again her koto was put in the alcove—maybe she came to the house more often than I knew.

One day in March, when I was eight years old, father called me into the veranda room to talk to me. I think it was after supper, about eight o'clock in the evening, when no one else was around.

"I have something to discuss with you, Tadasu," he began, in an unusually solemn tone. "I don't know how you feel about the lady who's been coming to visit us, but for various reasons —reasons that concern you as well as me—I'm thinking of marrying her. You'll be in the third grade this year, so I want you to try to understand what I'm saying. As you know, I had the greatest love for your mother. If she were only alive today I wouldn't want anyone else. Her death was a terrible blow to me—I couldn't get over it. But then I happened to meet this lady. You say you don't remember your mother's face very clearly, but you'll soon find that this lady resembles her in all sorts of ways. Of course no two people are quite alike, unless they're twins. That isn't what I mean by resembling her. I mean the impression she makes, the way she talks, the way she carries herself, her quiet, easygoing personality, sweet and gentle and yet deep—that's why I say she's like your mother. If I hadn't met her I'd never have wanted to marry again. It's only because there *is* such a person that I've come to feel this way. Maybe your mother saw to it that I happened to find this lady, for your sake as well as mine. If she'll come and stay with us, she'll be a wonderful help to you as you grow up. And now that the second anniversary of your mother's death has passed, this seems like a proper time for marrying her. What do you think, Tadasu? You understand what I've been telling you, don't you?"

Curiously enough, I had already given my consent long before he finished what he intended to say. Seeing my face light up, he added: "There's one thing more I'd like you to remember. When she comes you mustn't think of her as your second mother. Think that your mother has been away somewhere for a while and has just come home. Even if I didn't tell you so, you'd soon begin to look at it that way. Your two mothers will become one, with no distinction between them. Your first mother's name was Chinu, and your new mother's name is Chinu too. And in everything she says and does, your new mother will behave the way the first one did."

After that, father stopped taking me in to sit beside him during his morning and evening worship at the memorial tablet. The time he spent reading the sutras gradually became shorter. Then one evening in April the wedding ceremony was held in the veranda room. Maybe there was a reception afterward, in some restaurant, but I have no remembrance of that. The ceremony itself was a very quiet affair: only a few close relatives attended on either side. From that day on father called his bride "Chinu," and I, having been told to call her "mama," found that the word came to my lips with surprising ease.

For the past two or three years I had been accustomed to sleeping in the room next to father's, but from the night my new mother arrived I went back to sharing the little room across the corridor with Okane. Father seemed to be truly happy, and began living the same kind of tranquil domestic life he had enjoyed with my first mother. Even Okane and the maids, who had been with us for years and who might have been expected to gossip and criticize their new mistress, were won over completely by her. Probably it was because of her natural kindness and warmth—anyway, they served her as faithfully as they had her predecessor.

Our household returned to its old routine. Father would sit listening attentively while mother played the koto, just as he used to when my real mother was alive; and he always had the gold-lacquered koto brought out for the occasion. In summer the three of us would have supper beside the pond. Father would take his beer to cool under the spout of the bamboo mortar. Mother would dangle her feet in the pond. As I looked at her feet through the water I found myself remembering my real mother's feet. I felt as if they were the same; or rather, to put it more accurately, whenever I caught a glimpse of my new mother's feet I recalled that those of my own mother, the memory of which had long ago faded, had had the same lovely shape.

My stepmother also called the water plant we had in soup *nenunawa*, and told me how it was gathered at Mizoro Pond.

"I imagine that sooner or later you'll hear at school about the Court anthologies," she remarked one day. "Well, there's a poem in the earliest one that goes like this." And she recited a poem which had a pun on the word *nenunawa*.

As I have said before, I suspect that these incidents occurred during my real mother's lifetime and were only being repeated. No doubt father had instructed my present mother how to behave, and was trying his best to confuse me about what my two mothers had said or done, so that I would identify them in my mind.

One evening—I believe it was that autumn—mother came into my room just as I was about to go to sleep with Okane.

"Tadasu," she asked, "do you remember how your mama used to nurse you till you were about four years old?"

"Yes," I said.

"And do you remember how she always sang lullabies to you?"

"I remember."

"Wouldn't you still like to have your mama do those things?"

"I suppose so. . . ." I answered, flushing, aware that my heart had begun to pound.

"Then come and sleep with me tonight."

She took my hand and led me to the veranda room. The bed was ready for sleeping, but father had not yet come in. Mother herself was still fully dressed, still wearing her usual sash. The light was shining overhead. I could hear the clack of the bamboo mortar. Everything was the way it used to be. Mother got into her bed first, propped her head on the wooden pillow (her hair was done up in an old-fashioned chignon), and lifted the covers for me to crawl in after her. I was already too tall to bury myself easily under her chin, but being face to face with her made me feel so awkward that I shrank as far as I could under the covers. When I did, the neckline of her kimono was just at my nose.

Then I heard her whisper: "Tadasu, do you want some milk?" As she spoke, she bent her head down to look at me. Her cool hair brushed against my forehead.

"You must've been awfully lonely, with no one but Okane to sleep with for such a long time. If you wanted to sleep with mama, why didn't you say so earlier? Were you feeling shy about it?"

I nodded.

"What a funny little boy you are! Now, hurry up and see if you can find the milk!"

I drew the top of her kimono open, pressed my face between her breasts, and played with her nipples with both hands. Because she was still looking down at me, a beam of light shone in over the edge of the bedclothes. I held one nipple and then the other in my mouth, sucking and using my tongue avidly to start the flow of milk. But as hard as I tried, it wouldn't come.

"Ooh, that tickles!" mother exclaimed.

"I can't get a drop," I told her. "Maybe I've forgotten how."

"I'm sorry," she said. "Just be patient—I'll have a baby one of these days, and then there'll be lots of milk for you."

Even so, I wouldn't let go of her breasts, and kept sucking at them. I knew it was hopeless, but still I enjoyed the sensation of rolling around in my mouth those firm little buds at the tips of her soft, full breasts.

"I'm terribly sorry—and you've worked so hard at it! Do you want to go on trying anyway?"

Nodding my head, I kept on suckling. Once again, by some

strange association, I seemed to drift among the mingled scents of hair oil and milk that had hovered in my mother's bosom so long ago. That warm, dimly white dream world—the world I thought had disappeared forever—had unexpectedly returned.

Then mother began to sing the old lullaby, in the very rhythm that I knew so well:

> Go to sleep, go to sleep,
> Don't cry, there's a good child, go to sleep. . . .

But in spite of her singing I was too excited to relax that night, and I went on sucking away greedily at her nipples.

Within half a year, though I hadn't forgotten my real mother, I could no longer distinguish sharply between her and the present one. When I tried to remember my real mother's face, my stepmother's appeared before me; when I tried to remember her voice, my stepmother's echoed in my ears. Gradually the two images merged: I found it hard to believe that I had ever had a different mother. Everything turned out just as father had planned.

When I reached the age of twelve or thirteen, I began sleeping alone at night. But even then I would sometimes long to be held in my mother's bosom. "Mama, let me sleep with you!" I would beg. Drawing open her kimono, I would suck at her milkless breasts, and listen to her lullabies. And after drifting peacefully asleep I would awaken the next morning to find that in the meantime—I had no idea when—someone had carried me back and put me to bed alone in my own small room. Whenever I said: "Let me sleep with you!" mother was glad to do as I wished, and father made no objection.

For a long time I didn't know where this second mother was born, what her background was, or how she happened to marry my father; such subjects were never brought up in my presence. I knew I might have found some clue in the city records, but I obeyed my father's orders: "Think of her as your real mother. You mustn't take the attitude that she's a stepmother." Also, I had some qualms about what I might find. However, when I was about to enter higher school I had to get an abstract from the records, and at that time I learned that my stepmother's real name was not Chinu but Tsuneko.

The following year my nurse Okane, who was then fifty-seven, ended her long service with us and retired to her home town of Nagahama. One day in late October before she left I went along with her to visit the Shimogamo Shrine. She made an offering, prayed briefly before the main altar, and then said in a voice filled with emotion: "I don't know when I'll see this shrine again. . . ." After that she suggested we go for a little walk through the shrine forest, toward the Aoi Bridge.

As we were walking along she suddenly turned to me and said: "You know all about it, Tadasu, don't you?"

"Know about what?" I asked, surprised.

"If you haven't heard, I won't say any more. . . ."

"What are you talking about?"

"I wonder if I ought to tell you," she said, hesitating. Then still strangely evasive: "Tadasu, do you know much about your stepmother?"

"No," I answered. "I know that her real name is Tsuneko."

"How did you find that out?"

"I had to get an abstract from the city records last year."

"Is that really all you know?"

"That's all. Father said I shouldn't be too inquisitive about her, and you didn't tell me anything either, so I decided not to ask"

"As long as I was working at your house I didn't want to mention it, but once I go back to the country I can't say when I'll set eyes on you again. So I think maybe I ought to tell you after all. You mustn't let your father hear about it, though."

"Never mind then," I said, without really meaning it. "Don't tell me—I think I ought to do what father says."

But she insisted. "Anyway you're bound to find out sooner or later. It's something you ought to know."

I couldn't help being fascinated by her long, rambling story, told to me bit by bit as we walked along the shrine road.

"I've only heard this at second hand, so I can't be sure," Okane began, and went on to give me a full account of my stepmother's past.

It seems that she was born into a Kyoto family that owned a large stationery shop in the Nijo district, specializing in decorative papers and writing brushes. But when she was about nine years old the family went bankrupt; by the time of

Okane's story their shop no longer existed. At eleven she was taken in as an apprentice geisha at one of the houses in Gion; from twelve to fifteen she entertained at parties as a dancer. You could probably have discovered the professional name she used at that time, the name of the geisha house, and so on; but Okane didn't know. Then, at fifteen, she is supposed to have had her debts paid off by the son of a wholesale cotton merchant, and to have been taken into the family as his bride. Opinions differ as to whether or not she was his legal wife, some declaring that her name was never entered in the official records.

Anyhow, she enjoyed all the privileges of a wife, and for about three years lived comfortably as the young mistress of a prosperous household. But at eighteen, for one reason or another, she was divorced. Some say that family pressure drove her out; others that her dissipated husband simply tired of her. No doubt she received a considerable sum of money at the time, but she went back to her parents' drab little house in Rokujo, turned the upstairs room into a studio, and made her living by teaching flower arrangement and the tea ceremony to the young women of the neighborhood.

Apparently it was during those days that my father became acquainted with her. But no one knew how he happened to meet her, or where they were seeing each other before she came to Heron's Nest as his bride. Two and a half years passed from the time of my mother's death until father's second marriage. As vividly as the girl may have reminded him of his lost wife, he could hardly have fallen in love with her less than a year after the death of the woman he had so much adored; probably he made his mind up only a few months before the wedding took place. His first wife had died at twenty-two; his second was twenty when she married him; father himself was thirty-three, thirteen years her senior; and I, at eight, was almost that much younger.

Learning about my stepmother's background aroused strong curiosity in me, along with all sorts of other feelings. I had never dreamed that she was once a professional entertainer in Gion. Of course she was very different from the ordinary girl of that kind: she came from a respectable family, and had left the gay quarter after only a few years to take up the life of the young mistress of a well-to-do household, during which time she seemed to have acquired a number of polite feminine accomplishments. Yet I had to admire her for preserving her unaffected charm and graciousness, in spite of having been a Gion dancer. But what of the evident refinement of her voice, that soft speech in the tradition of the old Kyoto merchant class? Even if she had only spent two or three years in Gion one would expect to find some trace of it in her speech. Did her first husband and his parents make a point of correcting her?

I suppose it was natural for my father, at a time when he was sad and lonely, to be attracted by such a woman. And it was natural, too, for him to come to believe that a woman like her would have all the fine qualities of his former wife and could help me forget the sorrow of having lost my mother. I began to realize how much thought he had given to this, not merely for his own sake but for mine. Even if my stepmother shared his wish to make me think of my two mothers as a single woman, it was his own extraordinary effort that enabled him to mold her in the image of my real mother. I could see that the love he lavished on my stepmother and me only strengthened his love for his first wife all the more. And so, while it might seem that exposing the secrets of my new mother's earlier life had frustrated all of father's patient efforts, the result was to deepen my gratitude to him and my respect for my stepmother.

After Okane left we added another maid, so that there were four in all. And in January of the following year I learned that mother was pregnant. It was in the eleventh year of her marriage to my father. Since she had never had a child before, even by her former husband, both father and she seemed to be surprised that such a thing could happen, after all these years.

"I feel ashamed to be getting big like this, at my age," she used to say. Or again: "When you're past thirty it's hard to give birth for the first time, I hear." Both mother and father had concentrated all their parental love on me, and perhaps they worried about my reaction to this event. If they did, they needn't have: I cannot describe how pleased I was to think that, after all these years as an only child, I was about to have a little brother or sister. I suppose, too, that father's heart was darkened now and then by the ominous memory of my first mother's death in pregnancy. But what struck me as odd was that neither father nor mother seemed to want to bring up the matter; I began to notice that they looked strangely gloomy whenever the subject was mentioned.

"Since I have Tadasu I don't need another child," she would say, half-jokingly. "I'm too old to have a baby." Knowing her as I did, I thought it unlikely that she said such a thing merely to hide her embarrassment at being pregnant.

"What are you talking about, mother?" I would object. "You mustn't say foolish things like that!" But somehow father seemed to agree with her.

The doctor who examined her said that mother's heart was rather weak, but that it was not bad enough to be a cause for concern—on the whole, she had a strong constitution. And in May of that year she gave birth to a baby boy. Her delivery took place at our house: the little six-mat room that I had been using was given over to her. The baby was a healthy one, and in due time father gave it the name Takeshi. But when I came home from school one day—I believe it was about two weeks later—I was startled to find that Takeshi wasn't there.

"Father, where is Takeshi?" I asked.

"We've sent him out to Shizuichino for adoption," he told me. "Someday I think you'll understand, but for the present, please don't ask too many questions. I didn't plan this by myself—from the time we knew the child was coming your mother and I discussed it together every night. She wanted to do it even more than I did. Maybe we shouldn't have gone ahead without a word to you, but I was afraid that talking to you about it might do more harm than good."

For a moment I looked at him incredulously. Mother, who had left her bed only the day before, seemed to have deliberately slipped off somewhere, to leave us alone, "Where's mother?" I asked.

"I think she may have gone out to the garden," he said, as if he didn't know.

I went out to look for her at once. She was in the middle of the bridge, clapping her hands and calling the fish, and scattering food to them. When she saw me, she went over to the other side of the pond, sat down on a celadon porcelain drum beside one of those sinister-looking stone saints, and beckoned me to come and sit on the other drum, facing her.

"I was just talking to father," I said. "What on earth is the meaning of this?"

"Were you surprised, Tadasu?" Her soft, round face dimpled in a smile. The expression in her eyes was far too serene for a mother struggling to hold back her grief at having just been robbed of her beloved newborn infant.

"Of course I was."

"But haven't I always said that Tadasu is the only child I need?" Her calm expression remained unchanged. "Your father and I both thought it was for the best. Let's talk about it another time."

That night the room I had given up to mother and her baby was once again my bedroom. The more I thought about what had happened, the more puzzled I became. It was dawn before I fell asleep.

Here I should like to say a little about Shizuichino, the place to which Takeshi had been sent.

Shizuichino is the modern name for the Ichiharano district, where the legendary hero Raiko is supposed to have killed the two robber chiefs. Even now one of its villages is called Ichihara, and that is also the name of the local station on the electric-car line to Mount Kurama. However, it was only in recent years that the car line opened; before that, you had to make the six- or seven-mile trip from Kyoto to Shizuichino by ricksha, or go by carriage as far as Miyake-Hachiman and then walk about three and a half miles. For several generations we had had close ties with a family named Nose who were prosperous farmers in this district—I suppose one of my ancestors had been sent out to nurse at their house. Even in father's time, the head of the Nose family and his wife would come to pay their respects to us at the Bon Festival and at New Year's, bringing with them a cartload of fresh vegetables. Their Kamo eggplants and green soybeans were unobtainable at the market; we were always delighted to see them coming with their little handcart. Since we often went to stay overnight with them in the fall, to go mushroom hunting, I had been familiar with that region since childhood.

The road from the Nose house to the mushroom hill led along the Kurama River, one of the sources of the Kamo. We were already well above Kyoto: as we climbed still higher we could see the city lying below us. They say that the great scholar Fujiwara Seika retired here, after declining the invitation of the Shogun Ieyasu to come to Edo. The mountain villa Seika lived in has long since disappeared, but its site was in a wide bend of the meandering Kurama River. Not far away were the places he chose as the "Eight Scenic Beauties," to which he gave such names as Pillow-Stream Grotto and Flying-Bird Pool.

Another nearby point of interest was the Fudaraku Temple, popularly known as the Komachi Temple, where Ono-no-Komachi and her tormented suitor are said to lie buried. According to the *Illustrated Guide to the Capital*, this is also the temple which the Emperor Go-Shirakawa visited during his journey to Ohara, as related in the *Tales of the Heike*. There is a passage in one of the Noh plays about Komachi saying that many years ago a man who happened to be passing Ichiharano heard a voice from a clump of tall *susuki* grass recite this poem:

> When the autumn wind blows,
> Eyeless Komachi wails in pain.
> But where is her lovely face
> In this wilderness of *susuki*?

Whereupon the priest who recalls the poem decides to go to Ichiharano and pray for the repose of Komachi's soul. I have seen an old painting which shows *susuki* growing out of the eye sockets of what is presumably Komachi's skull; and in the Komachi Temple there was a "wailing stone" on which was carved the poem I have quoted. In my childhood, that whole area was a lonely waste covered with a rank growth of *susuki* grass.

A few days after I learned the astonishing news about Takeshi I decided that I had to make a secret visit to the Nose family in Shizuichino. Not that I was determined to steal Takeshi away from them and bring him home again. I am not the sort of person to do a thing like that on my own initiative. It was simply that I felt an overpowering rush of pity for my poor little brother, taken from his mother's arms to a house far away in the country. At least I could make sure that he was well, I thought, and then go home and urge father and mother to reconsider. If they didn't listen to me at first, I meant to go on visiting Takeshi regularly, keeping our link with him intact. Sooner or later they would understand how I felt.

I set out early in the morning and reached the house a little before noon. Fortunately, Nose and his wife had just returned from the fields, but when I asked to see Takeshi they seemed embarrassed.

"Takeshi isn't here," they told me.

"He isn't? Then where is he?"

"Well, now . . ." they began, exchanging worried glances as if they were at a loss for an answer.

But after I repeated my question several times, Nose's wife broke down and said: "We left him with some people a little farther out." Then they explained that because there wasn't anyone in the house just then to nurse a baby, and because my parents wanted Takeshi further away, they took him out to live with some old friends of theirs, people you could trust.

When I asked where "a little farther out" was, Nose seemed even more embarrassed. "Your parents know where it is," he said; "so please ask them. It wouldn't do for me to tell you myself."

His wife chimed in: "They said if you ever happened to ask us we shouldn't tell you!" But I was finally able to worm it out of them that the place in question was a village called Seriu.

There is a folk song with the line "Out beyond Kyoto, by Ohara and Seriu"; and the Kabuki play *The Village School* has a passage about "hiding their lord's child in the village of Seriu, nestled in the hills." But this Seriu is over the Ebumi Pass on the road from Shizuichino to Ohara, and now has a different name. The Seriu that Nose and his wife were talking about is a mountain village in Tanba, even more remote and isolated. To go there, you take the electric car to Kibune, the second stop after Shizuichino, and cross the Seriu Pass into Tanba. The pass is a difficult one, more than twice as high as the Ebumi Pass, and there is not a single house in the five miles from Kibune to Seriu.

Why would my parents have sent my little brother to such

a place? Even the Seriu in the play—the village "nestled in the hills" where a lord's child was kept in hiding—wasn't that far from Kyoto. Why had Takeshi been hidden away deep in the mountains of Tanba? I felt that I should try to find him that very day, but since all I knew was the name of the village I would have had to look for him from house to house. Anyway, there was hardly time for me to go on to Kibune and cross that steep mountain pass. Giving up for the time being, I went back home, thoroughly dejected, along the same road I had come that morning.

For the next two or three days my relations with my parents were strained; even at supper we seldom talked. Whether or not they had heard from the Nose family, they never said a word about my trip to Shizuichino, nor did I mention having gone. Mother was bothered by the swelling of her breasts and often secluded herself in the teahouse to use a milking device to relieve the pressure, or call one of the maids to massage her. Around this time my father seemed to be in poor health, and began taking afternoon naps in the veranda room, his head on a Chinese pillow of crimson papier-mâché. He seemed feverish too; I often saw him with a thermometer in his mouth.

I intended to go to Seriu as soon as possible, and was trying to think of an excuse to be away from home overnight. But one afternoon—it must have been late spring, since the silk tree my grandfather had been so proud of was in blossom —I decided to spend a little time reading in the pavilion. Taking along a novel, I went through the garden, past the flowering tree, and up the pavilion steps. Suddenly I noticed that mother was sitting there on a cushion before me, busily milking her breasts. That was something she did in the teahouse, I thought. I had never imagined I'd find her on the pavilion veranda in that state: leaning over in a languid pose, her kimono open so that her naked breasts were bared to my view. Startled, I turned to leave, but she called after me in her usual calm voice: "Don't go away, Tadasu."

"I'll come again later," I said. "I didn't mean to disturb you."

"It's stifling in the teahouse, so I thought I'd sit out here. Did you want to read?"

"I'll come later," I repeated, feeling very uncomfortable. But again she stopped me from leaving.

"You needn't go—I'll be done in a moment. Just stay where you are." And then: "Look! My breasts are so full they hurt!"

I said nothing, and she continued: "You must remember how you tried to nurse at them till you were twelve or thirteen. You used to fret because nothing would come out, no matter how hard you sucked."

Mother removed the milking device from her left nipple and placed it over the right one. Her breast swelled up inside the glass receptacle, almost filling it, and a number of tiny streams of milk spurted from her nipple. She emptied the milk into a drinking glass and held it up to show me.

"I told you I'd have a baby someday and there'd be lots of milk for you too, didn't I?" I had somewhat recovered from my initial shock and was watching her fixedly, though I hardly knew what to say.

"Do you remember how it tastes?" she asked. I lowered my gaze and shook my head.

"Then try a little," she said, holding the glass out to me. "Go on and try it!"

The next moment, before I realized what I was doing, my hand reached out for the glass, and I took a sip of the sweet white liquid.

"How is it? Does it remind you of how it used to taste? Your mother nursed you till you were four, I think." It was extraordinary for my stepmother to say "your mother" to me, distinguishing between herself and my father's first wife.

"I wonder if you remember how to nurse," she went on. "You can try, if you like." Mother held one of her breasts in her hand and offered me the nipple. "Just try it and see!"

I sat down before her so close that our knees were touching, bent my head toward her, and took one of her nipples between my lips. At first it was hard for me to get any milk, but as I kept on suckling, my tongue began to recover its old skill. I was several inches taller than she was, but I leaned down and buried my face in her bosom, greedily sucking up the milk that came gushing out. "Mama," I began murmuring instinctively, in a spoiled, childish voice.

I suppose mother and I were in each other's embrace for

about half an hour. At last she said: "That's enough for today, isn't it?" and drew her breast away from my mouth. I thrust her aside without a word, jumped down from the veranda, and ran off into the garden.

But what was the meaning of her behavior that afternoon? I knew she hadn't deliberately planned it, since we met in the pavilion by accident. Did our sudden encounter give her the impulse to embarrass and upset me? If our meeting was as much a surprise to her as it was to me, perhaps she merely yielded to a passing whim. Yet she had seemed far too cool to be playing such a mischievous trick: she had acted as if this were nothing out of the ordinary. Maybe she would have been just as calm even if someone had come upon us. Maybe, in spite of my having grown up, she still thought of me as a child. Mother's state of mind was a mystery to me, but my own actions had been equally abnormal. The moment I saw her breasts there before me, so unexpectedly revealed, I was back in the dream world that I had longed for, back in the power of the old memories that had haunted me for so many years. Then, because she lured me into it by having me drink her milk, I ended by doing the crazy thing I did. In an agony of shame, wondering how I could have harbored such insane feelings, I paced back and forth around the pond alone. But at the same time that I regretted my behavior, and tortured myself for it, I felt that I wanted to do it again—not once, but over and over. I knew that if I were placed in those circumstances again—if I were lured by her that way—I would not have the will power to resist.

After that I stayed away from the pavilion; and mother, possibly aware of how I felt, seemed to be using only the teahouse. Somehow the desire that had occupied such a large place in my heart—the desire to go to Seriu to see Takeshi—was no longer quite so strong. First of all, I wanted to find out why my parents had disposed of him in that way. Was it father's idea or mother's? As far as I could judge, it seemed likely that my stepmother—out of deference to my own mother—had decided that she ought not to keep her child here with us. And perhaps father shared her scruples. Undoubtedly his love for his former wife was still intense, and he may well have thought it wrong for him to have any other child than the one she left him. Perhaps that is why my stepmother gave up her baby. For her, such an act would have shown self-sacrificing devotion to my father—and wasn't she more attached to me than to her own son? I could only suppose that they had come to their decision for reasons of this sort. But why hadn't they confided in me, or at least given me some hint of their intentions? Why had they kept Takeshi's whereabouts such a dark secret?

I have mentioned that father's health seemed to be failing, and it occurred to me that that might have influenced his decision. Since about the end of the last year he had begun to look pale, and had become noticeably thinner. Although he seldom coughed or cleared his throat, he seemed to have a low fever, which made me suspect that he was suffering from some kind of chest trouble. Our family doctor was a man named Kato, whose office was on Teramachi at Imadegawa. During the early stages of his illness father never had him come to the house. "I'm going for a walk," he would say, and then take the streetcar to visit Dr. Kato. It was not until after the episode in the pavilion that I managed to find out where he was going.

"Father," I asked, "is anything wrong with you?"

"No, not in particular," he answered vaguely.

"But why do you have a prescription from Dr. Kato?"

"It isn't serious. I'm just having a little trouble passing water."

"Then it's inflammation of the bladder?"

"Yes," he said. "Something like that."

At last it became obvious to everyone that father had to urinate frequently. You could see that he was always going to relieve himself. Also, his coloring was worse than ever, and he had lost his appetite completely. That summer, after the rainy season, he began to spend most of the day resting, as if he felt exhausted; in the evening he sometimes came out to have dinner with us beside the pond, but even then he was listless and seemed to be making the effort out of consideration for mother and me.

I felt suspicious because he was so evasive about his illness, even concealing his regular visits to his doctor. One day I made a visit of my own to Dr. Kato's office and asked him about it.

"Father tells me he has inflammation of the bladder," I said. "I wonder if that's really all it is."

"It's true that he has an inflamed bladder," said Dr. Kato, who had known me all my life. "But hasn't he told you any more than that?" He looked a little surprised.

"You know how retiring and secretive father is. He doesn't like to talk about his illness."

"That puts me in a difficult position," Dr. Kato said. "Of course I haven't been too blunt with your father about it, but I've let him know his condition is serious. So I suppose that he and your mother are pretty well prepared for the worst —I can't understand why they've kept it from you. Probably they want to spare you any unnecessary grief. To my own way of thinking, I'm not sure it's wise to hide the truth from you, since you're already so worried. I've known your family for a good many years—your grandfather was a patient of mine—and so I don't think there should be any objection if I take it on myself to inform you." He paused a moment, and went on: "I'm sorry to have to say this, but as you must have gathered by now your father's condition is not at all hopeful." Then he told me the whole story.

It was last autumn that father noticed a change in the state of his health and went to be examined by Dr. Kato. He complained of various symptoms—fever, blood in his urine, pain after urinating, a sensation of pressure in his lower abdomen—and Dr. Kato found immediately, by touch, that both of his kidneys were swollen. He also discovered tuberculous bacilli in the urine. This is very serious, he thought; and he urged father to go to the urology department at the university hospital for a special examination, with X rays. Father seems to have been reluctant. However, he finally went, after Dr. Kato urged him repeatedly and gave him a letter of introduction to a friend of his at the hospital.

Two days later Dr. Kato learned the results of the examination from his friend: just as he had feared, both the cystoscope and the X rays showed clearly that the disease was tuberculosis of the kidneys, and that father's condition was fatal. If only one of his kidneys had been attacked he could probably have been saved by its removal. Even in such cases, the prognosis was bad: thirty or forty percent of the patients died. Unfortunately both of my father's kidneys were affected, so nothing could be done for him. Though he still didn't seem to be a very sick man, he would soon have to take to his bed—at the longest, he might live another year or two.

"This isn't the kind of thing you can afford to neglect," Dr. Kato had warned him at the time, in a roundabout way. "From now on I'll come to see you once or twice a week— you ought to stay at home and rest as much as possible." And he added: "I must ask you to refrain from sexual intercourse. There's no danger of respiratory contagion at present, so you needn't worry as far as the rest of the family is concerned. But your wife will have to be careful."

"Is it some kind of tuberculosis?"

"Well, yes. But it isn't tuberculosis of the lungs."

"Then what is it?"

"The bacilli have attacked the kidney. Since you have two kidneys, it's nothing to be so alarmed about."

Dr. Kato managed to gloss it over for the moment in that way, and father quietly accepted his advice. "I understand," he said. "I'll do as you've told me. But I like going out for walks, and as long as I'm able to get around I'll come to your office."

Father continued to visit Dr. Kato as usual, apparently not wishing to have him call at our house. Most of the time he came alone, but now and then mother accompanied him. Although Dr. Kato felt an obligation to inform her frankly of her husband's condition, he had not yet found an opportunity to do so.

Then one day father surprised him by saying: "Doctor, how much longer do I have, the way things are going?"

"Why do you talk like that?" Dr. Kato asked him.

Father smiled faintly. "You needn't keep anything from me. I've had a premonition about it all along."

"But why?"

"I don't know . . . maybe you'd call it instinct. It's just a feeling I've had. How about it, doctor? I know what to expect, so please tell me the truth."

Dr. Kato was well acquainted with father's character and took him at his word. Father had always been an acutely perceptive man; possibly he had been able to guess the nature of his illness from the way the specialists at the university treated him. Sooner or later I'll have to tell him or tell someone in his family, Dr. Kato thought; if he's so well prepared for it maybe I'd better do it now and get it over with. Indirectly, but without trying to evade my father's questions any longer, he confirmed his fears.

This is what Dr. Kato reported to me. Then he warned me that, since the disease often ended by invading the lungs, all of us—not just my mother—had to be careful.

I come now to the part of my narrative that I find most difficult.

I have tentatively given this narrative the title of "The Bridge of Dreams," and have written it, however amateurishly, in the form of a novel. But everything that I have set forth actually happened—there is not one falsehood in it. Still, if I were asked why I took it into my head to write at all, I should be unable to reply. I am not writing out of any desire to have others read this. At least, I don't intend to let anyone see it as long as I am alive. If someone happens across it after my death, there will be no harm in that; but even if it is lost in oblivion, if no one ever reads it, I shall have no regret. I write for the sake of writing, simply because I enjoy looking back at the events of the past and trying to remember them one by one. Of course, all that I record here is true: I do not allow myself the slightest falsehood or distortion. But there are limits even to telling the truth; there is a line one ought not to cross. And so, although I certainly never write anything untrue, neither do I write the whole of the truth. Perhaps I leave part of it unwritten out of consideration for my father, for my mother, for myself. . . . If anyone says that not to tell the whole truth is in fact to lie, that is his own interpretation. I shall not venture to deny it.

What Dr. Kato revealed to me about my father's physical condition filled my mind with wild, nightmarish fancies. If it was last fall that father became aware of his unhappy fate, he was then forty-three years old, mother was thirty, and I was eighteen. At thirty, however, mother looked four or five years younger—people took her for my sister. Suddenly I recalled the story of her earlier life, which Okane had told me as we walked through the shrine forest before she left us last year. "You mustn't let your father hear about it," she had said, but might she not have done so on his instructions? Perhaps he had reason to want to sever the connection between my real mother and my stepmother, who had become so closely linked in my mind.

Also, I thought of what had happened not long ago in the Silk-Tree Pavilion. Perhaps father had had something to do with *that*. I hardly think mother would have tried to tantalize me so shamelessly without his permission. The fact is, although I stayed away from the pavilion for several weeks after that incident, I went there to suckle at mother's breast more than once. Sometimes father was away, sometimes at home: it seems unlikely that he didn't realize what she was doing, or that she concealed it from him. Possibly, knowing he hadn't long to live, he was trying to create a deeper intimacy between mother and me, so that she would think of me as taking his place—and she made no objection. That is all I can bring myself to say. However, such a theory would explain why they sent Takeshi to Seriu. . . . It may seem that I have imagined the most preposterous things about my parents, but what father told me on his deathbed, as I shall relate presently, appears to bear me out.

I don't know when mother learned that father's days were numbered; perhaps he told her as soon as he knew. But that afternoon in the pavilion when she used the phrase "your mother"—was it really by chance, as it seemed then, or had she intended to say that? Indeed, father must have told her about his illness even before she gave birth to Takeshi in May. Once they anticipated what the future held in store for them they may have come to an understanding—even if they never discussed the matter openly—and sent Takeshi off for adoption.

What seemed strange was that, as far as I could tell, mother showed no sign of gloom or depression at the impending separation from her husband. It would have been contrary to her nature to display her emotions plainly—but was there even a shadow of secret grief across that bland, lovely face? Was she forcibly suppressing her tears, thinking she must not let me see her lose control of herself? Whenever I looked at them, her eyes were dry and clear. Even now I cannot say that I really understand how she felt, the complex emotions that seem to have existed beneath her surface calm. Until father was at his dying hour she never tried to talk to me about his death.

It was in August that father lost the strength to get out of bed. By then his entire body was swollen. Dr. Kato came to see him almost every day. Father grew steadily weaker, losing even the will to sit up to eat. Mother hardly left his bedside.

"You ought to hire a nurse," Dr. Kato told her.

But mother said: "I'll take care of him myself." She let no one else touch him. Evidently that was also my father's wish. All his meals—though he ate only a few bites—were carefully planned by her; she would order his favorite delicacies, such as sweetfish or sea eel, and serve them to him. As his urination became more and more frequent she had to be always ready to give him the bedpan. It was during the midsummer heat, and he suffered from bedsores, which she also cared for. Often, too, she had to wipe his body with a solution of alcohol. Mother never spared herself any pains at these tasks, all of which she did with her own hands. Father grumbled if anyone else tried to help him, but he never uttered a word of complaint about what she did. His nerves became so tense that the least sound seemed to bother him: even the bamboo mortar in the garden was too noisy, and he had us stop it. Toward the end he spoke only when he needed something, and then only to mother. Occasionally friends or relatives came to visit him, but he didn't seem to want to see them. Mother was busy with him day and night; whenever she was too exhausted to go on, her place was taken by my old nurse, Okane, who had come back to help us. I was amazed to discover that mother had so much stamina and perseverance.

It was one day in late September, the day after an unusually heavy rainstorm when the "Shallow Stream" overflowed its banks and backed up into our pond, clouding the water, that mother and I were summoned to father's bedside. He was lying on his back, but he had us turn him over on his side so that he could look into our faces more easily. Beckoning me to sit close to him, he said: "Come here, Tadasu. Your mother can listen from where she is." He kept his gaze fixed on me all the while he spoke, as if he were seeking something in the depths of my eyes.

"I haven't much longer," he said. "But this was meant to be, so I am resigned to it. When I go to the other world your mother will be waiting for me, and I'm happy at the thought of meeting her again after all these years. What worries me most is your poor stepmother. She still has a long life ahead of her, but once I'm gone she'll have only you to rely on. So please take good care of her—give her all your love. Everyone says you resemble me. I think so myself. As you get older you'll look even more like me. If she has you, she'll feel as if I am still alive. I want you to think of taking my place with her as your chief aim in life, as the only kind of happiness you need."

Never had he looked at me that way before, deep into my eyes. Though I felt I could not fully understand the meaning of his gaze, I nodded my consent; and he gave a sigh of relief. Then, after pausing a few minutes until he was breathing easily once more, he went on:

"In order to make her happy you'll have to marry, but instead of marrying for your own sake you must marry for your mother's, to have someone who will help you take care of her. I've been thinking of Kajikawa's daughter Sawako...."

Kajikawa was a gardener who had come to our house regularly for many years. (His father had been an apprentice of the man who laid out the garden at Heron's Nest.) We saw him frequently, since he and his helpers still worked in our garden several days a week. And we knew his daughter Sawako too: ever since she had been in Girls' High School she used to call on us once a year, on the day of the Aoi Festival.

Sawako had a fair complexion and a slender, oval face of the classic melon-seed shape, the kind of face you see in ukiyoe woodblock prints. I suppose some people would consider her beautiful. After graduating from high school, she began wearing extremely heavy makeup, and was even more striking. It had seemed to me that a girl with a lovely white skin needn't paint herself so; but the year before last she stopped by during the midsummer festival, after viewing the great bonfire in the Eastern Hills from the Kamo riverbank, and since she said she was hot we invited her to have a bath, which she did, reappearing later and passing so near me that I noticed a few freckles on her cheeks. That explains why she wears so much makeup, I thought. After that I didn't see her for a long time, but about ten days ago she and Kajikawa had come to pay a sick call. I found their visit rather disturbing. Father, who usually refused to see any visitors, asked that they be brought to his room and spent over twenty minutes talking with them. Realizing that something was up, I half expected what he had to say to me.

"I dare say you know a good deal about the girl," father continued; and he gave me a brief description of how Sawako had been brought up and what she was like. But there was nothing particularly new to me, since I had been hearing about her for years. She was nineteen, my own age, having also been born in 1906; she was intelligent and talented, and had been graduated from Girls' High School three years ago with an excellent record; after graduation she had kept busy taking lessons of one kind or another, acquiring a range of accomplishments far beyond what one might have expected of a gardener's daughter. Thus she had all the qualifications to make a fine bride for any family—except that 1906 was the Year of the Fiery Horse, by the old calendar, and she was a victim of the superstition that women born in that year are shrews. As a result, she had not yet received an attractive offer of marriage.

All this was long since familiar to me, and father concluded by asking me to take her as my wife. Then he added that both the girl and her parents would be delighted to accept such a proposal. "If you'll only agree to it, everything will be settled," he said. "But in that case there's one thing more I'd like to ask of you. If you have a child, send it elsewhere, just as your mother gave up her own child for your sake. There's no need to say anything to Sawako or her parents right away—you might as well keep this to yourself until the time comes when you have to tell them. The earlier you're married, the better. Have the ceremony as soon as the year of mourning is over. I can't think of a suitable go-between at the moment, but you and your mother can discuss that with Kajikawa and decide on someone."

After having talked for such a long time, father closed his eyes and drew a deep breath. He seemed suddenly reassured that I would obey his wishes. Mother and I turned him on his back again.

The next day father began to show symptoms of uremia. He could eat nothing whatever, his mind was hazy, and now and then he talked deliriously. He lived about three more days, until the beginning of October; but all that we could catch of his incoherent speech was my mother's name, "Chinu," and the broken phrase "the bridge . . . of dreams," a phrase he repeated over and over. Those were the last words I heard my father utter.

Okane had come back from the country in August to help us, and as soon as the Buddhist service of the Seventh Day was over she went home. Relatives we hadn't seen for years gathered at the house even for the services of the Thirty-fifth and Forty-ninth Days; but their number gradually dwindled until, on the Hundredth Day, only two or three people made an appearance.

The following spring I was graduated from higher school and entered the law department of the university. After the death of my unsociable father the guests who called at Heron's Nest, never very many, became so rare that at last there was hardly anyone but Sawako and her parents, who came about once a week. Mother would spend the whole day indoors, worshiping before father's memorial tablet or, if she needed diversion, taking out my first mother's koto and playing it for a while. Because our house seemed so lonely and quiet now, she decided to start up the bamboo mortar again after its long silence; and she had Kajikawa cut a piece of green bamboo for it. Once again I could hear the familiar clack, clack that I had always loved.

Mother had borne up well while she was nursing father the year before; even throughout the long series of Buddhist services that followed his death she always received our guests with dignity and self-control, and looked as full-cheeked and glowing with health as ever. But lately she seemed to show signs of fatigue, and sometimes had one of the maids massage her. Sawako offered her services whenever she was there.

One day when the silk tree was beginning to blossom I went out to the pavilion, knowing that I would find mother and Sawako. Mother was lying in her usual place, on two cushions, while Sawako was energetically rubbing her arms.

"Sawako's good at massaging, isn't she?" I said.

"She's really wonderful!" mother replied. "I don't know anyone who can equal her. She makes me so drowsy I almost drop off to sleep—it's a delicious feeling!"

"She *does* seem to know how to use her hands. Sawako, did you ever take lessons at this?"

"No, no lessons," she answered; "but I'm used to massaging my parents every day."

"That's what I thought," mother said. "No wonder she'd put even a professional to shame. Tadasu, let her try it on you."

"I don't need a massage. But maybe I'll be her pupil and learn how to do it."

"Why should you learn?" asked mother.

"Then I can massage you too. I ought to be able to learn that much."

"But your hands are too rough—"

"They're not rough, for a man. Isn't that so, Sawako? Just feel them!"

"Let's see," Sawako said, clasping my fingers in her own, and then stroking my palms. "My, you really do have nice smooth hands! You'll be fine!"

"It's because I've never gone in much for sports."

"Once you get the knack of it you'll soon be an expert!"

For some weeks after that I had Sawako teach me the various massaging techniques, and practiced them on mother. Sometimes she got so ticklish that she shrieked with laughter.

In July the three of us would sit by the pond together to enjoy the cool of evening. Like my father, I would take a few bottles of beer to put under the spout of the bamboo mortar. Mother drank too, several glasses if I urged her; but Sawako always refused.

Mother would dangle her bare feet in the water, saying:

"Sawako, you ought to try this. It makes you delightfully cool!"

But Sawako would sit there primly in her rather formal summer dress, with a heavy silk sash bound tightly around her waist. "Your feet are so pretty!" she would say. "I couldn't possibly show ugly ones like mine beside them!"

It seemed to me that she was too reserved. She might have been a little freer and more intimate with someone who would eventually become her mother-in-law. But she seemed too solicitous, too eager to please; often her words had a tinge of insincerity. Even her attitude toward me was curiously old-fashioned, for a girl who had been graduated from high school. Perhaps marriage would change her, but at the moment I couldn't help feeling that our relations were those of master and servant. Of course, it may have been precisely that quality in her which appealed to my father, and no doubt mother's strength and firmness made her seem retiring by contrast. Yet she seemed inadequate, somehow, for a young girl who was to become the third member of our small family.

A month or two after the silk-tree and pomegranate blossoms had fallen, when the crape myrtle was beginning to bloom and the plantain ripening, I had become fairly skillful at massaging and often asked mother to come out to the pavilion for a treatment.

"A few minutes then, if you like," she would reply.

Naturally I took Sawako's place whenever she wasn't there, but even when she was with us I would brush her aside and say: "Let me try it—you watch!" Unable to forget the days when mother had given her breasts to me, I now found my sole pleasure in massaging her. It was around then that Sawako, who had always worn her hair in Western style, began having it done up in a traditional high-piled Shimada, a coiffure that set off beautifully her ukiyoe-like face. She appeared to be getting ready for the Buddhist service that would be held on the first anniversary of my father's death, a time that was drawing near. Mother herself ordered new clothes for the occasion: among them, a formal robe of dark-purple figured satin with a hollyhock pattern on the skirt, and a broad sash of thick-woven white silk dyed with a pattern of the seven autumn flowers.

The anniversary service was held at a temple at Hyakumamben, and we had dinner served in the reception hall of its private quarters. Both mother and I noticed how cold and distant my relatives were. Some of them left as soon as they had burned incense, without stopping to join us at dinner. Ever since father had married a former entertainer my relatives had held an oddly hostile and disdainful attitude toward our family. And now, to make matters worse, I was engaged to marry the gardener's daughter: it was only to be expected that they would talk. Still, I hadn't thought they would treat us quite so brusquely. Mother carried it off with her usual aplomb; but Sawako, who had gone to great trouble to dress appropriately for the occasion, seemed so dejected that I had to feel sorry for her.

"I'm beginning to wonder how our wedding will turn out," I said to mother. "Do you suppose those people will come?"

"Why should you worry? You're not getting married for *their* benefit—it's enough if you and I and Sawako are happy." Mother seemed unconcerned, but before long I discovered that the hostility of our relatives was even more bitter than I had imagined.

Okane, who had come from Nagahama for the service, stayed with us a few days before going home. On the morning of the day she left, she suggested we go for another walk through the shrine forest.

"Okane, do you have something to tell me?" I asked.

"Yes, I do."

"I think I know what it is. It's about my wedding, isn't it?"

"That's not the only thing."

"Then what is it?"

"Well . . . but you mustn't get angry, Tadasu."

"I won't. Go ahead and say it."

"Anyway, you're sure to hear about it from somebody, so I guess it ought to come from me." Then, little by little, she told me the following story.

Of course it was true that my relatives were opposed to my forthcoming marriage, but that wasn't the only reason that they disapproved of us. Mother and I were the objects of their criticism, more than the match with Kajikawa's daughter. To put it bluntly, they believed that we were committing incest. According to them, Okane said, mother and I began carrying on that way while father was still alive, and father himself, once he knew he wouldn't recover, had tolerated it —even encouraged it. Some went so far as to ask whose baby had been smuggled out to Tanba, suggesting that Takeshi was my own child, not my father's.

I wondered how on earth these people, who had been avoiding us for years, could have heard anything that would make them spread such wild rumors. But Okane explained that everyone in our neighborhood had been gossiping this way about us for a long time. It seems they all knew that mother and I spent many hours alone together in the Silk-Tree Pavilion, which is probably why the rumors began to circulate. My relatives thought that my dying father arranged for me to marry Sawako because only a girl with her disadvantages would accept such a match. Most scandalous of all, his reason for wanting me to keep up appearances by taking a wife was presumably to have me continue my immoral relationship with mother. Kajikawa was well aware of these circumstances in giving his daughter, and Sawako was going to marry out of respect for her father's wishes—needless to say, they had their eyes on our property. And so my relatives were outraged first of all by my father's part in this, then by mother's, by mine, by Kajikawa's, and by his daughter's, in that order.

"Tadasu, be careful!" Okane ended by warning me. "Everybody knows people will talk, but they can say terrible things!" And she gave me a strange look out of the corner of her eye.

"Let them say what they please," I answered. "Nasty rumors like that will soon be forgotten."

"Well, maybe they'll come to the wedding next month after all," she said doubtfully as we parted.

I have no interest in going into detail about later events. But perhaps I should summarize the important ones.

Our wedding ceremony was held on an auspicious day in November of that year. To please mother, I wore a crested black silk kimono of father's instead of a morning coat. Hardly any of my relatives appeared for the wedding; even the ones on mother's side stayed away. Those who came were chiefly persons related to the Kajikawa family. Dr. Kato and his wife were kind enough to act as go-betweens. The doctor had been taking lessons in the Noh drama for many years, and he was more than happy to oblige by chanting the usual lines from *Takasago*. But as I listened to his sonorous voice my thoughts were far away.

After our marriage, Sawako's attitude toward mother and me showed no particular change. We spent a few days in Nara and Ise for our honeymoon, but I was always careful to take precautions against having a child—that was one thing I never neglected. On the surface, mother appeared to get along with her newly wed son and daughter-in-law in perfect harmony. After father's death, she had continued to sleep in the twelve-mat veranda room, and she stayed there even after Sawako came; Sawako and I slept in my little six-mat room. That was as it should be, we felt, since I was still going to school and was still a dependent. For the same reason, mother was in charge of all the household accounts.

As for mother's life in those days, anyone would have taken it to be enviably carefree and leisurely. She amused herself by practicing Konoe-style calligraphy, reading classical Japanese literature, playing the koto, or strolling in the garden; and whenever she felt tired, day or night, she would have one of us give her a massage. During the day she had her massages in the pavilion, but at night she always called Sawako to her bedroom. Occasionally the three of us would go out to the theatre, or on an excursion; but mother was inclined to be frugal and paid close attention to even trivial sums of money, warning us to do our best to avoid needless expense. She was especially strict with Sawako and caused her a good deal of worry over the food bills. Mother was looking fresher and more youthful than ever, and so plump that she was beginning to get a double chin. Indeed, she was almost too plump—as if now that father was dead her worries were over.

Our life went on in that way while I finished two more years at the university. Then about eleven o'clock one night in late June, shortly after I had gone to bed, I found myself being shaken by Sawako and told to get up.

"It's your mother!" she exclaimed, hurrying me off toward the other bedroom. "Something dreadful has happened!"

"Mother!" I called. "What's wrong?" There was no reply. She was lying there face down, moaning weakly and clutching her pillow with both hands.

"I'll show you what did it!" Sawako said, picking up a round fan from the floor near the head of the bed to reveal a large crushed centipede. Sawako explained that mother had wanted a massage, and she had been giving her one for almost an hour. Mother was lying on her back asleep, breathing evenly, as Sawako rubbed her legs all the way down to her ankles. Suddenly she gave a scream of pain, and her feet arched convulsively. When Sawako looked up in alarm she saw a centipede crawling across mother's breast, near the heart. Startled into action, she snatched up a nearby fan and brushed the insect away, luckily flicking it to the floor, where she covered it with the fan and then crushed it.

"If I'd only paid more attention . . ." Sawako said, looking deadly pale. "I was so busy massaging her . . ."

Dr. Kato came over immediately and took emergency measures, giving one injection after another; but mother's suffering seemed to increase by the moment. All her symptoms—her color, breathing, pulse, and the rest—showed that her condition was more serious than we had thought. Dr. Kato stayed by her side, doing his best to save her; but around dawn she took a turn for the worse, and died soon afterward.

"It must have been shock," Dr. Kato told us.

Sawako was weeping aloud. "I'm to blame, I'm to blame," she kept repeating.

I have no intention of trying to describe the feelings of horror, grief, despair, dejection, which swept over me then; nor do I think it reflects credit on myself to be suspicious of anyone without a shred of evidence. Yet I cannot escape certain nagging doubts. . . .

It was some forty years since my grandfather had built the house he called Heron's Nest, which was by then at its most beautiful, well seasoned, with the patina of age that suits a Japanese-style building of this kind. In grandfather's day the wood must have been too new to have such character, and as it grows older it will doubtless lose its satiny luster. The one really old building at Heron's Nest was the teahouse that grandfather had brought there; and during my childhood, as I have said, it was infested by centipedes. But after that centipedes began to be seen frequently both in the pavilion and in the main house. There was nothing strange about finding one of them in the veranda room, where mother was sleeping. Probably she had often seen centipedes in her room before, and Sawako, who was always going in to massage her, must have had the same experience. And so I wonder if mother's death was entirely accidental. Might not someone have had a scheme in mind for using a centipede, if one of them appeared? Perhaps it was only a rather nasty joke, with no thought that a mere insect bite could be fatal. But supposing that her weak heart had been taken into account, that the possibility had seemed attractive. . . . Even if the scheme failed, no one could prove that the centipede had been deliberately caught and placed there.

Maybe the centipede did crawl onto her by accident. But mother was a person who fell asleep very easily: whenever we massaged her she relaxed and dropped off into a sound sleep. She disliked a hard massage, preferring to have us stroke her so lightly and gently that her sleep was not disturbed. It would have been quite possible for someone to put a small object on her body without immediately awakening her. When I ran into her room, she was lying facedown writhing with pain; but Sawako said that earlier she had been lying on her back. I found it hard to believe that Sawako, who was massaging her legs, saw the centipede on mother's breast the moment she looked up. Mother wasn't lying there naked; she was wearing her night kimono. It was odd that Sawako happened to see the insect—surely it would have been crawling under the kimono, out of sight. Perhaps she knew it was there.

I wish to emphasize that this is purely my own assumption, nothing more. But because this notion has become so firmly lodged in my mind, has haunted me for so long, I have at last tried to set it down in writing. After all, I intend to keep this record secret as long as I live.

Three more years have passed since then.
When I finished school two years ago, I was given a job as a clerk at the bank of which father had been a director;

and last spring, for reasons of my own, I divorced Sawako. A number of difficult conditions were proposed by her family, and in the end I had to agree to their terms. The whole complicated affair was so unpleasant that I have no desire to write about it. At the same time that I took steps to be divorced I sold Heron's Nest, so full of memories for me, both happy and sad, and built a small house for myself near the Honen Temple. I had Takeshi come to live with me, insisting on bringing him back from Seriu in spite of his own reluctance as well as that of his foster parents. And I asked Okane, who was quietly living out her days at Nagahama, to come and look after him, at least for a few years. Fortunately, she is still in good health, at sixty-four, and still able to take care of children. "If that's what you want, I'll help out with the little boy," she said, and left her comfortable retirement to come and live with us. Takeshi is six. At first he refused to be won over by Okane and me, but now we have become very close. Next year he will begin going to school. What makes me happiest is that he looks exactly like mother. Not only that, he seems to have inherited something of her calm, open, generous temperament. I have no wish to marry again: I simply want to go on living as long as possible with Takeshi, my one link with mother. Because my real mother died when I was a child, and my father and stepmother when I was some years older, I want to live for Takeshi until he is grown. I want to spare him the loneliness I knew.

June 27, 1931 (the anniversary of mother's death)

Otokuni Tadasu

ARTHUR O. LEWIS was born in Wellsville, Pennsylvania, in 1920. He received his B.A. and M.A. in English from Harvard University in 1940 and 1942 respectively, and his Ph.D. in English from The Pennsylvania State University in 1951. Among his publications are *Of Men and Machines* (1963), a forty-one-volume reprint series, *Utopian Literature* (1971), and articles in professional journals. He has also collaborated on *A Case for Poetry* (1954; rev. ed. 1963), *Anglo-German and American-German Crosscurrents* (3 vols.: 1957, 1962, and 1967), and *Visions and Revisions in Modern American Criticism* (1962). Mr. Lewis is presently Professor of English and Associate Dean for Resident Instruction in the College of the Liberal Arts at The Pennsylvania State University. He is now at work on a bibliography of utopian materials in The Pennsylvania State University Library and on a book about utopias to be called *The Fall of Utopia*.

YOSHINOBU HAKUTANI was born in Osaka, Japan, in 1935. After completing his baccalaureate in English at Hiroshima University, he received his M.A. in English from the University of Minnesota in 1959 and his Ph.D. in English from The Pennsylvania State University in 1965. He is now Associate Professor of English at Kent State University. Mr. Hakutani's work on American and Japanese languages and literatures has appeared in various professional journals in Japan, the United States, and Europe. He is currently writing a book on the American novelist Theodore Dreiser and pursuing research on the influence of literary naturalism on modern Japanese and American fiction.